6

National Audubon Society Field Guide to North American Rocks and Minerals

Charles W. Chesterman
Honorary Curator of Mineralogy
California Academy of Sciences
Senior Scientist
California Division of
Mines and Geology

Scientific Consultant:
Kurt E. Lowe
Professor Emeritus of Geology
City College of the
City University of New York

Alfred A. Knopf, New York

This is a Borzoi Book.
Published by Alfred A. Knopf, Inc.

Copyright © 1979, 1998 by Chanticleer
Press, Inc. All rights reserved under
International and Pan-American
Copyright Conventions. Published in
the United States by Alfred A. Knopf,
Inc., New York, and simultaneously in
Canada by Random House of Canada
Limited, Toronto. Distributed by
Random House, Inc., New York.

Prepared and produced by
Chanticleer Press, Inc., New York.

Color reproductions by Amilcare Pizzi,
S.p.A., Milan, Italy. Type set in
Garamond by Dix Type Inc., Syracuse,
New York. Printed and bound by Dai
Nippon Printing Co., Ltd., Tokyo,
Japan.

Published May 25, 1979
Sixteenth Printing, March 1998

Library of Congress Cataloging-in-
Publication Number: 78-54893
ISBN: 0-394-50269-8

CONTENTS

NATIONAL AUDUBON SOCIETY

The mission of the NATIONAL AUDUBON SOCIETY *is to conserve and restore natural ecosystems, focusing on birds and other wildlife, for the benefit of humanity and the earth's biological diversity.*

With more than 560,000 members and an extensive chapter network, our staff of scientists, educators, lobbyists, lawyers, and policy analysts works to save threatened ecosystems and restore the natural balance of life on our planet. Through our sanctuary system we manage 150,000 acres of critical habitat. *Audubon* magazine, sent to all members, carries outstanding articles and color photography on wildlife, nature, and the environment. We also publish *Field Notes,* a journal reporting bird sightings, and *Audubon Adventures,* a bimonthly children's newsletter reaching 600,000 students.

NATIONAL AUDUBON SOCIETY produces television documentaries and sponsors books, electronic programs, and nature travel to exotic places.

For membership information:

NATIONAL AUDUBON SOCIETY
700 Broadway
New York, NY 10003-9562
(212) 979-3000

THE AUTHOR

Charles W. Chesterman, author of
more than 50 publications on
mineralogy, gemstones, and other areas
of geology, has been with the California
Division of Mines and Geology since
1947 and has been Honorary Curator of
Mineralogy at the California Academy
of Sciences since 1955. He has also
taught many popular courses for the
California Academy of Sciences and the
San Francisco Gem and Mineral
Society.

Professor Kurt E. Lowe (Scientific
Consultant) taught for many years at
City College of the City University of
New York, from which he retired in
1972, and was Chairman of the
Geology Department for 11 years. He
is now a prominent geological
consultant and is regarded as the
leading authority on the geology of
New York City and environs.

ACKNOWLEDGMENTS

The author extends his deep gratitude to Prof. Kurt E. Lowe, who contributed so generously to the chapters on rocks and mineral environments. I am also grateful to Thomas A. Peters, Capt. John Sinkankas, and Dr. Christopher Schuberth for their valuable comments and suggestions.

I am deeply indebted to Paul Steiner and the staff at Chanticleer Press: to Milton Rugoff for his unwavering faith in this book; to Gudrun Buettner for her invaluable ideas on layout and design; to Carol Nehring, who (with Tom Peters) selected and arranged the hundreds of photographs in the Visual Keys; and to Peter Salwen, who developed the Identification Keys, my special thanks and appreciation for his thorough editing and for his watchful eye over all phases of the project.

Finally, sincerest thanks to my wife, Norma C. Chesterman, who quietly gave her unlimited faith and support.

INTRODUCTION

In the past century, our knowledge of the mineral world has grown dramatically. Professional mineralogists can now determine what almost any mineral is made of, how it was formed, and where to find it. Maps, tools, and transportation are available to all, and even a relative beginner can soon acquire a respectable collection.
This field guide brings together all that a beginner will need to get a start collecting and studying minerals, gems, and rocks. Besides color photographs and descriptions of some 232 mineral species (including the 20 or so species that are used as gemstones) and 40 types of rock, it provides keys to their identification, descriptions of the natural rock environments in which the minerals occur, instructions on collecting procedures, and a mineralogical glossary and bibliography.

What Is a Mineral? To fully understand and enjoy mineral collecting, it is necessary to know exactly what we mean by the terms "mineral" and "rock," and how the two are related.
A mineral is usually defined as a homogenous, naturally occurring, inorganic solid. Each mineral has a definite chemical composition, which

may be fixed or variable within stated limits, and—most important—it has a characteristic crystalline structure, which results from the orderly arrangement of its atoms in space. A mineral may be a single native element, such as copper or gold. Or it may be a more or less complex compound.

The orderly arrangement of atoms in a mineral is responsible for its distinctive properties, such as hardness, crystal form, cleavage, and so on. A striking example of this fundamental relationship is the element carbon, which occurs in nature as several minerals, including graphite and diamond. These two are identical in chemical composition, but they are at the opposite ends of the hardness scale and show a number of other contrasting properties.

About 2,500 different minerals have been described, and new ones are discovered each year. Thus, choosing the minerals to be included in a field guide poses certain problems. Almost all experts will agree on the first 150 or so species, but beyond that point the choice becomes extremely personal. Some species are very beautiful but also very rare. Others are more widespread, but are not often collected because they rarely make attractive specimens. Each collector has a few personal favorites, and woe to the writer who fails to mention them!

We have included some 232 species from among the hundreds of possibilities. Some of these were chosen strictly for their beauty, others because they are "new" minerals—species that recently have become popular among collectors. In making our final selection we have been guided by the opinions of experts from several different regions of the country.

What Is a Gem?   Gems are minerals that have ornamental value. Most gemstones have three qualities that set them apart from common, run-of-the-mill minerals: beauty, durability, and some degree of rarity. About 20 mineral species may qualify as gemstones according to this definition. These occur in varieties that have the vividness of color, transparency, brilliance, and hardness to be cut and polished for use as jewels or decorative stones. Some gemstones are simply varieties of a single mineral species. Thus ruby and sapphire are varieties of corundum, and emerald, aquamarine, and morganite are varieties of beryl.

Altogether, the 20 most common gem minerals account for the 35 or so most common popular gemstones. A number of additional species would qualify as gems, but are so rare that there is little market for them. Other minerals sometimes, but only rarely, have the clarity and color required for gems, while still others lack hardness but are sometimes made into decorative pieces for special purposes. All these are placed in the general category of "rare and unusual" gemstones, and only a few of these will be discussed in this guide.

What Is a Rock? A rock may be thought of as an aggregate of minerals. Some rocks, such as limestone, consist almost entirely of a single mineral. In most cases, however, a rock consists of a few major (essential) minerals together with a number of minor (accessory) minerals. Accessory minerals do not greatly affect the bulk composition of a rock, and they have no bearing on how the rock is classified. By understanding the differences between rocks of many types, and how they were formed, geologists have been able to piece together a record of the earth's history, attempting even to reach back to the very formation of the planet more than 4.5 billion years ago.

From the mineralogist's point of view, a rock may be thought of as a "mineral environment." Each rock type was formed under certain specified conditions, resulting in the formation of a fairly predictable group of minerals. This field guide includes descriptions, color illustrations, and identification keys for most of the rocks you are likely to encounter on a field trip. By learning to understand the relations between particular rocks and their associated minerals, you will improve your chances of finding collecting localities for any given mineral.

Mineral Origins The mineral collector is most interested in finding places where minerals occur in concentrated form, preferably with well-formed, undamaged crystals. The collector wants to know, then, what minerals will be found within each type of rock, and how to recognize an area that promises good hunting. A crystal-lined geode, for instance, is most likely to be found in or near certain types of limestone, a sedimentary rock; other minerals, such as kyanite, are associated only with certain types of metamorphic rocks, usually mica schists and gneisses. A granite outcrop may lead the collector to a pegmatite, a coarse-grained rock that can yield excellent crystals of quartz, feldspar, beryl, and tourmaline, as well as other, rarer minerals.

In each of these cases, the mineral deposits that are of interest to the collector originated in a distinct manner, either precipitating out of a low-temperature solution, forming at depth under great heat and pressure, or crystallizing from hot liquids or gases of magmatic origin.

Mineral Environments In the examples just given, the minerals were formed by processes that are typical for each of the great rock classes. Thus a schist, for example, may be the mineral environment not only for kyanite, but also for garnet and other associated minerals such as staurolite and various types of feldspar and mica.

Because minerals, like rocks, can form under a variety of conditions, some are associated with more than one environment. It will help the collector, however, to know where and in what types of rock he is most likely to find a given mineral, and what other minerals are likely to occur nearby. This field guide therefore places great emphasis on mineral environments and mineral associations. In the chapter "The Common Minerals of North America," environments and mineral associations are listed for each species described, and in "The Common Rocks of North America," a list is provided of the principal minerals associated with each rock. Thus, if you wish to collect a particular mineral, the mineral description will indicate where it might be found, and which other minerals might be an indication that it is nearby. On the other hand, if you don't know what minerals to look for but you do know the type of rock in which you will be searching, the rock description will suggest the mineral species you are most likely to find.

In addition to the several types of igneous, sedimentary, and metamorphic mineral environments, deposits of two other types are particularly interesting to collectors: hydrothermal replacement deposits and vein environments. Both of these are formed through complex geological processes, and both often contain minerals that are of great economic or scientific interest. In all, the amateur mineralogist should become familiar with about a dozen principal mineral-forming environments in order to learn how minerals are developed and distributed. The chapter "Mineral Environments and Associations" briefly describes all the major environment types, indicating the rock types typical of each and explaining how the minerals of each environment came to be associated with one another. The explanations given there will help the collector in making the best use of the information given elsewhere in the book.

HOW TO USE THIS GUIDE

This field guide is designed to be used in three ways: as a tool for identifying minerals, as a guide to identifying rocks, and as a convenient reference and source book for mineral collecting in the field.

A few words of caution should be added with regard to both rock keys and mineral keys. Identifying minerals and rocks is not simple, and your first attempts at identification may be frustrating. But with a little practice you will soon become familiar with most of the interesting minerals and rocks, and your way is then open to explore the many fascinating byways of the mineral world.

Mineral Identification   To identify a mineral, first turn to the Visual Key to Minerals, beginning on page 39. The illustrations in this key are grouped by color, so that you can make a quick comparison of your specimen with the minerals in the plates. (Some minerals occur in several colors or forms, and are therefore illustrated more than once in the Visual Key.) Using the page references in the captions, you can then refer to the mineral descriptions, beginning on page 343, to confirm your identification.

If a visual inspection is not sufficient to

make an identification, use the Descriptive Key to Minerals, starting on page 281. In this key, all the common minerals are arranged by color, hardness, and cleavage, with additional descriptive remarks to aid in identification. As in the Visual Key, cross-references to the mineral descriptions are included to help confirm the identification. For readers not familiar with the physical properties used to identify minerals an explanatory chapter, "A Guide to Mineral Identification," precedes the Visual Key to Minerals.

Rock Identification   To identify a rock, refer to the Visual Key to Rocks, beginning on page 615. This key consists of close-up and distant views of most of the rocks you are likely to see in the field. The illustrations are arranged according to the four basic rock classes: igneous-volcanic, igneous-plutonic, sedimentary, and metamorphic.
To determine which group a rock belongs in, first turn to the Key to Rock Classes, which is illustrated with black-and-white drawings; it will guide you to the proper section of the color plates in the Visual Key. By comparing your specimen with those in the color plates you should be able to identify most of the rocks you find. As in the Visual Key to Minerals, cross-references are given to the detailed descriptions of the common rocks, which begin on page 681.
To help you use the keys to rocks, an introductory chapter, "A Guide to Rock Identification," precedes the Visual Key to Rocks.

The Study of Rocks and Minerals   The mineral descriptions are grouped according to their scientific classification, to emphasize the similarities and differences among related species. General readers who are interested in acquiring a basic understanding of mineralogy can use this section for study—as a reference that is systematic, yet not as difficult as an academic textbook. The rock descriptions are also grouped systematically, and will introduce the reader to the origins and distinguishing features of the most common rocks.

Mineral Collecting Even those who are familiar with minerals need guidance in finding and exploring good collecting sites. Part III, "Mineral Collecting," therefore offers information that is of particular use to the active "rockhound," or outdoor collector.

"Tools and Techniques for Collectors" offers basic instruction on the use of basic tools and equipment for collecting and organizing a mineral collection. Finally, the chapter "Mineral Environments and Associations" helps the reader interpret each rock type as a "mineral-forming environment," and determine the likely places to search for particular mineral species. It describes the major environment types and lists the favorite mineral species that collectors look for in each environment. Armed with this knowledge, even a relative beginner can take a practical approach to mineral hunting.

PART I: MINERALS

A GUIDE TO MINERAL IDENTIFICATION

Most of the minerals in this field guide can be identified using only a few simple tests and a minimum of equipment. Several physical properties will serve to identify most common minerals: color, streak, luster, hardness, cleavage, parting, specific gravity, fracture, tenacity, mineral habit, and the form of crystal aggregates. A number of minerals can also be recognized by other less common physical properties, such as taste, odor, feel, magnetism, fluorescence, and radioactivity.

Color Color is the most striking property of many minerals, especially those with a metallic luster. Some minerals can be identified by color: malachite is always green, azurite is deep blue, and realgar is red. But color alone is usually not enough to identify a mineral. In fact, for most nonmetallic minerals the color is extremely variable; quartz, calcite, fluorite, and tourmaline, to name just a few, may occur in at least a half-dozen colors. The explanation is that a mineral's "color" is often caused by impurities; these are present in quantities too small to affect its basic composition. Color can also be affected by variations in atomic structure or by structural defects in a crystal.

Quartz is an excellent example of this variation. Pure crystalline quartz, also called rock crystal, is colorless and glass-clear. If it contains minute traces of iron, it may take on a deep violet color; it is then called amethyst. Traces of manganese or titanium may result in a pink variety, rose quartz, and exposure to radioactivity, which is common at great depths underground, can change clear quartz to a brown variety called smoky quartz. Other impurities can result in blue, yellow, and other colors.

Streak   The streak of a mineral is its color when it is ground into a fine powder. This may be done by crushing a mineral fragment, placing the powder on a sheet of white paper, and observing the color. A more common (and convenient) procedure is to rub the mineral firmly across a tile of unglazed white porcelain (called a streak plate) to produce a line of powder whose color is called the streak of the mineral. This property may be distinctive when the color of the mineral is different from that of its streak, since the streak varies only slightly from one specimen to another. Streak is most useful for the identification of dark-colored minerals such as metallic sulfides and oxides; its usefulness is more limited when testing light-colored sulfates, carbonates, or silicates. Also, minerals having a hardness exceeding that of the streak plate (about 6½) cannot be tested in this manner.

Luster   The luster of a mineral is the way its surface reflects light. Luster is governed largely by the surface characteristics of the mineral's atomic structure and is slightly modified by its transparency. Luster should not be confused with color; minerals of different colors may have the same luster.
As with color, the luster of a mineral

should be observed on a cleavage surface or freshly broken, untarnished surface and described by comparing it with that of well-known materials. We may begin by deciding whether the luster is metallic (like that of any metal surface) or nonmetallic. Some minerals may have a luster, called submetallic, that falls between the above two categories by appearing only slightly metallic. Among the different kinds of nonmetallic luster, vitreous (glassy), adamantine (brilliant or gemlike), and resinous (resinlike) lusters are common. Other terms used to describe luster are self-explanatory, and include greasy, oily, pearly, waxy, and silky. The intensity or brilliance of a mineral's luster may be described as splendent (the brightest) down through shining, glistening, and glimmering (the dullest). A mineral with a rough, porous, or lusterless surface is described as dull or earthy.

Judgment of a luster is subjective. A mineral that looks, say, pearly to one collector may seem silky to another. It is best, therefore, to use luster only as a general guide.

Hardness The hardness of a mineral indicates how well it resists scratching or abrasion. It is measured on a numerical scale, from 1 (softest) to 10 (hardest):

1   talc
2   gypsum
3   calcite
4   fluorite
5   apatite
6   orthoclase feldspar
7   quartz
8   topaz
9   corundum
10 diamond

This scale was devised by the German mineralogist Frederick Mohs (1773–1839), who selected these ten minerals because they are common or readily available (with the possible exception of diamond, hardness 10). Each mineral in the Mohs scale can scratch any mineral with the same number or a lower number, and can itself be scratched by any mineral with a higher number.

A standard hardness testing kit, containing a labeled sample of each of the ten minerals on the Mohs scale (except diamond), can be ordered from most scientific supply houses. The numbers used in the Mohs scale are somewhat arbitrary. Diamond, the hardest known substance, is about four times as hard as corundum (hardness 9), but corundum is less than twice as hard as topaz (hardness 8). Hardness is very useful in mineral identification. To test a mineral's hardness, select a fresh firm surface on the back or underside of the specimen, so that scratching will not spoil the specimen for your collection. Holding the specimen firmly, attempt to scratch it with a test point—a sharp fragment of mineral from the hardness testing kit, beginning with the hardest mineral (corundum) and working down the scale. Press the test mineral firmly but lightly against the specimen. If the test point is harder than the specimen, you should feel a definite "catch" or "bite" as it cuts into the surface. If the specimen is harder than the test point, the point will slide across the surface. If the point is only slightly harder, it may barely catch the surface without digging in.

Perform the test several times, always using a sharp test point, and check with a hand lens to be sure that the point, and not the mineral, was doing the scratching. The hardness of the mineral is just below that of the lowest point that will scratch it. For example, if your specimen can be scratched by all the hardness points down to apatite (hardness 5) but not by fluorite (hardness 4), it may be assigned a hardness value of 4½, which is accurate enough for most purposes.

It is also useful to make several test scratches in different directions, since some minerals, such as kyanite and calcite, have different hardnesses depending on the direction of the scratch. The differences may be useful in identifying these minerals.

In casual field work, determinations of hardness may be even cruder. Often the only equipment used is a fingernail (hardness 2½), a penny (3), a knife blade or fragment of window glass (5½–6), a section of a hardened steel file (7+), or a small piece of emery cloth (between 8 and 9). It is important to test the hardness of a mineral on a fresh surface, and not to mistake the *brittleness* of a mineral for *softness*. Minerals that are fibrous, readily pulverized, scaly, or granular often crumble easily and may seem softer than they actually are.

The hardness of a mineral not only helps us determine its identity; it is also important when we think of minerals in their special character as gemstones. A number of attractive minerals, such as fluorite, can be cut into beautiful faceted stones, but are too soft to be regarded as valuable gemstones, because they would quickly be damaged if they were worn as jewelry. Most valuable gems are at least as hard as quartz (hardness 7); anything softer is liable to be damaged quickly in normal use. The most highly prized gemstones are usually also the hardest; typical are emerald and aquamarine (which are both varieties of beryl, hardness 8), sapphire and ruby (varieties of corundum, hardness 9) and, of course, diamond (hardness 10), the hardest of all minerals.

Cleavage When a mineral has the tendency to break along one or more smooth, flat lustrous surfaces, it is said to have cleavage. The way the mineral breaks is an indication of the way the atoms are arranged within the crystals. Minerals that break easily and cleanly in one or more directions are said to have *perfect* cleavage. If the break is less clean the cleavage may be described as *good, distinct,* or *poor.*

Perfect, one direction (muscovite)

Since cleavage is determined by atomic structure, some minerals will have no cleavage, whereas others may have more than one. When there are two or more cleavage planes, cleavage may not be equally good in each direction. Calcite will cleave equally well in three directions, whereas gypsum has perfect cleavage along one plane and poor cleavages along two others. Topaz has one perfect cleavage, augite and spodumene have two good cleavages, halite and galena have three, fluorite has four, and sphalerite six. Garnet and many other minerals do not cleave, and this lack is a clue to their identity.

Perfect, three directions (halite)

In many cases a mineral's cleavage can be observed without actually having to break the specimen apart. A transparent or translucent crystal may have cleavage planes that can be observed with the hand lens. In a number of opaque minerals, such as hornblende and augite, it is possible to see the cleavage planes even though the broken surface appears rough and uneven. The technique is to turn the specimen slowly, trying to catch the reflection of the sun or other light source. When the angle is exactly right, a cleavage plane can be recognized by the simultaneous reflection of light from many small, parallel lustrous surfaces, which are scattered at different levels along the break.

Good, two directions (augite)

Parting   Not to be confused with cleavage is parting, another physical property that is seen when a crystal is broken. Parting surfaces are smooth and flat, and closely resemble cleavage planes, but they are caused by structural imperfections in the mineral and not by the mineral's atomic structure. These imperfections are usually caused by strains that develop within the mineral crystal as it grows, or they may occur as planes of weakness between twin crystals. One crystal may show parting, while another crystal of the same species may not.

Specific Gravity The relative weight of any substance is referred to as its specific gravity or simply "gravity." The specific gravity of a mineral (or any other substance) is given as a number, comparing its weight with the weight of an equal volume of water. Thus, a mineral with a specific gravity of 4 is four times as heavy as water. To determine the specific gravity of a mineral accurately it is necessary to weigh a sample twice: once in the air and a second time while it is suspended in water. The difference between the two weights equals the weight of the volume of water the sample displaces. The specific gravity is then calculated by dividing the weight of the displaced water into the weight of the mineral. Obviously, this is a delicate procedure that requires special equipment.

Usually, it is possible, with practice, to make a fairly good estimate of gravity by the "heft" of a mineral in the hand. To make the estimate as accurate as possible, it is useful to compare an unknown mineral specimen with another one of comparable size whose gravity is known. Some common minerals and their specific gravities are quartz (2.6), calcite (2.7), feldspar (2.5–2.8), fluorite (3.2), pyrite (5.0), and galena (7.4–7.6). As a group, the nonmetallic minerals are lighter than the metallic ones, so it will be more useful, wherever possible, to compare an unknown mineral with a familiar one from the same group.

Fracture   The way a mineral fractures can sometimes help to identify it. Most fractures can be described by the following terms:

Uneven   Rough or irregular surface.
Conchoidal   "Shell-like," with a smooth curved surface.
Hackly   Sharp, jagged surfaces like broken metal.
Splintery   Forming elongated splinters (applies to fibrous minerals).
Earthy   Breaking like clay or chalk.

Tenacity   A mineral's tenacity is its capacity to resist the stress of crushing, tearing, bending, or breaking. Tenacity is usually described by the following terms:

Brittle   Easily broken into a powder by cutting or hammering.
Sectile   Can be cut by a knife into thin shavings.
Malleable   Can be hammered into thin sheets like gold or copper.
Flexible   Can be bent, but will not return to original form when stress is released.
Elastic   Can be bent (like a spring) and will return to original form when stress is released.

Crystal Form   For many collectors the most exciting aspect of minerals is their beautiful and often elegant crystal form, with regular geometric shapes and smooth flat surfaces, called crystal faces. This crystal form is only a visible expression of the mineral's invisible, internal atomic structure. The organization of atoms, which is responsible for the gross form of the crystal, also accounts for other physical properties such as hardness, cleavage, and fracture. Since the atomic structure—which is the heart of any crystal—is the same in every specimen of the same mineral, knowledge of crystal forms can be useful in identifying minerals.

Crystal Systems Mineral crystals come in a seemingly infinite range of shapes. But behind this tremendous diversity of form there is a strict order, because crystals always grow according to simple mathematical laws. By studying the crystal geometry, crystallographers can fit any crystal into one of only six basic crystal systems. These are called isometric, tetragonal, hexagonal, orthorhombic, monoclinic, and triclinic:

Isometric Crystals are generally blocky in appearance or ball-like, with many similar, symmetrical faces; characteristic forms are cubes, octahedrons, and dodecahedrons, either single or in varied combinations. Also called the cubic crystal system.

Tetragonal Crystals are often long and slender or even needle-like; characteristic forms are four-sided prisms, pyramids, and dipyramids.

Hexagonal Crystals are generally prismatic or columnar, with rounded triangular or hexagonal cross section; characteristic forms are three- or six-sided prisms, pyramids, and rhombohedrons. The very similar *trigonal system* is often included within the hexagonal system.

Orthorhombic Crystals are generally short, stubby, with diamond-shaped or rectangular cross section; characteristic forms are four-sided prisms, pyramids, and pinacoids (open forms made up of two parallel faces).

Monoclinic Crystals are mostly stubby, with tilted, matching faces at opposite ends suggesting a distorted rectangle; characteristic forms are prisms and pinacoids.

Triclinic Crystals are usually flattened, with sharp edges and sharp, thin cross section; no right angles on faces or edges; all forms are pinacoids.

The six crystal systems, with some representative crystal forms for each, are shown on the following two pages.

Isometric (or Cubic) System	Three axes of symmetry, all at right angles to one another and all of equal length.
Tetragonal System	Three axes of symmetry: two axes, of equal length, lie in a plane at 90°; the third is longer or shorter and is at right angles to the others.
Hexagonal (or Trigonal) System	Four axes of symmetry: three, of equal length, lie in a plane at 120°; the fourth axis is longer or shorter and is at right angles to the others.
Orthorhombic System	Three unequal axes, all at right angles to one another.
Monoclinic System	Three unequal axes: two axes, at right angles to each other, lie in a plane; the third axis is inclined to the plane of the other two. There is one twofold axis.
Triclinic System	Three axes, all of different length and none perpendicular to the others.

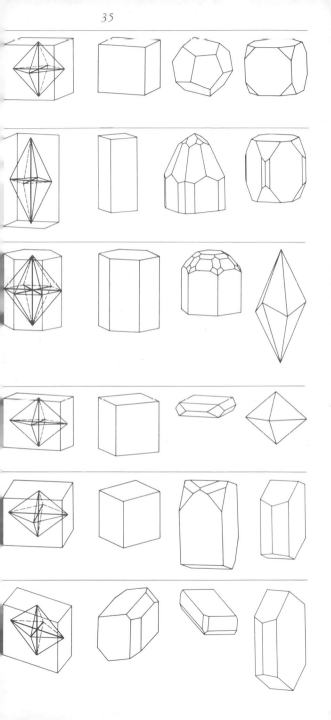

Symmetry As the descriptions on page 28 suggest, the crystals systems are defined in terms of symmetry. That is, there is always a balanced pattern in the arrangement of the crystal faces. It is possible to show that the angle between any two corresponding faces will be the same in every crystal of a particular type, even though the individual crystals, and their faces, may vary enormously in size or shape.

Crystals may have three types of symmetry: plane symmetry, axial symmetry, and symmetry about a center.

Plane Symmetry Plane symmetry, the type that is most familiar to us, means that if an object were cut along a plane each of the resulting halves would be a mirror image of the other. The human body, for example, is roughly symmetrical around a vertical plane from front to back.

Axial Symmetry Other objects, such as a snowflake (which is a crystal of water), are symmetrical about an axis. If a crystal is rotated around an axis of symmetry, the movement will bring identical faces into identical positions at regular intervals, until the crystal is returned to its starting position. Depending on how many times the faces come into similar positions, symmetry about an axis is described as a twofold, threefold, fourfold, or sixfold symmetry. A crystal may have several different axes of symmetry.

Symmetry about a Center Finally, a crystal may also be described as symmetrical about a center, if each face has a corresponding face parallel to it on the opposite side.

Of the six crystal systems, the isometric has the highest degree of symmetry. The tetragonal, hexagonal, and orthorhombic systems have less symmetry, but the axes are still at right angles. Symmetry is much less distinct in monoclinic crystals, and triclinic crystals, with their tilted faces, seem to show almost no symmetry at all.

Twinned Crystals

Quite frequently minerals will develop not as single crystals but as composites. In some minerals the individual parts of the composite are related to one another in a definite manner and they develop what are called twinned crystals. Many minerals occur as twins. In fact, the important rock-forming minerals occur more commonly as twins than as single crystals. Twinning may be a useful clue to mineral identification, and is not difficult to detect, a sharp V-shaped depression often marking the junction between the crystal pairs. The surface where the crystal pairs meet is called the composition plane.

There are three types of twin crystals: contact twins, penetration twins, and repeated twins. In contact twins, the two crystals are united by the composition plane. Penetration twins occur when two single crystals grow into each other, with the corners of each extending through the faces of the other. Repeated twinning is simply the parallel grouping of successive crystals, "back-to-back" in a series. It is best observed in the plagioclase feldspars, where it appears as fine parallel striations on the cleavage surfaces.

Mineral Habit and Form

Each mineral normally takes one or more characteristic forms, which can be useful in identification. These forms are determined by the manner of crystal growth and aggregation, and may have little or no resemblance to the "ideal" shape of an individual crystal. The term "habit" is used to refer to the mineral's preferred mode of growth—that is, to the arrangement and proportion of the faces on the single crystals. Some commonly seen crystal habits and forms are described and illustrated on the following four pages.

Mineral Habit   Some of the most common crystal habits are:

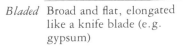

Acicular   Needlelike (e.g. natrolite).

Bladed   Broad and flat, elongated like a knife blade (e.g. gypsum)

Dendritic   Crystallizing in a "tree-like" or branching pattern (e.g. copper)

Equant   Having roughly the same diameter in every direction (e.g. garnet); an equivalent term is equidimensional.

Prismatic   Elongated in one direction (e.g. tourmaline).

Striated   Having very shallow, parallel grooves or depressions on one or more crystal faces (e.g. pyrite).

Tabular   Thick or thin flat plates (e.g. wulfenite).

Twinned Crystals	Twinned crystals may take a variety of forms. The most common types of twinning are:

Contact	Two simple crystals are joined at the composition plane (e.g. spinel).	

Penetration	Two single crystals grow into a single structure with the corners of each crystal protruding through the faces of the other (e.g. staurolite "cross"; orthoclase "Carlsbad" twin).	

Repeated	Crystals may grow "back-to-back" in parallel groups (e.g. albite) or twinning may occur at both ends of the crystal (e.g. rutile cyclic twin).	

Mineral Aggregates	Aggregates of mineral crystals may occur in many forms, including:

Botryoidal   Resembling a bunch of grapes; also called *globular* (e.g. malachite).

Columnar   Made up of slender, parallel columns (e.g. beryl).

Coxcomb   A serrated crustlike arrangement of twinned crystals (marcasite).

Druse   A coating or crust of small projecting crystals on the wall of a vein or cavity (e.g. quartz).

Fibrous   Showing threadlike fibers (e.g. serpentine).

Geode   A rounded, hollow nodule, lined with crystals, usually quartz or calcite (e.g. amethyst).

Mammillary   Forming smooth, rounded masses; "breastlike" (e.g. hematite).

Massive	Interlocking mineral grains, lacking apparent structure (e.g. limonite).	
Micaceous	Forming thin, flat, easily separated sheets (e.g. muscovite)	
Oolitic	Forming small spheres, 1–2 mm (0.04″–0.1″) across (e.g. hematite).	
Pisolitic	Forming spheres between 2 and 10 mm (0.1″–0.4″) across (e.g. bauxite).	
Radiating	Made up of crystals growing outward from a central point (e.g. wavellite).	
Reniform	Kidney-shaped (e.g. pyrolusite).	
Stalactitic	Slender, icicle-shaped formations (e.g. goethite).	
Wheat sheaf	A bundle-like aggregate of fine crystals (e.g. stilbite).	

In general, mineral identification depends on sensitivity to colors, especially to the subtler ones, and on the other physical properties previously discussed, such as hardness, specific gravity, cleavage, crystal form and habit, and mineral association.

Other Physical Properties
A small number of minerals may be identified by such minor physical properties as taste, odor, feel, magnetism, reaction with acid, and radioactivity.

To have any taste at all, a mineral must be soluble in water. Of the water-soluble minerals, halite (rock salt) can be readily identified by its salty taste, while epsomite is bitter, and chalcanthite and borax both have a peculiar sweetish, astringent taste. Few minerals can be recognized by their taste, and in any case only the tiniest particle should be sampled, as some minerals (e.g. chalcanthite) can be very poisonous.

Some minerals give off a characteristic odor. Arsenopyrite will develop an odor like that of garlic or arsenic when struck or heated. Pyrite and many other sulfide minerals will give a sulfurous odor. Kaolinite and a group of related (clay) minerals have an earthy, claylike odor when they are dampened or even breathed upon.

The "feel" of a mineral may be used to distinguish between such soft, white, earthy materials as kaolinite (a clay mineral), which is smooth to the touch, and chalk (a rock composed of microscopic fossil shells), which has a rough feel.

A few iron-bearing minerals will respond to a magnet in varying degrees or may be natural magnets such as lodestone, a variety of magnetite that has been used and studied for centuries. Franklinite and some varieties of hematite are weakly magnetic, and become more strongly magnetic if they are heated. Pyrrhotite is sometimes strongly magnetic and some specimens of chromite and ilmenite may also show weak magnetism (stronger if heated), depending on the proportion of iron they contain.

A simple acid test is useful in identifying the carbonate minerals (aragonite, calcite, dolomite, and several others). A small piece of the mineral can be crushed and a few drops of diluted acid mixed with the powder; this mixture will effervesce (bubble) as the acid reacts with the carbonate materials in the mineral. Calcite and aragonite both react so strongly to acid that they will bubble without being crushed first.

Radioactivity occurs in a number of minerals that contain elements, such as uranium and thorium, that are in a constant state of radioactive disintegration. These elements give off energy, in the form of gamma rays and other radiation, that can be detected with electronic equipment, principally a Geiger counter. Radioactive minerals are needed in science, medicine, and industry, and the search for such minerals is of great interest to the mining industry.

For amateurs who are interested in this subject, useful but inexpensive radiation-detecting equipment is available from some hobby and mineral shops. For the collector, the principal uranium minerals are carnotite, autunite, and uraninite; monazite is the commonest thorium-bearing mineral. A number of the radioactive minerals are rich orange, green, and yellow in color.

Fluorescence Many minerals will glow in a variety of colors, including yellow, blue, green, orange, and red, when exposed to ultraviolet (UV) light. This phenomenon, which is seen most easily when the minerals are in a dark room or a special display case, is called fluorescence. It is caused by impurities in the minerals, called activators, which respond to the invisible ultraviolet light by giving off visible colored light. The color of the visible light depends on the specific activator involved and also on the type of UV lamp (long-wave or short-wave) that is used.

Advanced amateurs will find a UV lamp a very useful piece of equipment, and testing for fluorescence in minerals can be exciting and rewarding. During World War II, numerous commercially valuable deposits of tungsten were discovered by amateur and professional geologists using UV lamps in a search for scheelite, a mineral with a distinctive bluish-white fluorescence. Fluorescence may also help in identifying a mineral, or it may confirm other identification tests. However, a mineral cannot be identified by fluorescence alone, since many different minerals exhibit similar fluorescent colors and a single mineral species may fluoresce in several colors.

Additional Tests for Identifying Minerals

Additional testing may be necessary to identify some minerals. Most of these tests are beyond the interest or ability of a beginner; for doubtful specimens it is best to ask the advice of a professional or well-informed amateur. Such people are often willing to be of help, and they can be located through a museum or university or through a gem or mineral club.

More advanced amateurs may wish to carry out their own tests. For this, the basic equipment needed (in addition to the field equipment already mentioned) includes: a mortar and pestle, to grind minerals into powder; a Bunsen burner, to test the reactions to heat and for use in a variety of chemical tests; a charcoal block on which the mineral can be placed for flame tests; a blowpipe for use with the Bunsen burner flame; a short length of platinum wire, which is used to hold a small bead of melted borax for bead tests; and forceps, an assortment of glass tubing, and various wet and dry chemicals. The surest method of mineral identification, especially for a small specimen, is x-ray diffraction. In this procedure, a beam of x-rays of uniform wave-length is directed toward a sample of the powdered mineral set in a slender glass or plastic tube at the center of a cylindrical camera. As they pass through the powdered mineral, the x-rays are diffracted (scattered) and produce a pattern of lines which is distinctive for each mineral.

Testing procedures are described in detail in several of the books listed in the bibliography.

VISUAL KEY TO MINERALS

The color plates on the following pages show examples of every mineral described in this guide. The illustrations have been arranged in the following groups, according to color:

Green
Blue
Violet to Pink
Red
Brown
Orange
Yellow
Colorless
White
Gray
Black
Multicolored or Banded
Metallic

An additional group of plates shows a selection of gem minerals, both in rough form and as cut or polished gems.
Because many minerals vary in color and form, a mineral may appear more than once in the Visual Key; the illustrations include all the color variations that are commonly found in North America. Also included are a number of minerals that rarely occur in North American mineral deposits but are readily available to collectors.

Procedures for Identifying Minerals

To identify a mineral specimen by color, turn to the color plate that most resembles it in color and form. If your specimen matches the mineral in the illustration, the caption will indicate the page containing the description of the mineral. If you cannot find the right color plate, turn to the appropriate color section of the Descriptive Key to Minerals; it will help you make a positive identification of most minerals.

Crystal Size and Quality

Outstanding, museum-quality crystals are very rare. Thus they would not be very helpful in a field guide intended for general use. Nevertheless, the minerals shown in the color plates are of finer quality than the amateur is likely to find; this is necessary to show clearly the distinctive qualities of color, crystal form, and habit. Most of the specimens are shown at 10 times actual size (10x) or more.

In general, the smallest mineral crystals are also the most perfect in form. By studying your specimen under a hand lens, you will often discover complete undamaged crystals that compare well with those in the color plates.

Localities

Most of the specimens illustrated here are from North American localities. Mineral collecting and trading is now a distinctly international activity, however, even among amateurs, and minerals from abroad are easily obtained at mineral shows or from dealers. A number of plates have therefore been included showing some from other countries. Because collectors are often interested in knowing exactly where a specimen was found, the locality for each is given in a list following the main text.

Minerals

The following color plates show the
most important minerals as they occur
in nature. Each specimen appears as it
was found, except for trimming and
cleaning.

Many of the plates show matrix
specimens, with the surrounding rock
material or other associated minerals
visible in the picture. Such associations
are often very useful in identifying
minerals.

Thumb Index

Since very few minerals can be
identified by color alone, the color
plates in this Key are arranged by habit
and form.
To aid you in finding the correct group
of plates quickly, a diagrammatic
symbol has been inset as a color spot at
the left-hand edge of each double-page
of plates, forming a "thumb index" to
the Visual Key. To use the thumb
index, flip through the pages until you
find the inset that most closely matches
your specimen in color and form.

The mineral forms are indicated in the
thumb index by the symbols on the
opposite page.

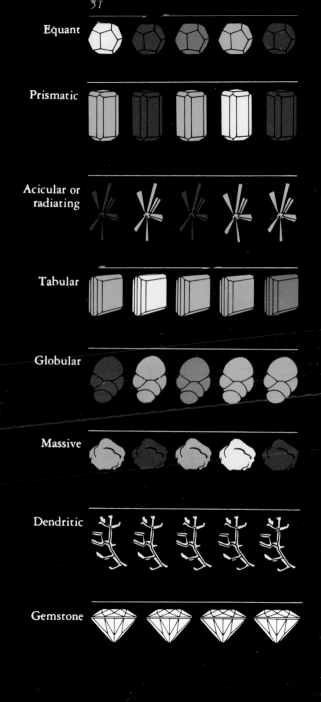

Equant

Prismatic

Acicular or
radiating

Tabular

Globular

Massive

Dendritic

Gemstone

1   Chrysoberyl with Garnet (Spessartine), *p. 420*

2   Diopside, *p. 545*

3   Garnet (Andradite), *p. 582*

4   Garnet (Grossular), *p. 582*

5   Fluorite on Pyrite, *p. 428*

6   Spodumene (Hiddenite), *p. 550*

7   Apophyllite, *p. 525*

8   Calcite with Malachite inclusions, *p. 432*

9   Olivine (Peridot), *p. 573*

10   **Garnet (Uvarovite),** *p. 582*

11   **Garnet (Grossular),** *p. 582*

12   **Fluorite,** *p. 428*

13　Orthoclase (Microcline, var. Amazonite), *p. 508*

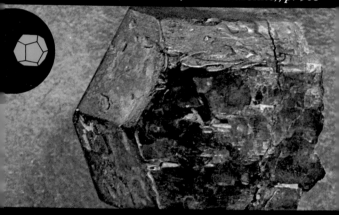

14　Scapolite, *p. 517*

15　Augite with Plagioclase (Albite), *p. 547*

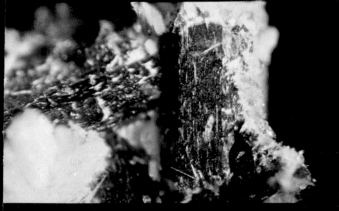

16   Hornblende, *p. 539*

17   Hedenbergite, *p. 546*

18   Actinolite, *p. 538*

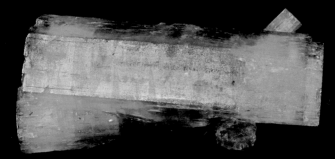

19   Beryl (Emerald), *p. 560*

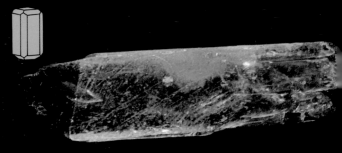

20   Spodumene (Hiddenite), *p. 550*

21   Malachite pseudomorph after Azurite, *p. 444*

22 Pyromorphite, *p. 484*

23 Willemite, *p. 576*

24 Chrysoberyl, *p. 420*

25   Orthoclase (Microcline, var. Amazonite), *p. 508*

26   Apophyllite, *p. 525*

27   Calcite with Malachite inclusions, *p. 432*

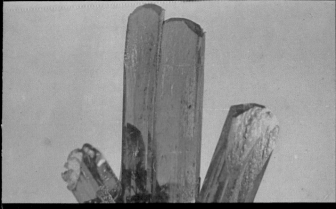

28   Vivianite, *p. 474*

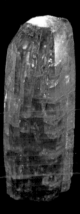

29   Beryl, *p. 560*

30   Brochantite, *p. 463*

31   Willemite, *p. 576*

32   Tourmaline (Elbaite), *p. 563*

33   Tourmaline (Elbaite), *p. 563*

34　Diopside, *p. 545*

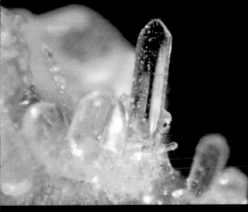

35　Vesuvianite, *p. 568*

36　Olivenite, *p. 480*

37 Topaz, *p. 580*

38 Apatite, *p. 482*

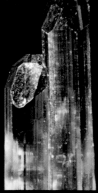

39 Clinozoisite, *p. 570*

40 Tourmaline (Elbaite), *p. 563*

1 Epidote, *p. 571*

2 Diopside with Garnet (Grossular), *p. 545*

Green Minerals

43   Aurichalcite, *p. 443*

44   Dioptase, *p. 559*

45   Brochantite, *p. 463*

46 Austinite with Conichalcite, *p. 478*

47 Turquoise, *p. 488*

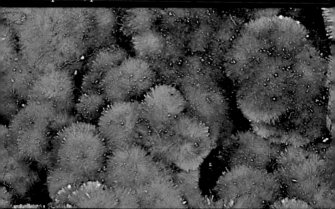

48 Aurichalcite, *p. 443*

49 Malachite, *p. 444*

50 Olivenite with Chrysocolla, *p. 480*

51 Wavellite, *p. 490*

52 Pumpellyite (center) with Actinolite, *p.* 567

53 Vivianite, *p.* 474

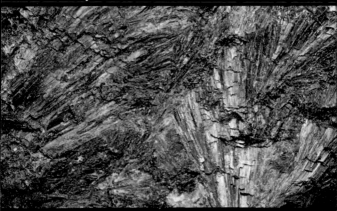

54 Hedenbergite, *p.* 546

55   Adamite, *p. 481*

56   Chrysocolla pseudomorph after Azurite, *p. 556*

57   Autunite, *p. 492*

58   Prehnite pseudomorph after Anhydrite, *p. 590*

59   Calcite with Colemanite, *p. 432*

60   Prehnite, *p. 590*

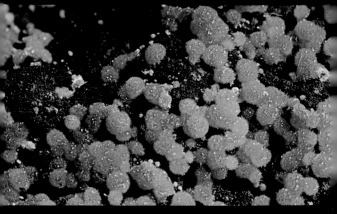

61   Conichalcite, *p. 477*

62   Variscite, *p. 476*

63   Wavellite, *p. 490*

64   Malachite with Azurite, *p. 444*

65   Malachite, *p. 444*

66   Smithsonite, *p. 436*

67 Torbernite, *p. 491*

68 Malachite replacing Azurite, *p. 444*

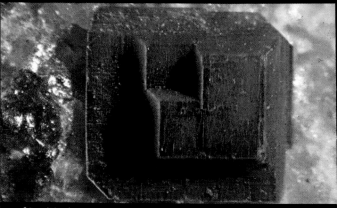

69 Torbernite, *p. 491*

70 Fluorite, *p. 428*

71 Chlorite, *p. 535*

72 Apatite on Muscovite, *p. 482*

73   Antigorite (Serpentine), *p. 527*

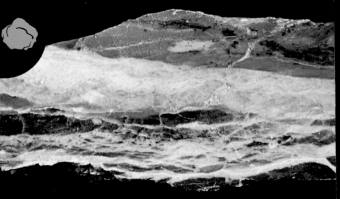

74   Chrysotile (Serpentine), *p. 527*

75   Muscovite, *p. 531*

76   Scapolite, *p. 517*

77   Turquoise, *p. 488*

78   Variscite, *p. 476*

79   Jadeite, *p. 549*

80   Pargasite with Phlogopite, *p. 541*

81   Olivine (Peridot), *p. 573*

82 Chalcedony (Chrysoprase), *p. 504*

83 Talc, *p. 530*

84 Zoisite with Corundum (Ruby), *p. 569*

85   Corundum, *p. 395*

86   Lazulite, *p. 487*

87   Benitoite, *p. 558*

88 Orthoclase (Microcline, var. Amazonite), *p. 508*

89 Orthoclase (Microcline, var. Amazonite), *p. 508*

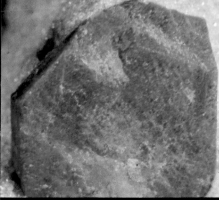

90 Lazulite, *p. 487*

91   Benitoite, *p. 558*

92   Azurite, *p. 445*

93   Lazulite, *p. 487*

94   Topaz with Tourmaline and Lepidolite, *p. 580*

95   Fluorite, *p. 428*

96   Fluorite, *p. 428*

97 Barite, *p. 455*

98 Celestite, *p. 456*

99 Vivianite, *p. 474*

100 Anhydrite on Quartz, *p. 458*

101 Kyanite, *p. 579*

102 Triphylite, *p. 472*

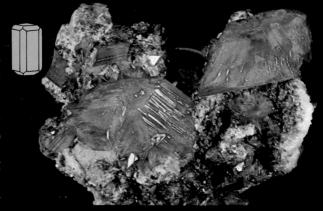

103   Tourmaline (Indicolite), *p. 563*

104   Linarite, *p. 464*

105   Chalcanthite, *p. 461*

106 Azurite, *p. 445*

107 Azurite, *p. 445*

108 Zoisite (Tanzanite), *p. 569*

109 Linarite on Barite, *p. 464*

110 Shattuckite, *p. 557*

111 Cyanotrichite with Brochantite, *p. 466*

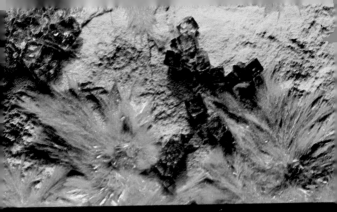

112 Aurichalcite with Fluorite, *p. 443*

113 Turquoise, *p. 488*

114 Chrysocolla pseudomorph after Azurite, *p. 556*

115   Chrysocolla encrusted with Quartz, *p. 556*

116   Hemimorphite, *p. 565*

117   Azurite, *p. 445*

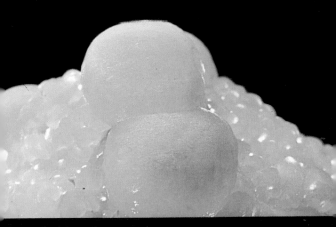

118 Smithsonite, *p. 436*

119 Chrysocolla with Quartz, *p. 556*

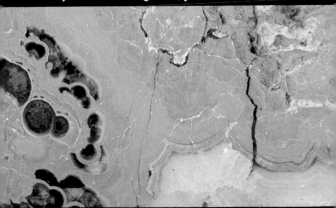

120 Chrysocolla, *p. 556*

121   Linarite, *p. 464*

122   Azurite with Cuprite, *p. 445*

123   Covellite, *p. 368*

124 Sodalite in Nepheline, *p. 515*

125 Sodalite, *p. 515*

126 Cordierite, *p. 562*

127   Lazurite with Pyrite, *p. 516*

128   Dumortierite, *p. 589*

129   Shattuckite, *p. 557*

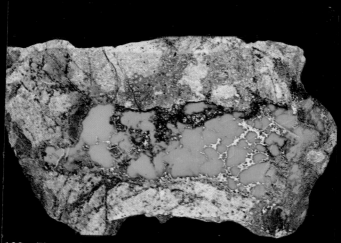

130   Turquoise, *p. 488*

131   Plagioclase (Labradorite), *p. 510*

132   Chalcedony, *p. 504*

133   Fluorite, *p. 428*

134   Spinel, *p. 416*

135   Halite, *p. 426*

138   Inesite, *p. 592*

139   Beryl (Morganite) and Plagioclase (Albite), *p. 5(*

140   Rhodochrosite, *p. 435*

141   Halite "hopper" crystals, *p. 426*

142 Chabazite, *p. 521*

143 Heulandite, *p. 518*

144 Lawsonite, *p. 566*

145   Fluorite, *p. 428*

146   Garnet (Grossular), *p. 582*

147   Fluorite, *p. 428*

148 Rhodonite with Franklinite in Calcite, *p. 553*

149 Rhodochrosite, *p. 435*

150 Orthoclase, *p. 508*

151   Anhydrite, *p. 458*

152   Rhodonite with Garnet (Andradite), *p. 553*

153   Quartz (Rose Quartz), *p. 502*

154 Quartz (Rose Quartz) "scepter" crystals, *p. 502*

155 Quartz (Amethyst), *p. 502*

156 Quartz (Amethyst), *p. 502*

157 Tourmaline (Elbaite), *p. 563*

158 Tourmaline (Elbaite) in Plagioclase, *p. 563*

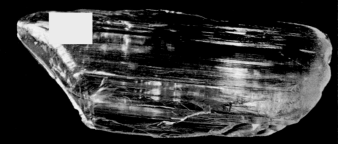

159 Spodumene (Kunzite), *p. 550*

160 Quartz (Rose Quartz), *p. 502*

161 Dolomite, *p. 442*

162 Inesite, *p. 592*

163　Erythrite, *p. 475*

164　Erythrite, *p. 475*

165　Dumortierite, *p. 589*

166 Hematite inclusions in Chalcedony, *p. 397*

167 Smithsonite, *p. 436*

168 Siderite, *p. 434*

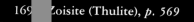

169 Zoisite (Thulite), *p. 569*

170 Corundum (Ruby), *p. 395*

171 Garnet (Pyrope, var. Rhodolite), *p. 582*

172   Lepidolite, *p. 534*

173   Muscovite, *p. 531*

174   Halite, *p. 426*

175 Garnet (Almandine) in Rhyolite, *p. 582*

176 Garnet (Spessartine) in Plagioclase, *p. 582*

177 Garnet (Pyrope), *p. 582*

178   Fluorite, *p. 428*

179   Huebnerite, *p. 496*

180   Cuprite, *p. 394*

181   Cuprite, *p. 394*

182   Rhodochrosite, *p. 435*

183   Vanadinite, *p. 486*

84 Hematite coating on Quartz, *p. 397*

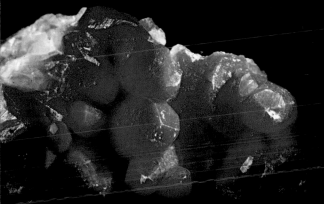

85 Cuprite (Chalcotrichite) in Calcite, *p. 394*

86 Realgar, *p. 370*

Red Minerals

187 Sphalerite, *p. 362*

188 Zincite, *p. 395*

189 Rhodochrosite, *p. 435*

190 Spinel, *p. 416*

191 Cassiterite, *p. 402*

192 Pyrargyrite, *p. 384*

193   Corundum (Ruby), *p. 395*

194   Garnet (Almandine), *p. 582*

195   Vanadinite, *p. 486*

196 Beryl, *p. 560*

197 Apatite, *p. 482*

198 Neptunite, *p. 555*

199   Rhodonite, *p. 553*

200   Corundum (Ruby), *p. 395*

201   Tourmaline (Rubellite), *p. 563*

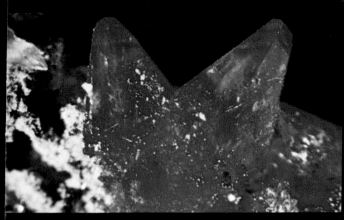

202 Cuprite inclusions in Calcite, *p. 394*

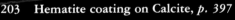

203 Hematite coating on Calcite, *p. 397*

204 Rhodonite with Calcite, *p. 553*

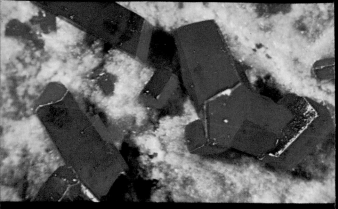

205   Realgar, *p. 370*

206   Vanadinite, *p. 486*

207   Proustite, *p. 385*

208 Pyrargyrite, *p. 384*

209 Pyrargyrite, *p. 384*

210 Huebnerite, *p. 496*

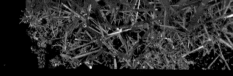

211 Cuprite (Chalcotrichite), *p. 394*

212 Crocoite, *p. 470*

213 Crocoite, *p. 470*

214 Cinnabar, *p. 369*

215 Realgar, *p. 370*

216 Descloizite, *p. 478*

217   Rhodonite, *p. 553*

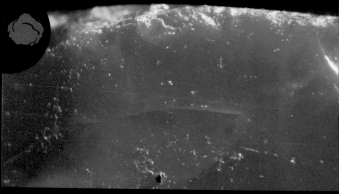

218   Chalcedony, *p. 504*

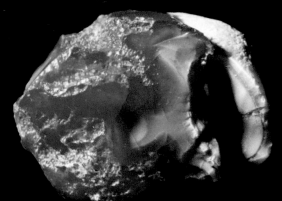

219   Opal (Fire Opal), *p. 506*

220 Chalcedony (Jasper), *p. 504*

221 Cinnabar, *p. 369*

222 Zincite, *p. 395*

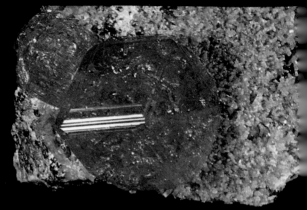

223   Garnet (Grossular) on Diopside, *p. 582*

224   Sphalerite, *p. 362*

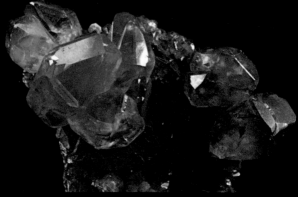

225   Calcite, *p. 432*

226 Fluorite with Calcite, *p. 428*

227 Jarosite, *p. 465*

228 Rutile with Muscovite, *p. 400*

229   Apatite, *p. 482*

230   Titanite, *p. 588*

231   Zircon, *p. 586*

32 Anglesite, *p. 457*

33 Fluorite, *p. 428*

34 Calcite twin crystals, *p. 432*

235 Monazite with Quartz, *p. 473*

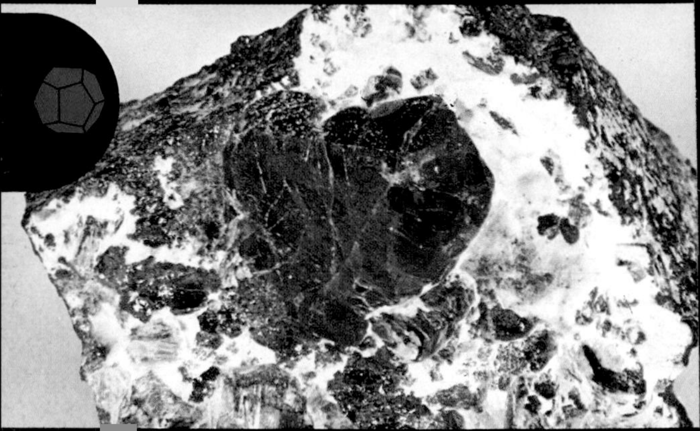

236 Chondrodite, *p. 587*

237 Descloizite, *p. 478*

238 Garnet (Almandine) in Schist, *p. 582*

239 Garnet (Andradite), *p. 582*

240 Garnet (Almandine), *p. 582*

241   Zircon, *p. 586*

242   Tourmaline (Dravite) with Tremolite, *p. 563*

243   Garnet (Grossular), *p. 582*

244   Zircon, *p.* 586

245   Scheelite, *p.* 497

246   Willemite on Calcite, *p.* 576

247   Siderite, *p. 434*

248   Limonite pseudomorph after Pyrite, *p. 413*

249   Staurolite in Schist, *p. 581*

250   Andalusite, *p. 577*

251   Apatite, *p. 482*

252   Phlogopite in Calcite, *p. 532*

253   Gypsum, *p. 459*

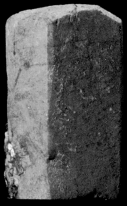

254   Orthoclase, *p. 508*

255   Vesuvianite, *p. 568*

256 Topaz, *p. 580*

257 Aragonite, *p. 438*

258 Calcite, *p. 432*

259   Barite with Calcite, *p. 455*

260   Hypersthene, *p. 544*

261   Calcite twin crystals, *p. 432*

262 Rutile in Quartz, *p. 400*

263 Rutile with Muscovite, *p. 400*

264 Scapolite, *p. 517*

265   Vanadinite with Descloizite, *p. 486*

266   Huebnerite, *p. 496*

267   Goethite, *p. 411*

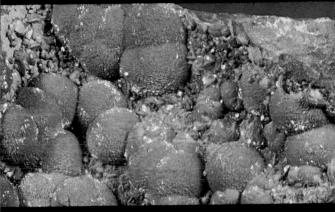

269 Siderite, *p. 434*

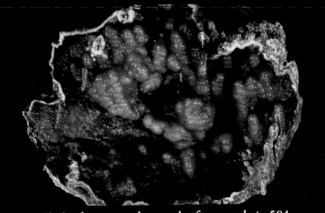

270 Chalcedony pseudomorph after coral, *p. 504*

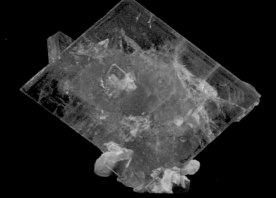

271 Barite, *p. 455*

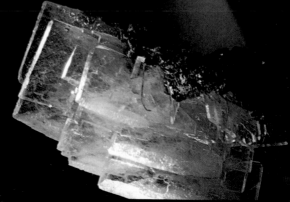

272 Muscovite, *p. 531*

273 Barite, *p. 455*

274 Axinite, *p.* 559

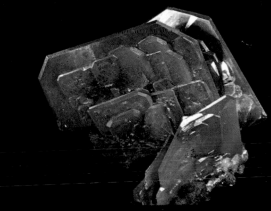

275 Wulfenite, *p.* 499

276 Axinite, *p.* 559

277   Dolomite, *p. 442*

278   Barite "rose," *p. 455*

279   Tephroite with Calcite, *p. 574*

280   Opal, *p. 506*

281   Chalcedony (Jasper), *p. 504*

282   Bauxite, *p. 410*

283   Gummite in Feldspar, *p. 404*

284   Willemite, *p. 576*

285   Topaz, *p. 580*

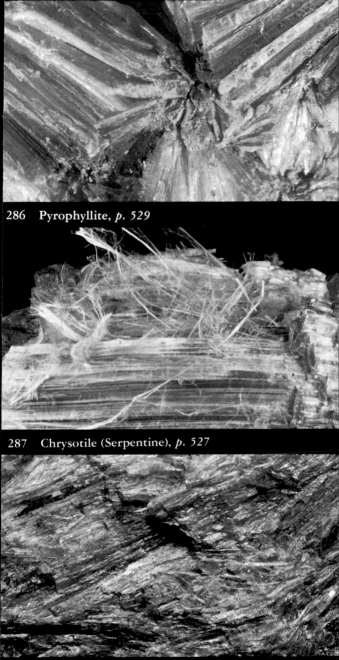

286 Pyrophyllite, *p. 529*

287 Chrysotile (Serpentine), *p. 527*

288 Sillimanite, *p. 578*

289   Scheelite, *p. 497*

290   Wulfenite, *p. 499*

291   Vanadinite, *p. 486*

292 Legrandite, *p. 489*

293 Orpiment, *p. 371*

294 Mimetite, *p. 485*

295   Mimetite, *p. 485*

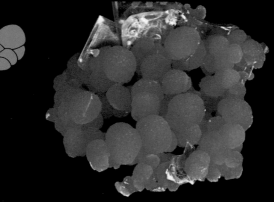

296   Mimetite with Wulfenite, *p. 485*

297   Zincite, *p. 395*

298 Wulfenite, *p. 499*

299 Wulfenite, *p. 499*

300 Wulfenite, *p. 499*

301   Amblygonite, *p. 480*

302   Orthoclase, *p. 508*

303   Fluorite on Limestone, *p. 428*

304 Sulfur, *p. 353*

305 Diamond, *p. 354*

306 Fluorite, *p. 428*

307   Topaz, *p. 580*

308   Monazite, *p. 473*

309   Garnet (Andradite, var. Topazolite), *p. 582*

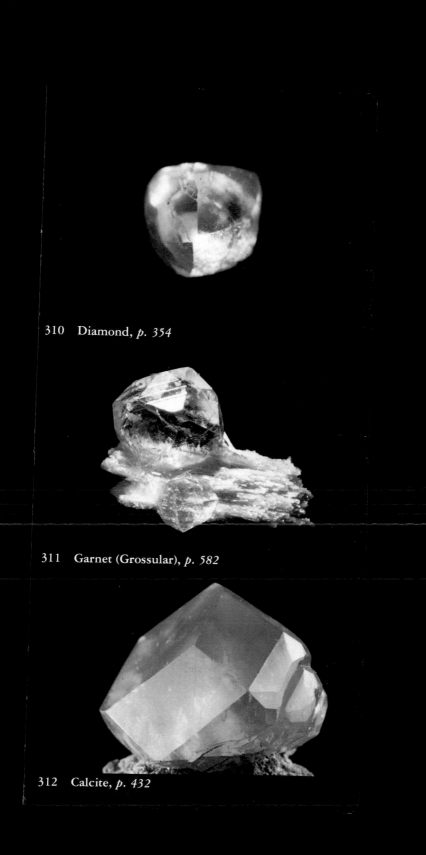

310   Diamond, *p. 354*

311   Garnet (Grossular), *p. 582*

312   Calcite, *p. 432*

313 Danburite, *p. 513*

314 Garnet (Grossular), *p. 582*

315 Halite, *p. 426*

316   Amblygonite, *p. 480*

317   Datolite, *p. 591*

318   Magnesite, *p. 433*

319   Plagioclase (Labradorite), *p. 510*

320   Calcite, *p. 432*

321   Scheelite on Quartz, *p. 497*

322 Diamond, *p. 354*

323 Anglesite, *p. 457*

324 Amblygonite, *p. 480*

325   Calcite, *p. 432*

326   Vesuvianite, *p. 568*

327   Beryl, *p. 560*

328 Adamite, *p. 481*

329 Apatite, *p. 482*

330 Epidote, *p. 571*

331 Sulfur, *p. 353*

332 Orpiment, *p. 371*

333 Legrandite, *p. 489*

334 Barite with Calcite, *p. 455*

335 Willemite, *p. 576*

336 Scapolite on Calcite, *p. 517*

337   Legrandite, *p. 489*

338   Orthoclase (Adularia) with Actinolite, *p. 508*

339   Vanadinite, *p. 486*

340 Adamite, *p. 481*

341 Legrandite, *p. 489*

342 Mimetite, *p. 485*

343 Barite, *p.* 455

344 Wulfenite, *p.* 499

345 Wulfenite, *p.* 499

346 Apophyllite on Prehnite, *p. 525*

347 Autunite, *p. 492*

348 Axinite, *p. 559*

349   Titanite, *p. 588*

350   Gummite, *p. 404*

351   Carnotite, *p. 494*

352　Axinite with Rhodonite on Franklinite, *p. 559*

353　Gummite with Uraninite, *p. 404*

354　Orpiment, *p. 371*

355 Dolomite, *p. 442*

356 Fluorite, *p. 428*

357 Topaz, *p. 580*

358   Topaz, *p. 580*

359   Phenakite with Fluorite, *p. 575*

360   Plagioclase (Anorthite), *p. 510*

361 Anglesite, *p. 457*

362 Diamond in Peridotite (Kimberlite), *p. 354*

363 Garnet (Grossular) on Diopside needle, *p. 582*

364 Calcite on Quartz (Amethyst), *p. 432*

365 Datolite, *p. 591*

366 Colemanite, *p. 450*

367 Topaz, *p. 580*

368 Pectolite, *p. 552*

369 Celestite with Calcite, *p. 456*

370   Quartz (Rock Crystal), *p. 502*

371   Willemite, *p. 576*

372   Quartz (Rock Crystal), *p. 502*

373   Barite, *p. 455*

374   Beryl, *p. 560*

375   Barite, *p. 455*

376 Cerussite twin crystals, *p. 441*

377 Gypsum, *p. 459*

378 Hemimorphite, *p. 565*

379   Austinite, *p. 478*

380   Colemanite, *p. 450*

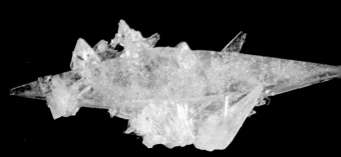

381   Prehnite, *p. 590*

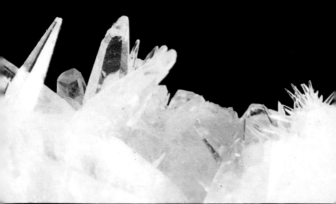

82 Calcite, *p. 432*

83 Danburite, *p. 513*

84 Kernite, *p. 448*

385   Quartz "Japanese" twin, *p. 502*

386   Kyanite, *p. 579*

387   Apophyllite, *p. 525*

388   Gypsum, *p. 459*

389   Natrolite, *p. 523*

390   Strontianite, *p. 440*

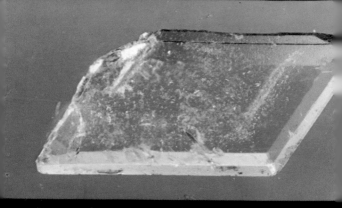

391   Amblygonite, *p. 480*

392   Datolite with Epidote, *p. 591*

393   Brucite, *p. 408*

394　Gypsum (Selenite), *p. 459*

395　Barite, *p. 455*

396　Quartz on Orthoclase (Adularia), *p. 502*

397   Amblygonite with Lepidolite on Quartz, *p. 480*

398   Witherite, *p. 439*

399   Orthoclase, *p. 508*

400 Beryl (Goshenite), *p. 560*

401 Plagioclase (Oligoclase), *p. 510*

402 Halite, *p. 426*

403   Heulandite with Chabazite, *p. 518*

404   Halite, *p. 426*

405   Datolite, *p. 591*

406   Glauberite, *p. 458*

407   Dolomite, *p. 442*

408   Colemanite, *p. 450*

409 Plagioclase (Anorthite), *p. 510*

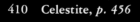

410 Celestite, *p. 456*

411 Apophyllite with Laumontite, *p. 525*

412 Analcime with Calcite, *p. 522*

413 Leucite, *p. 513*

414 Orthoclase (Microcline), *p. 508*

415   Witherite, *p. 439*

416   Calcite, *p. 432*

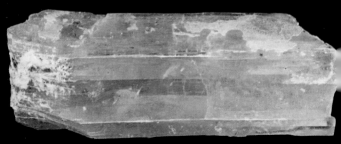

417   Kernite, *p. 448*

18   Willemite in Calcite, *p. 576*

19   Lawsonite on Glaucophane, *p. 566*

20   Scapolite, *p. 517*

421   Jadeite, *p. 549*

422   Wollastonite with Calcite and Pyroxene, *p. 55*

423   Celestite, *p. 456*

424 Barite, *p. 455*

425 Danburite, *p. 513*

426 Borax, *p. 448*

427   Calcite on Fluorite, *p. 432*

428   Stilbite, *p. 519*

429   Anhydrite, *p. 458*

430 Calcite, *p. 432*

431 Quartz pseudomorph after Anhydrite, *p. 502*

432 Hemimorphite, *p. 565*

433   Calcite, *p. 432*

434   Aragonite, *p. 438*

435   Colemanite, *p. 450*

436   Cerussite, *p. 441*

437   Laumontite, *p. 520*

438   Ulexite, *p. 449*

439   Ulexite on Colemanite, *p. 449*

440   Natrolite, *p. 523*

441   Aragonite, *p. 438*

442 Pectolite with Natrolite, *p. 552*

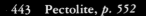

443 Pectolite, *p. 552*

444 Plagioclase (Albite) on Quartz, *p. 510*

445 Pectolite, *p. 552*

446 Pyrophyllite, *p. 529*

447 Mesolite, *p. 524*

448 Tremolite, *p. 537*

449 Strontianite, *p. 440*

450 Wollastonite, *p. 551*

451 Thenardite, *p. 454*

452 Chalcedony, *p. 504*

453 Pectolite, *p. 552*

454 Lawsonite, *p. 566*

455 Heulandite, *p. 518*

456 Borax, *p. 448*

457   Epsomite, *p. 462*

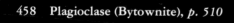

458   Plagioclase (Bytownite), *p. 510*

459   Muscovite, *p. 531*

460 Wollastonite, *p. 551*

461 Cryolite with Siderite, *p. 429*

462 Magnesite with Serpentine, *p. 433*

463   Melanterite, *p. 461*

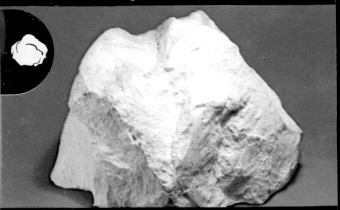

464   Kaolinite, *p. 526*

465   Plagioclase (Andesine) with Hornblende, *p. 510*

466 Orthoclase (Microcline, var. Perthite), *p. 508*

467 Talc, *p. 530*

468 Howlite, *p. 451*

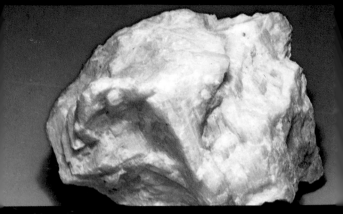

469 Cryolite, *p.* 429

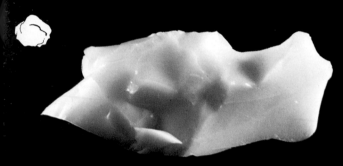

470 Opal, *p.* 506

471 Gypsum, *p.* 459

472 Gypsum, *p. 459*

473 Aragonite, *p. 438*

474 Serpentine (Chrysotile), *p. 527*

475 Fluorite with Rhodochrosite, *p. 428*

476 Cryolite, *p. 429*

477 Tremolite with Tourmaline (Dravite), *p. 537*

478 Tremolite, *p. 537*

479 Kernite, *p. 448*

480 Nepheline, *p. 514*

481   Thenardite, *p. 454*

482   Leucite in Rhyolite, *p. 513*

483   Apophyllite, *p. 525*

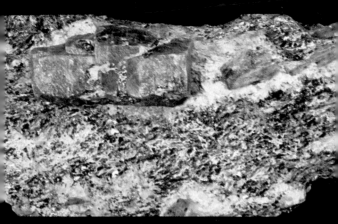

484 Corundum in Gneiss, *p. 395*

485 Andalusite in Quartz, *p. 577*

486 Scapolite, *p. 517*

487   Wavellite, *p. 490*

488   Pyrophyllite, *p. 529*

489   Tremolite, *p. 537*

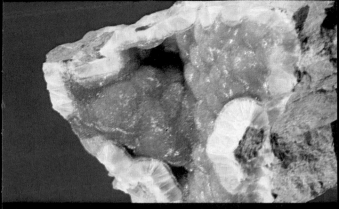

490 Wavellite, *p. 490*

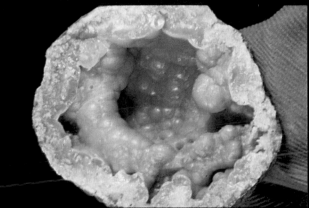

491 Chalcedony geode, *p. 504*

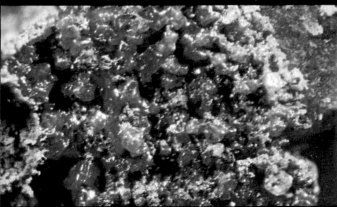

492 Chlorargyrite, *p. 426*

493 Barite with Siderite, *p. 455*

494 Barite, *p. 455*

495 Glauberite, *p. 458*

496   Anhydrite, *p. 458*

497   Plagioclase (Labradorite), *p. 510*

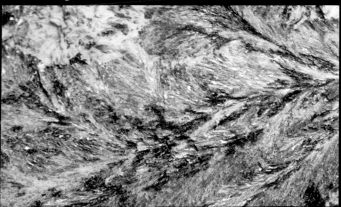

498   Muscovite, *p. 531*

499   Brucite, *p. 408*

500   Zoisite, *p. 569*

501   Chalcedony, *p. 504*

502   Nepheline, *p. 514*

503   Clinozoisite, *p. 570*

504   Bauxite, *p. 410*

505   Spinel, *p. 416*

506   Tourmaline, *p. 563*

507   Garnet (Almandine), *p. 582*

508 Descloizite, *p. 478*

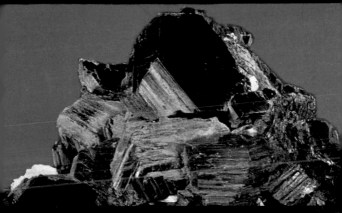

509 Phlogopite, *p. 532*

510 Augite, *p. 547*

511   Garnet (Andradite, var. Melanite), *p. 582*

512   Garnet (Andradite), *p. 582*

513   Hornblende, *p. 539*

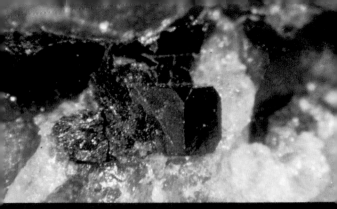

514 Uraninite, *p. 403*

515 Cassiterite, *p. 402*

517   Babingtonite, *p. 554*

518   Actinolite, *p. 538*

519   Cordierite, *p. 562*

520   **Hedenbergite,** *p. 546*

521   **Augite,** *p. 547*

522   **Epidote,** *p. 571*

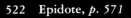

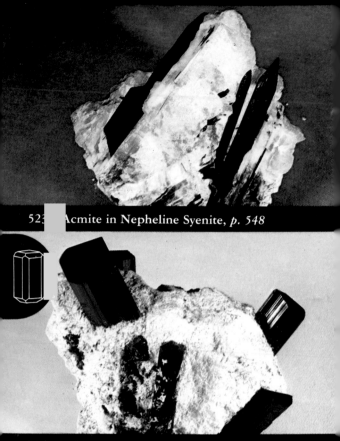

523 Acmite in Nepheline Syenite, *p. 548*

524 Epidote, *p. 571*

525 Neptunite in Natrolite, *p. 555*

526 Quartz (Smoky Quartz) on Feldspar, *p. 502*

527 Riebeckite with Quartz and Microcline, *p. 543*

528 Diopside with Calcite, *p. 545*

529   Vivianite, *p. 474*

530   Goethite, *p. 411*

531   Vivianite, *p. 474*

532 Pumpellyite (var. Chlorastrolite), *p. 567*

533 Hematite, *p. 397*

534 Axinite, *p. 559*

535   Actinolite, *p. 538*

536   Hornblende, *p. 539*

537   Glaucophane, *p. 542*

538 Staurolite twins in Schist, *p. 581*

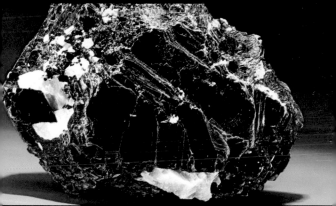

539 Biotite, *p. 533*

540 Chlorite on altered Pyroxene, *p. 535*

541   Tourmaline (Watermelon Tourmaline), *p. 563*

542   Tourmaline (Elbaite) on Quartz, *p. 563*

543   Tourmaline (Elbaite), *p. 563*

544 Vivianite, *p. 474*

54 Quartz with Hematite coating, *p. 502*

546 Vanadinite, *p. 486*

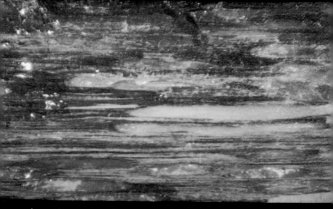

547   Opal (Precious Wood Opal), *p. 506*

548   Muscovite in polarized light, *p. 531*

549   Plagioclase (Labradorite), *p. 510*

550 Plagioclase ("Sunstone" Oligoclase), *p. 510*

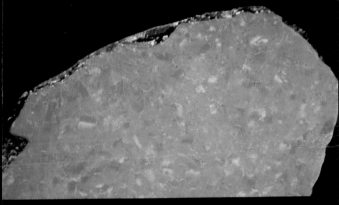

551 Opal (Precious Opal), *p. 506*

552 Plagioclase (Labradorite), *p. 510*

553   Opal (Precious Opal), *p. 506*

554   Chalcedony (Agate), *p. 504*

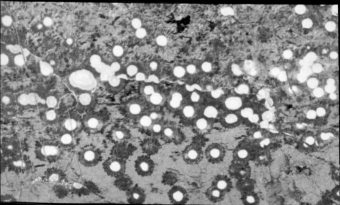

555   Chalcedony (Orbicular Jasper), *p. 504*

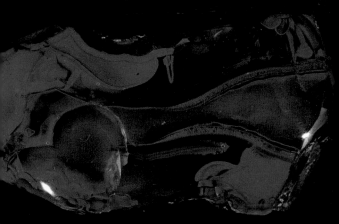

556 Chalcedony ("Apache Flame" Agate), *p. 504*

557 Opal (Fire Opal), *p. 506*

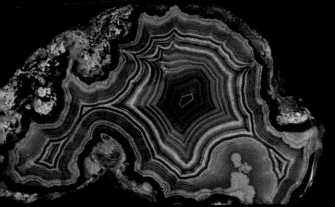

558 Chalcedony (Banded Agate), *p. 504*

559   Galena, *p. 361*

560   Chalcocite twin crystals, *p. 359*

561   Arsenopyrite twin crystals, *p. 377*

562   Gold, *p. 346*

563   Chalcopyrite twins on Quartz, *p. 363*

564   Chalcopyrite twins on Calcite, *p. 363*

565 Chalcopyrite with Quartz and Sphalerite, *p. 363*

566 Marcasite, *p. 376*

567 Chalcopyrite, *p. 363*

568   **Pyrite,** *p. 374*

569   **Pyrite,** *p. 374*

570   **Tetrahedrite with Quartz,** *p. 386*

571 Manganite, *p. 409*

572 Skutterudite, *p. 379*

573 Arsenopyrite, *p. 377*

574 Hematite, *p. 397*

575 Galena, *p. 361*

576 Hematite, *p. 397*

577 Tennantite with Pyrite and Quartz, *p. 386*

578 Sphalerite with Pyrite, *p. 362*

579 Sphalerite, *p. 362*

580 Bornite with Pyrite, *p. 360*

581 Pyragyrite, *p. 384*

582 Arsenopyrite, *p. 377*

583   Bixbyite on Topaz, *p. 399*

584   Cobaltite, *p. 375*

585   Bixbyite on Rhyolite, *p. 399*

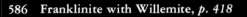

586 Franklinite with Willemite, *p. 418*

587 Franklinite with Calcite and Zincite, *p. 418*

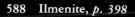

588 Ilmenite, *p. 398*

589   Chromite, *p. 419*

590   Magnetite, *p. 417*

591   Pyrargyrite with Quartz, *p. 384*

592 Chalcocite, *p. 359*

593 Columbite-Tantalite on Albite, *p. 422*

594 Enargite, *p. 388*

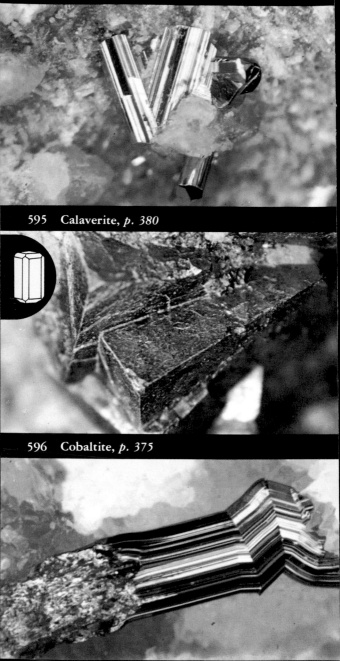

595 Calaverite, *p. 380*

596 Cobaltite, *p. 375*

597 Stibnite, *p. 372*

598   Marcasite twins, *p. 376*

599   Pyrargyrite with Quartz, *p. 384*

600   Pyrargyrite with Quartz (Amethyst), *p. 384*

601 Enargite, *p. 388*

602 Chalcocite on Quartz, *p. 359*

603 Manganite, *p. 409*

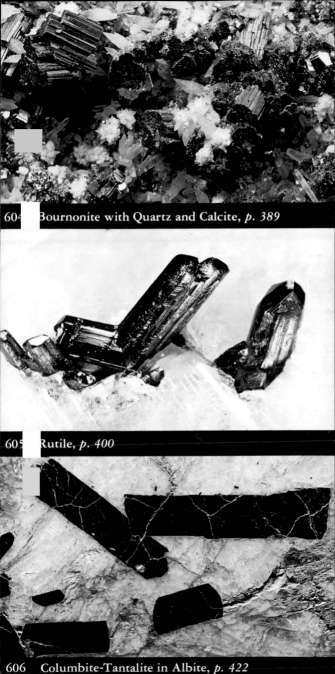

604   Bournonite with Quartz and Calcite, *p. 389*

605   Rutile, *p. 400*

606   Columbite-Tantalite in Albite, *p. 422*

607 Millerite in geode, *p. 366*

608 Jamesonite with Quartz and Pyrite, *p. 391*

609 Boulangerite with Quartz, *p. 390*

610 Bismuthinite with Pyrite and Calcite, *p. 373*

611 Goethite, *p. 411*

612 Goethite, *p. 411*

613 Goethite, *p. 411*

614 Manganite with Calcite, *p. 409*

615 Pyrolusite, *p. 401*

616 Pyrite "dollar," *p. 374*

617 Pyrite "dollar," *p. 374*

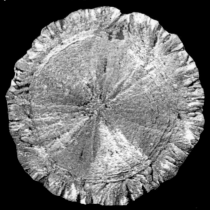

618 Pyrite "dollar," *p. 374*

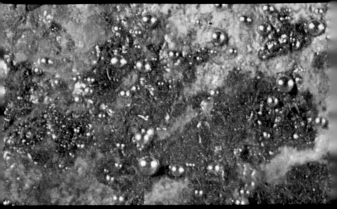

619   Mercury, *p. 370*

620   Goethite with Aurichalcite, *p. 411*

621   Hematite, *p. 397*

622 Psilomelane on Limonite, *p. 411*

623 Limonite, *p. 413*

624 Goethite, *p. 411*

625   Huebnerite, *p. 496*

626   Wolframite on Quartz, *p. 496*

627   Hematite with Quartz, *p. 397*

628   **Enargite,** *p. 388*

629   **Stephanite,** *p. 384*

630   **Covellite,** *p. 368*

631   Bornite, *p. 360*

632   Goethite, *p. 411*

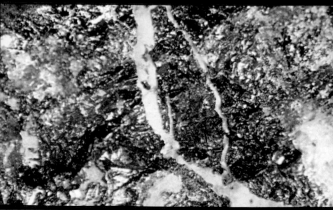

633   Bornite, *p. 360*

634   Pentlandite with Chalcopyrite, *p. 367*

635   Nickeline, *p. 366*

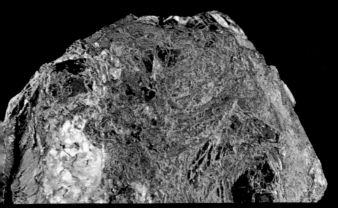

636   Pyrrhotite, *p. 364*

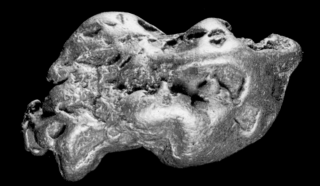

637   Gold nugget, *p. 346*

638   Gold on Quartz, *p. 346*

639   Gold vein in Quartz, *p. 346*

640   Platinum nugget, *p. 349*

641   Molybdenite with Quartz, *p. 378*

642   Antimony, *p. 351*

643   Arsenic, *p. 350*

644   Graphite, *p. 355*

645   Bismuth, *p. 352*

646 Acanthite, *p. 358*

647 Silver with Dyscrasite coating, *p. 347*

648 Sylvanite, *p. 381*

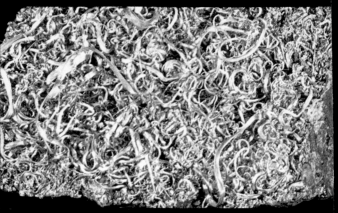

649   Silver, *p. 347*

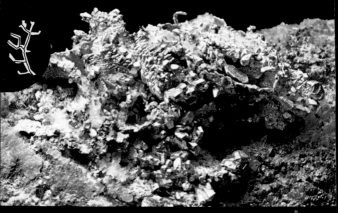

650   Gold with Arsenopyrite, *p. 346*

651   Silver (Copper-bearing wires), *p. 347*

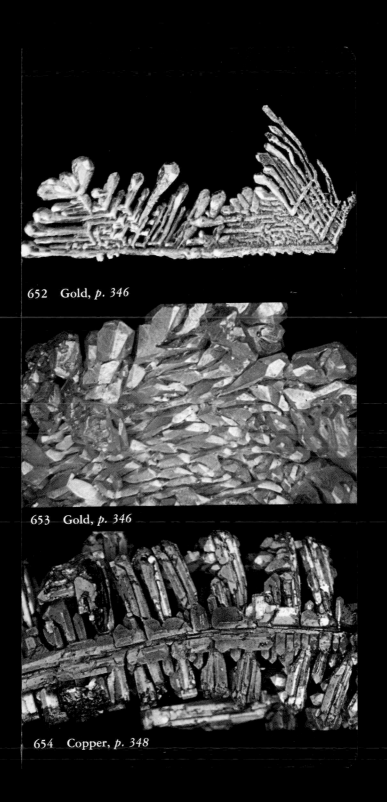

652   Gold, *p. 346*

653   Gold, *p. 346*

654   Copper, *p. 348*

Gemstones

Gemstones are minerals that have outstanding transparency, luster, color, "fire," and freedom from flaws, and are therefore prized for their beauty. Most gemstones also have sufficient hardness and tenacity to be used as personal jewelry or for similar decorative purposes.

Preparation of Gems A gemstone becomes a gem when it is cut, shaped, and polished for use as an ornament. The final form, depending on the type of stone and the preference of the lapidary artist, will be a faceted stone, a cabochon, or a carving. Faceted stones are cut so as to bring out the brilliance and sparkle of the gem. The cabochon cut—highly polished, but rounded or flattened rather than faceted—takes advantage of a stone's color and pattern, and is used for star and catseye gems and many others. Carving is a popular way of working suitable gemstones in larger sizes, including among others rock crystal (quartz), agate, turquoise, and jade. The color plates on the following pages show a selection of the best-known gem minerals, both as rough stones and as cut and polished gems.

655 Jade (Jadeite; Nephrite), *pp. 538, 549*

656 Chrysoprase (Chalcedony), *p. 504*

657 Amazonstone (Orthoclase, var. Microcline), *p. 50*

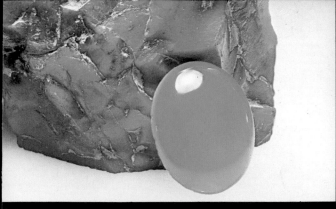

658 Chrysocolla, *p. 556*

659 Turquoise, *p. 488*

660 Labradorite (Plagioclase), *p. 510*

661 Tigereye (Quartz), *p. 502*

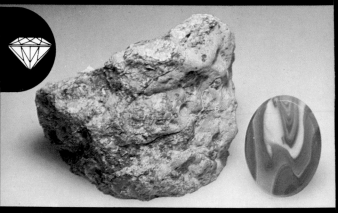

662 Agate (Chalcedony), *p. 504*

663 Jasper (Chalcedony), *p. 504*

664 Moonstone (Plagioclase, var. Oligoclase), *p. 510*

665 Opal, *p. 506*

666 Lapis Lazuli (Lazurite), *p. 516*

667   Ruby Spinel, *p. 416*

668   Ruby (Corundum), *p. 395*

669   Almandine (Garnet), *p. 582*

670 Pyrope (Garnet), *p. 582*

671 Almandine (Garnet), *p. 582*

672 Rubellite (Tourmaline), *p. 563*

673   Rose Quartz, *p. 502*

674   Amethyst (Quartz), *p. 502*

675   Fluorite, *p. 428*

676 **Morganite (Beryl),** *p. 560*

677 **Diamond,** *p. 354*

678 **Kunzite (Spodumene),** *p. 550*

679 Sapphire (Corundum), *p. 395*

680 Benitoite, *p. 558*

681 Tanzanite (Zoisite), *p. 569*

682 Aquamarine (Beryl), *p. 560*

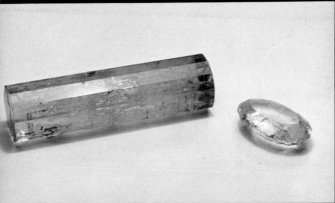

683 Emerald (Beryl), *p. 560*

684 Spinel, *p. 416*

685   Peridot (Olivine), *p. 573*

686   Zircon, *p. 586*

687   Elbaite (Tourmaline), *p. 563*

688 Heliodor (Golden Beryl), *p. 560*

689 Hiddenite (Spodumene), *p. 550*

690 Smoky Quartz, *p. 502*

691 Chrysoberyl, *p. 420*

692 Vesuvianite, *p. 568*

693 Demantoid (Garnet, var. Andradite), *p. 582*

694 Scapolite, *p. 517*

695 Titanite, *p. 588*

696 Apatite, *p. 482*

697   Grossular (Garnet), *p. 582*

698   Topaz, *p. 580*

699   Citrine (Quartz), *p. 502*

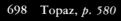

700   Fire Opal, *p. 506*

701   Carnelian (Chalcedony), *p. 504*

702   Spessartine (Garnet), *p. 582*

DESCRIPTIVE KEY TO MINERALS

This Key will allow you to identify any mineral you are likely to find, by making use of color, hardness, the quality and number of cleavages, and other physical properties.
To identify a specimen, first decide which of the following color groups it belongs in:

Green
Blue
Violet to Pink
Red
Brown
Orange
Yellow
Colorless
White
Gray
Black
Multicolored or Banded
Metallic

Within each color group, the minerals are arranged in order of increasing hardness (**H**), indicated by the number or numbers in the first column of the Key; the hardness test is explained on p. 21. Within each hardness group the minerals are arranged according to the quality and number of cleavages (**Cl**); cleavage is explained on p. 23. The following symbols are used in the

second column of the Key to indicate
cleavage quality:

```
+ + +   Perfect
+ +     Good or distinct
+       Poor
—       None
```

For example, this entry:

2+++

indicates a mineral, such as hornblende,
that has perfect cleavage in two
directions. This entry:

1+++
2++

indicates a mineral, such as barite, that
has perfect cleavage in one direction
and good or distinct cleavage in·two
others.

Additional remarks on each species, in
the third column, describe distinctive
features that will aid in identification.
The Key will help you to narrow down
the possibilities for any specimen to no
more than six or eight species. By
checking the descriptions on the pages
indicated you will be able to identify
most of the common minerals.

Example   For example, suppose you have a blue
mineral with a hardness of about 4 to
5. Turning to the "Blue" section of the
Key, first check all the species whose
hardness falls in this range. The Key
tells you that there are ten choices:

Azurite (H = $3\frac{1}{2}$–4)
Fluorite (H = 4)
Smithsonite (H = 4–$4\frac{1}{2}$)
Kyanite (H = 4–5)
Triphylite (H = 4–5)
Hemimorphite (H = $4\frac{1}{2}$–5)
Apatite (H = 5)
Lazurite (H = 5–$5\frac{1}{2}$)
Riebeckite (H = 5–6)
Turquoise (H = 5–6)

With the possibilities thus narrowed down, the next step is to test for cleavage. If we assume that your specimen cleaves easily in two directions, the choice is now narrowed down to only four species: azurite, kyanite, hemimorphite, and riebeckite. Looking in the "Distinctive Features" column, you see that only one of these, azurite, has a blue streak, which matches your specimen. Tentatively identifying your specimen as azurite, turn to the mineral description, whose page number follows the name of the mineral. By checking the details given in the description, you can confirm your identification. For minerals that are not readily identified, you may have to run through several of the possibilities listed in the Key. In difficult cases, it may be necessary to check with a museum or mineral club.

H	C1	Distinctive Features	Mineral
		GREEN MINERALS	
1	1+++	Extremely soft; greasy feel; micaceous habit and flaky cleavage	Talc, p. 530
1–2	1+++	Forms feathery masses of fine needlelike or lathlike crystals	Aurichalcite, p. 443
1–2	1+++	Usually as fine-grained masses, often foliated or fibrous; greasy feel; micaceous habit and flaky cleavage	Pyrophyllite, p. 529
1½–2	1+++	Thin flexible flakes and small tabular crystals; streak white turning to blue in light	Vivianite, p. 474
2	1+++ 1++	Bluish- to yellowish-green; sweetish astringent taste	Melanterite, p. 461
2–2½	1+++	Usually in flat translucent tabular crystals or aggregates; yellowish streak	Autunite, p. 492
2–2½	1+++	Extremely soft, often in flexible sheets; pearly luster on cleavage surface	Brucite, p. 408
2–2½	1+++	Usually in irregular, foliated masses; breaks into mica-like sheets	Chlorite, p. 535
2–2½	1+++	Cleaves into thin, flexible elastic plates; colorless and transparent in thin sheets	Muscovite, p. 531
2–2½	1+++	Square tabular crystals; micaceous cleavage	Torbernite, p. 491

H	Cl	Distinctive Features	Mineral
5–5½	1++	Usually as flattened, wedge-shaped crystals; brittle; parting common	Titanite, p. 588
5–5½	—	Usually as trapezohedral vitreous crystals lining cavities in volcanic rocks	Analcime, p. 522
5–5½	—	Usually as pale-colored, blunt, wedge-shaped crystals	Datolite, p. 591
5–6	2+++	Crystals usually slender, prismatic; prismatic cleavage at 56° and 124°	Actinolite, p. 538
5–6	2+++	Usually massive; cleaves at nearly right angles	Hedenbergite, p. 546
5–6	2+++	Nearly black color; cleavages at angles of 56° and 124°	Hornblende, p. 539
5–6	2+++	Prismatic crystals with diamond-shaped cross section	Pargasite, p. 541
5–6	1+++ 2++	Usually in coarsely crystalline aggregates; bronze or pearly luster; cleavages intersect at nearly right angles	Hypersthene, p. 544
5–6	2++	Two distinct cleavages at nearly right angles; often in short prismatic crystals	Augite, p. 547
5–6	2++	Short prismatic crystals with good terminations, often twinned; two cleavages at nearly right angles	Diopside, p. 545
5–6	2++	Short square prismatic crystals	Scapolite, p. 517

H	C1	Distinctive Features	Mineral
5–6	—	Bright sky-blue to apple-green; usually in compact masses or veins	Turquoise, p. 488
5½	2++	Short prismatic or rhombohedral crystals; luster usually resinous	Willemite, p. 576
5½–6½	—	Vitreous brittle masses; conchoidal fracture; may be milky or show internal play of colors	Opal, p. 506
6 ·	2++	Two good cleavages at right angles; usually as masses or grains; crystals, often twinned, common in pegmatites	Orthoclase, p. 508
6	2++	Narrow tabular or platy crystals or fibrous, bladed masses	Pumpellyite, p. 567
6–6½	2+++	Slender prismatic crystals ending in pointed pyramids; gray streak	Acmite, p. 548
6–6½	1++	Botryoidal crusts, usually as linings in cavities in volcanic rocks	Prehnite, p. 590
6–6½	1++	Long prismatic orthorhombic crystals with deep lengthwise striations; luster vitreous but pearly on cleavage surface	Zoisite, p. 569
6–7 4–5	1+++ 1++	Bladed crystals; hardness greater across crystals than lengthwise	Kyanite, p. 579
6–7	1+++	Long, slender, grooved prismatic crystals	Epidote, p. 571

H	Cl	Distinctive Features	Mineral
6½	1+	Crystals short, prismatic, with square cross section; also columnar, massive (like jade)	Vesuvianite, p. 568
6½–7	2++	Extremely tough, compact; cleavages at nearly right angles	Jadeite, p. 549
6½–7	2++	Usually in striated crystals, flattened and lathlike; a tough mineral; fracture splintery	Spodumene, p. 550
6½–7	2+	Indistinct cleavages at right angles; usually as rounded grains or granular masses	Olivine Group, p. 573
6½–7½	—	Crystals equant dodecahedrons or trapezohedrons; common in metamorphic rocks	Garnet Group, p. 582
7	1+++	Prismatic, monoclinic crystals; perfect lengthwise cleavage	Clinozoisite, p. 570
7	—	Smooth surface and conchoidal fracture; botryoidal form common; no visible crystals	Chalcedony, p. 504
7–7½	—	Slender prismatic, striated crystals, rounded-triangular in cross section	Tourmaline Group, p. 563
7½–8	1+	Crystals prismatic, hexagonal, striated lengthwise	Beryl, p. 560

H	C1	Distinctive Features	Mineral
7½–8	—	Octahedral crystals, often twinned	Spinel, p. 416
8	1+++	Usually as stubby or medium-long prismatic crystals with lengthwise striations; perfect cleavage across crystals	Topaz, p. 580
8½	1++ 2+	Vitreous tabular or prismatic crystals, often twinned	Chrysoberyl, p. 420
9	—	Crystals barrel-shaped; vitreous or adamantine luster; may break into cubic fragments with striated faces	Corundum, p. 395

BLUE MINERALS

H	C1	Distinctive Features	Mineral
1–2	1+++	Forms feathery masses of fine needlelike or lathlike crystals	Aurichalcite, p. 443
1½–2	1+++	Indigo or dark blue; cleaves into thin flexible sheets; streak lead-gray to black	Covellite, p. 368
1½–2	1+++	Thin flexible flakes and small tabular crystals; streak white turning to blue in light	Vivianite, p. 474
2–2½	3+++	Salty taste; cleaves easily into lusterless cubic fragments	Halite, p. 426
2–2½	1+++	Extremely soft, often in flexible sheets; pearly luster on cleavage surface	Brucite, p. 408

H	Cl	Distinctive Features	Mineral
2–4	—	Usually sky-blue or greenish blue; conchoidal fracture	Chrysocolla, p. 556
2½	1+++ 1+	Deep azure-blue masses and prismatic crystals; pale blue streak	Linarite, p. 464
2½	—	Deep color; often in short prismatic crystals; readily dissolves to form blue solution in water	Chalcanthite, p. 461
3	3+++	Cleaves into perfect rhombohedrons; clear specimens doubly refractive; bubbles easily in acid	Calcite, p. 432
3	—	Sky-blue to azure-blue plush- or wool-like aggregates; streak pale blue	Cyanotrichite, p. 466
3–3½	3+++	Rectangular cleavage; often in light, massive aggregates	Anhydrite, p. 458
3–3½	1+++ 2++	Usually in tabular crystals; heavy	Barite, p. 455
3–3½	1+++ 2++	Tabular crystals or cleavage masses; often with partial light blue tint	Celestite, p. 456
3½	2+++	Radiating clusters of fine prismatic crystals; occurs only near Bisbee, Arizona	Shattuckite, p. 557
3½–4	2++	Intense azure-blue crystals or masses; streak blue	Azurite, p. 445

H	Cl	Distinctive Features	Mineral
4	4+++	Usually in cubic crystals; perfect octahedral cleavage	Fluorite, p. 428
4–4½	3+++	Usually in translucent botryoidal masses; rhombohedral cleavage; bubbles in acid	Smithsonite, p. 436
4–5 6–7	1+++ 1++	Bladed crystals; hardness greater across crystals than lengthwise	Kyanite, p. 579
4–5	1+++ 2+	Usually massive, with the poor cleavages at right angles; occurs in granite pegmatites	Triphylite Series, p. 472
4½–5	1+++	Crystals usually small, thin, bladed, in fan-shaped aggregates; transparent to translucent	Hemimorphite, p.565
5	1+	Hexagonal prismatic crystals; sometimes tabular; greasy luster	Apatite, p. 482
5–5½	6+	Deep azure to greenish-blue; usually massive; vitreous	Lazurite, p. 516
5–6	2+++	Fibrous masses or prismatic crystals with diamond-shaped cross section; color quite dark	Riebeckite, p. 543
5–6	—	Bright sky-blue to apple-green; usually in compact masses or veins	Turquoise, p. 488
5½–6	1++	Distinct light- to dark-blue color; usually as bipyramidal crystals	Lazulite, p. 487

H	Cl	Distinctive Features	Mineral
5½–6	6+	Usually massive or as disseminated grains; vitreous; transparent to translucent	Sodalite, p. 515
5½–6½	—	Vitreous brittle masses; conchoidal fracture; may be milky or show internal play of colors	Opal, p. 506
6	2+++ 1++	Prismatic tabular crystals, often twinned; two perfect cleavages distinctive; luster vitreous to greasy	Lawsonite, p. 566
6	2+++ 1+	Cleavage masses or grains with fine parallel striations on best cleavage surface	Plagioclase Feldspar Group, p. 510
6	2+++	Fibrous masses of prismatic crystals with diamond-shaped cross section; color generally dark	Glaucophane, p. 542
6–6½	—	Well-formed tabular triangular crystals; occurs only in San Benito Co., California	Benitoite, p. 558
6–7; 4–5	1+++ 1++	Bladed crystals; hardness greater across crystals than lengthwise	Kyanite, p. 579
6½	1+	Crystals short, prismatic, with square cross section; also columnar, massive (like jade)	Vesuvianite, p. 568
7	1++ 1+	Usually as compact fibrous or columnar masses; bright color	Dumortierite, p. 589

H	C1	Distinctive Features	Mineral
7	—	Vitreous or greasy luster; massive or in hexagonal, horizontally striated crystals ending in double rhombohedrons; conchoidal fracture	Quartz, p. 502
7–7½	1+	In quartzlike masses or grains; color may seem to change when viewed from different angles	Cordierite, p. 562
7–7½	—	Slender prismatic, striated crystals, rounded triangular in cross section	Tourmaline Group, p. 563
7½–8	1+	Crystals prismatic, hexagonal, striated lengthwise	Beryl, p. 560
7½–8	—	Octahedral crystals, often twinned	Spinel, p. 416
8	1+++	Usually as stubby or medium-long prismatic crystals with lengthwise striations; perfect cleavage across crystals	Topaz, p. 580
9	—	Crystals barrel-shaped; vitreous or adamantine luster; may break into cubic fragments with striated faces	Corundum, p. 395

VIOLET TO PINK MINERALS

H	C1	Distinctive Features	Mineral
1½–2½	1+++	Usually as delicate, earthy crusts; color vivid red or pink; streak reddish or pink	Erythrite, p. 475

H	Cl	Distinctive Features	Mineral
2–2½	3+++	Salty taste; cleaves easily into lusterless cubic fragments	Halite, p. 426
2–2½	1+++	Cleaves into thin, flexible elastic plates; colorless and transparent in thin sheets	Muscovite, p. 531
2½–3	1+++	Cleaves into thin, elastic sheets; usually occurs as scaly aggregates	Lepidolite, p. 534
3–3½	3+++	Rectangular cleavage; often in light, massive aggregates	Anhydrite, p. 458
3½–4	3+++	Rhombohedral crystals, with curved faces; luster pearly; powder bubbles in acid	Dolomite, p. 442
3½–4	3+++	Usually in pinkish masses or crystals with curved faces; rhombohedral cleavage	Rhodochrosite, p. 435
3½–4	1++ 2+	Often as pseudohexagonal prisms or fibrous aggregates; poor prismatic cleavage	Aragonite, p. 438
4	4+++	Usually in cubic crystals; perfect octahedral cleavage	Fluorite, p. 428
4–4½	3+++	Usually in translucent botryoidal masses; rhombohedral cleavage; bubbles in acid	Smithsonite, p. 436
4–5	1+++ 2+	Usually massive, with the poor cleavages at right angles; occurs in granite pegmatites	Triphylite Series, p. 472

H	C1	Distinctive Features	Mineral
4–5	3+	Rhombohedral crystals, often twinned; poor rhombohedral cleavage	Chabazite, p. 521
5	1+	Hexagonal prismatic crystals; sometimes tabular; greasy luster	Apatite, p. 482
5–6	2+++	Crystals usually slender, prismatic; prismatic cleavage at 56° and 124°	Tremolite, p. 537
5–6	2++	Short square prismatic crystals	Scapolite, p. 517
5½–6	2++	Fine-grained cleavable to compact masses; good cleavages at almost right angles	Rhodonite, p. 553
5½–6½	—	Vitreous brittle masses; conchoidal fracture; may be milky or show internal play of colors	Opal, p. 506
6	1+++ 1++	Usually prismatic or fibrous; color rose, flesh-red; streak pale pinkish; rare	Inesite, p. 592
6	2++	Blocky orthorhombic crystals; good cleavages at 90°; rare except at Franklin, New Jersey	Tephroite, p. 574
6–6½	1++	Long prismatic orthorhombic crystals with deep lengthwise striations; luster vitreous but pearly on cleavage surface	Zoisite, p. 569
6½–7	2++	Extremely tough, compact; cleavages at nearly right angles	Jadeite, p. 549

H	C1	Distinctive Features	Mineral
6½–7	2++	Usually in striated crystals, flattened and lathlike; a tough mineral; fracture splintery	Spodumene, p. 550
6½–7½	—	Crystals equant dodecahedrons or trapezohedrons; common in metamorphic rocks	Garnet Group, p. 582
7	1++ 1+	Usually as compact fibrous or columnar masses; bright color	Dumortierite, p. 589
7	—	Vitreous or greasy luster; massive or in hexagonal, horizontally striated crystals ending in double rhombohedrons; conchoidal fracture	Quartz, p. 502
7–7½	1+	In quartzlike masses or grains; color may seem to change when viewed from different angles	Cordierite, p. 562
7–7½	—	Slender prismatic, striated crystals, rounded-triangular in cross section	Tourmaline Group, p. 563
7½	2++	Crystals stubby, square, lacking sharp edges; square cross section may show dark cross-shaped pattern	Andalusite, p. 577
7½–8	1+	Crystals prismatic, hexagonal, striated lengthwise	Beryl, p. 560

H	Cl	Distinctive Features	Mineral
7½–8	1+	Small, twinned crystals, usually flat hexagonal prisms, rhombohedrons; striated lengthwise	Phenakite, p. 575
7½–8	—	Octahedral crystals, often twinned	Spinel, p. 416
8	1+++	Usually as stubby or medium-long prismatic crystals with lengthwise striations; perfect cleavage across crystals	Topaz, p. 580
9	—	Crystals barrel-shaped; vitreous or adamantine luster; may break into cubic fragments with striated faces	Corundum, p. 395

RED MINERALS

H	Cl	Distinctive Features	Mineral
1	—	Earthy or as round grains in gray or yellow matrix	Bauxite, p. 410
1½–2	1+++ 2++	Often in flat rhombic crystals; breaks easily into thin flexible flakes	Gypsum, p. 459
1½–2	1++	Usually earthy; color deep red or orange; streak orange-yellow	Realgar, p. 370
1½–2½	1+++	Usually as delicate, earthy crusts; color vivid red or pink; streak reddish or pink	Erythrite, p. 475
2–2½	3+++	Bright red to brownish; usually granular, massive; heavy; streak scarlet	Cinnabar, p. 369

H	Cl	Distinctive Features	Mineral
2–2½	1++	Color and streak scarlet-vermillion; crystal forms usually distorted, complex	Proustite, p. 385
2½	1++	Dark (blackish) red; crystals prismatic, striated; streak red	Pyrargyrite, p. 384
2–3	1+++	Cleaves easily into thin, elastic sheets; color usually pale; associated with marble	Phlogopite, p. 532
2½ 3	1++ 2+	Bright orange-red prismatic crystals; streak orange-yellow; extremely rare	Crocoite, p. 470
2½–3	—	Color usually intense, with strong resinous luster; small prismatic hexagonal crystals	Vanadinite, p. 486
3	3+++	Cleaves into perfect rhombohedrons; clear specimens doubly refractive; bubbles easily in acid	Calcite, p. 432
3–3½	1+++ 2++	Usually in tabular crystals; heavy	Barite, p. 455
3½–4	6+++	Resinous or adamantine crystals; perfect dodecahedral cleavage	Sphalerite, p. 362
3½–4	3+++	Usually in pinkish masses or crystals with curved faces; rhombohedral cleavage	Rhodochrosite, p. 435
3½–4	1+++	Coffin-shaped or tabular crystals; crystals vitreous except pearly on cleavage surface	Heulandite, p. 518

H	C1	Distinctive Features	Mineral
3½–4	1+++	"Wheat-sheaf" aggregates of twinned crystals common	Stilbite, p. 519
3½–4	—	Octahedral or cubic crystals; streak brownish red; sometimes in long hairlike crystals	Cuprite, p. 394
4	1+++	Orange-yellow streak; usually as masses or grains; occurs only in Sussex Co., New Jersey	Zincite, p. 395
4–5	3+	Rhombohedral crystals, often twinned; poor rhombohedral cleavage	Chabazite, p. 521
5–5½	—	Usually as trapezohedral vitreous crystals lining cavities in volcanic rocks	Analcime, p. 522
5–6	—	Gray or black to red or brown; streak reddish brown; forms radiating or tabular crystals, botryoidal masses	Hematite, p. 397
5½	2++	Short prismatic or rhombohedral crystals; luster usually resinous	Willemite, p. 576
5½–6	2++	Fine-grained cleavage or compact masses; good cleavages at almost right angles	Rhodonite, p. 553
5½–6½	—	Vitreous brittle masses; conchoidal fracture; may show internal play of colors	Opal, p. 506
6	2+++ 1+	Cleavage masses or grains with fine parallel striations on best cleavage surface	Plagioclase Feldspar Group, p. 510

H	Cl	Distinctive Features	Mineral
6	2++	Two good cleavages at right angles; usually as masses or grains; crystals, often twinned, common in pegmatites	Orthoclase, p. 508
6	1++	Weakly magnetic; usually in short prismatic crystals; streak dark red	Columbite-Tantalite Series, p. 422
6–6½	1+	Prismatic or tabular crystals or disseminated grains in marble	Chondrodite, p. 587
6½–7½	—	Crystals equant dodecahedrons or trapezohedrons; common in metamorphic rocks	Garnet Group, p. 582
7	—	Smooth surface and conchoidal fracture; botryoidal form common; no visible crystals	Chalcedony, p. 504
7–7½	—	Slender prismatic, striated crystals, rounded-triangular in cross section	Tourmaline Group, p. 563
7½	2+	Heavy short tetragonal crystals with square cross section	Zircon, p. 586
7½–8	—	Octahedral crystals, often twinned	Spinel, p. 416
9	—	Crystals barrel-shaped; vitreous or adamantine luster; may break into cubic fragments with striated faces	Corundum, p. 395

H	Cl	Distinctive Features	Mineral
		BROWN MINERALS	
1	—	Earthy or as round grains in gray or yellow matrix	Bauxite, p. 410
1½–2	1+++ 2++	Often in flat rhombic crystals; breaks easily into thin flexible flakes	Gypsum, p. 459
2–2½	1+++	Cleaves into thin, flexible elastic plates; colorless and transparent in thin sheets	Muscovite, p. 531
2–3	1+++	Cleaves easily into thin, elastic sheets; color usually pale; associated with marble	Phlogopite, p. 532
2½	—	Usually massive with waxy luster; sectile	Chlorargyrite, p. 426
2½	—	Reddish yellow to reddish brown; streak pale yellow; greasy or waxy pitch-like masses	Gummite, p. 404
2½–3	—	Color usually intense, with strong resinous luster; small prismatic hexagonal crystals	Vanadinite, p. 486
2½–3½	1++	Small hexagonal or triangular crystals; also various massive forms; streak pale yellow	Jarosite, p. 465
3	3+	Crystals square, tabular; color usually brilliant; intense resinous, adamantine luster	Wulfenite, p. 499
3–3½	1+++ 2++	Usually in tabular crystals; heavy	Barite, p. 455

H	C1	Distinctive Features	Mineral
3–3½	—	Small pyramidal or prismatic crystals with uneven faces; occurs in hydrothermal replacement deposits	Descloizite Series, p. 478
3½	1+++	Tin-white with dark-gray tarnish; gives garlic odor when heated in flame; tin-white streak	Arsenic, p. 350
3½–4	6+++	Resinous or adamantine crystals; perfect dodecahedral cleavage	Sphalerite, p. 362
3½–4	3+++	Usually in pinkish masses or crystals with curved faces; rhombohedral cleavage	Rhodochrosite, p. 435
3½–4	3+++	Crystals rhombohedral with curved faces; rhombohedral cleavage; magnetic when heated	Siderite, p. 434
3½–4	1+++ 2++	Botryoidal crusts or hemispherical aggregates	Wavellite, p. 490
3½–4	1+++	"Wheat-sheaf" aggregates of twinned crystals common	Stilbite, p. 519
3½–4	—	Usually as hexagonal prisms or globular forms or crusts; luster resinous	Mimetite, p. 485
3½–4	—	Hexagonal crystals may be cavernous or barrel-shaped; streak white, pale yellow or green	Pyromorphite, p. 484
4	4+++	Usually in cubic crystals; perfect octahedral cleavage	Fluorite, p. 428

H	Cl	Distinctive Features	Mineral
4–4½	3+++	Usually in translucent botryoidal masses; rhombohedral cleavage; bubbles in acid	Smithsonite, p. 436
4–4½	1+++	Usually as dark bladed crystals, striated lengthwise on one face; streak brown-black	Wolframite Series, p. 496
4–5	1+++ 2+	Usually massive, with two poor cleavages at right angles; occurs in granite pegmatites	Triphylite Series, p. 472
4–5½	—	Amorphous, earthy masses; yellowish-brown streak; may occur as pseudomorphs after pyrite, marcasite, siderite	Limonite, p. 413
4½–5	1++ 2+	Octahedral crystals common; also massive; luster vitreous adamantine	Scheelite, p. 497
5	1+	Hexagonal prismatic crystals; sometimes tabular; greasy luster	Apatite, p. 482
5–5½	1+++	Submetallic, usually in botryoidal, mammillary or radiating masses; fibrous structure; yellowish-brown streak	Goethite, p. 411
5–5½	1++	Small grains or flattened crystals; cleaves obliquely into brittle splinters	Monazite, p. 473
5–5½	1++	Usually as flattened, wedge-shaped crystals; brittle; parting common	Titanite, p. 588

H	Cl	Distinctive Features	Mineral
5–6	2+++	Nearly black color; perfect cleavages at angles of 56° and 124°	Hornblende, p. 539
5–6	2+++	Prismatic crystals with diamond-shaped cross section; cleaves at angles of 56° and 124°; may have tan streak	Pargasite, p. 541
5–6	1+++ 2++	Usually in coarsely crystalline aggregates; bronze or pearly luster; cleavages intersect at nearly right angles	Hypersthene, p. 544
5–6	1+++	Well-formed prismatic crystals with square cross section; perfect lengthwise cleavage	Neptunite, p. 555
5–6	2++	Two distinct cleavages at nearly right angles; often in short prismatic crystals	Augite, p. 547
5–6	2++	Short square prismatic crystals	Scapolite, p. 517
5–6	—	Gray or black to red or brown; streak reddish brown; forms radiating or tabular crystals, botryoidal masses	Hematite, p. 397
5½	2++	Short prismatic or rhombohedral crystals; luster usually resinous	Willemite, p. 576
5½–6	3+	Greasy luster; usually in cleavable (prismatic) masses	Nepheline, p. 514
5½–6½	—	Vitreous brittle masses; conchoidal fracture; may be milky or show internal play of colors	Opal, p. 506

H	Cl	Distinctive Features	Mineral
6	2++	Two good cleavages at right angles; usually as masses or grains; crystals, often twinned, common in pegmatites	Orthoclase, p. 508
6	2++	Blocky orthorhombic crystals; good cleavages at 90°; rare except at Franklin, New Jersey	Tephroite, p. 574
6	1++	Weakly magnetic; usually in short prismatic crystals; streak dark red	Columbite-Tantalite Series, p. 422
6–6½	2+++	Slender prismatic crystals ending in pointed pyramids; gray streak	Acmite, p. 548
6–6½	1++	Long prismatic orthorhombic crystals with deep lengthwise striations; luster vitreous but pearly on cleavage surface	Zoisite, p. 569
6–6½	1+	Prismatic or tabular crystals or disseminated grains in marble	Chondrodite, p. 587
6–7	1+++	Usually in fibrous masses or radiating masses; extremely brittle with splintery fracture	Sillimanite, p. 578
6–7	2++	Crystals usually short, prismatic, twinned; streak light brown	Cassiterite, p. 402
6½	1+	Crystals short, prismatic, with square cross section; also columnar, massive	Vesuvianite, p. 568

H	Cl	Distinctive Features	Mineral
6½–7	2++	Extremely tough, compact; distinct cleavages at nearly right angles	Jadeite, p. 549
6½–7	1++	Striated tabular crystals with knifelike edges	Axinite Group, p. 559
6½–7	2+	Indistinct cleavages at right angles; usually as rounded grains or granular masses	Olivine Group, p. 573
6½–7½	—	Crystals equant dodecahedrons or trapezohedrons; common in metamorphic rocks	Garnet Group, p. 582
7	1+++	Prismatic, monoclinic crystals; perfect lengthwise cleavage	Clinozoisite, p. 570
7	—	Smooth surface and conchoidal fracture; botryoidal form common; no visible crystals	Chalcedony, p. 504
7	—	Vitreous or greasy luster; massive or in hexagonal, horizontally striated crystals ending in double rhombohedrons; conchoidal fracture	Quartz, p. 502
7–7½	1+	Occurs as single or commonly twinned prismatic crystals in metamorphic rocks	Staurolite, p. 581
7–7½	—	Slender prismatic, striated crystals, rounded-triangular in cross section	Tourmaline Group, p. 563

H	Cl	Distinctive Features	Mineral
7½	2++	Crystals stubby, square, lacking sharp edges; square cross section may show dark cross-shaped pattern	Andalusite, p. 577
7½	2+	Heavy short tetragonal crystals with square cross section	Zircon, p. 586
7½–8	1+	Small, twinned crystals, usually flat hexagonal prisms, rhombohedrons; striated lengthwise	Phenakite, p. 575
7½–8	—	Octahedral crystals, often twinned	Spinel, p. 416
8½	1++ 2+	Vitreous tabular or prismatic crystals, often twinned; extremely hard	Chrysoberyl, p. 420
9	—	Crystals barrel-shaped; vitreous or adamantine luster; may break into cubic fragments with striated faces	Corundum, p. 395

ORANGE MINERALS

H	Cl	Distinctive Features	Mineral
1½–2	1++	Usually earthy; color deep red or orange; streak orange-yellow	Realgar, p. 370
2½	—	Reddish yellow to reddish brown; streak pale yellow; greasy or waxy pitch-like masses	Gummite, p. 404
3	3+	Crystals square, tabular; color usually brilliant; intense resinous, adamantine luster	Wulfenite, p. 499

H	Cl	Distinctive Features	Mineral
3½–4	—	Octahedral or cubic crystals; streak brownish red; sometimes in long hairlike crystals	Cuprite, p. 394
3½–4	—	Usually as hexagonal prisms or globular forms or crusts; luster resinous	Mimetite, p. 485
4	1+++	Orange-yellow streak; usually as masses or grains; occurs only in Sussex Co., New Jersey	Zincite, p. 395
5	1+	Radiating aggregates; found only at Mexican localities; rare	Legrandite, p. 489
6½–7½	—	Crystals equant dodecahedrons or trapezohedrons; common in metamorphic rocks	Garnet Group, p. 582

YELLOW MINERALS

H	Cl	Distinctive Features	Mineral
1	—	Earthy or as round grains in gray or yellow matrix	Bauxite, p. 410
1–2	1+++	Usually as fine-grained masses, often foliated or fibrous; greasy feel; micaceous habit and flaky cleavage	Pyrophyllite, p. 529
1½–2	1+++ 2++	Often in flat rhombic crystals; breaks easily into thin flexible flakes	Gypsum, p. 459
1½–2	1+++	Lemon-yellow; streak lemon-yellow; cleaves into thin flexible flakes with pearly luster	Orpiment, p. 371

H	C1	Distinctive Features	Mineral
1½–2½	2+	Transparent yellow crystals or masses; very soft and brittle; streak pale yellow	Sulfur, p. 353
2	1+++	Usually bright yellow; massive or as powdery crystalline aggregates; streak yellow	Carnotite, p. 494
2–2½	1+++	Usually in flat translucent tabular crystals or aggregates; yellowish streak	Autunite, p. 492
2–2½	1+++	Earthy, easily broken masses or minute plates	Kaolinite, p. 526
2–2½	1+++	Cleaves into thin, flexible elastic plates; colorless and transparent in thin sheets	Muscovite, p. 531
2½	—	Reddish yellow to reddish brown; streak pale yellow; greasy or waxy pitch-like masses	Gummite, p. 404
2½–3	1+++	Bitter salty taste; dissolves slowly in water; crystal faces striated	Glauberite, p. 458
2½–3	1+++	Cleaves into thin, elastic sheets; usually occurs as scaly aggregates	Lepidolite, p. 534
2½–3½	1++	Small hexagonal or triangular crystals; also various massive forms; streak pale yellow	Jarosite, p. 465
3	3+++	Cleaves into perfect rhombohedrons; clear specimens doubly refractive; bubbles easily in acid	Calcite, p. 432

H	C1	Distinctive Features	Mineral
3	3+	Crystals square, tabular; color usually brilliant; intense resinous, adamantine luster	Wulfenite, p. 499
3–3½	1+++ 2++	Usually in tabular crystals; heavy	Barite, p. 455
3–3½	2++	Massive or in platy crystals; adamantine luster; brittle	Cerussite, p. 441
3–5	—	Massive or fibrous; luster waxy or silky; greasy feel, hardness extremely variable	Serpentine Group, p. 527
3½	1++ 1+	Honey-yellow to yellowish-green drusy crusts or wedge-shaped crystals	Adamite, p. 481
3½–4	1+++ 2++	Botryoidal crusts or hemispherical aggregates	Wavellite, p. 490
3½–4	1+++	"Wheat-sheaf" aggregates of twinned crystals common	Stilbite, p. 519
3½–4	—	Usually as hexagonal prisms or globular forms or crusts; luster resinous	Mimetite, p. 485
3½–4	—	Hexagonal crystals may be cavernous or barrel-shaped; streak white, pale yellow, or green	Pyromorphite, p. 484
3½–4½	3+++	Usually in cleavable porcelainlike masses	Magnesite, p. 433
4	4+++	Usually in cubic crystals; perfect octahedral cleavage	Fluorite, p. 428

H	C1	Distinctive Features	Mineral
4	1+++	Orange-yellow streak; usually as masses or grains; occurs only in Sussex Co., New Jersey	Zincite, p. 395
4–4½	1+++ 1++	Two cleavages at 90°; in short prismatic crystals or cleavable masses	Colemanite, p. 450
4–5	3+	Rhombohedral crystals, often twinned; poor rhombohedral cleavage	Chabazite, p. 521
4–5½	—	Amorphous, earthy masses; yellowish-brown streak; may occur as pseudomorphs after pyrite, marcasite, siderite	Limonite, p. 413
4½–5	1+++	Crystals cubelike, striated; luster vitreous, pearly on base	Apophyllite, p. 525
4½–5	1+++	Crystals usually small, thin, bladed, in fan-shaped aggregates	Hemimorphite, p. 565
5	1+	Hexagonal prismatic crystals; sometimes tabular; greasy luster	Apatite, p. 482
5	1+	Radiating aggregates; found only at Mexican localities; rare	Legrandite, p. 489
5–5½	1+++	Submetallic, usually in botryoidal, mammillary or radiating masses; yellowish-brown streak	Goethite, p. 411
5–5½	1++	Small grains or flattened crystals; cleaves into brittle splinters	Monazite, p. 473
5–5½	1++	Usually as flattened, wedge-shaped crystals; brittle; parting common	Titanite, p. 588

H	Cl	Distinctive Features	Mineral
5–5½	—	Usually as trapezohedral vitreous crystals lining cavities in volcanic rocks	Analcime, p. 522
5–6	2+++	Crystals usually slender, prismatic; prismatic cleavage at 56° and 124°	Tremolite, p. 537
5–6	2++	Short square prismatic crystals	Scapolite, p. 517
5½	2++	Short prismatic or rhombohedral crystals; luster usually resinous	Willemite, p. 576
5½–6	1+++ 3++	Usually as lath-shaped crystals or cleavable vitreous masses	Amblygonite, p. 480
5½–6½	—	Vitreous brittle masses; conchoidal fracture; may be milky or show internal play of colors	Opal, p. 506
6–6½	1++	Botryoidal crusts, usually as linings in cavities in volcanic rocks	Prehnite, p. 590
6–6½	1+	Prismatic or tabular crystals or disseminated grains in marble	Chondrodite, p. 587
6½	1+	Crystals short, prismatic, with square cross section; also columnar, massive	Vesuvianite, p. 568
6½–7	2++	Usually in striated crystals, flattened and lathlike; a tough mineral; fracture splintery	Spodumene, p. 550
6½–7½	—	Crystals equant dodecahedrons or trapezohedrons; common in metamorphic rocks	Garnet Group, p. 582

H	Cl	Distinctive Features	Mineral
7	—	Vitreous or greasy luster; massive or in hexagonal, horizontally striated crystals ending in double rhombohedrons; conchoidal fracture	Quartz, p. 502
7½	2+	Heavy short tetragonal crystals with square cross section	Zircon, p. 586
7½–8	1+	Crystals prismatic, hexagonal, striated lengthwise	Beryl, p. 560
7½–8	1+	Small, twinned crystals, usually flat hexagonal prisms, rhombohedrons; striated lengthwise	Phenakite, p. 575
8	1+++	Usually as stubby or medium-long prismatic crystals with lengthwise striations; perfect cleavage across crystals	Topaz, p. 580
8½	1++ 2+	Vitreous tabular or prismatic crystals, often twinned	Chrysoberyl, p. 420
9	—	Crystals barrel-shaped; vitreous or adamantine luster; may break into cubic fragments with striated faces	Corundum, p. 395
10	4+++	Extremely hard; usually in octahedral crystals; adamantine or greasy luster	Diamond, p. 354

COLORLESS MINERALS

1½–2	1+++ 2++	Often in flat rhombic crystals; breaks easily into thin flexible flakes	Gypsum, p. 459

H	Cl	Distinctive Features	Mineral
2–2½	3+++	Salty taste; cleaves easily into lusterless cubic fragments	Halite, p. 426
2–2½	1+++ 1++	Sweetish alkaline taste; dissolves easily in water	Borax, p. 448
2–2½	1+++ 1++	Usually in fibrous or botryoidal masses; forms encrustations on mine walls; salty bitter taste	Epsomite, p. 462
2–2½	1+++	Cleaves into thin, flexible elastic plates; colorless and transparent in thin sheets	Muscovite, p. 531
2–3	1+++	Cleaves easily into thin, elastic sheets; color usually pale; associated with marble	Phlogopite, p. 532
2½	1+++ 1++	Occurs as loose, silky "cotton ball" nodules	Ulexite, p. 449
2½	—	Occurs as translucent masses; no cleavage, pseudocubic parting; weak salty taste	Cryolite, p. 429
2½–3	1+++	Bitter salty taste; dissolves slowly in water; crystal faces striated	Glauberite, p. 458
2½–3	2++	Heavy masses or striated crystals; adamantine luster	Anglesite, p. 457
3	3+++	Cleaves into perfect rhombohedrons; clear specimens doubly refractive; bubbles easily in acid	Calcite, p. 432
3	2+++ 1++	Cleaves into long splinters; sweetish alkaline taste	Kernite, p. 448

H	Cl	Distinctive Features	Mineral
3–3½	3+++	Rectangular cleavage; often in light, massive aggregates	Anhydrite, p. 458
3–3½	1+++ 2++	Usually in tabular crystals; heavy	Barite, p. 455
3–3½	1+++ 2++	Tabular crystals or cleavage masses, often with partial light blue tint	Celestite, p. 456
3–3½	2++	Massive or in platy crystals; adamantine luster; brittle	Cerussite, p. 441
3½	1++ 1+	Honey-yellow to yellowish-green drusy crusts or wedge-shaped crystals	Adamite, p. 481
3½–4	3+++	Rhombohedral crystals, with curved faces; luster pearly; powder bubbles in acid	Dolomite, p. 442
3½–4	1+++ 1+	Usually massive or fibrous; may be in long, pointed crystals; bubbles in acid	Strontianite, p. 440
3½–4	1+++	Coffin-shaped or tabular crystals; crystals vitreous except pearly on cleavage surface	Heulandite, p. 518
3½– 4½	1++ 1+	Usually occurs as pale green or greenish-blue nodules or veins	Variscite, p. 476
4	4+++	Usually in cubic crystals; perfect octahedral cleavage	Fluorite, p. 428
4	2+++	Prismatic crystals with oblique terminations; surfaces usually powdery, white	Laumontite, p. 520

H	Cl	Distinctive Features	Mineral
4–4½	3+++	Usually in translucent botryoidal masses; rhombohedral cleavage; bubbles in acid	Smithsonite, p. 436
4–4½	1+++ 1++	Two cleavages at 90°; in short prismatic crystals or cleavable masses	Colemanite, p. 450
4½–5	2+++	Botryoidal and radiating fibrous aggregates; occurs in cavities in volcanic rocks	Pectolite, p. 552
4½–5	2+++	Occurs in limestones; usually as compact, cleavable masses; cleavages at nearly right angles	Wollastonite, p. 551
4½–5	1+++	Crystals cubelike, striated; luster vitreous, pearly on base	Apophyllite, p. 525
4½–5	1+++	Crystals usually small, thin, bladed, in fan-shaped aggregates	Hemimorphite, p.565
5	2+++	Usually as radiating groups of fine needlelike crystals in cavities in volcanic rocks	Mesolite, p. 524
5	1+++	Slender or needlelike prismatic crystals often lining cavities in volcanic rocks	Natrolite, p. 523
5	1+	Hexagonal prismatic crystals; sometimes tabular; greasy luster	Apatite, p. 482
5	1+	Radiating aggregates; found only at Mexican localities; rare	Legrandite, p. 489

H	Cl	Distinctive Features	Mineral
5–5½	—	Usually as trapezohedral vitreous crystals lining cavities in volcanic rocks	Analcime, p. 522
5–5½	—	Usually as pale-colored, blunt, wedge-shaped crystals with many facets	Datolite, p. 591
5–6	2+++	Crystals usually slender, prismatic; prismatic cleavage at 56° and 124°	Tremolite, p. 537
5–6	2++	Short prismatic crystals with good terminations, often twinned; two cleavages at nearly right angles	Diopside, p. 545
5–6	2++	Short square prismatic crystals	Scapolite, p. 517
5½–6	6+	Usually massive or as disseminated grains; vitreous; transparent to translucent	Sodalite, p. 515
5½–6	3+	Greasy luster; usually in cleavable (prismatic) masses	Nepheline, p. 514
5½–6	—	Trapezohedral translucent crystals, usually in dark rock	Leucite, p. 513
5½–6½	—	Vitreous brittle masses; conchoidal fracture; may be milky or show internal play of colors	Opal, p. 506
6	2+++ 1++	Prismatic tabular crystals, often twinned; two perfect cleavages distinctive; luster vitreous to greasy	Lawsonite, p. 566

H	Cl	Distinctive Features	Mineral
6	2+++ 1+	Cleavage masses or grains with fine parallel striations on best cleavage surface	Plagioclase Feldspar Group, p. 510
6	2++	Two good cleavages at right angles; usually as masses or grains; crystals, often twinned, common in pegmatites	Orthoclase, p. 508
6½–7½	—	Crystals equant dodecahedrons or trapezohedrons; common in metamorphic rocks	Garnet Group, p. 582
7	1+	Crystals vitreous, prismatic; may be quite long, slender, or blunt, chisel-like	Danburite, p. 513
7	—	Vitreous or greasy luster; massive or in hexagonal, horizontally striated crystals ending in double rhombohedrons; conchoidal fracture	Quartz, p. 502
7½	2+	Heavy short tetragonal crystals with square cross section	Zircon, p. 586
7½–8	1+	Crystals prismatic, hexagonal, striated lengthwise	Beryl, p. 560
7½–8	1+	Small, twinned crystals, usually flat hexagonal prisms, rhombohedrons; striated lengthwise	Phenakite, p. 575

H	C1	Distinctive Features	Mineral
8	1+++	Usually as stubby or medium-long prismatic crystals with lengthwise striations; perfect cleavage across crystals	Topaz, p. 580
8½	1++ 2+	Vitreous tabular or prismatic crystals, often twinned; extremely hard	Chrysoberyl, p. 420
10	4+++	Extremely hard; usually in octahedral crystals; adamantine or greasy luster	Diamond, p. 354

WHITE MINERALS

H	C1	Distinctive Features	Mineral
1	1+++	Extremely soft; greasy feel; micaceous habit and flaky cleavage	Talc, p. 530
1	—	Earthy or as round grains in gray or yellow matrix	Bauxite, p. 410
1–2	1+++	Usually as fine-grained masses, often foliated or fibrous; greasy feel; micaceous habit and flaky cleavage	Pyrophyllite, p. 529
1½–2	1+++ 2++	Often in flat rhombic crystals; breaks easily into thin flexible flakes	Gypsum, p. 459
2	1+++ 1++	Bluish- to yellowish-green; sweetish astringent taste	Melanterite, p. 461
2–2½	1+++ 1++	Sweetish alkaline taste; dissolves easily in water	Borax, p. 448
2–2½	1+++ 1++	Usually in fibrous or botryoidal masses; forms encrustations on mine walls; salty bitter taste	Epsomite, p. 462

H	Cl	Distinctive Features	Mineral
2–2½	1+++	Extremely soft, often in flexible sheets; pearly luster on cleavage surface	Brucite, p. 408
2–2½	1+++	Cleaves into thin, flexible elastic plates; colorless and transparent in thin sheets.	Muscovite, p. 531
2–2½	1+++	Earthy, easily broken masses or minute plates	Kaolinite, p. 526
2½	1+++ 1++	Occurs as loose, silky "cotton ball" nodules	Ulexite, p. 449
2½	—	Occurs as translucent masses; no cleavage, pseudocubic parting; weak salty taste	Cryolite, p. 429
2½–3	1+++	Bitter salty taste; dissolves slowly in water; crystal faces striated	Glauberite, p. 458
2½–3	1+++	Cleaves into thin, elastic sheets; usually occurs as scaly aggregates	Lepidolite, p. 534
2½–3	2++	Heavy masses or striated crystals; adamantine luster	Anglesite, p. 457
2½–3	1++	Dissolves readily; weak salty taste	Thenardite, p. 454
3	3+++	Cleaves into perfect rhombohedrons; clear specimens doubly refractive; bubbles easily in acid	Calcite, p. 432
3	2+++ 1++	Cleaves into long splinters; sweetish alkaline taste	Kernite, p. 448

H	Cl	Distinctive Features	Mineral
3–3½	3+++	Rectangualar cleavage; often in light, massive aggregates	Anhydrite, p. 458
3–3½	1+++ 2++	Usually in tabular crystals; heavy	Barite, p. 455
3–3½	1+++ 2++	Tabular crystals or cleavage masses; often with partial light-blue tint	Celestite, p. 456
3–3½	2++	Massive or in platy crystals; adamantine luster; brittle	Cerussite, p. 441
3–3½	1++ 2+	Crystals always twinned, forming pseudohexagonal prisms; bubbles in hydrochloric acid	Witherite, p. 439
3½	—	Compact nodular masses resembling porcelain or chalk; dissolves in hydrochloric acid	Howlite, p. 451
3½–4	3+++	Rhombohedral crystals, with curved faces; luster pearly; powder bubbles in acid	Dolomite, p. 442
3½–4	3+++	Crystals rhombohedral with curved faces; rhombohedral cleavage; magnetic when heated	Siderite, p. 434
3½–4	1+++ 2++	Botryoidal crusts or hemispherical aggregates	Wavellite, p. 490
3½–4	1+++ 1+	Usually massive or fibrous; may be in long, pointed crystals; bubbles in acid	Strontianite, p. 440

H	Cl	Distinctive Features	Mineral
3½–4	1+++	Coffin-shaped or tabular crystals; crystals vitreous, except pearly on cleavage surface	Heulandite, p. 518
3½–4	1+++	"Wheat-sheaf" aggregates of twinned crystals common	Stilbite, p. 519
3½–4	1++ 2+	Often as pseudohexagonal prisms or fibrous aggregates; poor prismatic cleavage	Aragonite, p. 438
3½–4½	3+++	Usually in cleavable porcelainlike masses	Magnesite, p. 433
4	4+++	Usually in cubic crystals; perfect octahedral cleavage	Fluorite, p. 428
4	2+++	Prismatic crystals with oblique terminations; surfaces usually powdery, white	Laumontite, p. 520
4–4½	3+++	Usually in translucent botryoidal masses; rhombohedral cleavage; bubbles in acid	Smithsonite, p. 436
4–4½	1+++ 1++	Two cleavages at 90°; in short prismatic crystals or cleavable masses	Colemanite, p. 450
4–4½	1++	Forms minute bladed or needlelike crystals; also as crusts, nodules; rare	Austinite, p. 478
4–5 6–7	1+++ 1++	Bladed crystals; hardness greater across crystals than lengthwise	Kyanite, p. 579
4–5	3+	Rhombohedral crystals, often twinned; poor rhombohedral cleavage	Chabazite, p. 521

H	C1	Distinctive Features	Mineral
4½–5	2+++	Botryoidal and radiating fibrous aggregates; occurs in cavities in volcanic rocks	Pectolite, p. 552
4½–5	2+++	Occurs in limestones; usually as compact, cleavable masses; cleavages at nearly right angles	Wollastonite, p. 551
4½–5	1+++	Crystals cubelike, striated; luster vitreous, pearly on base	Apophyllite, p. 525
4½–5	1+++	Crystals usually small, thin, bladed, in fan-shaped aggregates	Hemimorphite, p.565
4½–5	1++ 2+	Octahedral crystals common; also massive; vitreous, adamantine	Scheelite, p. 497
5	2+++	Usually as radiating groups of fine needlelike crystals in cavities in volcanic rocks	Mesolite, p. 524
5	1+++	Slender or needlelike prismatic crystals often lining cavities in volcanic rocks	Natrolite, p. 523
5	1+	Hexagonal prismatic crystals; sometimes tabular; greasy luster	Apatite, p. 482
5–5½	—	Usually as trapezohedral vitreous crystals lining cavities in volcanic rocks	Analcime, p. 522
5–6	2++	Short prismatic crystals with good terminations, often twinned cleaves	Diopside, p. 545
5–6	2++	Short square prismatic crystals	Scapolite, p. 517

H	C1	Distinctive Features	Mineral
5½	2++	Short prismatic or rhombohedral crystals; luster usually resinous	Willemite, p. 576
5½–6	1+++ 3++	Usually as lath-shaped crystals or cleavable masses with vitreous or greasy luster	Amblygonite, p. 480
5½–6	6+	Usually massive or as disseminated grains; vitreous; transparent to translucent	Sodalite, p. 515
5½–6	3+	Greasy luster; usually in cleavable (prismatic) masses	Nepheline, p. 514
5½–6	—	Trapezohedral translucent crystals, usually in dark rock	Leucite, p. 513
5½–6½	—	Vitreous brittle masses; conchoidal fracture; may be milky or show internal play of colors	Opal, p. 506
6	2+++ 1++	Prismatic tabular crystals, often twinned; two perfect cleavages distinctive; luster vitreous to greasy	Lawsonite, p. 566
6	2++	Two good cleavages at right angles; usually as masses or grains; crystals, often twinned, common in pegmatites	Orthoclase, p. 508
6	2+++ 1+	Cleavage masses or grains with fine parallel striations on best cleavage surface	Plagioclase Feldspar Group, p. 510
6–6½	1++	Botryoidal crusts, usually as linings in cavities in volcanic rocks	Prehnite, p. 590

H	Cl	Distinctive Features	Mineral
6–7 4–5	1+++ 1++	Bladed crystals; hardness greater across crystals than lengthwise	Kyanite, p. 579
6–7	1+++	Usually in fibrous masses or radiating masses; extremely brittle with splintery fracture	Sillimanite, p. 578
6–7	2++	Extremely tough, compact; distinct cleavages at nearly right angles	Jadeite, p. 549
6½–7	2++	Usually in striated crystals, flattened and lathlike; a tough mineral; fracture splintery	Spodumene, p. 550
6½–7½	—	Crystals equant dodecahedrons or trapezohedrons; common in metamorphic rocks	Garnet Group, p. 582
7	1+	Crystals vitreous, prismatic; may be quite long, slender, or blunt, chisel-like	Danburite, p. 513
7	—	Smooth surface and conchoidal fracture; botryoidal form common; no visible crystals	Chalcedony, p. 504
7	—	Vitreous or greasy luster; massive or in hexagonal, horizontally striated crystals ending in double rhombohedrons; conchoidal fracture	Quartz, p. 502

H	Cl	Distinctive Features	Mineral
7–7½	—	Slender prismatic, striated crystals, rounded-triangular in cross section	Tourmaline Group, p. 563
7½	2++	Crystals stubby, square, lacking sharp edges; square cross section may show dark cross-shaped pattern	Andalusite, p. 577
7½–8	1+	Small, twinned crystals, usually flat hexagonal prisms, rhombohedrons; striated lengthwise	Phenakite, p. 575
8	1+++	Usually as stubby or medium-long prismatic crystals with lengthwise striations; perfect cleavage across crystals	Topaz, p. 580

GRAY MINERALS

H	Cl	Distinctive Features	Mineral
1	—	Earthy or as round grains in gray or yellow matrix	Bauxite, p. 410
1–2	1+++	Usually as fine-grained masses, often foliated or fibrous; greasy feel; micaceous habit and flaky cleavage	Pyrophyllite, p. 529
1½–2	1+++ 2++	Often in flat rhombic crystals; breaks easily into thin flexible flakes	Gypsum, p. 459
2–2½	3+++	Salty taste; cleaves easily into lusterless cubic fragments	Halite, p. 426
2–2½	1+++ 1++	Sweetish alkaline taste; dissolves easily in water	Borax, p. 448

H	C1	Distinctive Features	Mineral
2–2½	1+++ 1++	Usually in fibrous or botryoidal masses; forms encrustations on mine walls; salty bitter taste	Epsomite, p. 462
2–2½	1+++	Extremely soft, often in flexible sheets; pearly luster on cleavage surface	Brucite, p. 408
2–2½	1+++	Earthy, easily broken masses or minute plates	Kaolinite, p. 526
2–2½	1+++	Cleaves into thin, flexible elastic plates; colorless and transparent in thin sheets	Muscovite, p. 531
2–3	1+++	Cleaves easily into thin, elastic sheets; color usually pale; associated with marble	Phlogopite, p. 532
2½	—	Usually massive with waxy luster; sectile	Chlorargyrite, p. 426
2½–3	1+++	Bitter salty taste; dissolves slowly in water; crystal faces striated	Glauberite, p. 458
2½–3	2++	Heavy masses or striated crystals; adamantine luster	Anglesite, p. 457
3	3+++	Cleaves into perfect rhombohedrons; clear specimens doubly refractive; bubbles easily in acid	Calcite, p. 432
3–3½	3+++	Rectangular cleavage; often in light, massive aggregates	Anhydrite, p. 458

H	C1	Distinctive Features	Mineral
3–3½	2++	Massive or in platy crystals; adamantine luster; brittle	Cerussite, p. 441
3–3½	1++ 2+	Crystals always twinned, forming pseudohexagonal prisms; bubbles in hydrochloric acid	Witherite, p. 439
3½–4	6+++	Resinous or adamantine crystals; perfect dodecahedral cleavage	Sphalerite, p. 362
3½–4	3+++	Rhombohedral crystals, with curved faces; luster pearly; powder bubbles in acid	Dolomite, p. 442
3½–4	1+++ 1+	Usually massive or fibrous; may be in long, pointed crystals; bubbles in acid	Strontianite, p. 440
3½–4	1+++	Luster submetallic; prismatic crystals, often in groups or bundles; streak reddish brown or black	Manganite, p. 409
3½–4	1+++	"Wheat-sheaf" aggregates of twinned crystals common	Stilbite, p. 519
3½–4	1++ 2+	Often as pseudohexagonal prisms or fibrous aggregates; poor prismatic cleavage	Aragonite, p. 438
3½–4	—	Hexagonal crystals may be cavernous or barrel-shaped; streak white, pale yellow or green	Pyromorphite, p. 484
3½–4½	3+++	Usually in cleavable porcelainlike masses	Magnesite, p. 433

H	Cl	Distinctive Features	Mineral
4–4½	1+++	Usually as dark bladed crystals, striated lengthwise on one face; streak brown-black	Wolframite Series, p. 496
4–4½	3+++	Usually in translucent botryoidal masses; rhombohedral cleavage; bubbles in acid	Smithsonite, p. 436
4–4½	1+++ 1++	Two cleavages at 90°; in short prismatic crystals or cleavage masses	Colemanite, p. 450
4–5 6–7	1+++ 1++	Bladed crystals; hardness greater across crystals than lengthwise	Kyanite, p. 579
4½–5	2+++	Botryoidal and radiating fibrous aggregates; occurs in cavities in volcanic rocks	Pectolite, p. 552
4½–5	2+++	Occurs in limestones; usually as compact, cleavable masses	Wollastonite, p. 551
4½–5	1+++	Crystals cubelike, striated; luster vitreous, pearly on base	Apophyllite, p. 525
5	1+++	Slender or needlelike prismatic crystals	Natrolite, p. 523
5–5½	1++	Usually as flattened, wedge-shaped crystals; brittle; parting common	Titanite, p. 588
5–5½	—	Usually as trapezohedral vitreous crystals lining cavities in volcanic rocks	Analcime, p. 522
5 6	2+++	Nearly black color; perfect cleavages at angles of 56° and 124°	Hornblende, p. 539

H	Cl	Distinctive Features	Mineral
5–6	2+++	Crystals usually slender, prismatic; prismatic cleavage at 56° and 124°	Tremolite, p. 537
5–6	1+++ 2++	Usually in coarsely crystalline aggregates; bronze or pearly luster; cleavages intersect at nearly right angles	Hypersthene, p. 544
5–6	2++	Short prismatic crystals with good terminations, often twinned; two cleavages at nearly right angles	Diopside, p. 545
5–6	2++	Short square prismatic crystals	Scapolite, p. 517
5–6	—	Submetallic masses, sometimes botryoidal or mammillary; streak black or brown, shiny	Psilomelane, p. 411
5½–6	1+++ 3++	Usually as lath-shaped crystals or cleavage masses with vitreous or greasy luster	Amblygonite, p. 480
5½–6	6+	Usually massive or as disseminated grains; vitreous; transparent to translucent	Sodalite, p. 515
5½–6	3+	Greasy luster; usually in cleavable (prismatic) masses	Nepheline, p. 514
5½–6	—	Trapezohedral translucent crystals, usually in dark rock	Leucite, p. 513
5½–6½	—	Vitreous brittle masses; conchoidal fracture; may be milky or show internal play of colors	Opal, p. 506

H	C1	Distinctive Features	Mineral
6	2+++ 1++	Prismatic tabular crystals, often twinned; two perfect cleavages distinctive; luster vitreous to greasy	Lawsonite, p. 566
6	2+++ 1+	Cleavage masses or grains with fine parallel striations on best cleavage surface	Plagioclase Feldspar Group, p. 510
6	2++	Two good cleavages at right angles; usually as masses or grains; crystals, often twinned, common in pegmatites	Orthoclase, p. 508
6	2++	Blocky orthorhombic crystals; good cleavages at 90°; rare except at Franklin, New Jersey	Tephroite, p. 574
6–6½	1++	Botryoidal crusts, usually as linings in cavities in volcanic rocks	Prehnite, p. 590
6–6½	1++	Long prismatic orthorhombic crystals with deep lengthwise striations; luster vitreous but pearly on cleavage surface	Zoisite, p. 569
6–7 4–5	1+++ 1++	Bladed crystals; hardness greater across crystals than lengthwise	Kyanite, p. 579
6½–7	2++	Extremely tough, compact; distinct cleavages at nearly right angles	Jadeite, p. 549
6½–7	2++	Usually in striated crystals, flattened and lathlike; a tough mineral; fracture splintery	Spodumene, p. 550

H	Cl	Distinctive Features	Mineral
7	1+++	Prismatic, monoclinic crystals; perfect lengthwise cleavage	Clinozoisite, p. 570
7	—	Smooth surface and conchoidal fracture; botryoidal form common; no visible crystals	Chalcedony, p. 504
7	—	Vitreous or greasy luster; massive or in hexagonal, horizontally striated crystals ending in double rhombohedrons; conchoidal fracture	Quartz, p. 502
7–7½	1+	In quartzlike masses or grains; color may seem to change when viewed from different angles	Cordierite, p. 562
7–7½	1+	Occurs as single or commonly twinned prismatic crystals in metamorphic rocks	Staurolite, p. 581
7½	2+	Heavy short tetragonal crystals with square cross section	Zircon, p. 586
9	—	Crystals barrel-shaped; vitreous or adamantine luster; may break into cubic fragments with striated faces	Corundum, p. 395

BLACK MINERALS

H	Cl	Distinctive Features	Mineral
1½–2	1+++	Thin flexible flakes and small tabular crystals; streak white turning to blue in light	Vivianite, p. 474
2–2½	1+++	Usually in irregular, foliated masses; breaks into mica-like sheets	Chlorite, p. 535

H	C1	Distinctive Features	Mineral
2½–3	1+++	Usually in irregular cleavage masses or tabular, barrel-shaped crystals; cleaves into tough, thin very elastic plates	Biotite, p. 533
3–3½	—	Small pyramidal or prismatic crystals with uneven faces; occurs in hydrothermal replacement deposits	Descloizite Series, p. 478
3½–4	6+++	Resinous or adamantine crystals; perfect dodecahedral cleavage	Sphalerite, p. 362
3½–4	1+++	Luster submetallic; prismatic crystals, often in groups or bundles; streak reddish brown or black	Manganite, p. 409
4	4+++	Usually in cubic crystals; perfect octahedral cleavage	Fluorite, p. 428
4–4½	1+++	Usually as short bladed crystals, striated lengthwise on one face; streak brown-black	Wolframite Series, p. 496
5–5½	1+++	Submetallic, usually in botryoidal, mammillary or radiating masses; fibrous structure; yellowish-brown streak	Goethite, p. 411
5–5½	1++	Usually as flattened, wedge-shaped crystals; brittle; parting common	Titanite, p. 588
5–6	2+++	Usually massive; cleaves more or less distinctly at nearly right angles	Hedenbergite, p. 546

H	Cl	Distinctive Features	Mineral
5–6	2+++	Stubby crystals, grains; perfect cleavages at angles of 56° and 124°	Hornblende, p. 539
5–6	2+++	Prismatic crystals with diamond-shaped cross section; cleaves at angles of 56° and 124°; may have tan streak	Pargasite, p. 541
5–6	2+++	Fibrous masses or prismatic crystals with diamond-shaped cross section	Riebeckite, p. 543
5–6	1+++	Well-formed prismatic crystals with square cross section; perfect lengthwise cleavage	Neptunite, p. 555
5–6	2++	Two distinct cleavages at nearly right angles; often in short prismatic crystals	Augite, p. 547
5–6	—	Submetallic masses, sometimes botryoidal or mammillary; streak black or brown, shiny	Psilomelane, p. 411
5–6	—	Brownish to pitch black, with black or olive-green streak; octahedral crystals; radioactive	Uraninite, p. 403
5½	2++	Short prismatic or rhombohedral crystals; luster usually resinous	Willemite, p. 576
5½–6	2++	Small striated crystals, with two cleavages at nearly right angles; weakly magnetic; rare	Babingtonite, p. 554

H	Cl	Distinctive Features	Mineral
6	2+++	Fibrous masses of prismatic crystals with diamond-shaped cross section	Glaucophane, p. 542
6	1++	Weakly magnetic; usually in short prismatic crystals; streak dark red	Columbite-Tantalite Series, p. 422
6–6½	2+++	Slender prismatic crystals ending in pointed pyramids; gray streak	Acmite, p. 548
6–7	1+++	Long, slender, grooved prismatic crystals	Epidote, p. 571
6–7	2++	Crystals usually short, prismatic, twinned; streak light brown	Cassiterite, p. 402
6½–7½	—	Crystals equant dodecahedrons or trapezohedrons; common in metamorphic rocks	Garnet Group, p. 582
7	—	Smooth surface and conchoidal fracture; botryoidal form common; no visible crystals	Chalcedony, p. 504
7	—	Vitreous or greasy luster; massive or in hexagonal, horizontally striated crystals ending in double rhombohedrons; conchoidal fracture	Quartz, p. 502
7–7½	1+	Occurs as single or commonly twinned prismatic crystals in metamorphic rocks	Staurolite, p. 581

H	Cl	Distinctive Features	Mineral
7–7½	—	Slender prismatic, striated crystals, rounded-triangular in cross section	Tourmaline Group, p. 563
7½–8	—	Octahedral crystals, often twinned	Spinel, p. 416
9	—	Crystals barrel-shaped; vitreous or adamantine luster; may break into cubic fragments with striated faces	Corundum, p. 395

MULTICOLORED OR BANDED MINERALS

H	Cl	Distinctive Features	Mineral
2½–3	—	Color usually intense, with strong resinous luster; small prismatic hexagonal crystals	Vanadinite, p. 486
5½–6½	—	Vitreous brittle masses; conchoidal fracture; may be milky or show internal play of colors	Opal, p. 506
6	2+++ 1+	Cleavage masses or grains with fine parallel striations on best cleavage surface	Plagioclase Feldspar Group, p. 510
7	—	Smooth surface and conchoidal fracture; botryoidal form common; no visible crystals	Chalcedony, p. 504
7	—	Vitreous or greasy luster; massive or in hexagonal, horizontally striated crystals ending in double rhombohedrons; conchoidal fracture	Quartz, p. 502

H	Cl	Distinctive Features	Mineral
7–7½	—	Slender prismatic, striated crystals, rounded triangular in cross section	Tourmaline Group, p. 563

METALLIC MINERALS

H	Cl	Distinctive Features	Mineral
1–1½	1+++	Bluish lead-gray; will make greenish-black streak on paper; cleaves into flexible sheets; feels greasy	Molybdenite, p. 378
1–2	1+++	Color and streak black or gray; feels greasy; breaks into flexible sheets	Graphite, p. 355
1½–2	1+++	Silver-white to steel-gray; streak black or nearly so; unstriated crystals or branched aggregates; melts in flame	Sylvanite, p. 381
2	1+++	Lead-gray to tin-white with yellow or iridescent tarnish; streak lead-gray; usually massive, foliated, or fibrous	Bismuthinite, p. 373
2	1+++	Lead-gray with black tarnish; will make dark lead-gray streak on paper; may be in bladed or curved striated crystals	Stibnite, p. 372
2–2½	1+++	Silver-white or reddish with brassy tarnish; can be cut with knife	Bismuth, p. 352
2–2½	2++	Dark lead-gray to black; streak iron-black; usually in short striated prismatic to tabular crystals	Stephanite, p. 384

H	Cl	Distinctive Features	Mineral
2–2½	—	Lead-gray to black; streak black, shining; can be cut with knife into thin layers	Acanthite, p. 358
2½	3+++	Usually as dark lead-gray cubes or octahedrons; perfect cubic cleavage; streak lead-gray	Galena, p. 361
2½	1++	Steel-gray, lead-gray, with iridescent tarnish; streak grayish-black; crystals needlelike, often in felted or feathery masses	Jamesonite, p. 391
2½–3	1++ 2+	Color and streak gray to black; short striated prismatic crystals, often in twinned, cruciform or wheel-like aggregates	Bournonite, p. 389
2½–3	1++	Flexible fibers or long deeply striated prismatic crystals; color lead-gray with gray or brown streak	Boulangerite, p. 390
2½–3	1+	Dark lead-gray; streak gray or black, shiny; can be cut with knife; very brittle	Chalcocite, p. 359
2½–3	—	Brass-yellow to silver-white; streak yellowish to greenish gray; striated bladed or lathlike crystals	Calaverite, p. 380
2½–3	—	Copper-red (may have black tarnish); malleable; usually granular, but sometimes in branched aggregates of crystals; shiny copper-red streak	Copper, p. 348

H	C1	Distinctive Features	Mineral
2½–3	—	Golden-yellow; extremely heavy; quite soft and malleable; shiny gold streak	Gold, p. 346
2½–3	—	Color silver-white; malleable; in grains or curving wires	Silver, p. 347
3	1+++ 2++	Color and streak grayish black; usually in striated tabular crystals or bladed aggregates	Enargite, p. 388
3	—	Coppery or bronze, with iridescent blue and purple (peacock) tarnish; streak pale gray-black	Bornite, p. 360
3–3½	2+++	Yellow metallic hairlike crystals, often in radiating groups; greenish-black streak	Millerite, p. 366
3–3½	1+++	Tin-white to light steel-gray; very brittle	Antimony, p. 351
3–4	—	Steel-gray to iron-black; streak gray, black, reddish brown; crystals tetrahedral	Tetrahedrite Series, p. 386
3½	1+++	Tin-white with dark gray tarnish; gives garlic odor when heated in flame; tin-white streak	Arsenic, p. 350
3½–4	1+	Tetrahedral crystals; deep brass or golden-yellow, with iridescent tarnish; greenish-black streak; very brittle	Chalcopyrite, p. 363
3½–4	—	Usually in light, bronze-yellow masses; light bronze-brown streak	Pentlandite, p. 367

H	C1	Distinctive Features	Mineral
½–1½	—	Bronze with dark brown tarnish; weakly magnetic	Pyrrhotite, p. 364
4–4½	—	Tin-white or gray; extremely heavy; occurs in grains or nuggets	Platinum, p. 349
4–5½	—	Amorphous, earthy masses; yellowish-brown streak; may occur as pseudomorphs after pyrite, marcasite, siderite	Limonite, p. 413
5–5½	1+++	Botryoidal, mammillary or radiating masses; fibrous structure; yellowish-brown streak	Goethite, p. 411
5–5½	—	Light copper-red; brownish-black streak; heavy; rare	Nickeline, p. 366
5–6	—	Gray or black to red or brown; streak reddish brown; usually as radiating or tabular crystals or botryoidal masses	Hematite, p. 397
5–6	—	Color and streak black or brownish black; weakly magnetic	Ilmenite, p. 398
5½	1+++	Silver-white, gray, reddish to black; streak gray-black; in striated cubes, pyritohedrons; also massive	Cobaltite, p. 375
5½	—	Weakly magnetic; iron-black masses with dark brown streak	Chromite, p. 419
5½–6	2++	Massive or as cubic, octahedral crystals; color and streak tin-white to silver; crystals rare	Skutterudite Series, p. 379

H	Cl	Distinctive Features	Mineral
5½–6	1++	Silver-white to steel-gray; streak grayish black; usually massive or in prismatic crystals	Arsenopyrite, p. 377
5½–6½	—	Weakly magnetic; black octahedral crystals or masses; streak reddish brown, black	Franklinite, p. 418
5½–6½	—	Strongly magnetic; color and streak black; octahedral crystals	Magnetite, p. 417
6–6½	2+++	Color and streak black; brittle, with splintery fracture, powdery	Pyrolusite, p. 401
6–6½	2++ 1+	Red, reddish brown, black, with pale streak; striated prismatic crystals, often in knee-shaped twins	Rutile, p. 400
6–6½	2++	Pale brass-yellow to white with yellow or brown tarnish; streak dark green to black; often as coxcombs, spears, or radiating groups	Marcasite, p. 376
6–6½	1+	Crystals nearly perfect cubes; color and streak black; luster brilliant metallic to submetallic; rare	Bixbyite, p. 399
6–6½	—	Pale-yellow to brass-yellow; streak greenish black; often in striated cubes or pyritohedrons or in masses or nodules	Pyrite, p. 374

THE COMMON MINERALS OF NORTH AMERICA

Minerals, like trees, animals, and other natural objects, are classified into groups of similar species. This helps the scientist or collector to recognize similarities and differences within each class of mineral, while emphasizing the differences between the classes.

Mineral Classes   In this book we follow the classification used in Dana's *System of Mineralogy* (7th Edition), the standard reference to minerals. Every mineral species included belongs in one of 15 classes, beginning with "native elements" and ending with "silicates." The minerals are classified on the basis of their crystal chemistry—that is, their chemical makeup and crystal structure.
In the following pages each group of mineral descriptions is preceded by a short description of the mineral class.

Mineral Species   For each mineral species, the following information is given:
1. The chemical description and formula.
2. The physical properties of the mineral, including color, luster, streak, hardness, cleavage, and such other data as specific gravity, tenacity, and fracture. (These terms are explained in

the preceding section, "A Guide to
Mineral Identification.")
3. A description of the crystals and
mineral form.
4. The best field marks for identifying
the mineral. These may include crystal
form, color, hardness or softness, or any
other characteristic that helps in
recognition. Even taste is used as a field
mark in some cases.
5. Notes on similar mineral species
that might cause confusion in making
an identification.
6. The mineral environments where
the species is most likely to be found.
7. Important occurrences—that is,
localities where outstanding specimens
have been found.
8. Gemstone data for precious and
semiprecious minerals.
9. The origin of the name, and general
information—historical, economic, or
esthetic—on the occurrence and use of
the mineral.

The number or numbers preceding each
mineral description correspond to the
illustration number(s) in the Visual Key
to Minerals, pages 41 through 280.

Native Elements

Native elements are those elements that occur in the free, uncombined state, and include metallic elements (gold, silver), semimetallic elements (arsenic, antimony), and nonmetallic elements (carbon, sulfur). The metals are more numerous, and because they are malleable and have a metallic appearance, they are readily recognized.

562, 637, 638,	**Gold**
639, 650, 652,	Native, with some silver, copper, and
653	iron
	Au

Color and luster: Gold-yellow, brass-yellow, pale yellow; does not tarnish; metallic; streak gold-yellow, shiny.

Hardness: 2½–3

Cleavage: None.

Other data: *Specific gravity* 15.6 to 19.3; *fracture* hackly; ductile and malleable.

Crystals: Isometric; commonly octahedral, dodecahedral, and cubic; commonly distorted; also grains, scales, lumps, also plates, leaves, and wires.

Best field marks: Gold-yellow color, high gravity, and malleability.

Similar species: Pyrite and chalcopyrite are lighter in weight than gold; are brittle; and will yield small fragments and powder when the minerals are hammered.

Environment: Although a considerable amount of gold has been recovered by the mining of clastic placer sedimentary deposits, the gold was originally deposited in veins, igneous rocks, and hydrothermal replacement deposits. Gold occurs with pyrite and arsenopyrite in lode hydrothermal replacement deposits.

Occurrence: Many mines in North America have become famous for the value in gold they produced and for the great span in years the mines were in continuous operation. No attempt will be made here to enumerate these famous mines; only those mines, large or small, that have yielded fine gold specimens are listed.

In California fine specimens showing well-formed crystals have come from the Empire Mine in Grass Valley and the Red Ledge Mine near Washington, both in Nevada Co. Beautiful crystals of gold in white quartz have come from Red Mountain Pass, San Juan Co., Colorado, and from several mines in the Mexican states of Chihuahua, Hidalgo, Sonora, and Zacatecas. The Hollinger

and Dome mines in the famous
Porcupine district of Ontario have also
produced fine gold specimens, as well
as being among the most productive
mines in the world.

The name is thought to be Anglo-
Saxon, and of uncertain origin. Gold
itself, since it rarely combines with
other elements, is mined as the ore of
gold.

647, 649, 651	Silver
	Native, often with much gold or mercury, and lesser amounts of arsenic and antimony
	Ag

Color and luster:	Silver-white; tarnish yellow, brown, black; metallic; streak silver-white to light lead-gray, shining.
Hardness:	2½–3
Cleavage:	None.
Other data:	*Specific gravity* 10.1 to 11.1; *fracture* hackly; malleable and ductile.
Crystals:	Isometric; crystals (rare) are cubes, octahedrons, and dodecahedrons or in groups of parallel cubes or octahedrons; also grains, scales, plates, wire, reticulated, arborescent.
Best field marks:	White color, malleability, and hardness.
Similar species:	Silver is whiter and harder than lead, and softer than platinum.
Environment:	Silver is widely distributed in small amounts and occurs in volcanic rocks and in various types of veins. Large irregular masses and sheets of silver occur with copper, chalcocite, and pumpellyite in basalt of volcanic rocks, and with quartz, uraninite, and nickeline in hypothermal and mesothermal veins.
Occurrence:	There are several excellent collecting localities in North America. Notable among them are the famous mines on the Keweenaw Peninsula, Michigan,

where silver occurs with copper, prehnite, calcite, and analcime in cavities in amygdaloidal basalt. Irregular masses and small plates of silver occur with chalcocite at Bisbee, Cochise Co., Arizona, and fine microspecimens have been found at Creede, Mineral Co., Colorado. Sheets and masses of silver many inches across have been collected from the veins at Cobalt, Timiskaming District, Ontario, and wire and arborescent silver at Batopilas, Chihuahua, Mexico.

The name is said to be Anglo-Saxon, but its ultimate origin is not known. Silver is mined as an ore of silver.

654 Copper
Native, often with small amounts of arsenic, antimony, bismuth, iron, and silver
Cu

Color and luster:	Copper-red; tarnish black, blue, green; metallic; streak copper-red, shiny.
Hardness:	2½–3
Cleavage:	None.
Other data:	*Specific gravity* 8.9; *fracture* hackly; ductile and malleable.
Crystals:	Isometric; usually cubic and dodecahedral, rarely octahedral; often flattened, elongated, distorted; also scales, plates, lumps, branching aggregates.
Best field marks:	Malleability and copper color on fresh surface.
Similar species:	None.
Environment:	Native copper commonly develops in basalt of volcanic rocks by the reaction of copper-bearing solutions on the iron-oxide minerals in the basalt. A few of the associated minerals in this environment are calcite, cuprite, and zeolites. Native copper forms also in disseminated hydrothermal replacement deposits, and here it is usually

associated with cuprite and calcite.

Occurrence:

The copper mines of the Keweenaw Peninsula in Michigan have yielded excellent specimens of native copper. Crystals up to 2.5 cm (1 inch) across and specimens of copper that contain as much native silver as copper are not uncommon in the Michigan mines. These mines also yield crystals of calcite that enclose untarnished copper wire and platelets. Some of the copper mines in Arizona, especially those at Ajo, Pima Co., have yielded spectacular specimens of native copper, as crystals and masses. Native copper has been obtained from New Mexico, Oregon, Alaska, New Jersey, and Nova Scotia.

The name is from the Greek *Kyprios,* the island Cyprus, where copper was early found and mined. Native copper is used as an ore of copper.

---

640 Platinum

Native, with minor amounts of iridium, osmium, rhodium, and palladium; also contains iron, copper, gold, or nickel
Pt

Color and luster:	Tin-white, steel-gray; does not tarnish; metallic; streak light steel-gray, shining.
Hardness:	4–4½
Cleavage:	None.
Other data:	*Specific gravity* 14 to 19; *fracture* hackly; malleable, ductile.
Crystals:	Isometric; usually distorted cubes; commonly as grains, scales, lumps or nuggets.
Best field marks:	Specific gravity and weak magnetism of the iron-rich particles.
Similar species:	Platinum is heavier than silver and is also slightly magnetic.
Environment:	Although platinum develops in peridotites of plutonic rocks, where it occurs associated with chromite,

olivine, and enstatite, much of the world's supply of the metal is derived from clastic placer deposits, which in places also produce considerable amounts of gold.

Occurrence: Seldom has platinum been found in nuggets much larger than a pea, and because it lacks the appeal of gold nuggets or a cluster of silver crystals, it is not a common mineral in collections. Platinum is widely distributed throughout the world and has been found in North America in gold-bearing placer deposits in Rutherford and Burke Cos., North Carolina; in Trinity and Butte Cos., California; at Cape Blanco, Curry Co., Oregon; in Beauce Co., Quebec, and in the Kamloops mining district, British Columbia.

The name is from the Spanish *plata,* "silver." It is the only ore of platinum and related elements. Native platinum always contains other members of its chemical group, the heavy metals iridium, osmium, rhodium, and palladium. Their presence accounts for platinum's great range of specific gravity.

643 Arsenic
Native, usually with some antimony, iron, nickel, silver, and sulfur
As

Color and luster: Tin-white, tarnishing quickly to dark gray; metallic; streak tin-white.
Hardness: 3½
Cleavage: Perfect, one direction.
Other data: *Specific gravity* 5.6 to 5.7; *fracture* uneven, brittle; gives garlicky odor when heated (**caution:** fumes are poisonous).
Crystals: Hexagonal, pseudocubic; natural crystals rare; usually granular, massive; also mammillary, stalactitic, reniform.

Best field marks:	Garlicky odor; otherwise difficult to distinguish from antimony, with which it is easily confused.
Similar species:	Antimony.
Environment:	Arsenic is not a common mineral and is found largely in mesothermal and epithermal veins, where it is associated with barite, nickeline, and cinnabar.
Occurrence:	Excellent collecting localities seem to be largely in Europe, especially in France, Germany, England, and Italy. It does occur sparingly as spherical masses up to several pounds in weight at Washington Camp, Santa Cruz Co., Arizona, and at Atlin, British Columbia.

The name is from the Greek *arsenikon* and was originally applied to orpiment.

---

642   Antimony
Native, sometimes containing arsenic, iron, and silver
Sb

Color and luster:	Tin-white to light steel-gray; metallic; streak tin-white to light steel-gray.
Hardness:	3–3½
Cleavage:	Perfect, one direction.
Other data:	*Specific gravity* 6.6 to 6.7; *fracture* uneven; very brittle.
Crystals:	Hexagonal, sometimes pseudocubic; generally massive, lamellar, and distinctly cleavable; also radiated, botryoidal, or reniform.
Best field marks:	Antimony is difficult to distinguish by physical tests from arsenic, with which it is confused.
Similar species:	Arsenic.
Environment:	Antimony is restricted in its environments and is most commonly found associated with stibnite, nickeline, and sphalerite in mesothermal veins.
Occurrence:	Occurrences of antimony are scarce in North America, but fine pure masses, some as much as several hundred

pounds, have come from small mines on Erskine Creek, near Kernville, Kern Co., California. Nodules of antimony several inches across have come from mines at Arechuybo, Chihuahua, Mexico, and several occurrences have been reported at South Ham, Wolfe Co., Quebec.

The name is from the Medieval Latin *antimonium,* which was originally applied to stibnite.

---

645 **Bismuth**
Native, with small amounts of sulfur, arsenic, and antimony
Bi

Color and luster: Silver-white, reddish; tarnish often brassy; metallic; streak silver-white with reddish hue, shining.

Hardness: 2–2½

Cleavage: Good, one direction across long direction of crystal.

Other data: *Specific gravity* 9.7 to 9.8; sectile; somewhat malleable when heated.

Crystals: Hexagonal; crystals rare, but in parallel groups; also laminated, granular, branching, disseminated.

Best field marks: Pinkish, silver-white hue, and broad cleavage surfaces.

Similar species: May be mistaken for antimony, from which it can be distinguished by its pinkish silver-white hue.

Environment: Bismuth is not a common mineral, yet it occurs in several environments. It occurs with bismuthinite and quartz in granite pegmatites; with gold, cassiterite, and quartz in hypothermal and mesothermal veins, and with gold, acanthite, and cassiterite in massive hydrothermal replacement deposits.

Occurrence: Excellent specimens have come from Schneeberg and Annaberg in Saxony, Germany, and from Fahlun, Sweden. It occurs sparingly in North America, but fine specimens have been found associated with silver ores at Cobalt, Timiskaming district, Ontario, and in the pitchblende veins at Great Bear Lake, Mackenzie district, Northwest Territory. Small amounts of bismuth have been found in the Chesterfield district of South Carolina, and in fine brilliant masses with bismuthinite at the El Carmen Mine, Durango, Mexico.

The name is said to be from the German *Wismut*, of unknown origin. It is a minor ore of bismuth.

304, 331 Sulfur
Native sulfur, sometimes with small amounts of selenium
S

Color and luster:	Yellow, greenish or reddish yellow, brown, gray; greasy, resinous, adamantine; streak white.
Hardness:	1½–2½
Cleavage:	Poor, two directions.
Other data:	*Specific gravity* 2.0 to 2.1; *fracture* conchoidal; very brittle; transparent to translucent.
Crystals:	Orthorhombic; usually steep bipyramids, sometimes tabular; also granular, fibrous, compact, earthy; reniform, stalactitic, incrusting.
Best field marks:	Transparent yellow crystals and softness.
Similar species:	There are very few common minerals with which sulfur can be confused.
Environment:	Sulfur is generally deposited as a direct sublimation product from volcanic gases. It is often associated with cinnabar and stibnite, and frequently occurs in basalt of volcanic rocks.
Occurrence:	Sulfur deposits at Agrigento and Cattolico in Sicily have been the sources for excellent display specimens. North American localities where fine crystal specimens may be obtained are not common. Sulfur occurs in rhyolite tuff

at Sulphurdale, Beaver Co., Utah; around the fumaroles in Yellowstone National Park; at Sulphur Bank, Lake Co., California, and on Lassen Peak, Tehama Co., California.

Origin of the name is unknown. Sulfur has many uses, especially in the manufacture of sulfuric acid.

305, 310, 322, 362, 677	**Diamond** Carbon C

Color and luster: White, colorless; pale shades of yellow, red, orange, blue, green, brown; frequently black; adamantine, greasy.

Hardness: 10

Cleavage: Perfect, four directions.

Other data: *Specific gravity* 3.5; *fracture* conchoidal; brittle; transparent to translucent; some stones strongly fluorescent.

Crystals: Isometric; mostly octahedrons; less commonly dodecahedral; rarely cubic; usually with curved faces; also rounded and irregular grains.

Best field marks: Extreme hardness and greasy (adamantine) luster.

Similar species: Diamond is most easily confused with quartz pebbles, but the luster and hardness of diamond will suffice to distinguish one from the other.

Environment: Although a substantial proportion of diamonds are mined from placer sedimentary deposits, diamond is actually formed in peridotite of plutonic rocks, where it is associated with olivine, magnetite, and phlogopite.

Occurrence: India was the earliest source of diamonds. They were discovered in Brazil in 1729, in South Africa in 1867, and in Pike Co., Arkansas, in 1906. A few colorless diamonds were recovered along with gold in placer mining of gravels in several northern

Mother Lode counties, California.

Gemstone data: Gem varieties of diamond include *colorless,* which may be colorless or faintly tinted, commonly with yellow or brown and less commonly with green or blue; and *fancies,* diamonds with decided tint or depth of color. In fancy diamonds, browns are very common, orange, violet, strong yellow (or canary), and yellowish greens are common, and red, blue, and deep pure green are rarest. *Black diamonds* are rarely used in jewelry, and bort and carbonado, because they are aggregates of very minute crystals, are used only as abrasives. Fancy diamonds of the rarer colors are the most valuable. Diamonds are faceted for their ultimate use in jewelry. Principal sources of diamonds are in Africa (Zaire, South Africa, South-West Africa) and Brazil. Some diamonds have been found in Arkansas and California.

The name is from the Greek *adamas,* "invincible." Diamonds have many uses, but principally as gems and as an abrasive. Diamond is the birthstone for April.

Diamond also occurs in two quite distinct varieties. *Bort* occurs as rough rounded masses with radial or confused structure, without distinct cleavage; it is grayish black with a specific gravity of 3.5. *Carbonado,* or black diamond, is opaque, granular to compact, and without cleavage; its specific gravity is 3.1 to 3.3.

---

644 **Graphite**
Carbon, often impure due to admixed clay and iron oxide
C

Color and luster: Steel-gray to iron-black; metallic; streak grayish to black, shining.

Hardness: 1–2

Cleavage: Perfect, one direction; thin flakes flexible, sectile.

Other data: *Specific gravity* 1.9 to 2.3; feels greasy.

Crystals: Hexagonal tablets; also foliated, scaly, granular, earthy.

Best field marks: Perfect cleavage and inelastic flexible laminae.

Similar species: Easily confused with molybdenite, which is heavier.

Environment: Graphite results from the metamorphism of carbonaceous material in sedimentary rocks and is therefore found with quartz and muscovite in schists of regional metamorphic rocks and in marble.

Occurrence: Graphite is seldom found in mineral collections because of the scarcity of good specimens, but fine crystals have been found in the marbles at the Sterling Hill Mine at Ogdensburg, Sussex Co., New Jersey; in the schists in Clay Co., Alabama; and in massive veins near Ticonderoga, Essex Co., New York.

The name is derived from the Greek *graphein*, "to write," in allusion to its use as a crayon. Its principal use is in lubricants.

Sulfides, Arsenides, and Tellurides

The sulfides are simple compounds of one or more metallic elements or semimetals with sulfur, a nonmetallic element. Typical sulfide minerals, such as galena and sphalerite, are relatively soft, heavy, and brittle, with a distinct metallic luster; a few, such as pyrite, give off a sulfurous odor when struck with a hammer. The semimetallic elements tellurium and selenium or arsenic may substitute for one or more of the sulfur atoms. The mineral thus formed, which is described as a telluride or an arsenide, shows physical properties much like those of the simple sulfides.

Most sulfides are readily altered by weathering at the earth's surface. The water-soluble sulfide minerals may then be carried far underground with heated groundwater, later to be redeposited at great depth. This process of secondary enrichment, also called sulfide enrichment, may result in rich deposits of copper, lead, zinc, or other metallic ores.

646 Acanthite (Argentite)
Silver sulfide, often with some copper
Ag_2S

Color and luster: Lead-gray to black; metallic; streak black, shining.
Hardness: $2–2\frac{1}{2}$
Cleavage: Indistinct; perfectly sectile; cuts like lead.
Other data: *Specific gravity* 7.2 to 7.4; *fracture* hackly.
Crystals: Isometric; crystals (rare) in cubes and octahedrons, or dodecahedral; often in groups of parallel individuals; reticulated, arborescent, massive, and as a coating.
Best field marks: Sectility and lack of distinct cleavage.
Similar species: Acanthite lacks the perfect cleavage of galena and does not exhibit the conchoidal fracture which is so characteristic of chalcocite.
Environment: Acanthite occurs with barite, bornite, and galena in massive hydrothermal replacement deposits and with quartz, gold, and pyrite in epithermal veins.
Occurrence: Excellent crystals of acanthite have come from the famous silver mines at Kongsberg, Norway, where it occurs with native silver. In North America good collecting localities are not abundant, but acanthite was especially abundant in the silver mines at Pachuca, Guanajuato, and Zacatecas, Mexico; at Butte, Montana; at Aspen and Leadville, Colorado; and at the famous Comstock Lode, Virginia City, Nevada.

Acanthite is named from the Greek word for "thorn," *akantha,* with reference to the crystal form. The alternate name, argentite, comes from the Latin *argentum,* "silver." At temperatures above 173°C acanthite alters to a twinned form and is correctly called argentite. At room temperatures, acanthite is the only stable form of Ag_2S.

560, 592, 602 **Chalcocite**
Copper sulfide
Cu_2S

Color and luster:	Dark lead-gray; tarnish dull black; metallic; streak dark gray to black, shining.
Hardness:	2½–3
Cleavage:	Poor, one direction.
Other data:	*Specific gravity* 5.5 to 5.8; *fracture* conchoidal; brittle; imperfectly sectile.
Crystals:	Orthorhombic; short prismatic or tabular, striated on one face; also granular compact, disseminated.
Best field marks:	Gray color; less sectile than other sulfide minerals; associated with other copper minerals; very brittle.
Similar species:	Chalcocite is less sectile than acanthite; does not have the cleavage of galena; and is gray in color.
Environment:	One of the most abundant of copper minerals, chalcocite occurs in several distinct environments, especially with galena, pyrite, and quartz in mesothermal veins; with native copper and calcite in basalt of volcanic rocks; and with chalcopyrite, bornite, and pyrite in massive, lode, and disseminated hydrothermal replacement deposits.
Occurrence:	Although significant deposits of chalcocite have been mined at Butte, Montana, the best North American occurrence for fine crystals was an old mine in Bristol, Connecticut. Other localities include the famous copper mines at Miami, Morenci, Bisbee, and Ray in Arizona; at Bingham, Tooele Co., Utah; at Santa Rita, New Mexico; and at Kennecott in the Copper River district, Alaska.

The name is derived from the Greek *chalkos,* for "copper." Chalcocite is an important ore of copper.

580, 631, 633   Bornite
Copper iron sulfide
Cu_5FeS_4

Color and luster: Copper-red to bronze-brown; tarnish deep blue, purple, variegated; metallic; streak grayish black.

Hardness: 3

Cleavage: None.

Other data: *Specific gravity* 4.9 to 5.1; *fracture* uneven, conchoidal; brittle.

Crystals: Isometric; crystals (rare) cubic, dodecahedral, rarely octahedral; compact, granular.

Best field marks: Occurrence with other copper minerals and colorful tarnish, which is referred to as *peacock*.

Similar species: Pyrrhotite is magnetic, and nickeline is harder and heavier than bornite. Pyrrhotite and nickeline do not exhibit the peacock tarnish.

Environment: Bornite is a common and widespread copper-sulfide mineral, and occurs in several environments. It occurs with pyrite, barite, and calcite in carbonatites; with andradite, galena, and calcite in skarn of hydrothermal metamorphic rocks; with quartz, enargite, and pyrite in mesothermal veins; and with chalcopyrite, chalcocite, and pyrite in massive, lode, and disseminated hydrothermal replacement deposits.

Occurrence: Fine crystals of bornite are rare, but there are many places in North America where excellent specimens of massive bornite can still be found. Small crystals were found in druses at Butte, Silver Bow Co., Montana, and at Bristol, Hartford Co., Connecticut. Massive bornite occurs at the Evergreen Mine, near Apex, Gilpin Co., Colorado; the Magma Mine at Superior, Pinal Co., Arizona; at Kennecott in the Copper River district, Alaska; at Butte, Montana; at the Acton Mine, Bagot Co., Quebec; and at the Marble Bay Mine, Texada Island, British Columbia.

It is named after Ignaz von Born
(1742–1791), famous Austrian
mineralogist. Bornite is an important
copper-ore mineral.

559, 575 Galena
Lead sulfide
PbS

Color and luster:	Dark lead-gray; metallic; streak dark lead-gray.
Hardness:	2½
Cleavage:	Perfect in three directions at 90°.
Other data:	*Specific gravity* 7.4 to 7.6; *fracture* subconchoidal (rare); brittle.
Crystals:	Isometric; commonly in cubes and combinations of cubes and octahedrons; dodecahedrons less frequent; also massive and in cleavage fragments, coarse- or fine-grained, fibrous.
Best field marks:	Cubic cleavage and lead-gray color.
Similar species:	The cubic cleavage and dark lead-gray color will distinguish galena from sphalerite, jamesonite, and stibnite.
Environment:	Galena is the commonest of all lead minerals and occurs in several environments. It is associated with andradite, pyrite, and chalcopyrite in skarn of hydrothermal metamorphic rocks; with quartz, bornite, and sphalerite in hypothermal and mesothermal veins; and most significantly with barite, sphalerite, and marcasite in lode and disseminated hydrothermal replacement deposits.
Occurrence:	Fine crystals and crystal groups of galena have come from famous European mines, but the Joplin district of Oklahoma, Kansas, and Missouri is equally famous for its beautiful cubes and octahedrons. Fine specimens of galena have also come from the Leadville, Aspen, Georgetown, and San Juan districts of Colorado; and it has been found in a siderite-quartz gangue at the lead-silver mines of the Coeur d'Alene region of Idaho, and with

scheelite, sphalerite, and pyrite at Darwin, Inyo Co., California.

The name is from the Latin *galena*, which was applied to lead ore or the dross from melted lead. It is the most important ore of lead, and during the heyday of the crystal-detector radio receiver, galena was well known for its use as the crystal in the radio.

187, 224, 578, 579

Sphalerite
Zinc sulfide, usually with some iron, manganese, and cadmium
ZnS

Color and luster: Yellow, brown, red, green, black; rarely white or pale gray (cleiophane); resinous, adamantine, submetallic; streak light brown (always lighter than specimen).

Hardness: 3½–4

Cleavage: Perfect, six directions.

Other data: *Specific gravity* 3.9 to 4.1; *fracture* conchoidal; brittle; transparent to translucent (dark iron-rich varieties nearly opaque); fluorescent occasionally.

Crystals: Isometric; tetrahedral and dodecahedral forms common; faces often rounded; also cleavage masses, granular, compact, botryoidal.

Best field marks: Red-brown to green color, adamantine luster, and cleavage.

Similar species: Sphalerite is not as heavy as galena and lacks the cubic cleavage. Sphalerite is heavier than siderite, which has only three cleavage directions.

Environment: Sphalerite shares many environments with galena. It occurs with galena, fluorite, and cerussite in carbonatites and sedimentary (limestone) deposits; with galena, arsenopyrite, and quartz in hypothermal and mesothermal veins; and with galena, pyrite, and chalcopyrite in massive, lode, and disseminated hydrothermal replacement deposits.

Occurrence: Many specimens showing well-formed crystals have been obtained from the famous tri-state region near Joplin, Missouri. Fine pale-green (cleiophane) crystals were found in the zinc mines at Franklin, Sussex Co., New Jersey. Pale-green to deep-green crystals, sometimes complexly twinned, occur in calcite and quartz at Cananea, Sonora, Mexico. Masses of coarsely crystalline sphalerite occur in many small zinc mines scattered throughout W United States.

The name is from the Greek *sphaleros,* "treacherous," in allusion to its similarity to other minerals, with which it was often confused. Sphalerite is the principal ore of zinc.

563, 564, **Chalcopyrite**
565, 567 Copper iron sulfide, often with some silver and gold
$CuFeS_2$

Color and luster: Brass-yellow, golden-yellow; tarnish often iridescent or deep blue, purple, and black; metallic; streak greenish black.

Hardness: $3\frac{1}{2}-4$

Cleavage: Poor, one direction.

Other data: *Specific gravity* 4.1 to 4.3; *fracture* uneven; brittle.

Crystals: Tetragonal; commonly tetrahedral; crystal faces usually uneven and some may contain striations in different directions; often massive, compact, granular, disseminated.

Best field marks: Hardness, color, and brittleness.

Similar species: Pyrite is harder than chalcopyrite, but less yellow in color. Gold is not brittle, whereas chalcopyrite is.

Environment: Chalcopyrite is one of the most widely distributed copper minerals. It is found in a number of environments and occurs associated with barite and bornite in carbonatites; with glaucophane and lawsonite in the blue schists of regional metamorphic rocks; with pyrite, andradite, and molybdenite in skarn of hydrothermal metamorphic rocks; and most commonly with pyrite, chalcocite, and gold in hypothermal and mesothermal veins.

Occurrence: Because of the widespread occurrence of sites where specimens can be collected, only a few of the exceptional localities will be listed here. Chalcopyrite is found in large but usually tarnished crystals at the French Creek mines, Chester Co., Pennsylvania; in fine iridescent, tarnished tetrahedral crystals with quartz at La Bufa, Chihuahua, Mexico; in the lead-zinc mines with galena, marcasite, and sphalerite in the tri-state district of Missouri, Kansas, and Oklahoma; with garnet at Silver Bell, Pima, Arizona; with pyrite, tourmaline, and quartz at the Cactus Mine, San Francisco district, Utah; with pyrrhotite, pyrite, and sphalerite in quartz veins at the Noranda Mine, Rouyn district, Quebec; and with other sulfides and gold at Flin Flon, Manitoba.

The name is from the Greek *chalkos*, "copper," and *pyrites*, "fiery." Chalcopyrite is quite abundant and is an important ore of copper.

636 Pyrrhotite

Iron sulfide, with small amounts of nickel and cobalt
$Fe_{1-x}S$, in which x ranges between 0 and 0.2

Color and luster: Yellowish to brownish bronze; tarnish dark brown; metallic; streak dark grayish black.
Hardness: $3\frac{1}{2}-4\frac{1}{2}$
Cleavage: None; basal parting distinct.
Other data: *Specific gravity* 4.5 to 4.6; *fracture* uneven; strongly to weakly magnetic.
Crystals: Orthorhombic (pseudo-hexagonal);

commonly tabular to platy, some faces striated; also massive, granular.

Best field mark: Magnetism.

Similar species: Pyrrhotite is magnetic; the similar species pentlandite, pyrite, and chalcopyrite are not.

Environment: Pyrrhotite is more widely distributed than pentlandite, one of its associated minerals, and occurs in several distinct environments, including pegmatites, carbonatites, metamorphic rocks, and hydrothermal replacement deposits. Pyrrhotite occurs with sodalite, wollastonite, and albite in nepheline syenite pegmatites; with scapolite, barite, and tetrahedrite in carbonatites; with andradite, scheelite, and hedenbergite in skarn of hydrothermal metamorphic rocks; and with gold, pyrite, and galena in massive and lode hydrothermal replacement deposits.

Occurrence: Famous localities at Kisbanya, Rumania, Andreasberg, Germany, and Falun, Sweden, have produced excellent well-formed crystals of pyrrhotite. In North America there are several important localities, including the Standish Mine in Maine, where pyrrhotite occurs with andalusite, and at Trumbull, Fairfield Co., Connecticut, where it occurs with topaz. Pyrrhotite occurs abundantly in the zinc ores at Ducktown, Polk Co., Tennessee, and in a massive form in shale and sandstone at Island Mt., Mendocino Co., California. Twinned crystals of pyrrhotite occur in calcite veins at Elizabethtown and Webster, Ontario, and with pentlandite at Sudbury, Ontario. Large crystals, often highly iridescent, occur at the Potosí Mine, Santa Eulalia, Chihuahua, Mexico.

The name is from the Greek *pyrrhotes,* "redness."

635 Nickeline (Niccolite)
Nickel arsenide, frequently with some antimony
NiAs

Color and luster:	Light copper-red; tarnish gray to blackish; may have coating of green annabergite; metallic; streak brownish black.
Hardness:	5–5½
Cleavage:	None.
Other data:	*Specific gravity* 7.8; *fracture* uneven.
Crystals:	Hexagonal; crystals rare, often distorted and striated; usually massive, reniform with columnar structure.
Best field mark:	Copper color.
Similar species:	None.
Environment:	Nickeline is not a common mineral. It occurs most commonly with chalcopyrite, pyrrhotite, and pentlandite in mesothermal veins.
Occurrence:	Well-crystallized specimens of nickeline have come from Eisleben, Germany. It has been found sparingly at Franklin, Sussex Co., New Jersey, and occurs with pyrrhotite and pentlandite at Sudbury, Ontario, and in veins in Sinaloa, Mexico.

The name is derived from the Latin *nicolum,* referring to its composition. Nickeline is an ore of nickel.

---

607 Millerite
Nickel sulfide, usually with small amounts of cobalt, iron, and copper
NiS

Color and luster:	Brass-yellow; metallic; streak greenish black.
Hardness:	3–3½
Cleavage:	Perfect in two directions, but difficult to observe.
Other data:	*Specific gravity* 5.3 to 5.5; *fracture* splintery, uneven; brittle; slender crystals elastic.
Crystals:	Hexagonal; usually very slender to

capillary crystals, often in radiating groups; also in columnar tufted coatings.

Best field marks: Slender capillary crystals, yellow color, and mineral association.

Similar species: Tourmaline and rutile. Neither of these minerals when found in the capillary form occurs in limestone or with nickel minerals, and they rarely are yellow.

Environment: Because the formation of millerite does not require high temperatures, it is commonly found associated with calcite, chalcopyrite, and quartz in disseminated hydrothermal replacement deposits.

Occurrence: Famous European localities are Freiberg, Johanngeorgenstadt, and Saarbrücken in Germany, and Glamorgan in Wales. In North America it is found with ankerite in cavities in hematite at the Sterling Mine, Antwerp, St. Lawrence Co., New York; as thin coatings with velvety surface on pyrrhotite at the Gap Mine, Lancaster Co., Pennsylvania; with calcite, dolomite, and fluorite in geodes at Keokuk, Iowa, and St. Louis, Missouri; and with grossular in Sherbrooke, Quebec.

The name is after W. H. Miller (1801–1880), an English mineralogist.

634 Pentlandite
Sulfide of iron and nickel
$(Fe,Ni)_9S_8$

Color and luster: Light bronze-yellow; metallic; streak light bronze-brown.

Hardness: 3½–4

Cleavage: None; parting in one direction.

Other data: *Specific gravity* 4.6 to 5.1; *fracture* uneven, conchoidal; brittle.

Crystals: Isometric; usually massive and in granular aggregates.

Best field marks: Massive occurrence with pyrrhotite and chalcopyrite; lack of magnetism.

Similar species: Pyrrhotite is magnetic, pentlandite is not.

Environment: Pentlandite is usually intimately associated with pyrrhotite and less commonly with chalcopyrite in gabbro of plutonic rocks. It is often in parallel intergrowths with pyrrhotite and chalcopyrite, and because of this specimens of relatively pure pentlandite are rare.

Occurrence: Collecting localities for pentlandite are uncommon, but the mineral does occur at the Key West Mine, Nye Co., Nevada; on Yakobi Island, SW Alaska; and most significantly with pyrrhotite at Sudbury, Ontario, where it is mined for its nickel content.

Named after the Irish scientist J. B. Pentland (d. 1873), who discovered it. Pentlandite is mined with pyrrhotite as an ore of nickel.

123, 630 **Covellite**
Copper sulfide, often with a small amount of iron
CuS

Color and luster: Dark indigo-blue or darker, often highly iridescent in brass-yellow and deep red; submetallic; streak lead-gray to black.

Hardness: 1½–2

Cleavage: Perfect, one direction.

Other data: *Specific gravity* 4.6 to 4.8; *fracture* uneven; thin laminae flexible; brittle.

Crystals: Hexagonal; rarely in good crystals; commonly massive, less commonly disseminated and in thin crusts.

Best field marks: Platy characteristics, blue color (which should not be confused with the iridescent film on chalcopyrite and bornite), and association with other copper minerals.

Similar species: When chalcopyrite and bornite are covered by deep-blue iridescent film (which can easily be removed by a sharp blow with a hammer), they could be confused with covellite.

Environment: Covellite is not a common mineral but when encountered it occurs with chalcopyrite and pyrite in massive and lode hydrothermal replacement deposits, and with pyrite, bornite, and chalcopyrite in skarn of hydrothermal metamorphic rocks.

Occurrence: Significant amounts of covellite have been mined along with other copper-ore minerals at Kennecott in the Copper River district of Alaska and at Butte, Montana. Some of the finest covellite has come from Sardinia, but fine crystals and crystal groups have been collected at Butte, Montana. Other North American localities include Summitville, Rio Grande Co., Colorado; Wagon Wheel Gap, Mineral Co., Colorado; and La Sal district, San Juan Co., Utah.

Covellite was first found at Vesuvius by the Italian mineralogist Niccolò Covelli (1790–1829) and named in his honor. It is a minor ore of copper.

214, 221, 619 **Cinnabar**
Mercury sulfide
HgS

Color and luster: Bright red, purplish red to brownish red; adamantine to dull; streak scarlet to brownish red.

Hardness: 2–2½

Cleavage: Perfect in three directions at 60° and 120°.

Other data: *Specific gravity* 8.0 to 8.2; *fracture* uneven; brittle to sectile; translucent to transparent.

Crystals: Hexagonal; rhombohedral and thick tabular; also granular, earthy, incrustations.

Best field marks: Bright-red color, softness, and unusual heaviness.

Similar species: Cinnabar is harder and heavier than

realgar, but softer than cuprite.

Environment: Cinnabar is formed at low temperature, usually near hot springs or where there has been volcanic activity. It also forms in epithermal veins, associated with opal, chalcedony, and dolomite.

Occurrence: Almadén, Ciudad Real, Spain, is a famous locality for cinnabar. In North America important cinnabar deposits occur in California, Nevada, Oregon, and Texas. In California fine crystals of cinnabar have come from the Almaden Mine in Santa Clara Co. and the New Idria Mine in San Benito Co. Beautiful crystals occur in calcite at the Cahill Mine, Humboldt Co., Nevada.

The name is said to have come from India. Cinnabar is the principal ore of mercury. *Native mercury*, a liquid, is rare and usually occurs with cinnabar as heavy, tin-white metallic drops.

186, 205, 215 **Realgar**
Arsenic sulfide
AsS

Color and luster: Deep red to orange, becoming yellow upon exposure to light; resinous, adamantine, dull; streak orange-yellow.

Hardness: 1½–2

Cleavage: Good, one direction lengthwise.

Other data: *Specific gravity* 3.5 to 3.6; *fracture* conchoidal; translucent to transparent; slightly sectile.

Crystals: Monoclinic; usually prismatic, but crystals rare; also granular, earthy, incrusting, disseminating.

Best field marks: Color, softness, and prismatic crystals.

Similar species: Realgar can easily be confused with cinnabar, but cinnabar is slightly harder and has higher gravity.

Environment: Realgar forms in low-temperature veins and occurs with cinnabar, stibnite, and orpiment in epithermal veins.

Occurrence: Fine crystals of realgar occur in cavities at Mercur, Tooele Co., Utah; in dark-gray clayey matrix at the Getchell Mine, Humboldt Co., Nevada; with stibnite and cinnabar at Manhattan, Nye Co., Nevada; and with ulexite and colemanite at Boron, Kern Co., California.

The name is from the Arabic *rahj al-ghar,* "powder of the mine." Realgar is used as an ore of arsenic.

293, 332, 354 Orpiment
Arsenic trisulfide
As_2S_3

Color and luster:	Lemon-yellow, orange; resinous, pearly on cleavage; streak lemon-yellow.
Hardness:	$1\frac{1}{2}$–2
Cleavage:	Good, one direction.
Other data:	*Specific gravity* 3.4 to 3.5; thin flakes flexible; slightly sectile; translucent to transparent.
Crystals:	Monoclinic; poorly formed crystals rare; usually foliated, granular, earthy incrustations.
Best field marks:	Cleavage with pearly luster and color.
Similar species:	Sulfur does not have the perfect cleavage of orpiment.
Environment:	Orpiment develops along with cinnabar, realgar, and calcite in epithermal veins. It also forms as a sublimation in fumaroles.
Occurrence:	Large micaceous crystals of orpiment have been obtained at Mercur, Tooele Co., Utah. In Nevada, crystals up to 1.25 cm ($\frac{1}{2}$") across occur with realgar at the Getchell Mine, Humboldt Co., and coarse foliate masses with stibnite, cinnabar, and realgar at Manhattan, Nye Co.

The name is from the Latin *auripigmentum,* in reference to the mineral's vivid gold hue. Orpiment is used as an ore of arsenic.

597   **Stibnite**
Antimony trisulfide; small amounts of
iron, copper, or lead may be present
Sb_2S_3

Color and luster: Lead-gray; tarnish black, sometimes
iridescent; metallic; streak dark lead-
gray.
Hardness: 2
Cleavage: Perfect, one direction lengthwise.
Other data: *Specific gravity* 4.6; *fracture* uneven;
crystals slightly flexible; brittle;
slightly sectile.
Crystals: Orthorhombic; stout to slender,
striated lengthwise; often bent or
twisted; also bladed, in radiated
groups, columnar masses, granular.
Best field marks: Low gravity for a sulfide, and ability to
bend slightly.
Similar species: Easily confused with bismuthinite,
which is heavier but will not bend
without breaking.
Environment: Stibnite is the commonest of all
antimony minerals. It occurs
abundantly with realgar, orpiment, and
calcite in epithermal veins.
Occurrence: Mineral collections throughout the
world usually will contain specimens of
the fine crystals of stibnite from the
island of Shikoku, Japan, or from the
famous mines of Felsöbanya, Rumania.
North America has prominent localities
where outstanding crystal groups of
stibnite have been collected, among
them the Coeur d'Alene district,
Shoshone Co., Idaho; the Manhattan
district, Nye Co., Nevada; the Stayton
district, near Hollister, San Benito Co.,
California; and South Ham, Wolfe Co.,
Quebec.

The name is derived from the Greek
stibi, used for antimony. Stibnite was
employed as a cosmetic preparation by
the ancients. It is the most important
ore of antimony.

610 Bismuthinite
Bismuth trisulfide; may contain small amounts of lead, copper, and iron
Bi_2S_3

Color and luster:	Lead-gray to tin-white, with yellowish or iridescent tarnish; metallic; streak lead-gray.
Hardness:	2
Cleavage:	Perfect, one direction lengthwise.
Other data:	*Specific gravity* 6.8; *fracture* uneven; crystals flexible; brittle; somewhat sectile.
Crystals:	Orthorhombic; long striated prismatic crystals, often acicular; usually massive with foliated or fibrous texture.
Best field marks:	Gravity and hydrothermal-vein mineral environment.
Similar species:	Easily confused with stibnite when occurring in massive form. It is heavier than stibnite and is rarely found associated with cinnabar, orpiment, or realgar.
Environment:	Bismuthinite is not a common mineral but is usually found with arsenopyrite, gold, and chalcopyrite in hypothermal veins; with quartz and microcline in granite pegmatites; and with chalcopyrite and covellite in massive hydrothermal replacement deposits.
Occurrence:	Excellent specimens of bismuthinite have come from famous localities in Europe, South America, and Australia, but in North America localities are scarce. It occurs with chrysoberyl at Haddam, Connecticut; with almandine and barite in the Granite mining district, Beaver Co., Utah; with scheelite, epidote, and andradite at several tungsten prospects in E Kern Co., California; at several places in Temiscaming Co., Quebec, and at Guanajuato, Mexico.

The origin of the name is uncertain, as is the case for bismuth. Bismuthinite is an ore of bismuth.

568, 569, 616, 617, 618	**Pyrite** Iron disulfide, often with substantial amounts of nickel and cobalt FeS_2

Color and luster:	Pale yellow to brass-yellow, often tarnished with brown film of iron oxide; sometimes iridescent; metallic; streak greenish black.
Hardness:	6–6½
Cleavage:	None.
Other data:	*Specific gravity* 4.9 to 5.2; *fracture* uneven; brittle.
Crystals:	Isometric; predominately in cubes and pyritohedrons with parallel striations on faces, less commonly in octahedrons; also in nodules and massive forms; fine to coarse granular, fibrous, mammillary, stalactitic.
Best field marks:	Brass-yellow color; hardness; striations on crystal faces; usually lack of tarnish; striking with steel will produce sparks.
Similar species:	Chalcopyrite, pyrrhotite, and other similar iron sulfides are softer; chalcopyrite is more yellow; pyrrhotite is darker; marcasite is paler in color.
Environment:	The most widespread and abundant of the sulfide minerals, pyrite occurs in rocks of many types and in all types of hydrothermal veins. It is associated with quartz, microcline, and biotite in granite pegmatites and many other rock types; with albite and hornblende in nepheline syenite pegmatites; with acmite and barite in carbonatites; with chalcopyrite and lawsonite in blue schists of regional metamorphic rocks; with andradite and hedenbergite in skarn of hydrothermal metamorphic rocks; with quartz, gold, and acanthite in mesothermal and epithermal veins; and with chalcopyrite, enargite, and sphalerite in lode and disseminated hydrothermal replacement deposits.
Occurrence:	Excellent collecting localities are numerous throughout North America. Among the most prominent are the American Mine in Bingham Canyon, Salt Lake Co., Utah; Park City,

Summit Co., Utah (large, well-developed crystals); Gilman, Leadville, and Rico, Colorado (large crystals); Sparta, Illinois ("pyrite dollars"—spectacular discoidal concretions in coal shales); and French Creek Mine in Chester Co., Pennsylvania (roughly octahedral crystals).

Pyrite (from the Greek *pyr,* "fire") is the well-known "fool's gold," so called because it is easily mistaken for native gold. In fact, pyrite really can be associated with gold, and thus can be an important gold ore. Pyrite has had commercial importance as a source of sulfur, used in the manufacture of sulfuric acid; iron may also be produced as a by-product.

584, 596	**Cobaltite** Sulfarsenide of cobalt, with much iron (Co,Fe)AsS
Color and luster:	Silver-white to gray, sometimes reddish; also steel-gray, with violet tinge, or grayish black when containing much iron; metallic; streak grayish black.
Hardness:	5½
Cleavage:	Perfect, one direction.
Other data:	*Specific gravity* 6.3; *fracture* uneven; brittle.
Crystals:	Isometric; commonly in cubes and pyritohedrons, with striated crystal faces; also in compact and granular masses.
Best field marks:	Crystal form, striations on crystal faces, color, and hardness.
Similar species:	Arsenopyrite and marcasite are harder than cobaltite, and lack the cubic or pyritohedral crystal form. Cobaltite does not have the yellow color of pyrite.
Environment:	Cobaltite is most commonly found associated with chalcopyrite and pyrite in mesothermal veins and less commonly in hornfels of regional

metamorphic rocks associated with
pyrite.

Occurrence: Cobaltite is rare. The best collecting
localities are at Cobalt, Timiskaming
district, Ontario, and especially at the
Columbus claim, where fine octahedral
crystals have been found.

The name is taken from the German
Kobold, "underground spirit" or
"goblin," in allusion to the fact that
certain cobalt-bearing ores did not
smelt properly, as though bewitched.
Cobaltite is an ore of cobalt.

566, 598 **Marcasite**
Disulfide of iron
FeS_2

Color and luster: Pale brass-yellow to almost white;
tarnish deeper yellow to brown;
metallic; streak dark greenish to
brownish.

Hardness: $6-6\frac{1}{2}$

Cleavage: Distinct, two directions.

Other data: *Specific gravity* 4.8 to 4.9; *fracture*
uneven; brittle.

Crystals: Orthorhombic; dipyramidal; commonly
tabular, rarely capillary; also stalactitic
with radiating structure and botryoidal
or reniform crusts. Twin crystals
showing coxcomb and spear shapes are
common.

Best field marks: White on fresh surface and harder than
most other sulfide minerals.

Similar species: Marcasite is whiter than pyrite; it lacks
the cubic form of either cobaltite or
pyrite; and is slightly harder than
arsenopyrite.

Environment: Marcasite is not a rare mineral and is
often found associated with bornite and
galena in skarn of hydrothermal
metamorphic rocks, and with
chalcocite, pyrite, and quartz in
massive, lode, and disseminated
hydrothermal replacement deposits.

Occurrence: Marcasite is of very little use, but it is

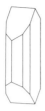

mined along with galena and sphalerite at Joplin, Missouri. Excellent collecting localities for marcasite are found throughout North America, especially in the Joplin district of Missouri, Oklahoma, and Kansas, where it occurs as well-formed crystals and coxcomb groups on galena and sphalerite; and at Guanajuato, Mexico.

"Marcasite" is believed to derive from an Arabic word once used for pyrite. The amateur will find that the marcasite in his collection is among the first minerals to disintegrate, unless it is carefully protected, developing into a white powder that no longer resembles the original mineral.

561, 573, 582 **Arsenopyrite**
Iron arsenide sulfide, usually with some cobalt
FeAsS

Color and luster:	Silver-white to steel-gray; metallic; streak grayish black.
Hardness:	5½–6
Cleavage:	Distinct, one direction.
Other data:	*Specific gravity* 6.0 to 6.2; *fracture* uneven; brittle.
Crystals:	Monoclinic; prismatic; formerly thought to be orthorhombic; striated faces; also granular, compact, columnar.
Best field mark:	Shape of the crystals.
Similar species:	Cobaltite usually occurs in cubes, marcasite in tabular crystals.
Environment:	Arsenopyrite is the most abundant arsenic mineral and commonly occurs in hypothermal veins associated with quartz, chalcopyrite, and gold, and less commonly in pegmatites associated with quartz, muscovite, and orthoclase.
Occurrence:	Famous European localities include the nickel-silver mines at Freiberg, Germany, and the tin mines at Cornwall, England. Notable among the

many North American localities are the Westinghouse Mine, Buckfield, and Mt. Mica, Maine (pegmatites); Lewis, near Keeseville, Essex Co., New York (fine crystals with smaltite and nickeline); the Haynes-Stellite Mine, Blackbird district, Lemhi Co., Idaho; the Tres Hermanos Mts., New Mexico (star-shaped twins); many of the gold-quartz veins of the Sierra Nevada of California; the O'Brien Mine at Cobalt, Timiskaming district, Ontario; the Nickel Plate Mine, British Columbia (with gold and pyrite); and Mapimi, Durango, Mexico.

Because arsenopyrite resembles pyrite and contains arsenic, the word "arsenopyrite" was coined as a contraction of "arsenical pyrites." It is frequently mined for its gold content, but more commonly as an ore of arsenic.

---

641   Molybdenite
Molybdenum sulfide
MoS_2

Color and luster:	Bluish lead-gray; metallic; streak grayish black, greenish on white unglazed porcelain.
Hardness:	1–1½
Cleavage:	Perfect, one direction.
Other data:	*Specific gravity* 4.6 to 5.1; sectile; thin flakes are flexible; feels greasy.
Crystals:	Hexagonal; well-formed crystals common but may be misshapen because they are tabular and bend easily; also occurs in scales, foliated masses, rarely as fine granular.
Best field marks:	Perfect cleavage and flexible laminae.
Similar species:	May be confused with graphite, which is blacker but lighter in weight.
Environment:	Molybdenite is the most common molybdenum-bearing mineral. It occurs with quartz, cassiterite, and chalcopyrite in hypothermal veins; with

pyrite, scheelite, and garnet in skarn of hydrothermal metamorphic rocks; and with pyrite and barite in carbonatites.

Occurrence: Excellent specimens have been collected from only a few localities in North America. Well-formed crystals up to 7.5 cm (3″) in diameter have been found in skarns at Aldfield, Pontiac Co., Quebec; associated with quartz and beryl at the Urad Mine, Clear Creek Co., Colorado; excellent crystals in quartz near Lake Chelan, Okanogan and Chelan Cos., Washington; with scheelite, epidote, and garnet on Pine Creek, Inyo Co., California, and near La Trinidad, Sahuaripa district, Sonora, Mexico (groups on galena and sphalerite); and at Guanajuato, Mexico.

The word derives from the Greek *molybdos,* "lead." Molybdenite is an important ore of molybdenum.

---

572 Skutterudite Series
A three-member series consisting of skutterudite, the cobalt-rich end member, smaltite, the intermediate member, and chloanthite, the nickel-rich end member
$(Co,Ni)As_3$ (skutterudite, smaltite)
$(Ni,Co)As_3$ (chloanthite)

Color and luster: Tin-white to silver-gray, sometimes with gray iridescent tarnish; metallic; streak tin-white to silver-gray.
Hardness: 5½–6
Cleavage: Distinct, two directions.
Other data: *Specific gravity* 6.1 to 6.9; *fracture* uneven; brittle.
Crystals: Isometric; cubic and octahedral crystals are most common, but crystals are rare; usually massive and granular.
Best field marks: Cubic or octahedral metallic crystals.
Similar species: Arsenopyrite is similar, but forms monoclinic crystals; skutterudite crystals are cubic or octahedral. Cobaltite and the skutterudite minerals

both crystallize in the isometric system
as cubes and octahedrons, but cobaltite
can be distinguished by its perfect
cleavage.

Environment: The skutterudite minerals develop in
mesothermal veins, in association with
cobaltite, nickeline, arsenopyrite,
native silver, calcite, siderite, and
quartz.

Occurrence: Members of the series are found in
Canada and United States. Chloanthite
occurs in crystals and the massive form
at Franklin, New Jersey, and in the
Rose Mine in Grant Co., New Mexico.
Skutterudite has come from the Horace
Porter Mine, Gunnison Co., Colorado.
Members of the skutterudite series are
important ores of cobalt and nickel in
silver mines at Cobalt, Ontario, and at
other Ontario mines, particularly at
South Lorrain, Gowganda, and
Sudbury.

It is difficult to distinguish among the
members of this series. Skutterudite
alters to magenta-colored erythrite and
chloanthite alters to green annabergite.
Skutterudite is named for its original
locality in Skutterud, Norway; smaltite
is named for its use as a source of smalt,
a deep-blue ceramic glaze; chloanthite
(also called "nickel-skutterudite") is
named from the Greek words *chloe* and
anthoe, "green flower," in reference to
the coating of green annabergite
commonly found on the mineral. All
three are ores of cobalt and nickel.

595   **Calaverite**
Ditelluride of gold, often with small
amount of silver
$AuTe_2$

Color and luster: Brass-yellow to silver-white; metallic;
streak yellowish to greenish gray.
Hardness: 2½–3
Cleavage: None.

Other data: *Specific gravity* 9.1 to 9.4; *fracture* conchoidal; brittle.

Crystals: Monoclinic; usually in bladed or lathlike crystals and short slender prisms that are striated; also granular.

Best field mark: Striated elongated crystals.

Similar species: Sylvanite resembles calaverite, but has a good cleavage.

Environment: Calaverite is not a common mineral and is usually found associated with pyrite, native gold, and quartz in mesothermal and epithermal veins.

Occurrence: Localities where calaverite may be found are not abundant, but good

specimens have come from the Melones and Stanislaus mines at Carson Hill, Calaveras Co., California; it occurs as fine crystals associated with fluorite, quartz, and celestite at Cripple Creek, Teller Co., Colorado; also in the Kirkland Lake and Boston Creek areas, Ontario.

The name is derived from the first reported occurence in Calaveras Co., California. Calaverite is an ore of gold.

---

648 **Sylvanite**
Telluride of gold and silver, with gold-to-silver ratio approximately 1:1
$AuAgTe_4$

Color and luster: Silver-white to steel-gray, inclining to yellow; metallic; streak black or nearly so.

Hardness: 1½–2

Cleavage: Perfect, one direction.

Other data: *Specific gravity* 8.2; *fracture* uneven; brittle.

Crystals: Monoclinic; prismatic; also branching aggregates, bladed, columnar, granular.

Best field marks: Hardness and lack of striations on crystal faces.

Similar species: Calaverite is harder and has striations; arsenopyrite is harder; and jamesonite is harder and lighter in weight.

Environment: Sylvanite is the commonest of all gold-silver telluride minerals and occurs principally in low-temperature epithermal veins, where it is associated with quartz, calaverite, acanthite, pyrite, fluorite, and rhodochrosite.

Occurrence:

Collecting localities are not abundant in North America, but mention can be made of the Melones and Stanislaus mines in Calaveras Co., California. It occurs with calaverite at Cripple Creek, Teller Co., Colorado; at Idaho Springs, Clear Creek Co., Colorado; and in Canada at Bigstone Bay and at the Dome Mine, Kirkland Lake, Ontario.

Originally found in Transylvania and named in allusion to *sylvanium*, one of the names first proposed for the element tellurium. Sylvanite is mined for its gold and silver content.

Sulfosalts

The sulfosalts are rare compounds of one or more metallic elements with sulfur plus a semimetal (antimony, arsenic, bismuth). Sulfosalt minerals are soft, heavy, and brittle, and generally occur in small crystals or masses. They form in low-temperature environments and are among the last minerals to develop in epithermal veins.

629 Stephanite
Silver antimony sulfide
Ag_5SbS_4

Color and luster:	Dark lead-gray to iron-black; metallic; streak iron-black.
Hardness:	2–2½
Cleavage:	Distinct, two directions.
Other data:	*Specific gravity* 6.2 to 6.5; *fracture* uneven; brittle.
Crystals:	Orthorhombic; usually short prismatic to tabular, less commonly elongated; striated; also compact and disseminated.
Best field mark:	Good orthorhombic crystal shape.
Similar species:	Stephanite is not sectile as is acanthite; it is softer and heavier than tetrahedrite; and it lacks the cleavage of galena.
Environment:	Stephanite rarely occurs in large masses; it is most often associated with pyrite, quartz, and galena in epithermal veins.
Occurrence:	Excellent collecting localities are not common throughout North America, but crystals up to several inches across have come from the Pedrazzini Mine, Arizpe, Sonora, Mexico. It was an important ore mineral in the Comstock Lode, Virginia City, Nevada, and occurs in small well-formed crystals in gold-bearing quartz veins at Bodie, Mono Co., California.

Stephanite is named after Archduke Stephan (d. 1867), an early Mining Director of Austria. It is an ore of silver.

192, 208, 209, 581, 591, 599, 600 Pyrargyrite
Silver antimony sulfide, with small amount of arsenic
Ag_3SbS_3

Color and luster:	Dark (blackish) red; adamantine; streak purplish red, cherry-red.
Hardness:	2½
Cleavage:	Distinct, one direction.

Other data: *Specific gravity* 5.8 to 5.9; *fracture* conchoidal, uneven; brittle.

Crystals: Hexagonal; commonly prismatic with striations; also disseminated, incrusting, compact.

Best field marks: Dark-red color and striated prismatic crystals.

Similar species: Cuprite is in octahedral-shaped crystals.

Environment: Pyrargyrite occurs with quartz, calcite, and rhodochrosite in mesothermal and epithermal veins.

Occurrence: Pyrargyrite has been found in many of the silver districts of W United States and Mexico. It occurs with native silver and tetrahedrite in the Ruby district, Gunnison Co., Colorado; was abundant in the Comstock Lode, Virginia City, Nevada; in the Poorman Mine, Silver City district, Owyhee Co., Idaho; in the California Rand Silver Mine at Red Mt., San Bernardino Co.; at Guanajuato, Durango, Mexico; and in the silver veins at Cobalt, Timiskaming district, Ontario.

The name is from the Greek *pyr,* "fire," and *argyros,* "silver," in reference to color and silver content.

207 Proustite
Silver arsenic sulfide, with small amounts of antimony
Ag_3AsS_3

Color and luster: Scarlet-vermillion, darkens upon exposure to light; adamantine to submetallic; streak bright red.

Hardness: 2–2½

Cleavage: Distinct, one direction.

Other data: *Specific gravity* 5.6; *fracture* conchoidal to uneven; brittle; translucent.

Crystals: Hexagonal; usually poorly formed prismatic crystals showing hexagonal shape; also massive, compact.

Best field marks: Deep-red color and silvery luster.

Similar species: Resembles pyrargyrite, but proustite is significantly lighter in color.

Environment: Develops in epithermal veins, commonly associated with tetrahedrite, calcite, and quartz.

Occurrence: In North America, well-formed crystals have come from the Keeley Mine, South Lorrain, in the Cobalt district, Ontario. Proustite has been found in mines at Red Mountain, San Juan Co., and at Georgetown, Clear Creek Co., Colorado, and in small granular masses at several silver mines in California and Nevada. A large crystalline mass, weighing over 225 kg (500 lb), was found in the Poorman Mine, Silver Creek district, Owyhee Co., Idaho. Well-formed crystals up to 6 mm (¼") across have been found with native silver at Batopilas, Chihuahua, Mexico.

The mineral is named for Joseph Louis Proust (1754–1826), French chemist. Proustite is a minor ore of silver.

570, 577   **Tetrahedrite Series**
A two-member series consisting of tetrahedrite, the antimony-rich end member, and tennantite, the arsenic-rich end member
$Cu_{12}Sb_4S_{13}$ (tetrahedrite)
$(Cu,Fe)_{12}As_4S_{13}$ (tennantite)

Color and luster: Steel-gray to iron-black; metallic; streak dark gray, black, reddish brown.

Hardness: 3–4

Cleavage: None.

Other data: *Specific gravity* 4.6 to 5.1; *fracture* uneven to subconchoidal; brittle.

Crystals: Isometric; predominantly in tetrahedrons; sometimes as groups of parallel crystals; also compact, coarse- to fine-granular.

Best field marks: Tetrahedral form of crystals, nearly conchoidal fracture, and lack of cleavage.

Similar species: Enargite forms tabular and prismatic crystals; chalcopyrite is brass-yellow in color, and sphalerite has excellent cleavage, which is absent in tetrahedrite.

Environment: Tetrahedrite and tennantite are common copper-bearing minerals and they form in several environments. They occur with galena and bornite in carbonatites; with pyrite, quartz and chalcopyrite in mesothermal and epithermal veins; and with pyrite and chalcopyrite in massive hydrothermal replacement deposits.

Occurrence: Tetrahedrite is a widespread mineral. In addition to famous European localities, especially in Germany, excellent localities are scattered throughout North America. Very fine lustrous crystals as much as 1.25 cm (½″) across occur at Bingham, Salt Lake Co., Utah. Tetrahedrite occurs with siderite at the Sunshine Mine, Kellogg, Shoshone Co., Idaho; with pyrite, sphalerite, and quartz at Mina Bonanza, Concepcion del Oro, Zacatecas, Mexico, and at the Kootenai Mine, Windermere district, British Columbia.

Tennantite is not as widely distributed as tetrahedrite, but it has been found associated with siderite and arsenopyrite at the Freeland Lode and the Crockett Mine, Idaho Springs, in Clear Creek Co., Colorado; at the Elridge Mine, Buckingham Co., Virginia; in Barrie Township, Frontenac Co., Ontario; and in Lillooet district, British Columbia.

Tetrahedrite is named for its predominant crystal form, the tetrahedron. Tennantite is named after Smithson Tennant (1761–1815), an English chemist. Both are important copper-ore minerals.

594, 601, 628   **Enargite**
Copper arsenic sulfide, often with
several percent antimony
Cu_3AsS_4

Color and luster: Grayish black to iron-black; tarnishing
dull; metallic; streak grayish black.

Hardness: 3

Cleavage: Perfect in one direction; distinct in two
others.

Other data: *Specific gravity* 4.4 to 4.5; *fracture*
uneven; brittle.

Crystals: Orthorhombic; predominately tabular,
also prismatic; striated on several faces;
also compact, granular, columnar.

Best field mark: Tabular or prismatic crystal shape.

Similar species: Manganite is harder than enargite and
has reddish-brown streak.

Environment: Enargite is a common copper mineral.
It occurs associated with galena, pyrite,
and chalcopyrite in mesothermal veins,
and with chalcopyrite, pyrite, and
bornite in disseminated hydrothermal
replacement deposits.

Occurrence: Excellent collecting localities are
numerous throughout North America.
It occurs with bornite, covellite, and
pyrite at Butte, Montana; associated
with sphalerite and galena at Bingham
Canyon, Salt Lake Co., and the Tintic
district, Juab Co., Utah; at the
Morningstar Mine, Alpine Co.,
California; with chalcocite and bornite
at Kennecott in the Copper River
district, Alaska; and with bornite,
tennantite, barite, and alunite at the
Caridad Mine, Sonora, Mexico.

It is an important ore of copper and
derives its name from the Greek *enargos,*
"visible," in allusion to its distinct
cleavage.

604 Bournonite

Lead copper antimony sulfide, often
with some arsenic
$PbCuSbS_3$

Color and luster:	Steel-gray to black, inclining to blackish lead-gray or iron black; metallic; streak gray to black.
Hardness:	2½–3
Cleavage:	Good, one direction, and two others fair at right angles to the good one.
Other data:	*Specific gravity* 5.83; *fracture* subconchoidal to uneven; brittle.
Crystals:	Orthorhombic; usually short prismatic striated crystals in subparallel groups; also massive, granular, compact. Twinning is repeated, forming cruciform or wheel-like aggregates.
Best field mark:	Twinned crystals.
Similar species:	Bournonite resembles enargite but is somewhat heavier. When the characteristic wheel-like twinning is absent it is difficult to distinguish between the two species.
Environment:	Bournonite develops in mesothermal veins, where it is commonly associated with galena, tetrahedrite, sphalerite, chalcopyrite, pyrite, siderite, and quartz.
Occurrence:	Bournonite is widespread in occurrence, but localities are scarce for good crystals. Beautiful brilliant crystals have been found coating crystals of tetrahedrite at the Mina Bonanza, Concepción del Oro, Zacatecas, Mexico; large crystals of bournonite occur with siderite and sphalerite at Park City, Utah; at the Boggs Mine in the Big Bug district, Yavapai Co., Arizona; and at the Cerro Gordo Mine, Inyo Co., California.

The name is after Count J. L. de
Bournon (1751–1825), a French
crystallographer and mineralogist.
Bournonite is a minor ore of lead and
copper.

609 Boulangerite
Lead antimony sulfide
$Pb_5Sb_4S_{11}$

Color and luster: Bluish lead-gray; metallic; streak brownish gray to brown.

Hardness: 2½–3

Cleavage: Good, one direction.

Other data: *Specific gravity* 6.23; *fracture* uneven; thin fibers flexible; brittle.

Crystals: Monoclinic; deeply striated, long prismatic to acicular crystals common; also plumose, fibrous, and in compact fibrous masses.

Best field marks: Color, flexibility of fibers.

Similar species: Jamesonite can be distinguished by its brittle fibers; other minerals similar to boulangerite are hard to distinguish from one another.

Environment: Boulangerite forms in mesothermal and epithermal veins and is commonly associated with stibnite, galena, sphalerite, pyrite, arsenopyrite, quartz, and siderite.

Occurrence: Boulangerite is found principally in W United States. It has been found in the lead-zinc mines in the Coeur d'Alene and Wood River districts in Idaho; in the Iron Mt. Mine at Superior, Montana; at Augusta Mt., Gunnison Co., Colorado; and in columnar to fibrous masses with sphalerite, arsenopyrite, galena, and siderite at the Cleveland Mine, Stevens Co., Washington. Masses of acicular boulangerite have been found in the El Triumfo and San Antonio districts, Baja California, Mexico.

The mineral is named after C. L. Boulanger (1810–1849), a French mining engineer. It is a minor ore of lead.

608 Jamesonite
Lead and iron antimony sulfide, often with substantial amounts of copper and zinc
$Pb_4FeSb_6S_{14}$

Color and luster: Steel-gray to dark lead-gray; sometimes tarnished iridescent; metallic; streak grayish-black.

Hardness: 2½

Cleavage: Good, one direction crosswise.

Other data: *Specific gravity* 5.5 to 6.0; *fracture* uneven; brittle.

Crystals: Monoclinic; prismatic; commonly in felted masses of needles; compact; sometimes radial or plumose.

Best field mark: Felted masses of brittle needles.

Similar species: Stibnite is similar, but is less brittle than Jamesonite.

Environment: Jamesonite is commonly found in mesothermal veins associated with quartz, gold, and tetrahedrite.

Occurrence: Pribram, Bohemia, and Felsobanya in Rumania are famous Old World localities from which choice mineral specimens have been collected, but excellent specimens have come from localities in Canada, Mexico, and the United States. Occurs with stibnite in Sevier Co., Arkansas; at Slate Creek, Custer Co., Idaho; at Park City, Utah; in dolomite near Barrie, Simcoe Co., Ontario; and as felted masses on brilliant crystals of pyrite at the Mina Noche Buena near Mazapil, Zacatecas, Mexico.

Jamesonite is sometimes called "feather ore" because it resembles feathers in general form. It was named after Robert Jameson (1774–1854), of Edinburgh, Scotland, for material found at Cornwall, England. It is a minor ore of lead.

Simple Oxides

The simple oxides are compounds of metallic elements with oxygen. They are called simple oxides because of their simple crystal structure and chemical composition. Water, hydrogen oxide (i.e. ice), is a mineral, and the commonest of all. This mineral group shows great range of hardness and color; some are opaque, others are transparent. Some are rare gems, and others are important ores. The simple oxides show similar variation in their origins, some of them forming deep in the earth's crust, and others developing at shallow depths or even on the surface.

180, 181, 185,   **Cuprite**
202, 211   Copper oxide
         Cu_2O

Color and luster: Ruby-red, reddish black; submetallic, adamantine or dull; streak brownish red.

Hardness: $3\frac{1}{2}-4$

Cleavage: Poor.

Other data: *Specific gravity* 6.1; *fracture* uneven; translucent; brittle.

Crystals: Isometric; usually octahedral, less often dodecahedral or cubic; also compact, granular, earthy, capillary (chalcotrichite).

Best field marks: Crystal shape and hardness.

Similar species: Cuprite forms as octahedral-shaped crystals, whereas those of pyrargyrite are prismatic; realgar forms as monoclinic prismatic crystals and has lower gravity; and zincite is generally associated with willemite and franklinite.

Environment: Cuprite is a secondary copper mineral and forms in the zone of alteration in disseminated hydrothermal replacement deposits, where it occurs with native copper, malachite, and calcite.

Occurrence: Fine specimens, sometimes with crystals up to 1.25 cm (½″) across, have been found at Bisbee, Cochise Co., Arizona, where magnificent specimens also have been found of "plush copper"—a surface covered by chalcotrichite fibers so densely packed as to resemble plush or velvet—which commonly line cavities in hard brown limonite. Beautiful ruby-red crystals of cuprite occur with native copper at Ray, Pinal Co., Arizona; at the Chino Pit, Santa Rita, Grant Co., New Mexico; and at Bingham, Tooele Co., Utah.

The name "cuprite" is from the Latin *cuprum,* "copper."

188, 222, 297   Zincite
Zinc oxide; may contain manganese and some iron
$(Zn,Mn)O$

Color and luster: Deep red to orange, yellow, or brown; adamantine; streak orange-yellow.

Hardness: 4

Cleavage: Perfect, one direction; also basal parting.

Other data: *Specific gravity* 5.4 to 5.7; *fracture* conchoidal; translucent to transparent; brittle.

Crystals: Hexagonal; crystals rare and usually pyramidal; usually massive, lamellar, granular.

Best field marks: Deep-red color and association with willemite and franklinite.

Similar species: The mineral association of zincite with willemite and franklinite is alone sufficient to distinguish it from either cinnabar or cuprite.

Environment: Zincite is a rare mineral and forms along with many minerals, but especially with willemite, calcite, and franklinite in massive hydrothermal replacement deposits.

Occurrence: The premier North American locality for zincite is at Franklin and Ogdensburg, Sussex Co., New Jersey.

The name derives from the mineral's composition. Many mineralogists believe that manganese is the cause of the red color, since pure zinc oxide is white. Zincite is an ore of zinc.

85, 170, 193,   Corundum
200, 484, 668,   Aluminum oxide
679 Al_2O_3

Color and luster: White, gray, brown to black, deep red (ruby), blue (sapphire), black from admixture of magnetite, hematite or spinel (emery); vitreous, adamantine; streak white.

Hardness: 9

Cleavage: None; often conspicuous parting in three directions.

Other data: *Specific gravity* 3.9 to 4.1; *fracture* uneven, conchoidal; transparent to translucent; fluorescent; brittle.

Crystals: Hexagonal; sometimes tapering prismatic; also pyramidal, tabular; often striated.

Best field marks: Hardness, high specific gravity, and striations on parting faces.

Similar species: Feldspars. The fine striations on parting faces might lead to confusion with the plagioclase feldspars, but corundum may be recognized by its superior hardness and high gravity.

Environment: Corundum forms in several distinctive environments. It occurs associated with albite and acmite in nepheline syenite pegmatites; with andalusite and cordierite in hornfels of contact metamorphic rocks; and with muscovite, almandine, and oligoclase in gneiss and hornfels of metamorphic terrains.

Occurrence: Gem-quality ruby and sapphire have been found at only a few places in North America: at Yogo Gulch, Judith Basin Co., Montana, and at several places in North Carolina. Fine stubby, cigar-shaped crystals are abundant in nepheline syenite in Hastings Co., Ontario. Large deposits of emery occur near Peekskill, New York. Loose crystals were formerly abundant at Corundum Hill, near Unionville, Chester Co., Pennsylvania. Crystals as much as 35 cm (14″) in length have been observed in gneiss near Salesville, Gallatin Co., Montana, and in mica schist on San Jacinto Peak, Riverside Co., California.

Gemstone data: Blood-red corundum is called *ruby* and is the rarest and most valuable gemstone. All other gem-quality corundum is called *sapphire,* and may be pink, blue, green, violet, gray, yellow, or other colors. May be clear or contain bundles of tubelike inclusions, giving "star" or "catseye" effect in cut or polished stones. The most highly valued specimens are clear ruby and deep blue or green sapphire and the extremely rare orange variety called *padparadschah*. Some rubies and sapphires are faceted, but most are worked into cabochons. Star and catseye varieties are fashioned as cabochons. Thailand, Ceylon, and Burma are the principal sources for ruby and sapphire. Some ruby has been found in North Carolina and sapphire in Montana. Ruby is the birthstone for July, sapphire for September.

The name is from *kuruntam*, a Tamil word derived from Sanskrit *kuruvinda*, "ruby." Corundum is used as an abrasive.

166, 184, 203, 533, 574, 576, 621, 627	**Hematite** Iron oxide Fe_2O_3
Color and luster:	Steel-gray, red, reddish brown, black; metallic; streak dark red, cherry-red, brownish red.
Hardness:	5–6
Cleavage:	None.
Other data:	*Specific gravity* 4.9 to 5.3; *fracture* uneven, splintery; brittle.
Crystals:	Hexagonal; thick to thin tabular, often as subparallel growths or as rosettes; striated; also compact, granular, radiated, reniform, botryoidal, columnar; micaceous (specular), earthy (red ocher).
Best field marks:	Red streak, color, and hardness.
Similar species:	The deep-red streak of hematite is sufficient to distinguish it from limonite and ilmenite, and the lack of magnetism distinguishes it from magnetite.
Environment:	The former huge bodies of iron ore, composed largely of hematite, worked in the Lake Superior region are of sedimentary origin. Hematite has

formed also in igneous and metamorphic rocks. It occurs with biotite, albite, and barite in carbonatites; with diopside and epidote in hornfels of contact and regional metamorphic rocks; with quartz and siderite in mesothermal and epithermal veins; and with fluorite, barite, and calcite in lode and disseminated replacement deposits.

Occurrence: Hematite has been reported from many localities in North America. It occurs as bright drusy crystals in mines near Edwards, Gouverneur, and Antwerp, St. Lawrence Co., New York. It occurs as dark reddish-brown reniform masses in the iron mines of Michigan and Minnesota, and on Aztec Peak, Gila Co., Arizona. Sharp, brilliant black hematite crystals occur with quartz near Bouse, Yuma Co., Arizona.

The name "hematite" is from the Greek *haimatites,* "bloodlike," in reference to the vivid red color of the powder. Hematite is the principal ore of iron.

588 Ilmenite

Iron titanium oxide, often with considerable magnesium and manganese
$FeTiO_3$

Color and luster: Iron-black, brownish black; metallic, submetallic; streak iron-black, brownish black.
Hardness: 5–6
Cleavage: None; sometimes parting.
Other data: *Specific gravity* 4.5 to 4.7; *fracture* conchoidal; brittle; weakly magnetic.
Crystals: Hexagonal; commonly thick tabular; also granular, compact, disseminated.
Best field marks: Black streak, hardness, and weak magnetism.
Similar species: Hematite has reddish-brown streak; magnetite is strongly magnetic; columbite is heavier than ilmenite; and rutile is nonmagnetic.

Environment: Although a considerable amount of ilmenite is recovered in placer mining operations, its principal environment is in gabbro of plutonic rocks, where it is associated with magnetite, labradorite, and hornblende.

Occurrence: Masses of ilmenite are a common feature in the emery mines of Chester, Hampden Co., Massachusetts, where it also occurs in fine crystals. It occurs with magnetite, garnet, and apatite in dikes at Roseland, Nelson Co., Virginia; as huge solid ilmenite-magnetite dikes in gabbro at Iron Mt., Wyoming, and with rutile, spinel, and biotite in veinlets in gabbro at St. Urbain, Charleroix, Quebec.

Ilmenite derives its name from a locality in the Ilmen Mts. of the USSR. Its principal use is as an ore of titanium.

583, 585 Bixbyite
Iron manganese oxide, with some titanium
$(Mn, Fe)_2O_3$

Color and luster: Black; brilliant metallic to submetallic; streak black.
Hardness: 6–6½
Cleavage: Poor, one direction.
Other data: *Specific gravity* 4.9; *fracture* irregular; brittle.
Crystals: Isometric; usually as cubes, sometimes highly modified.
Best field marks: Nearly perfect cubes, association with topaz.
Similar species: Other black manganese minerals, which are softer, lack crystal form and are fibrous or columnar.
Environment: A rare mineral found in cavities in rhyolite, associated with topaz, pink beryl, garnet, and hematite, and in metamorphosed manganese deposits.
Occurrence: Bixbyite occurs in nearly perfect crystals associated with topaz,

hematite, pink beryl, and garnet in cavities in rhyolite in the NE part of the Thomas Range, Juab County, Utah, and at San Luis Potosí, Mexico.

Bixbyite is named for Maynard Bixby. Although rare, bixbyite is a popular mineral and is prized for its perfect crystals and unusual mineral association.

228, 262, 263, 605	**Rutile** Titanium dioxide; may contain substantial amounts of iron TiO_2
Color and luster:	Red, reddish brown, black; adamantine, submetallic; streak white, gray, pale brown.
Hardness:	6–6½
Cleavage:	Distinct, sometimes good, two directions, poor in a third.
Other data:	*Specific gravity* 4.2 to 4.3; *fracture* uneven; brittle; translucent to transparent in thin pieces.
Crystals:	Tetragonal; commonly long, striated prismatic crystals; knee-shaped and rosette twins; also acicular, compact, disseminated.
Best field marks:	Gravity, twinned and striated crystals, and strong luster.
Similar species:	Cassiterite is heavier, and lacks the striated, lustrous, prismatic crystals of rutile.
Environment:	Rutile forms in plutonic and metamorphic rocks. It is associated with orthoclase, barite, and acmite in carbonatites; with albite, lawsonite, and glaucophane in blue schists of regional metamorphic rocks; and with pyrophyllite in massive hydrothermal replacement deposits.
Occurrence:	Splendid crystals of rutile have come from Graves Mt., Lincoln Co., Georgia; from Magnet Cove, Garland Co., Arkansas; and from the Champion Mine near Laws, Inyo Co., California.

Prismatic crystals up to 2.5 cm (1″) in length have been found on Tiburon Peninsula, Marin Co., California.

The name "rutile" is from the Latin *rutilus,* "reddish," in allusion to its color. Rutile is the principal ore of titanium and is also used as a gemstone and in ceramic glazes.

---

615 Pyrolusite
Manganese dioxide
MnO_2

Color and luster: Black to steel-gray, sometimes bluish where massive; metallic to dull; streak black, bluish black.

Hardness: 6–6½

Cleavage: Perfect in one direction.

Other data: *Specific gravity* 4.4 to 5; *fracture* splintery, uneven; brittle.

Crystals: Tetragonal; rarely in large well-formed crystals; usually massive columnar or fibrous and frequently divergent, acicular, radial, granular to powdery, massive, dendritic growths on fracture surfaces; crystals pseudomorphous after manganite are common.

Best field marks: Sooty black character of the streak.

Similar species: It is practically impossible to distinguish one manganese-oxide mineral from another lacking distinct crystals, except by X-ray tests. Pyrolusite is the commonest of all manganese-oxide minerals, and it is reasonably safe to apply the name "pyrolusite" to any black powdery mineral or any fibrous-looking mass of black manganese-oxide minerals.

Environment: Pyrolusite is one of the most abundant manganese minerals. It occurs with barite and hematite in massive hydrothermal replacement deposits and with calcite in epithermal veins.

Occurrence: There are many occurrences throughout North America, but specific collecting localities are few. There are manganese deposits in the Cartersville district, Bartow Co., Georgia, where crystallined geodes occur, and in the Maroco Mine, Ironton, Crow Wing Co., Minnesota.

The name is of Greek origin from *pyr*, "fire," and *louein* "to wash." Pyrolusite was used as an oxidizing agent in the manufacture of glass, to rid the molten silica of the greenish cast imparted by iron.

191, 515   Cassiterite
Tin oxide, often with some iron
SnO_2

Color and luster:	Brown, black; rarely yellow, gray; greasy or adamantine to dull; streak white, light brown.
Hardness:	6–7
Cleavage:	Distinct.
Other data:	*Specific gravity* 6.8 to 7.1; *fracture* uneven; transparent to translucent; brittle.
Crystals:	Tetragonal; generally in short prismatic twinned crystals; also granular, disseminated, reniform with radiating fibrous structure ("wood-tin").
Best field marks:	Light-brown streak, high gravity, and hardness.
Similar species:	Cassiterite has higher gravity than black tourmaline, rutile, columbite, and magnetite.
Environment:	Cassiterite is the commonest tin-bearing mineral and develops in hypothermal veins, where it is associated with tourmaline, molybdenite, and bismuthinite. Cassiterite also occurs with apatite, hedenbergite, and calcite in hornfels of contact metamorphic rocks. It is mined from placer clastic sedimentary deposits, but does not form there.
Occurrence:	Famous collecting localities include Llallagua, Bolivia, and Cornwall, England. Fine sharp crystals occur in

pegmatites at Amelia, Amelia Co., Virginia, and at Silver Hill, Spokane Co., Washington. Cassiterite occurs as rounded and irregularly shaped grains with limonite in S Kern Co., California, where it has been successfully mined on a commercial basis.

The name is from the Greek *kassiteros,* "tin." Cassiterite is the principal ore of tin.

---

514 Uraninite
Uranium oxide, often with substantial amounts of thorium
UO_2

Color and luster:	Greenish to brownish black, pitch-black (pitchblende); pitchlike, submetallic, dull; streak brownish black, grayish black, olive-green.
Hardness:	5–6
Cleavage:	None.
Other data:	*Specific gravity* 6.5 to 10; *fracture* conchoidal; most material is opaque; radioactive; brittle.
Crystals:	Isometric; usually octahedrons and cubes, less often as dodecahedrons; also massive (pitchblende), dense, botryoidal, granular, lamellar or columnar.
Best field marks:	Octahedral crystals, gravity, and radioactivity.
Similar species:	Magnetite is strongly magnetic, and uraninite is nonmagnetic; spinel is lighter in weight; columbite occurs in orthorhombic crystals.
Environment:	Uraninite occurs in several environments, including pegmatites, veins, and hydrothermal replacement deposits. It commonly occurs with pyrite, orthoclase, zircon, and nepheline in granite and nepheline syenite pegmatites; with arsenopyrite, cassiterite, and chalcopyrite in hypothermal veins; and with pyrite and

quartz in lode hydrothermal
replacement deposits.

Occurrence: Excellent collecting localities are not
abundant in North America. Large
crystals up to several inches across were
found associated with calcite, purple
Wilberforce, Renfrew Co., Ontario,
and sharp black cubes up to 2.5 cm (1″)
on edge occurred with quartz and
feldspar in a pegmatite in the Rock
Landing Quarry, near Portland,
Middlesex Co., Connecticut. Colorful
specimens of dendritic uraninite in
feldspar, surrounded by alteration
products, have come from the Ruggles
Mine, Grafton Co., New Hampshire.
Uraninite occurs abundantly as
colloform masses in veins associated
with pyrite, chalcopyrite, sphalerite,
and galena near Central City, Gilpin
Co., Colorado.

The name is derived from the mineral's
composition. Uraninite alters easily and
is commonly found in pegmatites as
rounded bodies generally surrounded by
brightly colored yellow, orange-red, or
green alteration products. Uraninite is
highly radioactive and is easily
recognized by any of the several
radiation detection instruments.
Although once considered almost
worthless, uraninite is much sought
after and is now an important ore of
uranium.

283, 350, 353 **Gummite**
Mixture of oxides and silicates of
uranium

Color and luster: Reddish yellow to orange-red, reddish
brown; greasy, waxy; streak pale
yellowish.
Hardness: 2½
Cleavage: None.
Other data: *Specific gravity* 3.9 to 4.2; *fracture*
uneven; translucent; radioactive.

Crystals: Massive; usually in rounded or flattened pieces resembling gum; compact.

Best field marks: Yellow to brown color, luster, and radioactivity.

Similar species: None.

Environment: Gummite is a mixture of secondary minerals, formed by the alteration of uraninite. It occurs in granite pegmatites, where it forms dendritic growths in feldspars or pseudomorphs after uraninite, and is found with uraninite (pitchblende) in hypothermal veins and in lode hydrothermal replacement deposits.

Occurrence: Spectacular red-orange gummite has been found at Rajputana, India. In North America fine masses of gummite have come from pegmatites in Mitchell Co., North Carolina, and splendid dendrites in feldspar from the Ruggles Mine, Grafton Co., New Hampshire. Gummite occurs sparingly in pitchblende ores at Great Bear Lake, Northwest Territories.

The name is probably derived from its gumlike nature. Gummite is a minor ore of uranium.

407

Hydroxides

The hydroxides are compounds of
metallic elements with water or
hydroxyl (the OH radical). Hydroxides
are generally softer than the simple
oxides.

393, 499   Brucite
Magnesium hydroxide, often with substantial amounts of manganese and iron
$Mg(OH)_2$

Color and luster: White, colorless, grayish, bluish, greenish; waxy, vitreous, pearly on cleavage; streak white.

Hardness: $2-2\frac{1}{2}$

Cleavage: Perfect, one direction.

Other data: *Specific gravity* 2.3 to 2.4; sectile; thin flakes and fibers flexible; transparent.

Crystals: Hexagonal; broad tabular, often subparallel aggregates of plates; also foliated, scaly, fibrous.

Best field marks: Hardness and inelasticity, pearly cleavage on face.

Similar species: Talc and pyrophyllite are softer than brucite; muscovite is slightly harder and is elastic.

Environment: Brucite forms at low temperatures and occurs with calcite and wollastonite in nepheline syenite pegmatites; with magnesite and talc in serpentinites of hydrothermal metamorphic rocks; and with aragonite and magnesite in hornfels of contact and regional metamorphic rocks.

Occurrence: Brucite is not a common mineral and there are only a few localities in North America where suitable specimens may be obtained. It was originally found at Hoboken, New Jersey. Excellent crystal specimens have been found at Wood's and Low's mines at Texas, Lancaster Co., Pennsylvania; with aragonite in dolomite near Reading and Sinking Springs, Berks Co., Pennsylvania; and with magnesite at Gabbs, Nevada.

Brucite is named for Archibald Bruce (1777–1818), the American mineralogist who first described the mineral. Brucite is used as a source of magnesium metal and magnesia.

571, 603, 614 Manganite
Basic manganese oxide
MnO(OH)

Color and luster:	Steel-gray to iron-black; submetallic; streak reddish brown to black.
Hardness:	3½–4
Cleavage:	Perfect, one direction lengthwise.
Other data:	*Specific gravity* 4.2 to 4.4; *fracture* uneven; translucent in thin splinters.
Crystals:	Monoclinic; short crystals striated lengthwise; frequently in groups or bundles; also columnar to coarse fibrous; rarely granular.
Best field marks:	Brown or black streak, mineral association.
Similar species:	Enargite has a distinct metallic luster and a grayish-black streak; tourmaline is harder than manganite; and pyrolusite seldom develops well-formed shining black crystals.
Environment:	Manganite is commonly found in association with several manganese minerals. It occurs with galena and quartz in granite pegmatites, and with quartz, pyrolusite, cinnabar, barite, and acanthite in epithermal veins.
Occurrence:	The finest crystals of manganite have come from localities in Germany, England, and China. In North America well-crystallized manganite has been found at Powell's Fort, near Woodstock, Shenandoah Co., Virginia; in the Cartersville district, Bartow Co., Georgia; with garnet at the Sterling Hill Mine at Ogdensburg, Sussex Co., New Jersey; mixed with pyrolusite and psilomelane at the Ladd Mine in Stanislaus Co., California; and at Cheverie, Walton, in Hants Co., Nova Scotia.

Manganite is named for its manganese content.

282, 504 Bauxite

In general, a basic aluminum hydroxide. Bauxite, like limonite, is not a specific mineral but a term applied to a mixture of hydrated aluminum oxides including gibbsite, boehmite, and diaspore

$Al(OH)_3$ (gibbsite)
$AlO(OH)$ (boehmite)
$HAlO_2$ (diaspore)

Color and luster: White, gray, yellow, red, brown; dull; streak white.

Hardness: 1–3

Cleavage: None.

Other data: *Specific gravity* 2.4 to 2.6; *fracture* earthy.

Crystals: Massive to microcrystalline; earthy, oolitic, sometimes small spherical brown masses in gray or yellow matrix (pisolitic).

Best field marks: Pisolitic structure and hardness.

Similar species: Bauxite is harder than most clays, and the clays usually lack the pisolitic structure.

Environment: Bauxite is a secondary material, usually formed at the surface by the alteration of minerals and rocks rich in aluminum.

Occurrence: Bauxite mining commenced in North America in 1888 from deposits in N Georgia, and in 1895 in Arkansas. Some bauxite has been mined in Alabama, Mississippi, Tennessee, and Virginia, but about 90 percent of US production is in Arkansas.

The name is for the locality of Baux (or Beaux), France. Bauxite is the principal ore of aluminum.

622 Psilomelane

Basic oxide of barium and manganese, often with small amounts of copper, cobalt, nickel, and magnesium
$BaMn^{2+}Mn_8^{4+}O_{16}(OH)_4$

Color and luster:	Iron-black, bluish black, steel-gray; submetallic, dull; streak black, brownish black, shining.
Hardness:	5–6
Cleavage:	None.
Other data:	*Specific gravity* 4.5 to 4.7; *fracture* conchoidal, uneven; may have coating of sooty black pyrolusite; brittle.
Crystals:	Monoclinic, but found only as massive; compact, botryoidal or mammillary crusts; also stalactitic, earthy, powdery.
Best field marks:	Massive appearance and association with other manganese minerals.
Similar species:	Pyrolusite is similar but is usually in crystalline form, and is harder and heavier than psilomelane. Psilomelane is usually found associated with other manganese minerals.
Environment:	Psilomelane is a widespread manganese mineral and commonly occurs with pyrolusite and barite in massive and disseminated hydrothermal replacement deposits.
Occurrence:	Although widely distributed, excellent collecting localities of psilomelane are rare, but are known to occur at Austinville, Wythe Co., Virginia, and near Tucson, Arizona.

The name derives from the Greek words *psilos,* "smooth," and *melas,* "black." Psilomelane is an important ore of manganese.

267, 530, 611, 612, 613, 620, 624, 632 Goethite

Hydrogen iron oxide, often with some manganese
$HFeO_2$

Color and luster:	Yellow, yellowish brown, dark brown, black, or with multicolored tarnish;

submetallic, adamantine, dull; streak
yellow, yellowish brown.

Hardness: 5–5½

Cleavage: Perfect, one direction lengthwise.

Other data: *Specific gravity* 3.3 to 4.3; *fracture* uneven, splintery.

Crystals: Orthorhombic; small, black, shining, prismatic; crystals rare; commonly acicular, flattened plates; also compact, granular, foliated, earthy.

Best field marks: Brownish-yellow to yellow streak and silky, fibrous structure.

Similar species: Hematite has a reddish-brown streak, and limonite lacks the silky, fibrous structure of goethite.

Environment: Goethite is a secondary iron mineral and forms in the zone of alteration in all types of hydrothermal replacement deposits, where it is commonly associated with psilomelane, manganite, calcite, and quartz.

Occurrence: Many materials formerly considered to be limonite are now identified as goethite, principally on the basis of X-ray studies. Good druses of goethite occur in many of the iron mines in the Lake Superior area, especially at the Jackson and Superior mines near Marquette, Marquette Co., Michigan. Exceptionally outstanding are the bladed crystals up to 5 cm (2″) in length that form rosettes on quartz and feldspar in cavities in pegmatites in the Crystal Peak area, Teller Co., Colorado.

The name is after Johann Wolfgang von Goethe (1749–1832), German poet, philosopher, and amateur mineralogist. In some areas, particularly in Europe, goethite is an important iron ore.

248, 623   Limonite
A mixture of hydrous iron oxides; of
indefinite composition
$FeO(OH) \cdot nH_2O$

Color and luster: Yellow, brown; glassy or silky to dull;
streak yellowish brown.

Hardness: 4–5½

Cleavage: None.

Other data: *Specific gravity* 2.7 to 4.3; *fracture*
conchoidal, splintery, uneven, earthy;
frequently varnish-like surface.

Crystals: Amorphous, earthy, fibrous,
botryoidal, stalactitic; commonly
pseudomorphous after pyrite,
marcasite, siderite.

Best field marks: Streak and earthy structure.

Similar species: Goethite has a silky, fibrous structure.

Environment: Limonite is a mixture of secondary iron
minerals and results from the alteration
of iron-bearing minerals, especially
sulfides such as pyrite, marcasite, and
arsenopyrite, near the earth's surface.

Occurrence: Limonite is widespread in distribution.
It is a coloring matter of soils and gives
the characteristic rusty-brown color to
the weathered surfaces of rocks.
Limonite formed extensive beds at
Salisbury and Kent in Litchfield Co.,
Connecticut, in Dutchess Co., New
York, and in Berkshire Co.,
Massachusetts. Large pseudomorphs of
limonite after pyrite cystals were found
near Fruitvale, Lancaster Co.,
Pennsylvania; at Pelican Point, Utah;
and at Londonderry, Colchester Co.,
Nova Scotia.

The name is from the Greek word
leimons, "meadow," in allusion to its
occurrence in bogs. Limonite is an ore
of iron and is used in the manufacture
of paints. The material usually called
limonite is actually cryptocrystalline
goethite with absorbed water. The
name is retained here as a field term for
natural hydrous iron oxides whose
precise identity is not specified.

Multiple Oxides

Multiple oxides are compounds of two metallic elements with oxygen, as in chromite, $FeCr_2O_4$. Some of the multiple oxides are soft, but many are hard and can be used as gemstones when transparent and flawless.

134, 190, 505, **Spinel**
667, 684 Magnesium aluminum oxide, in which magnesium can be partly or completely replaced by iron, zinc, or manganese
$MgAl_2O_4$

Color and luster: Red, green, blue, brown, black; vitreous, dull; streak white.
Hardness: 7½–8
Cleavage: None.
Other data: *Specific gravity* 3.6 to 4.0; *fracture* conchoidal; brittle; transparent to opaque; sometimes fluorescent.
Crystals: Isometric; usually in octahedrons; cubes and dodecahedrons rare; also granular, compact, disseminate.
Best field marks: Crystal shape and hardness.
Similar species: Magnetite is magnetic; chromite and zircon have higher gravity; and garnet does not crystallize in octahedral form.
Environment: Spinel forms in plutonic and metamorphic rocks. It is associated with olivine and hornblende in gabbro of plutonic rocks, and with pargasite, phlogopite, and chondrodite in hornfels and marbles of metamorphic rocks.
Occurrence: Perhaps the finest spinel comes from localities in Ceylon and Burma. Fine sharp cyrstals have been found in calcite veins in Ross Township, Renfrew Co., Ontario, and in St. Lawrence Co., New York. Sharp spinel crystals, some of them measuring more than 12.5 cm (5″) on the edge, have come from the Sterling Hill Mine at Ogdensburg, Sussex Co., New Jersey. Pink, green, black, and lavender crystals have come from a body of metamorphic rock in E Fresno Co., California.
Gemstone data: Gem quality spinel was known for many years as a substitute for ruby and sapphire. Spinel occurs in many colors: red, pink, rose, and yellow to orange spinel is called *rubicelle;* purple spinel is called *almandine spinel,* and blue or dark green to black spinel is called *pleonast.* Because spinel usually contains fewer flaws than ruby, it was frequently substituted for the rubies in the crowns

of England and Russia. Spinels are faceted. The best gem spinel comes from Ceylon and Burma, although small colorful stones have been found at several places in California, New Jersey, New Mexico, and North Carolina.

The name is of uncertain origin, but is probably from the Latin *spina,* "thorn," in reference to its sharply pointed crystals. The magnesium in spinel may be replaced by varying amounts of iron, zinc, or manganese, forming a series of related but separately named minerals called the *spinel series.* The mineral described here is the magnesium-rich variety most familiar to collectors.

---

590 Magnetite

Iron oxide; sometimes contains small amounts of manganese, nickel, chromium, and titanium
Fe_3O_4

Color and luster: Iron-black, metallic; streak black.

Hardness: $5\frac{1}{2}$–$6\frac{1}{2}$

Cleavage: None; may have octahedral parting in four directions.

Other data: *Specific gravity* 4.9 to 5.2; *fracture* subconchoidal, uneven; strongly magnetic; brittle.

Crystals: Isometric; usually octahedrons, sometimes dodecahedrons with striations; also massive, coarse or fine granular, lamellar.

Best field marks: Magnetism and dark streak.

Similar species: Magnetite has darker streak than ilmenite, and is more magnetic than chromite and franklinite.

Environment: Magnetite is one of the most abundant and widespread of all oxide minerals and occurs in a wide variety of environments. In general it is a common constituent of many igneous rocks, including diorite, gabbro, monzonite, and nepheline syenite, and of many clastic sedimentary rocks. It occurs more specifically associated with hedenbergite and andradite in hornfels of contact metamorphic rocks; with almandine, talc, and andradite in talc schist and quartzite of regional metamorphic rocks; with calcite, andradite, and chlorite in skarn of hydrothermal metamorphic rocks; and with barite and fluorite in massive and lode hydrothermal replacement deposits.

Occurrence: Because of its widespread distribution throughout North America, only those localities from which noteworthy material has been obtained will be mentioned here. Fine large crystals, some weighing over 180 kg (400 pounds), were collected near Faraday, Hastings Co., Ontario; beautiful brilliant black crystals have been collected from volcanic rocks in Kings and Annapolis Cos., Nova Scotia; lustrous sharp dodecahedral cyrstals occur in calcite at the Tilly Foster iron mine, Brewster, Putnam Co., New York. Sharp octahedrons up to 1.25 cm (½″) across occur with pyrite cubes in chlorite schist near Chester, Windsor Co., Vermont. Fine magnetite crystals occur at Fierro, New Mexico; in the Iron Springs district of S Utah; and at Heroult, Shasta Co., California.

Some magnetite (lodestone) is naturally magnetized and will attract small pieces of iron and steel. The name derives from Magnesia, an ancient district bordering on Macedonia. Magnetite is an important ore of iron.

586, 587   Franklinite
Zinc iron oxide, often with substantial amounts of manganese
$(Zn,Mn,Fe^{2+})\,(Fe^{3+},Mn^{3+})_2O_4$

Color and luster: Iron-black; metallic, dull; streak black, brownish black, reddish brown.

Hardness:	5½–6½
Cleavage:	None; indistinct octahedral parting in four directions.
Other data:	*Specific gravity* 5.1 to 5.2; *fracture* subconchoidal, uneven; weakly magnetic; brittle.
Crystals:	Isometric; usually octahedral, less frequently dodecahedral; also compact, granular, rounded disseminated grains.
Best field marks:	Weak magnetism and associated minerals.
Similar species:	Magnetite is strongly magnetic, and spinel is nonmagnetic.
Environment and Occurrence:	On a worldwide basis, franklinite is a rare mineral, but at Franklin and Sterling Hill, Sussex Co., New Jersey, it is the dominant mineral of a great zinc deposit, where it occurs with many minerals but especially with calcite, willemite, and zincite in a massive hydrothermal replacement deposit. Franklinite does not fluoresce, but the associated calcite and willemite do in beautiful brilliant colors. The name derives from the New Jersey locality where it was first found. Franklinite is an important ore of zinc.

---

589 Chromite
Iron chromium oxide
$FeCr_2O_4$

Color and luster:	Iron-black, brownish black, metallic; submetallic, dull; streak dark brown.
Hardness:	5½
Cleavage:	None; indistinct parting in four directions.
Other data:	*Specific gravity* 4.3 to 5.0; *fracture* conchoidal, uneven; may be slightly magnetic; brittle.
Crystals:	Isometric; crystals octahedral, rare; usually disseminated, granular, compact.
Best field marks:	Dark streak and weak magnetism.
Similar species:	Magnetite is strongly magnetic, and spinel does not have dark streak.

Environment: Chromite is of igneous origin and forms in peridotite of plutonic rocks. It also occurs in serpentinite, but since the serpentinite was developed through hydrothermal alteration of peridotite, the chromite in the original peridotite remains unchanged and appears as a constituent of the serpentinite. Uvarovite, the chromium garnet, is commonly associated with chromite.

Occurrence: Chromite occurs in the Bare Hills near Baltimore, Maryland, and at Wood's Mine, near Texas, Lancaster Co., Pennsylvania. Significant quantities of chromite have been mined in California, especially in Del Norte, Fresno, Glenn, San Luis Obispo, and Siskiyou Cos., and from mines in North Carolina, Oregon, and Wyoming.

The name derives from the mineral's chromium content (from the Greek *chroma,* "color"). Chromite is the principal ore of chromium.

1, 24, 691 Chrysoberyl
Beryllium aluminum oxide, often with small amounts of iron and chromium $BeAl_2O_4$

Color and luster: Yellowish green, deep green, greenish white, greenish brown, yellow; vitreous; streak white.

Hardness: $8\frac{1}{2}$

Cleavage: Good in one direction, poor in two others.

Other data: *Specific gravity* 3.5 to 3.8; *fracture* conchoidal, uneven; transparent to translucent; brittle.

Crystals: Orthorhombic; usually tabular or prismatic crystals; also disseminated plates; forms heart-shaped or pseudohexagonal twins.

Best field marks: Superior hardness and gravity.

Similar species: Chrysoberyl is harder and heavier than

beryl, with which it is usually associated.

Environment: Chrysoberyl occurs with beryl, microcline, and tourmaline in granite pegmatites, and with albite and almandite in schist of regional metamorphic rocks.

Occurrence: The finest alexandrite comes from near Sverdlovsk, in the Ural Mtns. of the USSR. Twin crystals, some of them chatoyant and spear-shaped, occur in pegmatites in the New England states and at Greenfield, Saratoga Co., New York. Large crude crystals up to 12.5 cm (5″) across were obtained from a pegmatite near Golden, Jefferson Co., Colorado.

Gemstone data: Dark yellow-green to slightly bluish-green chrysoberyl that appears red, purplish, or purplish violet under artificial light is called *alexandrite*. All other colors, including yellow to greenish-yellow, yellowish-brown, and bluish-green to green, are known simply as chrysoberyl. Some pale yellow to dark bluish-green and golden brown stones exhibit a floating billowy light, which moves as the stone is rotated, an effect called *cymophane*. When the cymophane effect is confined to a narrow band, *precious catseye* or *chrysoberyl* (also in alexandrite) *catseye* is produced. Alexandrite and chrysoberyl are faceted, whereas catseye and cymophane must be fashioned as cabochons. Most gem-quality chrysoberyl comes from foreign sources, including Brazil, Ceylon, China, Rhodesia, and Russia.

The name is from the Greek *chrysos* and *beryllos,* in allusion to its golden-yellow color and to beryl, of which it was once considered a variety. Alexandrite is a birthstone for June.

593, 606   Columbite-Tantalite Series
A two-member series, consisting of
columbite and tantalite in all
gradations, sometimes with tin and
tungsten
$(Fe,Mn)(Nb,Ta)_2O_6$ (columbite)
$(Fe,Mn)(Ta,Nb)_2O_6$ (tantalite)

Color and luster: Iron-black to brownish black;
submetallic, greasy, dull; streak dark
red to brown or black.

Hardness: 6

Cleavage: Good, one direction.

Other data: *Specific gravity* 5.3 (columbite) to 7.9
(tantalite); *fracture* subconchoidal,
uneven; columbite is opaque, tantalite
transparent in thin splinters.

Crystals: Orthorhombic; commonly short
prismatic; also equant, granular,
disseminated.

Best field marks: Iridescent (bluish) fracture surfaces,
high gravity, and weak magnetism.

Similar species: Columbite and tantalite are not as
magnetic as magnetite; are not
radioactive as is uraninite; are heavier
than black tourmaline; and lack the
perfect cleavage of wolframite.

Environment: Columbite and tantalite are the most
common and widespread of all minerals
that contain niobium and tantalum.
They generally are found in granite
pegmatites, where they occur associated
with albite, corundum, orthoclase, and
quartz. Both minerals will develop as
single crystals or as clusters, usually
with the columbite forming near the
walls of the pegmatite and the tantalite
near the core.

Occurrence: Good specimens have come from
pegmatite localities in Canada and the
United States. Fine crystals up to 2.5
cm (1″) in length have come from the
Woodcox Mine, Renfrew Co., Ontario,
and crystals up to 7.5 cm (3″) across
and subparallel aggregates of thin
blades have been found in the
Rutherford Mine, near Amelia, Amelia
Co., Virginia. Other localities are in
the Bridger Mts., in Wyoming, in

Colorado, and at the gem-bearing pegmatites in San Diego Co., California.

Both minerals are used as important ores of niobium and tantalum. They were named for their columbium (an old name for the element niobium) and tantalum content.

Halides

The halides are compounds in which a halogen element (chlorine, fluorine, iodine, or bromine) is the sole anion, as in halite, NaCl. These minerals are relatively soft, weak, and brittle, and many of them will dissolve readily in water. Those that are not soluble in water generally crystallize in the isometric crystal system and develop as cubes.

135, 141, 174,	**Halite**
315, 402, 404	Sodium chloride
	NaCl

Color and luster: Colorless, or tints of gray, yellow, red, blue; vitreous; streak white.

Hardness: 2–2½

Cleavage: Perfect, three directions at 90°.

Other data: *Specific gravity* 2.16; *fracture* conchoidal; transparent; salty taste; fluorescent; brittle.

Crystals: Isometric; usually the simple cube, rarely octahedral; faces are commonly cavernous and develop into "hopper" crystals; also granular, cleavage fragments, compact.

Best field marks: Salty taste and lusterless cubic crystals.

Similar species: Halite is readily soluble in water and has a salty taste, whereas cryolite has neither of these properties and is also harder than halite.

Environment: Halite is widespread in evaporite deposits of chemical sedimentary rocks and is commonly associated with gypsum, thenardite, and borax.

Occurrence: Famous European localities include those at Strassfurt, Germany, and at Salzburg, Austria. In North America bedded deposits, of which many are accessible only in underground mines, occur in central and W New York, in Michigan, and in Salina, Kansas. The surface of Searles Lake, a dry lake in San Bernardino Co., California, is a sheet of brilliant white halite.

The name "halite" is from the Greek *hals,* "salt." Halite finds wide use in the chemical industry and as a source of chlorine and sodium.

492	**Chlorargyrite (Cerargyrite)**
	Silver chloride
	AgCl

Color and luster: Pearl-gray to brown; colorless when fresh, but becomes violet or brown

	upon exposure to light; resinous, adamantine, waxy; streak white.
Hardness:	2½
Cleavage:	None.
Other data:	*Specific gravity* 5.5 to 5.6; *fracture* uneven; tough; sectile, ductile, and plastic; transparent to translucent.
Crystals:	Isometric, usually cubic; ordinarily massive, incrusting, columnar, stalactitic.
Best field marks:	High gravity, waxy appearance, and high sectility.
Similar species:	Calomel (mercury chloride, not described in this field guide) has three distinct cleavages at 90°.
Environment:	Chlorargyrite is a secondary mineral and generally develops in the zone of alteration in epithermal veins, where it occurs with acanthite, stephanite, and calcite, and in massive hydrothermal replacement deposits, where it occurs with acanthite and barite.
Occurrence:	Chlorargyrite localities, mostly in W United States and Mexico, are generally at silver mines. Masses of chlorargyrite, of which one weighed over 6 tons, were found at Treasure Hill, Nevada, and significant quantities were obtained from the silver ores mined at the famous Comstock Lode, Lincoln Co., Nevada. Well-formed cubes were found in massive chlorargyrite mined in the Silver City district, Owyhee Co., Idaho.

The name "chlorargyrite" is from the mineral's chlorine content and the Greek *argyros,* "silver," in allusion to the mineral's luster. Chlorargyrite is an ore of silver.

Fluorite
Calcium fluoride, with small amounts
of yttrium and cerium
CaF_2

Color and luster: Violet, blue, green, yellow, brown,
bluish black, pink, rose-red, colorless,
white; vitreous; streak white.

Hardness: 4

Cleavage: Perfect in four directions, forming an
octahedron.

Other data: *Specific gravity* 3.0 to 3.2; *fracture*
uneven; transparent to translucent;
fluorescent; brittle.

Crystals: Isometric; usually cubic or as
penetration twins; less frequently
octahedral and rarely dodecahedral; also
cleavage masses, granular, columnar;
penetration twins common.

Best field marks: Perfect octahedral cleavage, crystal
shape as cubes, and hardness.

Similar species: Fluorite is harder than calcite, but
much softer than quartz.

Environment: Fluorite develops in several
environments of widely different
character. It is associated with albite
and pyrite in carbonatites; with calcite
and spinel in hornfels of contact
metamorphic rocks; with calcite,
rhodochrosite, and chalcedony in
epithermal veins; and with galena,
barite, and pyrite in lode hydrothermal
replacement deposits.

Occurrence: Superb crystal groups have come from
the lead mines in England, especially at
Weardale, Durham, and Tavistock. In
North America excellent material has
come from a number of localities,
notably Rosiclare, Hardin Co., Illinois;
Marion, Crittenden Co., Kentucky;
Rimer, Putnam Co., and Clay Center,
Ottawa Co., Ohio. Superb, flawless,
sharp sea-green cubes occur with barite
in Madoc, Marmara, and Huntingdon,
Hastings Co., Ontario. Large blue
etched cubes and pale-green

octahedrons have come from the
Barstow Mine, Ouray Co., Colorado.
Colorless cubes on galena have been
obtained from mines near Mapimi,
Durango, Mexico. Colorless crystals
occur with calcite, mica, apatite,
scapolite, and uraninite near
Wilberforce, Haliburton Co., Ontario.

The name is from the Latin *fluere*, "to
flow," because fluorite melts easily and
is used as a flux in the smelting of
metallic ores. Fluorite is used in the
manufacture of steel and hydrofluoric
acid.

461, 469, 476 Cryolite
Sodium aluminum fluoride
Na_3AlF_6

Color and luster:	White, colorless; vitreous; streak white.
Hardness:	2½
Cleavage:	None; parting frequently in three directions at nearly right angles.
Other data:	*Specific gravity 2.9 to 3.0; fracture* uneven; transparent to translucent; weak salty taste; brittle.
Crystals:	Monoclinic; prismatic; usually massive with pseudocubic parting, coarse, granular.
Best field marks:	White translucent mineral lacking cleavage but usually enclosing brown siderite and gray galena.
Similar species:	None.
Environment:	Cryolite occurs in granite pegmatites, associated with quartz, feldspar, galena, and siderite.
Occurrence:	The principal occurrence of cryolite is at Ivigtut, Arsuk Fjord, Greenland, where it occurs in a pegmatite. It also occurs in limited amounts in a pegmatite at the southern base of Pikes Peak, El Paso Co., Colorado.

The name is from the Greek *kryos*,
"frost," and *lithos*, "stone." Cryolite is

used in the recovery of aluminum from bauxite. An interesting fact about cryolite is that when the powdered mineral is put in water the mineral will be invisible, because of the similarity of its refraction of light to that of water.

Carbonates

The carbonates are compounds of one or more metallic elements or semimetals with the carbonate radical. One member of this class, calcite, is sufficiently common to form large bodies of limestone, a sedimentary rock. The carbonates are brittle minerals, and many of them break easily along crystal directions to develop the characteristic rhombohedral cleavage. A few carbonate minerals are in bright colors, but many of them are white, colorless, or transparent.

8, 27, 59, 225, 234, 258, 261, 312, 320, 325, 364, 382, 416, 427, 430, 433	**Calcite** Calcium carbonate $CaCO_3$
Color and luster:	White, colorless, pale shades of gray, yellow, red, green, blue, brown to black when impure; vitreous, dull; streak white.
Hardness:	3
Cleavage:	Perfect in three directions, forming a rhombohedron.
Other data:	*Specific gravity* 2.7; *fracture* conchoidal, seldom observed; transparent to translucent; fluorescent.
Crystals:	Hexagonal; crystals commonly showing rhombohedron, scalenohedron, and prism; also tabular, acicular, cleavable, granular, compact, stalactitic, oolitic, earthy; twinned crystals very common.
Best field marks:	Perfect rhombohedral cleavage and hardness; effervesces vigorously in acid; double refraction in clear specimens (an object viewed through the crystal appears as a double image).
Similar species:	Aragonite lacks the rhombohedral cleavage. Optical tests are required to distinguish calcite from dolomite.
Environment:	Calcite is the commonest of all carbonate minerals and develops in many kinds of environments. It occurs with acmite, apatite, and fluorite in nepheline syenite pegmatites; with barite, albite, and scapolite in carbonatites; with zeolites and prehnite in basalt of volcanic rocks; with gypsum in limestone of chemical and organic sedimentary rocks; with tremolite and wollastonite in hornfels of contact metamorphic rocks; with grossular, wollastonite, and diopside in hornfels and marble of regional metamorphic rocks; with hedenbergite and andradite in skarn of hydrothermal metamorphic rocks; with quartz, dolomite, and fluorite in hypothermal, mesothermal, and epithermal veins; and with cerussite, marcasite, and sphalerite

Occurrence:

in disseminated hydrothermal replacement deposits. Because of its abundance, fine specimens of calcite are easy to obtain. Crystals up to roughly 450 kg (1,000 lb) in weight were found in a cave in limestone near Sterlingbush, Lewis Co., New York. Splendid colorless crystals up to 7.5 cm (3″) across enclosing brilliant native copper have come from copper mines on Keweenaw Peninsula, Michigan. Excellent clusters of well-formed crystals were found in abundance in the lead-zinc mines of the tri-state district of Oklahoma, Kansas, and Missouri. Beautiful blue coarse-cleavage calcite occurs in the Crestmore quarries near Riverside, California, and large flat crystals have been found at a number of localities in the states of Durango, Sonora, and Sinaloa, Mexico.

The name "calcite" is from the Greek *chalx,* "lime." Calcite is used in the manufacture of steel, cement, and glass.

318, 462 Magnesite
Magnesium carbonate, frequently with substantial amounts of iron and calcium
$MgCO_3$

Color and luster:	White, yellowish, grayish, brown; vitreous, dull; streak white.
Hardness:	3½–4½
Cleavage:	Perfect in three directions, forming a rhombohedron.
Other data:	*Specific gravity* 3.0 to 3.1; *fracture* conchoidal; transparent to translucent; tough to brittle.
Crystals:	Hexagonal; distinct crystals rare but usually rhombohedral; also compact like unglazed porcelain, granular, cleavable masses.
Best field marks:	White color, dull luster, and fine-grained porcelaneous masses.
Similar species:	Calcite and dolomite are softer and less

dense than magnesite, and lack the dull porcelaneous appearance. Datolite also occurs in porcelaneous masses, but it is harder than magnesite.

Environment: Magnesite has developed in several environments. It is associated with brucite in hornfels of contact metamorphic rocks; with brucite in serpentinite of hydrothermal metamorphic rocks; and with brucite in lode hydrothermal replacement deposits.

Occurrence: Good crystals of magnesite are rare, but in the massive form it is common. Deposits of magnesite are widely distributed in the serpentinite bodies scattered throughout the Coast Ranges of California. Massive magnesite occurs with brucite at Gabbs, Nevada, and in the South Canyon district and Target Range Canyon in Dona Ana Co., New Mexico. Magnesite occurs in Argenteuil Co., Quebec, and on the Yukon River in the Yukon.

Magnesite is named for its Mg content. It is used as a source of magnesium metal and magnesia.

168, 247, 269 **Siderite**
Iron carbonate; may contain some manganese, zinc, and cobalt
$FeCO_3$

Color and luster: Light to dark brown, reddish brown, white; vitreous, pearly, dull; streak white, pale yellow.
Hardness: $3\frac{1}{2}-4$
Cleavage: Perfect in three directions, forming a rhombohedron.
Other data: *Specific gravity* 3.8 to 3.9; *fracture* uneven; translucent; brittle.
Crystals: Hexagonal; commonly rhombohedral with curved faces; prismatic and scalenohedral forms less common; also granular, cleavable masses, compact, massive, botryoidal, fibrous.

Best field marks: Brown color, rhombohedral cleavage, and curved faces; becomes magnetic when heated.

Similar species: Sphalerite, dolomite, and calcite do not, like siderite, become magnetic when heated; siderite effervesces slightly in acid, calcite does so vigorously; sphalerite does not effervesce.

Environment: Siderite forms large deposits in sedimentary rocks of shale, clay, or coal seams. It occurs with barite and chalcopyrite in carbonatites; with calcite, rhodochrosite, and galena in hypothermal veins; and with galena, pyrite, and sphalerite in lode hydrothermal replacement deposits.

Occurrence: There are many interesting occurrences of siderite in North America. Large cleavage rhombs up to 30 cm (12″) across were obtained along with cryolite at Ivigtut, Greenland, and a large vein deposit was mined at Roxbury, Connecticut. Light-brown crystals were found lining cavities in massive siderite in several mines of the Gilman district, Eagle Co., Colorado, and fine granular brown stalactitic siderite covered by small iridescent siderite crystals was found in the Campbell shaft, Bisbee, Cochise Co., Arizona.

The name is from the Greek *sideros*, "iron," in reference to its composition. Siderite is a minor ore of iron.

140, 149, 182, **Rhodochrosite**
189 Manganese carbonate; often contains calcium, iron, magnesium, and zinc $MnCO_3$

Color and luster: Pink, rose-red, dark red, brown; darkens on exposure to atmosphere; vitreous, pearly; streak white.
Hardness: 3½–4
Cleavage: Perfect in three directions, forming a rhombohedron.

Other data: *Specific gravity* 3.4 to 3.6; *fracture*
uneven; subtransparent to translucent;
brittle.

Crystals: Hexagonal; most often in
rhombohedrons; also cleavage masses,
granular, compact, botryoidal,
incrusting; distinct crystals uncommon.

Best field marks: Rhombohedral cleavage and color.

Similar species: Rhodonite does not have the
rhombohedral cleavage and is harder
than rhodochrosite. The pink of
rhodochrosite will distinguish it from
other minerals with rhombohedral
cleavage.

Environment: Rhodochrosite is a common constituent
of veins and occurs with chalcopyrite,
galena, and sphalerite in hypothermal,
mesothermal, and epithermal veins,
and with sphalerite, bornite, and
tetrahedrite in massive hydrothermal
replacement deposits.

Occurrence: A famous locality is at Kapnik,
Rumania. In North America excellent
specimens have come from a number of
localities, but perhaps the finest crystals
were found at the St. Elmo and Mary
Murphy mines, Chaffee Co., and the
Sweet Home Mine, Park Co.,
Colorado. Massive pale-pink
rhodochrosite was mined at Philipsburg
and Butte, Montana. Rhodochrosite
occurs with manganese-oxide minerals
at Batesville, Arkansas; at Poland,
Maine; and at Placenta Bay,
Newfoundland.

The name is from the Greek *rhodon*
"rose," and *chros,* "color," in reference
to the rose-red color of the mineral.
Rhodochrosite is an ore of manganese.

66, 118, 167   Smithsonite
Zinc carbonate, often with some iron
$ZnCO_3$

Color and luster: White, gray, colorless, green, blue,
yellow, purple, pink, brown; vitreous,

adamantine, pearly; streak white.

Hardness: 4–4½

Cleavage: Perfect in three directions, forming a rhombohedron.

Other data: *Specific gravity* 4.3 to 4.5; *fracture* uneven, splintery; translucent; brittle.

Crystals: Hexagonal; crystals rare, usually botryoidal, reniform, stalactitic; also incrusting, coarsely granular, compact, cellular.

Best field marks: Botryoidal form, cleavage, hardness, and high gravity; effervesces in hydrochloric acid.

Similar species: Smithsonite is harder and heavier than most carbonates; it is softer than prehnite and heavier and harder than wavellite.

Environment: Smithsonite is a secondary mineral and occurs chiefly in the oxidized zone of massive hydrothermal replacement deposits, where it is associated with galena, cerussite, azurite, and malachite.

Occurrence: Famous localities include Laurium, Greece; Aachen, Germany; Bleiberg in Carinthia, Austria; Tsumeb in South-West Africa; and the Broken Hill Mine in N Rhodesia. Localities in North America include scattered occurrences near Friedensville, Lehigh Co., and at Bamford, Lancaster Co., Pennsylvania; in the lead mines at Yellville, Marion Co., Arkansas; and in the Tintic district, Juab Co., and the Ophir district in Utah. Masses of beautiful blue-green smithsonite were found in the mines at Kelly, near Magdalena, Socorro Co., New Mexico, and pale greenish-blue smithsonite in the lead-zinc mines at Cerro Gordo, Inyo Co., California.

The name is for James Smithson (1765–1829), founder of the Smithsonian Institution. Smithsonite is an ore of zinc.

257, 434, 441, **Aragonite**
473 Calcium carbonate; may contain some
strontium, lead, and zinc
$CaCO_3$

Color and luster: White, gray, colorless, yellow, pale
green, violet, brown; vitreous, resinous;
streak white.

Hardness: 3½–4

Cleavage: Good in one direction, poor in two
others.

Other data: *Specific gravity* 2.9 to 3.0; *fracture*
subconchoidal; transparent to
translucent; fluorescent; brittle.

Crystals: Orthorhombic, usually short to long
prismatic; also fibrous acicular,
columnar, stalactitic aggregates;
untwinned crystals very rare; twinned
crystals show pseudohexagonal prisms
and spear- or chisel-shaped forms.

Best field marks: Prismatic cleavage and pseudohexagonal
twin-crystal forms.

Similar species: Calcite lacks prismatic cleavage and
does not form the same shapes in twin
crystals.

Environment: Aragonite is not as common a mineral
as calcite, and it forms in fewer
environments. Aragonite occurs in
evaporite deposits of chemical
sedimentary rocks, where it is
associated with gypsum and calcite;
with glaucophane, albite, and lawsonite
in blue schists of regional metamorphic
rocks, and with azurite, chalcopyrite,
and cuprite in massive and
disseminated hydrothermal replacement
deposits.

Occurrence: Good North American localities for
aragonite are uncommon. Fine crystals
were found associated with calcite and
cerussite in the Magdalena district,
Socorro Co., and as hexagonal tablets
near Lake Arthur, Chaves Co., New
Mexico. Fine stalactitic masses were
found in the Turquoise district, Cochise
Co., Arizona.

Named after Aragon province, Spain,
where it was first found.

398, 415 **Witherite**
Barium carbonate
$BaCO_3$

Color and luster: White, gray, yellowish-gray; vitreous, greasy; streak white.

Hardness: $3-3\frac{1}{2}$

Cleavage: Distinct, one direction.

Other data: *Specific gravity* 4.3 to 4.4; *fracture* uneven; transparent to translucent; fluorescent; brittle.

Crystals: Orthorhombic; always twinned, forming pseudohexagonal dipyramids; also compact, granular, radial fibrous, lamellar.

Best field marks: High gravity and hardness.

Similar species: Witherite is heavier than strontianite and aragonite, but lighter in weight than cerussite, which also has good cleavage.

Environment: Witherite is an uncommon mineral and occurs associated with barite, calcite, and galena in epithermal veins.

Occurrence: Excellent specimens have come from lead mines at Fallowfield, Hexham, in Northumberland, England. In North America large crystals have been found in the fluorite mines near Rosiclare, Hardin Co., Illinois. It was mined on a commercial basis with barite from veins near El Portal, Mariposa Co., California; occurs with lead ores in the Castle Dome district, Yuma Co., Arizona; and has been reported from a silver-bearing vein in Gillies Township, Thunder Bay district, Ontario.

The mineral is named after W. Withering (1741–1799), English mineralogist. It is used as a source of barium.

390, 449 Strontianite
Strontium carbonate, usually with some calcium
$SrCO_3$

Color and luster: White, colorless, grayish, greenish, yellowish; vitreous, greasy; streak white.

Hardness: 3½–4

Cleavage: Perfect in one direction, poor in another.

Other data: *Specific gravity* 3.7; *fracture* uneven; transparent to translucent; brittle.

Crystals: Orthorhombic; crystals rare, commonly long, sharply pointed individuals; also acicular, fibrous, columnar, divergent, compact, granular, pseudohexagonal intergrowths.

Best field marks: Hardness, but difficult to distinguish from similar species on the basis of physical properties alone.

Similar species: Strontianite is slightly softer than aragonite, and lighter in weight than cerussite and witherite.

Environment: Strontianite is a low-temperature mineral and develops in several environments. It occurs most commonly with celestite and calcite in evaporite deposits of chemical sedimentary rocks, and with calcite and fluorite in epithermal veins.

Occurrence: Good crystals of strontianite are rare, and mineral collections will usually contain a massive form admixed with celestite and calcite. It occurs with aragonite in limestone near Mt. Union, Mifflin Co., Pennsylvania; in the Strontium Hills, north of Barstow, San Bernardino Co., California; near Lake Conner, Skagit Co., Washington; and in veins in limestone at Nepean, Carleton Co., Ontario.

The name is after the locality of Strontian, Argyll, Scotland. Strontianite is used as a source of strontium.

376, 436 Cerussite
Lead carbonate
$PbCO_3$

Color and luster:	White, gray, colorless, yellow, brown; adamantine, greasy, silky; streak white.
Hardness:	3–3½
Cleavage:	Good, in one direction.
Other data:	*Specific gravity* 6.5 to 6.6; *fracture* conchoidal; transparent to translucent; fluorescent; brittle.
Crystals:	Orthorhombic; flat tabular plates found only in small crystals that are striated; also intergrown to form skeletal lattices and star-shaped groups; massive, granular, fibrous, compact.
Best field marks:	Adamantine luster, high gravity, twinned crystals, and brittleness.
Similar species:	Cerussite is slightly harder and lacks the cleavage of anglesite.
Environment:	Cerussite is a secondary lead mineral and generally forms from galena in the zone of alteration in massive and disseminated hydrothermal replacement deposits. Associated minerals are galena, malachite, barite, and smithsonite. It also occurs with galena and barite in carbonatites.
Occurrence:	Cerussite has been found in the Wheatley mines, Phoenixville, Pennsylvania; as an important ore at Leadville, Colorado; as heart-shaped twins from the Organ district, Dona Ana Co., New Mexico; in choice vee-twins and reticulated groups in the Mammoth-St. Anthony Mine, Tiger, Pinal Co., Arizona; at Cerro Gordo, Inyo Co., California; and at Moyie and the H. B. Mine at Salmo, British Columbia.

The name derives from the Latin *cerussa*, "ceruse," a white lead pigment. Cerussite is an ore of lead.

161, 277, 355, 407 Dolomite

Calcium magnesium carbonate; sometimes contains minor amounts of manganese and iron
$CaMg(CO_3)_2$

Color and luster:
: White, colorless, pink, gray, green, brown, black; vitreous, pearly; streak white.

Hardness:
: $3\frac{1}{2}$–4

Cleavage:
: Perfect in three directions, forming a rhombohedron.

Other data:
: *Specific gravity* 2.8 to 2.9; *fracture* conchoidal, uneven; transparent to translucent; brittle.

Crystals:
: Hexagonal, commonly rhombohedral, with curved faces; also granular, compact, massive (as dolomite rock), and cleavage masses.

Best field marks:
: Curved faces and pearly luster; powder will effervesce in acid.

Similar species:
: Unlike calcite, dolomite rarely fluoresces and is further distinguished by its curved faces, pearly luster, and slightly greater density.

Environment:
: The mineral dolomite develops in several environments. It occurs with barite and fluorite in dolomite rock of chemical sedimentary rocks; with calcite in dolomitic marble of contact and regional metamorphic rocks; with calcite, siderite, and rhodochrosite in hypothermal, mesothermal, and epithermal veins; and with galena, calcite, and gypsum in massive and disseminated hydrothermal replacement deposits.

Occurrence:
: Dolomite rock is found in many places in North America, but localities where well-formed crystals of dolomite may be obtained are not abundant. Small pink crystals occur in cavities in limestone in the Ontario peninsula between Lakes Erie, Ontario, and Huron. Beautiful pink crystals were found in abundance associated with the lead-zinc ores in the Mississippi Valley, and sharp well-formed crystals of dolomite occur in vugs in gold-bearing quartz veins of the

Mother Lode district (W Sierra Nevada) of California.

The name is after Deodat de Dolomieu (1750–1801), French mineralogist. Dolomite is used to make magnesia for industrial and medical use.

43, 48, 112 Aurichalcite
A basic carbonate of zinc and copper $(Zn,Cu)_5(CO_3)_2(OH)_6$

Color and luster:	Pale green to greenish blue and sky-blue, silky to pearly; streak pale greenish or bluish.
Hardness:	1–2
Cleavage:	Perfect, one direction.
Other data:	*Specific gravity* 3.64; *fracture* uneven; translucent.
Crystals:	Orthorhombic; usually in delicate acicular or lathlike crystals that form tufted, feathery, or plumose incrustations; rarely columnar, laminated, or granular.
Best field marks:	Softness and feathery incrustations.
Similar species:	None.
Environment:	Aurichalcite is a secondary mineral and forms in the alteration zone in massive hydrothermal replacement deposits, where it occurs with malachite, azurite, and limonite.
Occurrence:	Excellent specimens of aurichalcite have come from Bisbee, Cochise Co., Arizona; Cottonwood Canyon, Salt Lake Co., Utah; the Magdalena district, Socorro Co., New Mexico; the No. 79 Mine, Banner district, Gila Co., Arizona; and the Darwin district, Inyo Co., California. The finest North American material comes from the Ojuela Mine, Mapimi, Durango, Mexico.

The name is thought to come from the Greek *oreichalkon*, "copper."
Aurichalcite is a minor ore of zinc.

21, 49, 64, 65,   **Malachite**
68   Basic copper carbonate
$Cu_2CO_3(OH)_2$

Color and luster: Emerald-green, grass-green, dark green; adamantine, silky, dull; streak light green.

Hardness: 3½–4

Cleavage: Perfect, one direction crosswise.

Other data: *Specific gravity* 3.9 to 4; *fracture* conchoidal, splintery; translucent; brittle.

Crystals: Monoclinic; crystals rare and usually short or long prismatic; also radial, fibrous, botryoidal, stalactitic, incrusting, earthy.

Best field marks: Green color and concentric color-banding when massive.

Similar species: Malachite rarely occurs in prismatic crystals, as does brochantite, and brochantite rarely occurs in the botryoidal masses characteristic of malachite.

Environment: Malachite is a secondary copper mineral and develops in the zone of alteration in massive, lode, and disseminated hydrothermal replacement deposits. Associated minerals are azurite, limonite, and chalcopyrite.

Occurrence: The copper mines at Bisbee, Cochise Co., Arizona, are famous for their fine specimens of massive malachite and pseudomorphs of malachite after azurite. Mines at Morenci in Greenlee Co., and at Globe in Gila Co., Arizona, have yielded beautiful malachite specimens, of which some consist of alternating layers of green malachite and blue azurite. Fine malachite has also come from copper mines in California, Nevada, Utah, Pennsylvania, and Tennessee.

The name is from the Greek *moloche,* "mallow," in allusion to the mineral's leaf-green color. Malachite is used as an ore of copper and as a gemstone.

92, 106, 107,   **Azurite**
117, 122   Basic copper carbonate
$Cu_3(CO_3)_2(OH)_2$

Color and luster: Azure-blue, dark blue; vitreous, dull; streak blue.

Hardness: $3\frac{1}{2}$–4

Cleavage: Good, two directions.

Other data: *Specific gravity* 3.7 to 3.8; *fracture* conchoidal; transparent in thin chips; brittle.

Crystals: Monoclinic; usually in well-formed equidimensional or tabular crystals; also radiating, botryoidal, incrusting, earthy.

Best field marks: Intense azure-blue color and association with malachite.

Similar species: Azurite is softer than lazulite and lazurite, and is usually associated with malachite.

Environment: Azurite is a secondary copper mineral and develops in the zone of alteration in all types of hydrothermal replacement deposits, where it commonly occurs with malachite, limonite, and chalcopyrite.

Occurrence: The copper deposits at Tsumeb, South-West Africa, have yielded some of the finest azurite crystals in the world. The copper deposits in Arizona and Utah that yielded many fine specimens of malachite also yielded outstanding specimens of azurite. Fine azurite crystals have also been found in the San Carlos Mine, Mazapil, Zacatecas, Mexico.

The name is from the characteristic azure-blue color of the mineral. Azurite is an ore of copper and a minor ornamental stone.

Borates

The borates are compounds of one or
more metallic elements with the borate
radical. There are two types of borates:
the first, primary type is anhydrous
(without water), and develops in
igneous and metamorphic
environments, where it is both rare and
stable; the second type, the hydrous
borates, develop in sedimentary rocks at
the bottom of playas in arid regions.
Many of the hydrous borates are readily
soluble in water, and the dryness of
their environment aids greatly in their
preservation. The hydrous borates are
brittle and relatively soft, and are
white, colorless, or transparent. The
anhydrous borates are dark in color and
heavy.

384, 417, 479   Kernite
Hydrous sodium borate
$Na_2B_4O_7 \cdot 4H_2O$

Color and luster: White, colorless, gray; vitreous, dull and powdery upon exposure to air; streak white.

Hardness: 3

Cleavage: Perfect in two directions, good in a third, forming long splinters.

Other data: *Specific gravity* 1.95; *fracture* splintery; transparent when fresh; dissolves readily in water; has sweetish alkaline taste.

Crystals: Monoclinic; nearly equant and striated; commonly aggregates of long crystals; massive.

Best field marks: Hardness and cleavage.

Similar species: Kernite is harder than borax and gypsum.

Environment: Kernite is restricted in its occurrences to evaporite-type chemical sedimentary rocks, where it is usually associated with ulexite and colemanite.

Occurrence: Excellent specimens of kernite have been obtained in North America from the famous Kramer borate district in Kern Co., California.

Kernite is named after the county in California in which it was discovered. It is an important source of borax and other boron compounds and has many uses in various industries.

426, 456   Borax
Hydrous sodium borate
$Na_2B_4O_7 \cdot 10H_2O$

Color and luster: Colorless, white, grayish to greenish white; vitreous, greasy; streak white.

Hardness: 2–2½

Cleavage: Perfect in one direction, good in another.

Other data: *Specific gravity* 1.7; *fracture* conchoidal; brittle; has sweetish alkaline taste; translucent to opaque.

Crystals: Monoclinic; usually short, well-formed

prismatic crystals; also compact, earthy, incrusting.

Best field marks: Dissolves in water and has a sweetish alkaline taste.

Similar species: None.

Environment: Borax forms in evaporated deposits in muds of saline lakes. It is not a common mineral and usually occurs with halite, ulexite, and kernite.

Occurrence: Although borax was first obtained from the salt lakes of Kashmir and Tibet, the principal deposits are in W United States. Well-formed crystals up to 15 cm (6″) long have been obtained from the mud at Borax Lake, Lake Co., California. Most significant is the deposit at Searles Lake, San Bernardino Co., California, where crystals of borax occur with halite and thenardite; further south, at Boron in Kern Co., borax occurs with ulexite and kernite. Borax also occurs with other saline minerals in Rhodes Marsh and Teel Marsh in Esmeralda Co., Nevada, and at Alkalı Flat, Dona Ana Co., New Mexico.

The name is from the Arabic *buraq,* which referred both to borax and to "niter" (potassium nitrate). Borax is used in many industrial applications (especially as a flux) and as a source of boric acid.

438, 439   Ulexite
Hydrous sodium calcium borate
$NaCaB_5O_9 \cdot 8H_2O$

Color and luster: White; vitreous, satiny, silky; streak white.

Hardness: 2½

Cleavage: Perfect in one direction, good in another.

Other data: *Specific gravity* 1.9; *fracture* uneven, splintery; transparent to translucent.

Crystals: Triclinic; distinct crystals rare; usually in small nodular, rounded, or lenslike

crystals; sometimes loose in texture
("cotton balls").

Best field mark: Association with other borate minerals.

Similar species: Difficult to distinguish by physical tests
from fibrous asbestos or other fibrous
minerals. Association and fibrous
masses are the best aids in
identification.

Environment: Ulexite usually develops in evaporite
deposits of chemical sedimentary rocks
and is generally associated with
colemanite, kernite, and calcite.

Occurrence: Fine fibrous ulexite occurs as seams in
clay at Boron, Kern Co., and tufted
"cotton ball" aggregates occur at Mt.
Blanco, Death Valley, Inyo Co., and at
a small spring in Red Rock Canyon,
Kern Co.; all are in California.

The name is after Georg Ludwig Ulex
(1811–1883), German chemist. Ulexite
is used as a source of boron and in the
manufacture of glass wool.

366, 380, 408, 435   **Colemanite**
Hydrous calcium borate
$Ca_2B_6O_{11} \cdot 5H_2O$

Color and luster: Colorless, white, grayish to yellowish
white; vitreous, dull; streak white.

Hardness: 4–4½

Cleavage: Perfect in one direction, distinct in
another.

Other data: *Specific gravity* 2.4; *fracture* uneven,
subconchoidal; transparent to
translucent.

Crystals: Monoclinic; commonly short prismatic;
equant; also massive, cleavable,
granular, compact, incrusting.

Best field marks: Shape of crystals, hardness, cleavage,
and mineral association.

Similar species: Calcite has perfect cleavage in three
directions, is softer than colemanite,
and is not commonly associated with
the borate minerals.

Environment: Colemanite is a low-temperature
mineral and usually occurs in evaporite

deposits of chemical sedimentary rocks, associated with ulexite and borax.

Occurrence: Localities where colemanite may be obtained are principally in W United States. It was first found in Death Valley, Inyo Co., California, in 1887 in deposits from which magnificent museum specimens are being obtained today. Nodules of colemanite containing beautiful blue crystals of celestite occur in the Calico district, north of Yermo, San Bernardino Co., California. Colemanite occurs as sharp-pointed crystals with ulexite and kernite at Boron, Kern Co., California, and at White Basin and Callville Wash in the Muddy Mts., Clark Co., Nevada.

Named after William T. Coleman, a San Francisco merchant and mine owner. Colemanite is used in the manufacture of glass and as a source of boron.

---

468 Howlite
Hydrated calcium silico-borate
$Ca_2B_5SiO_9(OH)_5$

Color and luster: White; subvitreous, glimmering, dull; streak white.
Hardness: 3½
Cleavage: None.
Other data: *Specific gravity* 2.53 to 2.59; *fracture* conchoidal, smooth; translucent in thin splinters; brittle.
Crystals: Monoclinic; crystals tabular, up to 1 mm (⅟₂₅″) across, very rare; usually occurs as compact, dense, structureless nodular masses that resemble unglazed porcelain; sometimes scaly, earthy, chalklike.
Best field marks: Porcelaneous or chalklike masses; hardness; dissolves in hydrochloric acid.
Similar species: Datolite is harder than howlite and will not dissolve in hydrochloric acid.
Environment: Howlite develops in evaporite deposits

in sedimentary rocks and usually occurs with ulexite and colemanite as nodules in clay.

Occurrence: Howlite was first found as nodules in anhydrite associated with ulexite near Windsor, Hants Co., Nova Scotia. In California it occurs abundantly as nodules, sometimes several hundred pounds in weight, especially with colemanite at Lang, Los Angeles Co., and with ulexite near Daggett, San Bernardino Co.

Howlite is named after Henry How (d. 1879), the Nova Scotia chemist, geologist, and mineralogist who first described the mineral. It has been used in polished form as a decorative stone.

Sulfates

The sulfates are compounds of one or
more metallic elements with the sulfate
radical. This is a large class of minerals,
whose members have few properties in
common. In general they are light in
color and transparent to translucent.
None are hard, and most are fragile.

451, 481   Thenardite
Sodium sulfate
Na_2SO_4

Color and luster: White to brownish white, gray; vitreous; streak white.

Hardness: 2½–3

Cleavage: Perfect, one direction.

Other data: *Specific gravity* 2.7; *fracture* uneven to hackly; transparent to translucent; soluble in water; has weak salty taste; somewhat brittle.

Crystals: Orthorhombic; commonly in intergrown clusters; also granular, massive; distinct tabular, short prismatic crystals uncommon; sometimes in sharp crossed twin crystals.

Best field marks: Dissolves readily, is fluorescent in shortwave ultraviolet light, and has weak salty taste.

Similar species: Thenardite lacks the cubic cleavage of halite, and dissolves quicker than glauberite. Thenardite fluoresces white.

Environment: Thenardite forms in chemical sedimentary evaporite deposits in lakes and playas in desert climates. It occurs in bedded deposits associated with halite and borax.

Occurrence: Thenardite was originally described from its occurrence in the salt lake of Espartinas in the province of Madrid, Spain. It occurs at many places throughout the world. In North America the most significant deposits are in California, Arizona, Nevada, and Canada. Fine twinned crystals up to 7.5 cm (3″) in length have come from Soda Lake, on the Carrizo Plain, San Luis Obispo Co., California, and layers of thenardite as much as 1.5 m (5′) thick occur at Searles Lake, San Bernardino Co., California.

The name is after Louis Thenard (1777–1857), French chemist. Thenardite is used in the glass- and paper-making industries.

Barite
Barium sulfate, often with small amounts of strontium
$BaSO_4$

Color and luster: White, gray, colorless, or shades of yellow, brown, red, blue; vitreous, pearly; streak white.

Hardness: $3–3\frac{1}{2}$

Cleavage: Perfect in one direction, good in a second, and distinct in a third.

Other data: *Specific gravity* 4.3 to 4.6; *fracture* uneven; transparent to translucent.

Crystals: Orthorhombic; usually thin to thick tabular crystals; also prismatic crystals, divergent groups, compact, lamellar, fibrous, granular.

Best field mark: High density for light-colored mineral.

Similar species: Calcite and fluorite have different cleavages; feldspars are harder.

Environment: Barite is the commonest barium-bearing mineral. It occurs with anhydrite, apatite, and calcite in carbonatites; with calcite, quartz, and fluorite in mesothermal and epithermal veins, and with gypsum, dolomite, and cerussite in massive hydrothermal replacement deposits.

Occurrence: There is an abundance of localities in North America for fine barite specimens. Spectacular specimens of yellow tabular barite crystals on pale-green fluorite octahedrons have been found at Grand Forks, British Columbia; splendid tabular blue barite crystals in clay near Sterling, Weld Co., Colorado; rich yellow-brown prismatic crystals in barite concretions in Mead Co., South Dakota; and tabular colorless crystals in barite veins in the Palos Verdes hills, Los Angeles Co., California.

The name is from the Greek *barys,* "heavy," in allusion to the mineral's high specific gravity. Barite is used in oil-well-drilling muds and in the manufacture of glass and paints.

98, 369, 410, 423 **Celestite**
Strontium sulfate, sometimes with much barium
SrSO₄

Color and luster:	White, colorless, bluish, reddish; vitreous, pearly; streak white.
Hardness:	3–3½
Cleavage:	Perfect in one direction, good in a second, and distinct in a third.
Other data:	*Specific gravity* 3.9 to 4.0; *fracture* uneven; brittle; transparent to translucent; sometimes fluorescent.
Crystals:	Orthorhombic; usually thin to thick tabular crystals; also fibrous, cleavage masses, nodular; rarely granular or lamellar.
Best field marks:	Light-blue color, which tints only part of a white or colorless crystal.
Similar species:	Celestite is lighter in weight than barite and anglesite, and color zoning of celestite aids in distinguishing it from barite.
Environment:	Celestite forms principally in evaporite deposits of chemical sedimentary rocks, and is usually associated with halite and strontianite.
Occurrence:	The finest celestite specimens come from the United States. It was discovered in excavating the Erie Canal in Niagara Co., New York, and large pale-blue crystals up to 45 cm (18″) in length were obtained in a cave in dolomite at Put-In-Bay, South Bass Island, Lake Erie. Excellent crystals with blue color and sharp crystal form occur at numerous localities in Ohio. Pale-blue celestite occurs with strontianite in geodes of colemanite in the Calico Hills district, San Bernardino Co., California, and large, pale blue, terminated crystals to 8.75 cm (3½″) in length have come from Matehuala, San Luis Potosí, Mexico.

Also called celestine. The name derives from the Latin *caelestis,* "of the sky," in allusion to the mineral's blue color.

Celestite is used in the manufacture of
caustic soda and special glasses.

232, 323, 361 **Anglesite**
Lead sulfate
PbSO$_4$

Color and luster: White, colorless, gray, yellow, green;
adamantine; streak white to grayish.
Hardness: 2½–3
Cleavage: Good in one direction, distinct in
another.
Other data: *Specific gravity* 6.4; *fracture* conchoidal;
transparent to translucent, brittle.
Crystals: Orthorhombic; commonly thin to thick
striated tabular crystals; also granular,
compact, massive, nodular, stalactitic.
Best field marks: Adamantine luster, untwinned crystals,
and high gravity.
Similar species: White color and adamantine luster will
aid in distinguishing anglesite from
barite and celestite. Cerussite has twin
crystals, and anglesite does not.
Environment: Anglesite generally forms in the zone of
alteration in massive hydrothermal
replacement deposits and occurs
associated with barite, anhydrite, and
galena.
Occurrence: Fine crystals have been found in many
mines in W United States and colorless
crystals were obtained from the
Wheatley mines, near Phoenixville,
Chester Co., Pennsylvania. Beautiful
well-formed crystals have been found in
cavities in massive galena at the
Hypotheek Mine, near Kingston,
Shoshone Co., Idaho, and also from the
Yellow Pine Mine, near Good Springs,
Clark Co., Nevada. Anglesite was
abundant in the massive form at Potosi,
Chihuahua, and in crystals in sulfur at
Los Lamentos, Chihuahua, Mexico.

The name is from the Isle of Anglesey,
Wales, where it was discovered.
Anglesite is used as an ore of lead.

100, 151, 429, Anhydrite
496 Calcium sulfate
$CaSO_4$

Color and luster: White, grayish, bluish, reddish to brick-red, pale lavender; vitreous, pearly on one cleavage; streak white to grayish.

Hardness: $3–3\frac{1}{2}$

Cleavage: Good, three directions at 90°.

Other data: *Specific gravity* 2.9 to 3.0; *fracture* uneven; transparent to translucent; sometimes fluorescent; brittle.

Crystals: Orthorhombic; crystals rare; usually massive; also granular, compact, fibrous, cleavable.

Best field marks: Rectangular cleavage fragments, low specific gravity.

Similar species: Gypsum is softer than anhydrite, and calcite does not have 90° cleavages.

Environment: Anhydrite is an important rock-forming mineral in evaporite deposits of chemical sedimentary rocks, where it is associated with halite and gypsum, and it occurs with barite and gypsum in carbonatites.

Occurrence: Anhydrite was first found in the salt deposit near Innsbruck, Austria. Cleavage masses occur at McLaren's Mine, North Burgess, Lanark Co., Ontario, and as large lilac cleavages up to 3.75 cm ($1\frac{1}{2}''$) across in a copper mine at Ajo, Pima Co., Arizona. It also occurs with gypsum and halite in the bedded potash deposits in the Carlsbad district, Eddy Co., New Mexico.

The name is from the Greek and means "without water."

406, 495 Glauberite
Sodium calcium sulfate
$Na_2Ca(SO_4)_2$

Color and luster: Colorless, yellowish, grayish; white powdery coating forms on exposure to air; vitreous, greasy; streak white.

Hardness:	2½–3
Cleavage:	Perfect, one direction.
Other data:	*Specific gravity* 2.7 to 2.8; *fracture* conchoidal; slightly salty taste; brittle.
Crystals:	Monoclinic, tabular; striated on several faces.
Best field marks:	Bitter, salty taste; dissolves slowly in water.
Similar species:	Glauberite lacks the cubic cleavage of halite and dissolves less quickly; calcite is harder than glauberite and has no salty taste.
Environment:	Glauberite is a common constituent of salt deposits. It is usually associated with halite, anhydrite, and thenardite in evaporite deposits of chemical sedimentary rocks.
Occurrence:	The former presence of glauberite, along with anhydrite, is indicated by casts in prehnite and quartz in cavities in basalt at Paterson and Great Notch, Passaic Co., New Jersey, formed when the glauberite was dissolved out of the surrounding mineral matrix. Glauberite occurs with thenardite and halite in the salt beds of Verde Valley, Yavapai Co., Arizona, and as well-formed single crystals in the clays of Saline Valley, Inyo Co., California.

Glauberite is so named because it contains a considerable quantity of the salt Na_2SO_4, which was formerly called Glauber's salt after the German chemist Johann Rudolf Glauber (1604–1668). It is not a common mineral and is not often found in mineral collections, principally because it lacks luster. It is of interest mainly to crystal collectors.

253, 377, 388,	**Gypsum**
394, 471, 472	Hydrous calcium sulfate
	$CaSO_4 \cdot 2H_2O$

Color and luster:	White, colorless, gray, yellow, red, brown, vitreous, pearly on cleavage surfaces; streak white.

Hardness: 1½–2

Cleavage: Perfect in one direction, distinct in two others.

Other data: *Specific gravity* 2.3 to 2.4; *fracture* conchoidal, splintery; transparent to translucent; brittle; thin flakes flexible.

Crystals: Monoclinic; untwinned single crystals showing rhombic form common; may be twinned as arrowhead shape with beveled edges; also granular, massive, fibrous ("satin spar"), earthy.

Best field marks: Softness; flexibility; flat crystals.

Similar species: Gypsum is softer than muscovite, brucite, and calcite. It is not elastic as is muscovite, and it commonly occurs as flat rhombic crystals.

Environment: Gypsum is a very common sulfate mineral. Although it may be found in several rock types, it develops principally in sedimentary rocks of chemical origin, where it forms rock gypsum deposits in beds that may be 10 m (30′) in thickness. It also occurs associated with dolomite and barite in hydrothermal replacement deposits.

Occurrence:  Excellent collecting localities are numerous in North America. At Lockport, Niagara Co., New York, beautiful transparent crystals occur lining cavity walls in dolomite. Large crystals have been found at South Wash, Wayne Co., Utah; clear "textbook" crystals up to 6.5 cm (2½″) in length at Ellsworth, Mahoning Co., Ohio; clusters of brown bladed crystals near Jet, Alfalfa Co., Oklahoma; massive beds near Hillborough, Albert Co., New Brunswick; and crystals up to 1.2 m (4′) long in the Maravilla Mine, Naica, Chihuahua, Mexico.

The name is from *gypsos,* Greek for gypsum or plaster; gypsum is still used for plaster and cement. The colorless transparent variety is called selenite (Greek *selenites,* "moon stone"). Dense granular gypsum is called alabaster, and is used for artistic stone carving.

105 Chalcanthite
Hydrous copper sulfate
$CuSO_4 \cdot 5H_2O$

Color and luster:	Deep blue, sky-blue, greenish blue; vitreous, dull; streak white.
Hardness:	2½
Cleavage:	Distinct.
Other data:	*Specific gravity* 2.28; *fracture* conchoidal, earthy; translucent to transparent; sweetish metallic taste (use taste test cautiously—mineral is poisonous).
Crystals:	Triclinic; usually short prismatic, less commonly thick tabular crystals; also incrusting, stalactitic.
Best field mark:	Readily dissolves in water and produces a blue solution.
Similar species:	Melanterite is green, whereas chalcanthite is blue.
Environment:	Chalcanthite is a secondary copper mineral that forms near the surface in the zone of alteration in all types of hydrothermal replacement deposits; it is commonly associated with aragonite and calcite. Because of the ready solubility of chalcanthite in water, fine specimens must be preserved immediately.
Occurrence:	Excellent chalcanthite has been found in the copper mines at Ducktown, Polk Co., Tennessee, and at Bingham Canyon, Salt Lake Co., Utah; sharp wedge-shaped crystals have been found in small copper mines near Imlay, Pershing Co., Nevada.

The name is from the Greek *chalkos,* "copper," and *anthos,* "flower."

463 Melanterite (Copperas)
Hydrous iron sulfate
$FeSO_4 \cdot 7H_2O$

Color and luster:	White, green, yellowish green; dull yellowish on exposure to air; vitreous, dull; streak white.
Hardness:	2

Cleavage: Perfect in one direction, distinct in another.

Other data: *Specific gravity* 1.9; *fracture* conchoidal, earthy; subtransparent to translucent; taste sweetish, astringent, metallic; brittle.

Crystals: Monoclinic; equant to short prismatic and tabular crystals; also capillary, fibrous, compact, stalactitic, concretionary, powdery.

Best field marks: Sweetish astringent taste and green color.

Similar species: Epsomite can be distinguished by its bitter salty taste.

Environment: Melanterite is a secondary mineral and is generally formed by the oxidation of pyrite or other iron-sulfide minerals in the zone of alteration in massive hydrothermal replacement deposits.

Occurrence: Beautiful deep-green melanterite has been found at The Geysers in Sonoma Co., and in the Alma Mine near Leona Heights, Alameda Co., California. It was found in the zinc mines at Ducktown, Polk Co., Tennessee; in the copper mines at Butte, Montana; at Bingham Canyon, Salt Lake Co., Utah; and at the Comstock Lode, Lincoln Co., Nevada.

Melanterite is named from the Greek *melanteria*, a black metallic pigment made with melanterite. The popular name "copperas" is from the Greek *copperas*, "copper water," which referred to a process of obtaining copper in which a compound of melanterite composition was formed as a by-product.

---

457 Epsomite
Hydrous magnesium sulfate, sometimes with considerable iron
$MgSO_4 \cdot 7H_2O$

Color and luster: White, colorless, gray; vitreous, dull; streak white.

Hardness: 2–2½
Cleavage: Good in one direction, poor in another.
Other data: *Specific gravity* 1.7; *fracture* conchoidal; bitter, salty taste; transparent to translucent; brittle.
Crystals: Orthorhombic; seldom well-crystallized; usually fibrous, botryoidal or reniform masses or crusts.
Best field marks: Salty bitter taste and ready solubility.
Similar species: Melanterite has a green color and a sweetish astringent taste.
Environment: Epsomite generally forms near the surface in fractures and walls of mine workings in the zone of alteration in disseminated hydrothermal replacement deposits. It is usually associated with gypsum and aragonite.
Occurrence: Specific localities where one can collect specimens of epsomite are uncommon, but general localities include the mine workings in the Comstock Lode, Lincoln Co., Nevada, and the Alma Mine near Leona Heights, Alameda Co., California. It occurs with mirabilite (hydrous sodium sulfate) in saline lakes on Kruger Mt., near Oroville, Washington, and as lake deposits near Ashcroft, British Columbia.

The name is from an occurrence at Epsom, England. Epsomite is used medicinally as "Epsom salts."

30, 45   Brochantite
Basic copper sulfate
$Cu_4(SO_4)(OH)_6$

Color and luster: Emerald-green, blackish green; vitreous, pearly on cleavage; streak pale green.
Hardness: 3½–4
Cleavage: Perfect, one direction.
Other data: *Specific gravity* 4.0; *fracture* uneven, conchoidal; transparent to opaque.
Crystals: Monoclinic; small, short prismatic to acicular, sometimes long prismatic or

tabular crystals; also granular, massive, drusy incrustations, loosely incoherent aggregates of acicular crystals.

Best field marks: Vivid green color and occurrence commonly in acicular crystals.

Similar species: Brochantite is a rarer mineral than malachite. Chemical tests are necessary to distinguish between the two.

Environment: Brochantite is a secondary mineral and commonly forms in the zone of alteration in all types of hydrothermal replacement deposits, where it is associated with cerussite, cyanotrichite, and chalcopyrite.

Occurrence: North American localities for brochantite are all in W United States. It occurs in the Alder Creek district, Custer Co., and the Seven Devils district, Adams Co., Idaho. Beautiful deep-emerald-green brochantite formerly occurred in abundance with malachite and azurite at Bisbee, Cochise Co., and in the copper mines at the Clifton-Morenci district, Greenlee Co., Arizona. Fine acicular crystals have come from the Monarch Mine in Chaffee Co., Colorado, and from the mines in the Tintic district, Juab Co., and the Apex Mine in the St. George district, Washington Co., Utah. It has also been found as acicular crystals at the Cerro Gordo Mine, Inyo Co., California.

The name is after A. T. M. Brochant de Villiers (1731–1840), French mineralogist and geologist.

104, 109, 121 Linarite
Basic sulfate of lead and copper
$PbCu(SO_4)(OH)_2$

Color and luster: Deep azure-blue; vitreous to subadamantine; streak pale blue.

Hardness: 2½

Cleavage: Perfect in one direction, poor in another.

Other data: *Specific gravity* 5.35; *fracture* conchoidal;
brittle; transparent to translucent.

Crystals: Monoclinic; elongated prismatic
crystals, often tabular; also in groups or
crusts of nonoriented prismatic crystals.

Best field marks: Deep blue color, hardness, and specific
gravity.

Similar species: Linarite is softer and heavier than
azurite.

Environment: Linarite is a secondary mineral and
forms in the zone of alteration in all
types of hydrothermal replacement
deposits, especially those that contain
lead and copper minerals. Associated
minerals include malachite, cerussite,
smithsonite, and brochantite.

Occurrence: Linarite is not a common mineral, but
it is widespread in small amounts,
principally in copper and lead mines in
W United States. Magnificent crystals,
some of them as much as 10 cm (4″) in
length, have been found in the
Mammoth Mine at Tiger, Pinal Co.,
Arizona. Linarite is known to occur at
Butte, Montana; at Park City and in
the Tintic district at Eureka, both in
Juab Co., Utah; and in Idaho in the
Bay Horse district, Custer Co., and the
Coeur d'Alene district, Shoshone Co.
Well-formed crystals of linarite have
been found in the silver-lead mines at
Cerro Gordo, Inyo Co., California.
Linarite has also come from Beaver
Mt. in the Slocan district and from
the Atlin district, British Columbia.

The name is after the locality at
Linares, Jaen province, Spain.

227 **Jarosite**
Basic hydrous potassium iron sulfate
$KFe_3^{3+}(SO_4)_2(OH)_6$

Color and luster: Amber-yellow, dark brown; vitreous,
resinous; streak pale yellow.

Hardness: 2½–3½

Cleavage: Good, one direction.

Other data: *Specific gravity* 2.9 to 3.3; *fracture* uneven; translucent; brittle.

Crystals: Hexagonal; usually small and indistinct, and either tabular or pseudocubic; also granular, massive, fibrous, incrusting, nodular.

Best field marks: Hexagonal crystals and softness.

Similar species: Although jarosite is softer than limonite, it is a difficult mineral to identify without crystals.

Environment: Jarosite is a secondary mineral and commonly forms in the zone of alteration in massive hydrothermal replacement deposits, where it occurs with barite, turquoise, and galena.

Occurrence: Jarosite is not a common mineral, but it does occur in North America at several places. It forms brilliant crystals in seams and cavities in hematite at the Iron Arrow Mine, Chaffee Co., Colorado, and brownish-yellow crusts on cellular quartz in the Vulture Mine, Maricopa Co., Arizona. Jarosite occurs in hexagonal scales on hematite in the Shattuck-Arizona Mine at Bisbee, Cochise Co., Arizona; as thick tabular brown crystals at Cherry Creek, Mackay district, Custer Co., Idaho; and in veins with turquoise in San Bernardino Co., California.

The name is from the original locality in the Jaroso ravine, Sierra Almagrera, Spain.

---

111 **Cyanotrichite**
Hydrous basic sulfate of copper and aluminum
$Cu_4Al_2SO_4(OH)_{12} \cdot 2H_2O$

Color and luster: Sky-blue to azure-blue; silky; streak pale blue.

Hardness: 3

Cleavage: None.

Other data: *Specific gravity* 2.74; brittle; translucent.

Crystals: Orthorhombic, usually as plush- or wool-like aggregates and coatings of small acicular crystals; also radial-fibrous or tufted.

Best field marks: Plush- or wool-like aggregates and color.

Similar species: Aurichalcite is transparent and is rarely dark blue.

Environment: Cyanotrichite is a secondary mineral and forms in the zone of alteration in all types of hydrothermal replacement deposits.

Occurrence: Excellent cyanotrichite has come from Laurium, Greece, and Leadhills, Scotland. In North America fine specimens have come from the Grandview Mine, Grand Canyon, Coconino Co., Arizona; from the American Eagle Mine, Tintic district, Juab Co., Utah; and from Majuba Hill, Pershing Co., Nevada.

The name is from the Greek words *kyanos* and *thrix*, "blue" and "hair," in reference to the color and typical tufted or hairlike habit.

Chromates

The chromates are compounds of
metallic elements with the chromate
radical. This is a small class of
minerals, and its members are usually
brightly colored. Only one species,
crocoite, is of interest to most
collectors.

212, 213 Crocoite
Lead chromate
$PbCrO_4$

Color and luster: Bright orange-red; adamantine, vitreous; streak orange-yellow.

Hardness: 2½–3

Cleavage: Distinct, one direction; poor in two other directions.

Other data: *Specific gravity* 5.9 to 6.1; *fracture* conchoidal, uneven; brittle and sectile; translucent.

Crystals: Monoclinic; usually prismatic, striated lengthwise; also acicular, granular, columnar, incrusting.

Best field marks: Prismatic crystals, bright orange-red color.

Similar species: Wulfenite does not form in long prismatic crystals; vanadinite forms six-sided prisms; realgar is softer and less dense.

Environment: Crocoite is a secondary lead mineral and forms in the zone of alteration in massive hydrothermal replacement deposits. It is usually associated with wulfenite, cerussite, and vanadinite.

Occurrence: A very rare mineral. The finest specimens come from mines in Tasmania, Australia. In California crocoite has been found with wulfenite at the lead mines at Darwin, Inyo Co., and at the El Dorado Mine, Indio, Riverside Co. A few specimens were also found with wulfenite and vanadinite at the Mammoth Mine at Tiger, Pinal Co., Arizona.

Crocoite is named from the Greek *krókos,* "saffron," in reference to the mineral's deep orange color. It is not regarded as a "North American" species, but is included here because its rarity and spectacular color make crocoite of great interest to collectors.

Phosphates, Arsenates, and Vanadates

This is a large class of minerals and includes compounds of metallic elements with the phosphate, arsenate, and the vanadate radicals. Several members of this class, including apatite and monazite, are primary minerals, but most are secondary and are formed through alteration of metallic-ore minerals, such as sulfides of copper, iron, lead, and zinc. In general, most of these minerals are soft and brittle, and often occur in small inconspicuous masses or crystals. Many are brightly colored and yield very colorful specimens.

102   Triphylite Series

A two-member series consisting of triphylite, the iron-rich end member, and lithiophilite, the manganese-rich end member

Li $(Fe^{2+},Mn^{2+})PO_4$ (triphylite)
Li $(Mn^{2+},Fe^{2+})PO_4$ (lithiophilite)

Color and luster: Gray-blue to gray-blue-green (triphylite), or pinkish to greenish brown (lithiophilite); vitreous to subresinous; streak colorless to grayish white.

Hardness: 4–5

Cleavage: Perfect in one direction, poor in two others at right angles.

Other data: *Specific gravity* 3.34 (lithiophilite) to 3.58 (triphylite); *fracture* uneven; brittle; transparent to translucent.

Crystals: Orthorhombic; crystals rare; usually massive, cleavage masses, compact.

Best field marks: Right-angle cleavages, resinous luster, and occurrence with other granite pegmatite minerals.

Similar species: None is known; occurrence of this series in granite pegmatites is an excellent clue to their identity.

Environment: Triphylite and lithiophilite develop in granite pegmatites, especially complex pegmatites containing lithium and phosphate minerals. Associated minerals include spodumene, albite, beryl, amblygonite, and lepidolite.

Occurrence: Triphylite occurs abundantly in pegmatites in central New Hampshire, especially at the Palermo and other mines at North Groton; at Peru, Newry, Lords Hill, Stoneham, and Black Mtn. in Maine; in the Keystone district, South Dakota, and at Pala, San Diego Co., California. Lithiophilite has been found at Branchville and Portland, Connecticut; at Buckfield, Poland, and Norway in Oxford Co., Maine; in large amounts in the Custer district, South Dakota; at Pala, San Diego Co., California, and in the Yellowknife-Beaulieu area, Northwest Territories, Canada.

The name triphylite is derived from the Greek *phylon,* "tribe," and can be literally interpreted as "threefold family," a reference to the three related cations in the mineral. Lithiophilite is also named from the Greek *philos,* "friend," in allusion to the mineral's affinity for lithium. Members of the triphylite-lithioplhilite series readily alter to a number of secondary minerals, including oxides of manganese and iron.

235, 308 **Monazite**
Phosphate of cerium and lanthanum; usually contains some yttrium, thorium, and uranium
$(Ce,La,Y,Th)PO_4$

Color and luster:	Yellow, yellowish brown, reddish brown; resinous, vitreous; streak white.
Hardness:	$5-5\frac{1}{2}$
Cleavage:	Distinct; sometimes parting in one direction.
Other data:	*Specific gravity* 4.6 to 5.4; *fracture* conchoidal, uneven; transparent to translucent; radioactive; brittle.
Crystals:	Monoclinic; equant, flattened or elongated crystals rare; usually small grains.
Best field marks:	Crystal form, reddish-brown color, and radioactivity.
Similar species:	Zircon is harder than monazite.
Environment:	Monazite develops in igneous and metamorphic rocks. It occurs with quartz and microcline in granite pegmatites; with biotite, albite, and acmite in carbonatites; and in schist and gneiss of regional metamorphic rocks.
Occurrence:	Large crystals, sometimes measuring 27.5 cm (11″) across, have come from pegmatites at Mars Hill, Madison Co., North Carolina. Fine museum specimens with crystals 20 cm (8″) across have been found in pegmatites in the Trout Creek Pass district, Chaffee

Co., Colorado. Small flat crystals of monazite occur in gneisses and schists in North Carolina, where monazite has also been recovered commercially from placer clastic sedimentary deposits.

The name is from the Greek *monazein,* "to be alone," in reference to its rarity when first found. Monazite is used as an ore of thorium and the rare-earth elements cerium, lanthanum, and yttrium.

28, 53, 99,   **Vivianite**
529, 531, 544   Hydrous phosphate of iron
$Fe_3(PO_4)_2 \cdot 8H_2O$

Color and luster:	Blue, green; colorless when fresh, becomes dark blue upon exposure to light; dull, vitreous, pearly on cleavage; streak white, blue, greenish blue.
Hardness:	1½–2
Cleavage:	Perfect, one direction.
Other data:	*Specific gravity* 2.6 to 2.7; *fracture* splintery, earthy; transparent to translucent; sectile; thin flakes flexible.
Crystals:	Monoclinic; usually in short to long prismatic crystals; also radial fibrous, earthy.
Best field marks:	Blue color and streak and micaceous tabular crystals.
Similar species:	Brucite is harder than vivianite and does not become darker upon exposure to light.
Environment:	Vivianite is found as a minor constituent in several environments, including sedimentary rocks, vein deposits, and pegmatites, but its principal occurrence is in disseminated hydrothermal replacement deposits, where it is associated with muscovite, sphalerite, and quartz.
Occurrence:	Vivianite occurs as masses of radiating blades at Mullica Hill, Gloucester Co., New Jersey; and at localities in Maryland; as well-developed crystals in the Ibex Mine, Leadville, Lake Co.,

Colorado; in beautiful blue-green crystals up to 5 cm (2″) in length associated with siderite in the Blackbird district, Lemhi Co., Idaho; and at Côte St. Charles, Vaudreuil Co., Quebec.

The mineral was named after J. G. Vivian, 19th-century English mineralogist.

163, 164 Erythrite
A hydrous arsenate of cobalt and nickel
$Co_3(AsO_4)_2 \cdot 8H_2O$

Color and luster: Deep purple red to bluish pink; vitreous, pearly on cleavage plane; streak pale red to light pink.

Hardness: 1½–2½

Cleavage: Perfect, one direction lengthwise.

Other data: *Specific gravity* 3.06; laminae flexible; sectile; transparent to translucent.

Crystals: Monoclinic; crystals rare but occur in radiating groups of striated acicular and prismatic crystals; usually as pink earthy crusts and in globular or reniform shapes with drusy surfaces.

Best field marks: Vivid purple-red color and the habit of forming thin crusts.

Similar species: None known.

Environment: Erythrite is a secondary mineral and forms by the alteration of arsenides and sulfides of cobalt and nickel in the oxidation zone of mesothermal veins and in hornfels of contact metamorphic rocks, where it occurs with malachite, adamite, and calcite.

Occurrence: Magnificent specimens of erythrite have come from mines at Bou Azzer, Morocco, and Schneeberg, Saxony, Germany. It is a common mineral in the Cobalt area of the Timiskaming district, Ontario, but only as micro crystals. Encrustations of micro crystals have been obtained from the mines in the Blackbird district, Lemhi Co., Idaho, and beautiful acicular crystals up to about 0.5 cm (⅛″) long were found recently in Mina Sara Alicia, near Alamos, Sonora, Mexico.

The name erythrite, a reference to the mineral's color, is from the Greek *erythos,* "red." Erythrite is the cobalt-rich member of a two-member series consisting of erythrite and a closely related nickel-rich mineral, *annabergite,* $(Ni,Co)_3(AsO_4)_2 \cdot 8H_2O$, which usually occurs only as earthy masses or crusts.

62, 78 Variscite
Hydrated phosphate of aluminum and iron
$(Al,Fe)PO_4 \cdot 2H_2O$

Color and luster:	Pale green to emerald-green, also bluish green, colorless; vitreous, waxy; streak white.
Hardness:	4–4½
Cleavage:	Good in one direction, poor in second direction.
Other data:	*Specific gravity* 2.57; *fracture* uneven, splintery, conchoidal; transparent in crystals, translucent to opaque in massive form; brittle.
Crystals:	Orthorhombic; crystals very rare; usually as fine-grained masses, nodules, veinlets, crusts.
Best field marks:	Green color and occurrence usually as nodules.
Similar species:	Turquoise usually has a bluish color and is slightly denser than variscite.
Environment:	Variscite is a low-temperature mineral and generally occurs associated with apatite, chalcedony, and limonite in massive hydrothermal replacement deposits.
Occurrence:	Localities in North America where variscite may be found appear to be located only in W United States. The finest material comes from Clay Canyon, near Fairfield, Utah Co., Utah. Variscite also occurs in Esmeralda and Mineral Cos., Nevada.

The name is from Variscia, an ancient district in Germany where the mineral was first found. Variscite is used as a gemstone.

---

61 Conichalcite
Basic arsenate of calcium and copper
$CaCu(AsO_4)(OH)$

Color and luster:	Grass-green to yellowish green; vitreous, greasy; streak green.
Hardness:	4½
Cleavage:	None.
Other data:	*Specific gravity* 4.33; *fracture* uneven; subtranslucent.
Crystals:	Orthorhombic; usually equant to stubby prismatic; also as botryoidal to reniform crusts and masses with radial fibrous structure.
Best field mark:	Vivid grass-green color.
Similar species:	Unlike brochantite, conichalcite has no cleavage and is grass-green in color.
Environment:	Conichalcite is a secondary copper mineral and generally develops in the zone of alteration in all types of hydrothermal replacement deposits, where it is associated with linarite, azurite, and malachite.
Occurrence:	Fine specimens of conichalcite have come from the American Eagle Mine, Tintic district, Juab Co., Utah; from the Higgins Mine at Bisbee, Cochise Co., Arizona; from the Bristol Mine, Lincoln Co., the Empire-Nevada Mine, near Yerington, Lyon Co., and from Good Springs, Clark Co., Nevada.

The name is from the Greek *konis,* "powder," and *chalx,* "lime."

46, 379   Austinite
Basic arsenate of calcium and zinc
$CaZnAsO_4OH$

Color and luster: Colorless to pale yellowish white or bright green; subadamantine; streak white to pale green.

Hardness: $4–4\frac{1}{2}$

Cleavage: Good, one direction lengthwise.

Other data: *Specific gravity* 4.13; *fracture* uneven; transparent to translucent.

Crystals: Orthorhombic; usually in minute elongated bladed or acicular crystals; also as radial fibrous crusts and nodules.

Best field marks: Minute bladed crystals, color, and occurrence in hydrothermal replacement environments.

Similar species: Adamite has two cleavage directions and is softer and more dense than austinite.

Environment: Austinite is a secondary mineral and forms in the zone of alteration in hydrothermal replacement deposits, where it occurs with adamite in cavities in massive limonite.

Occurrence: Austinite is an uncommon mineral and has been reported mainly at Gold Hill, Tooele Co., Utah, and in Mina Ojuela, Mapimi, Durango, Mexico.

Austinite is named for the American mineralogist Austin F. Rogers (1877–1957).

216, 237, 508   Descloizite Series
A two-member series, of which the more common member is descloizite, the zinc-rich end member, and the other member is mottramite, the copper-rich end member
$Pb(Zn,Cu)VO_4OH$ (descloizite)
$Pb(Cu,Zn)VO_4OH$ (mottramite)

Color and luster: Brown, reddish-brown to black (descloizite), becoming grass-green to olive-green in mottramite; greasy; streak orange to brownish-red and yellow (descloizite), and greenish (mottramite).

Hardness: 3–3½

Cleavage: None.

Other data: *Specific gravity* 6.2 (descloizite) to 5.9 (mottramite); *fracture* uneven to conchoidal; brittle; transparent to opaque.

Crystals: Orthorhombic; usually small pyramidal or prismatic crystals with uneven faces; also stalactitic and mammillary crusts; massive and granular.

Best field marks: Pyramidal or prismatic crystals, color, and association with other alteration minerals.

Similar species: None.

Environment: Descloizite and mottramite are secondary minerals, occurring in the zone of alteration in hydrothermal replacement deposits, especially those of copper, lead, and vanadium; they are associated with vanadinite, wulfenite, pyromorphite, and cerussite.

Occurrence: North American localities for the descloizite minerals seem to be confined to the W United States and Mexico. Descloizite and mottramite occur together in the Mammoth Mine, Pinal Co., Arizona, and mottramite occurs by itself in the Silver Star district, Montana. Descloizite is a common mineral in the Georgetown district, Grant Co., New Mexico.

Descloizite was named after Alfred L. O. L. Des Cloizeau (1817–1897), a French mineralogist. Mottramite was named after Mottram St. Andrews, the locality in Cheshire, England, where the mineral was first found. They are minor ores of copper, lead, and zinc.

301, 316, 324,   **Amblygonite**
391, 397   Basic fluophosphate of aluminum,
sodium, and lithium
$(Li,Na)Al(PO_4)(F,OH)$

Color and luster: Colorless, white (milky to creamy),
yellowish, beige, green, blue, gray;
vitreous, greasy, pearly on cleavage;
streak white.

Hardness: 5½–6

Cleavage: Perfect in one direction, good in three
others.

Other data: *Specific gravity* 3.1; *fracture* uneven to
subconchoidal; transparent to
translucent; fluorescent; brittle.

Crystals: Triclinic; usually equant to short
prismatic crystals; also compact, large
cleavage masses.

Best field mark: Lath-shaped crystals.

Similar species: It is difficult to distinguish between
orthoclase and amblygonite by physical
properties, but amblygonite commonly
occurs as lath-shaped crystals.

Environment: Amblygonite occurs almost exclusively
in granite pegmatites along with
lepidolite, spodumene, and tourmaline.

Occurrence: Very fine crystals up to 11.25 cm (4½″)
in diameter have come from a
pegmatite on Plumbago Mt. near
Newry, Oxford Co., Maine, and large
masses embedded in quartz or feldspar
in pegmatites occur in the Black Hills
of South Dakota and San Diego Co.,
California.

The name is from the Greek
amblygonios, "blunt angle."
Amblygonite is used as a source of
lithium and as a minor gemstone.

36, 50   **Olivenite**
Basic arsenate of copper
Cu_2AsO_4OH

Color and luster: Olive-green, greenish-brown, brown,
yellowish; vitreous to subadamantine;
streak colorless.

Hardness: 3

Cleavage: Poor, two directions.

Other data: *Specific gravity* 3.9 to 4.5; *fracture* conchoidal to irregular; translucent to opaque; brittle.

Crystals: Orthorhombic; often elongated or short prismatic to acicular crystals, rarely tabular; also in globular and reniform shapes with fibrous structure; massive, granular, earthy, nodular.

Best field marks: Dissolves readily in hydrochloric acid and fuses easily.

Similar species: Olivenite is much softer than epidote, which is also not soluble in hydrochloric acid.

Environment: Olivenite is a secondary mineral and forms in the alteration zone of hydrothermal replacement deposits, where it occurs with adamite, malachite, azurite, and limonite.

Occurrence: Olivenite originally came from the famous copper mines at Cornwall, England, but in North America it seems to be found largely in mines in W United States. It is associated with cassiterite and tourmaline in rhyolite at Majuba Hill, Pershing Co., Nevada, and occurs in the Blackbird district, Lemhi Co., Idaho. Good specimens have been found in the American Eagle and Mammoth mines in the Tintic district, Juab Co., Utah.

Olivenite is named from the German *Olivenerz,* "olive ore," with reference to its color. It is most popular with micromount collectors.

55, 328, 340 **Adamite**
Basic arsenate of zinc; some copper may be present
$Zn_2(AsO_4)(OH)$

Color and luster: Light yellow, honey-yellow, brownish yellow, pale green, yellowish green, rarely colorless; vitreous; streak white to pale greenish.

Hardness: 3½

Cleavage: Good in one direction, poor in second direction.

Other data: *Specific gravity* 4.32 to 4.48; *fracture* uneven; transparent to translucent; fluoresces yellow-green.

Crystals: Orthorhombic; usually prismatic or horizontally elongated; often as drusy crusts or aggregates.

Best field marks: Wedge-shaped drusy crystals, brilliant fluorescence, and color.

Similar species: Smithsonite does not fluoresce as does adamite.

Environment: Adamite is usually found with limonite and calcite in the so-called oxidized zone of lode hydrothermal replacement deposits.

Occurrence: Superb crystals have come from Cap Garonne, Le Pradet, near Hyeres, France, and several localities in North America have yielded excellent specimens. Beautiful, strongly fluorescent adamite occurs as well-formed crystals in cavities in massive limonite at Ojuela Mine, Mapimi, Durango, Mexico. Small crystals that make fine micromounts occur in the Gold Hill Mine, Gold Hill, Tooele Co., Utah, and colorless crystals occur at Chloride Cliff, Death Valley, Inyo Co., California.

The name is after Gilbert-Joseph Adam (1795–1881), French mineralogist.

38, 72, 136, **Apatite**
197, 229, 251, Calcium fluorine-chlorine-hydroxyl
329, 696 phosphate, often with some manganese and cerium
$Ca_5(PO_4)_3(F,Cl,OH)$

Color and luster: Green, brown, red, yellow, violet, pink, white, colorless; greasy, vitreous; streak white.

Hardness: 5

Cleavage: Poor, one direction crosswise.

Other data: *Specific gravity* 3.1 to 3.2; *fracture*

uneven, conchoidal; transparent to translucent; brittle.

Crystals: Hexagonal; usually short to long prismatic; frequently tabular; also massive, coarse granular to compact, stalactitic, earthy, oolitic.

Best field marks: Shape of crystals, hardness, and greasy luster.

Similar species: Beryl is harder than apatite, and green tourmaline is usually striated lengthwise. Tourmaline does not develop in six-sided crystals, the characteristic form of apatite.

Environment: Apatite is the commonest of all phosphorous-bearing minerals. It develops in many igneous rocks as a minor accessory mineral and is also formed in certain metamorphic rocks. It occurs with titanite and magnetite in many plutonic rocks; with albite and muscovite in granite pegmatites; with acmite and nepheline in nepheline syenite pegmatites; and with andradite and phlogopite in hornfels of contact metamorphic rocks.

Occurrence: Some of the most beautiful apatite has come from Ehrenfriedersdorf, Saxony, Germany, and from Spain, but North America is not without several excellent localities. Some very large crystals, up to 30 cm (12″) in length, have come from marble deposits in Ottawa Co., Ontario. Beautiful crystals up to 7.5 cm (3″) in length occur with actinolite at Pelham, Hampshire Co., Massachusetts. Crystals of apatite closely resembling green tourmaline occur in the Himalaya Mine, Mesa Grande, San Diego Co., California, and splendid yellow apatite crystals occur in iron mines at Ciudad Durango, Durango, Mexico.

The name derives from the Greek *apate*, "deceit," in allusion to its being confused with other minerals such as aquamarine, olivine, and fluorite. Apatite is widely used in the manufacture of phosphate fertilizers.

22   Pyromorphite

Lead chlorophosphate; may contain a small amount of arsenic
$Pb_5(PO_4)_3Cl$

Color and luster: Green, yellow, brown, white, gray; resinous, greasy, adamantine; streak pale yellow, white, greenish yellow.

Hardness: 3½–4

Cleavage: None.

Other data: *Specific gravity* 7.1; *fracture* subconchoidal, uneven; translucent; brittle.

Crystals: Hexagonal; usually prismatic, barrel-shaped, often with cavernous basal terminations; also incrusting, reniform, disseminated.

Best field marks: Cavernous crystals, lack of transparency, and luster.

Similar species: Vanadinite is generally bright red-brown-orange, whereas pyromorphite is usually green. Mimetite rarely appears in cavernous hexagonal crystals. Otherwise blowpipe tests are necessary to distinguish one from the other.

Environment: Pyromorphite is formed in the zone of alteration in massive hydrothermal replacement deposits and is usually associated with barite and vanadinite.

Occurrence: Excellent pyromorphite occurs with cerussite and galena on the Society Girl claim, Steel mining district, British Columbia, and beautiful drusy green crystals occur at several mines in the Coeur d'Alene district, Shoshone Co., Idaho. Pale greenish-gray pyromorphite crystals occur with wulfenite at the Ojuela Mine, Mapimi, Durango, Mexico.

The name is from the Greek *pyr,* "fire," and *morphe,* "form," in reference to the fact that a melted globule assumes a crystalline shape on cooling.
Pyromorphite is a minor ore of lead.

294, 295, 296, **Mimetite**
342 Lead chloroarsenate
$Pb_5(AsO_4)_3Cl$

Color and luster: Yellow, orange, brown; resinous; streak
nearly white.
Hardness: $3\frac{1}{2}$–4
Cleavage: Poor.
Other data: *Specific gravity* 7.0 to 7.3; *fracture*
subconchoidal to uneven; transparent to
translucent; brittle.
Crystals: Monoclinic; pseudohexagonal;
generally slender to thick needles,
rarely tabular; also globular, reniform,
incrusting.
Best field marks: Luster and frequent globular form
Similar species: Because of the close similarity between
mimetite, pyromorphite, and
vanadinite, one must rely upon
blowpipe tests to distinguish between
them.
Environment: Mimetite is formed in the zone of
alteration in massive hydrothermal
replacement deposits, and is generally
associated with barite, galena, and
vanadinite.
Occurrence: Mimetite is less common than
pyromorphite, but some excellent
exhibit specimens have come from
Tsumeb, South-West Africa, and
Broken Hill, New South Wales,
Australia. Mimetite was found at
Phoenixville, Chester Co.,
Pennsylvania; as bright orange-yellow
globular masses in the No. 79 Mine,
Banner district, Gila Co., Arizona; and
at the Bilbao Mine, Ojo Caliente,
Zacatecas, Mexico.
The name is from the Greek *mimetes,*
"imitator," from its resemblance to
pyromorphite. Mimetite is a minor ore
of lead.

183, 195, 206, **Vanadinite**
265, 291, 339, Lead chlorovanadate, sometimes with
546 small amount of arsenic
$Pb_5(VO_4)_3Cl$

Color and luster: Ruby-red, orange, brown, yellow,
multicolored; greasy, adamantine,
resinous; streak white, pale yellow.

Hardness: 3

Cleavage: None.

Other data: *Specific gravity* 6.7 to 7.2; *fracture*
uneven, conchoidal; transparent to
translucent; brittle.

Crystals: Hexagonal; usually small prismatic
crystals, sometimes hollow; also
fibrous, incrusting, compact, globular.

Best field marks: Red color and lustrous nature.

Similar species: Pyromorphite and mimetite rarely
occur in red lustrous crystals; crocoite
crystals are striated.

Environment: Vanadinite is a secondary mineral and
generally develops in the zone of
alteration in massive hydrothermal
replacement deposits, where it is
associated with galena, wulfenite, and
barite.

Occurrence: Many of the North American localities
for vanadinite are in SW United States
and Mexico. Exceptionally fine yellow,
red, and brown crystals up to 1.5 cm
(½″) in length have come from the
Sierra Grande Mine, Hillsboro district,
Sierra Co., New Mexico, and brilliant
red crystals from the Apache Mine,
Globe district, Gila Co., Arizona.
Good specimens of red crystals have
been found in the El Dorado Mine, near
Indio, Riverside Co., California. Red-
brown vanadinite crystals up to 1.5 cm
(½″) in length occur in calcite at Villa
Ahumada, Sierra Los Lamentos district,
Chihuahua, Mexico.

The name is derived from the mineral's
composition. Vanadinite is used as a
minor ore of lead.

86, 90, 93 Lazulite
A basic phosphate of magnesium, iron, and aluminum
$(Mg,Fe)Al_2(PO_4)_2(OH)_2$

Color and luster:	Deep blue, sky-blue, pale greenish blue; vitreous to dull; streak white.
Hardness:	5½–6
Cleavage:	Distinct, one direction.
Other data:	*Specific gravity* 3.0 to 3.1; *fracture* uneven; transparent to opaque; brittle.
Crystals:	Monoclinic; usually bipyramidal or tabular; also granular, compact.
Best field marks:	Light- to dark-blue color and bipyramidal crystals.
Similar species:	Vesuvianite is harder and denser than lazulite, and both sodalite and lazurite have lower specific gravity than lazulite.
Environment:	Lazulite forms in plutonic and metamorphic rocks. It is associated with quartz and muscovite in schist of regional metamorphic rocks; and with quartz, muscovite, hematite, and topaz in massive hydrothermal replacement deposits.
Occurrence:	Sharp pale-blue crystals of lazulite occur in granular quartz on Graves Mt., Lincoln Co., Georgia. Lazulite masses and prismatic crystals occur with quartz, hematite, muscovite, and topaz at the Champion Mine, Mono Co., and in Stevenson Meadow, Madera Co., California.

The name is from an old Arabic word *lazaward,* "heaven," a reference to the mineral's blue color. Lazulite is used as a gemstone.

47, 77, 113,   **Turquoise**
130, 659   Hydrous basic phosphate of copper and
aluminum; may contain some iron
$CuAl_6(PO_4)_4(OH)_8 \cdot 4-5H_2O$

Color and luster: Sky-blue, bluish green, apple-green;
waxy, dull, streak white, pale green.

Hardness: 5–6

Cleavage: None.

Other data: *Specific gravity* 2.6 to 2.8; *fracture*
conchoidal; subtranslucent to opaque.

Crystals: Triclinic; crystals rare; usually compact,
reniform, stalactitic, incrusting, thin
seams, disseminated.

Best field mark: Bright blue-green color.

Similar species: Turquoise can be distinguished from
variscite only on the basis of blowpipe
tests; chrysocolla is softer.

Environment: Turquoise forms as a secondary mineral
in the zone of alteration in disseminated
hydrothermal replacement deposits.

Occurrence: The finest turquoise comes from the
southwest slope of the Ali-Mirsa-Kuh
Mts., near Nishapur, Khurasan, Iran.
In North America turquoise is found
mostly in SW United States and rarely
in Virginia and Mexico. Nodular
masses, several weighing over 70 kg
(150 pounds) each, were found near
Battle Mt., Lander Co., Nevada, and
at No. 8 Mine, Lynn district, New
Mexico. Arizona, California, and
Colorado have yielded fair turquoise.
Microscopic crystals of turquoise occur
in fractured quartz in a small copper
prospect near Lynch Station, Campbell
Co., Virginia.

Gemstone data: Gem-quality turquoise ranges in color
from pale blue to bright blue. Vein
turquoise is usually poor in quality and
does not take the polish that can be
given to nodular turquoise. Much
turquoise is porous, but it can be
plastic-impregnated before use.
Turquoise is used for cabochons or
carved. The finest specimens come from
Iran, but some fine material has come
from mines in SW United States.
Turquoise is a birthstone for December.

The name was originally French, *turquoise,* "Turkish." It originally referred to material from the great localities in Persia (now Iran), which had passed through Turkey via the old trade routes and was mistakenly believed to have been excavated there.

292, 333, 337, 341   **Legrandite**
Hydrous basic zinc arsenate
$Zn_2(AsO_4)(OH) \cdot H_2O$

Color and luster:	Colorless to canary-yellow, orange; vitreous; streak white.
Hardness:	5
Cleavage:	Poor, one direction.
Other data:	*Specific gravity* 4.01; *fracture* uneven; transparent; brittle.
Crystals:	Monoclinic; usually radiating aggregates of prismatic crystals.
Best field mark:	Yellow radiating aggregates in limonite.
Similar species:	Adamite is similar but lacks the intense yellow color.
Environment:	Legrandite is a secondary mineral and develops in the zone of alteration in massive hydrothermal replacement deposits that contain arsenopyrite and sphalerite. Minerals usually associated with legrandite are limonite, siderite, adamite, pyrite, and sphalerite.
Occurrence:	Legrandite has been collected at the Flor de Peña Mine, Lampazos, Nuevo León, Mexico, where it occurs on massive sphalerite. The premier locality is the Ojuela Mine, Mapimi, Durango, Mexico.

The mineral is named for a Belgian mine manager named Legrand, who first collected the material at the Flor de Peña Mine.

51, 63, 487, **Wavellite**
490 Hydrous basic aluminum phosphate,
often with some fluorine and iron
$Al_3(PO_4)_2(OH)_3 \cdot 5H_2O$

Color and luster: Green, yellow, white, gray, brown;
vitreous, pearly; streak white.

Hardness: $3\frac{1}{2}$–4

Cleavage: Perfect in one direction, good in two
others.

Other data: *Specific gravity* 2.3 to 2.4; *fracture*
uneven, conchoidal; transparent to
translucent.

Crystals: Orthorhombic; stout to long prismatic
and striated, but rare; usually radial
fibrous and globular hemispheres with
crystalline surface (botryoidal crusts);
also stalactitic.

Best field marks: Distinctive botryoidal crusts and green
color.

Similar species: Wavellite is not a striking mineral and
its form in botryoidal crusts might be
mistaken for chalcedony, but it is
softer.

Environment: Wavellite is a secondary mineral and
commonly develops in the zone of
alteration in hornfels of contact
metamorphic rocks, where it is
associated with quartz and muscovite,
and in the upper alteration zone of
epithermal veins, where it occurs with
turquoise, limonite, and quartz.

Occurrence: The finest specimens of wavellite have
come from Garland, Hot Springs, and
Montgomery Cos., Arkansas. Small
colorless crystals that make attractive
micromounts occur at Moores Hill,
Cumberland Co., Pennsylvania, and
thin crusts of pale-gray crystals occur in
the King turquoise mine, near Villa
Grove, Saguache Co., Colorado.

The name is after William Wavell
(d. 1829), an English physician who
discovered the mineral.

67, 69   Torbernite
Hydrated phosphate of copper and uranium
$Cu(UO_2)_2(PO_4)_2 \cdot 8–12H_2O$

Color and luster: Emerald- and grass-green, sometimes leek-green, apple-green, or siskin-green; pearly on cleavage, vitreous to subadamantine in other directions; streak greenish.

Hardness: $2–2\frac{1}{2}$

Cleavage: Perfect, one direction; micaceous.

Other data: *Specific gravity* 3.22; *fracture* not visible; transparent to translucent; laminae somewhat brittle.

Crystals: Tetragonal; usually thin to thick square tabular crystals; also forms foliated, micaceous, and scaly aggregates.

Best field marks: Square outline of crystals and distinct green color.

Similar species: Torbernite has a stronger green color than autunite. Autunite is also fluorescent in UV light; torbernite is not.

Environment: Torbernite is a secondary mineral and forms along with autunite in the alteration zone of hydrothermal veins and pegmatites that contain uraninite and copper sulfides.

Occurrence: Torbernite occurs as an alteration product of uraninite in pegmatites at Haddam Neck, Connecticut; in pegmatites of the Black Hills, South Dakota; and at Chalk Mt., Mitchell Co., North Carolina. Beautiful specimens have come from Mina Candelaria, Moctezuma, Sonora, Mexico.

Torbernite is named after Torbern Bergmann (1735–1784), a Swedish chemist. It is a minor ore of uranium.

57, 347   **Autunite**
Hydrous phosphate of calcium and
uranium, often with some barium and
magnesium
$Ca(UO_2)_2(PO_4)_2 \cdot 10-12H_2O$

Color and luster: Lemon- to sulfur-yellow, yellowish-
green, green; pearly, subadamantine;
streak yellowish.

Hardness: 2–2½

Cleavage: Perfect, one direction.

Other data: *Specific gravity* 3.1 to 3.2; flakes brittle;
transparent to translucent; strongly
fluorescent (pale yellow-green).

Crystals: Tetragonal; usually thin tabular
crystals; also foliated, scaly micaceous
aggregates.

Best field marks: Vivid lemon-yellow color and yellow
streak, flat tabular crystals, and strong
fluorescence.

Similar species: Willemite has similar response to UV
light, but is harder than autunite, has
higher gravity, and is not found in
pegmatites.

Environment: Autunite is a secondary uranium
mineral and develops in the zones of
alteration in granite pegmatites and
hypothermal veins, where it occurs
with uraninite and microcline.

Occurrence: The finest North American material
comes from the Daybreak Mine, Mt.
Spokane, Spokane Co., Washington,
where magnificent specimens
containing well-formed crystals and
divergent aggregates of vivid yellow-
green coloration have been obtained.
The Ruggles Mine, near Grafton
Center, Grafton Co., New Hampshire,
has yielded some fine specimens of
autunite, and so have pegmatites in
mines at Spruce Pine and Penland in
North Carolina, near Keystone in South
Dakota, and in the White Signal
district, Grant Co., New Mexico.

The name is after the locality at Autun,
Saône-et-Loire, France. Autunite is an
ore of uranium.

Vanadium Oxysalts

The vanadium oxysalts are compounds of metallic elements with the vanadate radical. This is a small class of minerals of which the most interesting for collectors is carnotite, an important ore of uranium. Members of this class are soft, brittle, and brightly colored.

351   **Carnotite**
Hydrous potassium uranium vanadate
$K_2(UO_2)_2(VO_4)_2 \cdot 1–3H_2O$

Color and luster: Bright yellow, lemon-yellow, greenish yellow; dull, earthy, pearly, silky when coarsely crystalline; streak yellow.

Hardness: 2

Cleavage: Perfect, one direction.

Other data: *Specific gravity* 4 to 5; sectile.

Crystals: Monoclinic; usually powdery, loosely coherent, fine crystalline aggregates, disseminated.

Best field mark: Bright-yellow color.

Similar species: None.

Environment: Carnotite is a secondary uranium mineral that occurs chiefly in sandstones, where it was formed by the action of water on preexisting uranium and vanadium materials. Carnotite also forms in massive hydrothermal replacement deposits.

Occurrence: Important deposits of carnotite occur in SW Colorado, SE Utah, NE Arizona, and NW New Mexico. Carnotite occurs in the Pottsville conglomerate near Mauch Chunk, Carbon Co., Pennsylvania.

The name is after Marie-Adolfe Carnot (1839–1920), French engineer and chemist. Carnotite is an important ore of uranium.

Molybdates and Tungstates

The molybdates and tungstates are compounds of metallic elements with the molybdate and tungstate radicals, respectively. These minerals as a rule are heavy, soft, brittle, and dark or vividly colored.

179, 210, 266, 625, 626 **Wolframite Series**

A three-member series consisting of huebnerite, the manganese-rich end member, wolframite, the iron-manganese intermediate member, and ferberite, the iron-rich end member

$MnWO_4$(huebnerite)

$(Fe,Mn)WO_4$(wolframite)

$FeWO_4$(ferberite)

Color and luster: Reddish-brown (huebnerite) to black (ferberite); submetallic to resinous (huebnerite); streak reddish-brown (huebnerite) to black (ferberite).

Hardness: 4–4½

Cleavage: Perfect, one direction lengthwise; parting in some specimens.

Other data: *Specific gravity* 7.12 to 7.51; *fracture* uneven; huebnerite is transparent and ferberite nearly opaque; ferberite is weakly magnetic.

Crystals: Monoclinic; huebnerite usually in long prismatic striated crystals; wolframite in short prismatic, flattened striated crystals; ferberite in elongated striated crystals, rarely flattened. All may be granular massive or bladed. Twinning (usually as simple contact twins) is common in all members.

Best field marks: Single cleavage, high gravity, crystal form, and brown to black color.

Similar species: Huebnerite resembles goethite in color, but is heavier and softer; their cleavage and crystal form distinguish members of the wolframite series from cassiterite and columbite-tantalite.

Environment: Members of the wolframite series are found in hypothermal and mesothermal veins and in pegmatites that are very closely associated with granitic rocks. Associated minerals include cassiterite, arsenopyrite, hematite, tourmaline, lepidolite, topaz, fluorite, quartz, and feldspar.

Occurrence: Colorado has produced many fine specimens of ferberite and huebnerite. Beautiful black crystals of ferberite occur with hematite, scheelite, pyrite, and adularia in mesothermal veins in

Boulder and Gilpin Cos., Colorado, and huebnerite has come from mines in the Uncompahgre district in Ouray Co. and near Silverton and Gladstone in San Juan Co., Colorado. Huebnerite occurs in the Blue Wing district, Lemhi Co., Idaho, with ferberite in veins and pegmatites near Deadwood, Custer Co., South Dakota, and in mines near Ellsworth, Nye Co., Nevada. Specimens have been taken from numerous mines in Arizona and New Mexico, and red-brown crystals of huebnerite have been found recently in quartz veins near Townesville, Vance Co., North Carolina.

Huebnerite was named for Adolph Huebner, a metallurgist of Freiberg, Saxony. Ferberite was named for Adolph Ferber of Gera, Germany. Wolframite was named for tungsten (*Wolfram* in German), of which it is an ore. There is some question as to how *Wolfram* itself was named. The 16th-century mineralogist Agricola suggested that the name derived from the words *volf*, "wolf," and *rahm*, "cream," in allusion to an objectionable scum that formed during the smelting of ores containing tungsten. Huebnerite and ferberite are also important ores of tungsten.

245, 289, 321 **Scheelite**
Calcium tungstate, frequently with small amounts of molybdenum
$CaWO_4$

Color and luster: White, colorless, gray, yellowish, orange, brownish, greenish; vitreous, adamantine; streak white to yellowish.
Hardness: $4\frac{1}{2}$–5
Cleavage: Distinct in one direction, poor in two others.
Other data: *Specific gravity* 5.9 to 6.1; *fracture* conchoidal, uneven; transparent to

translucent; strongly fluorescent.

Crystals: Tetragonal; usually dipyramidal (pseudo-octahedral), frequently tabular; also incrusting, granular, compact.

Best field marks: High gravity, softness, and pseudo-octahedral crystals.

Similar species: Fluorite often fluoresces a bluish-white color, similar to that of scheelite, but the high gravity of scheelite is sufficient to differentiate it.

Environment: Scheelite develops principally in metamorphic rocks, but also in veins and pegmatites. It is associated with grossular, epidote, and calcite in hornfels of contact metamorphic rocks; with quartz and stibnite in epithermal veins; and with green beryl, oligoclase, muscovite, and quartz in granite pegmatites.

Occurrence: Scheelite has been mined at many localities in North America, especially in British Columbia and W United States. The largest operating mine is on Pine Creek, near Bishop, Inyo Co., California, where scheelite occurs with garnet, epidote, and molybdenite in metamorphosed limestone. Fine orange-brown crystals have been obtained from the Mineral Mts., near Milford, Beaver Co., Utah, and from the Cohen Mine, Cabezas Mts., Cochise Co., Arizona. Colorless etched crystals and masses of sufficient size to be cut into brilliant gems of many carats have come from mines on Greenhorn Mt., Kern Co., California. Large masses of pale-gray, coarsely crystalline scheelite, weighing as much as 8 metric tonnes (10 tons), have been mined from veins at Atolia, San Bernardino Co., California. Scheelite was mined along with stibnite in the antimony mines at Yellow Pine, Idaho, and coarsely crystalline scheelite was mined from a pegmatite at Oreana, Pershing Co., Nevada. Scheelite occurs with stibnite in the Bridge River district, British Columbia, and in quartz veins in Halifax Co., Nova Scotia.

Scheelite is named for Karl Wilhelm Scheele (1742–1786), Swedish chemist, who determined the presence of tungstic oxide in scheelite. It is an important ore of tungsten.

275, 290, 298, 299, 300, 344, 345   **Wulfenite**
Lead molybdate
$PbMoO_4$

Color and luster:	Yellow, orange, brown, yellowish gray, whitish; resinous, adamantine; streak white.
Hardness:	3
Cleavage:	Distinct, one direction.
Other data:	*Specific gravity* 6.5 to 7.0; *fracture* subconchoidal, uneven; transparent to translucent.
Crystals:	Triclinic, pseudo-tetragonal due to twinning; commonly square tabular, sometimes extremely thin; infrequently cube-like; also massive, coarse to fine granular.
Best field marks:	Brilliant colors and tabular habit.
Similar species:	None.
Environment:	Wulfenite is a secondary mineral and generally forms in the zone of alteration in massive hydrothermal replacement deposits that contain significant lead mineralization. Barite, sphalerite, and molybdenite are common associates. Wulfenite also occurs with molybdenite, barite, and calcite in carbonatites.
Occurrence:	Many of the choice collecting localities for wulfenite are in SW United States and Mexico. Beautiful bright orange-red crystals have come from the Red Cloud and Hamburg mines in the Trigo Mts., Yuma Co., and thin tabular orange-yellow crystals, about 1.5 cm (½″) across, from the Rawley Mine, near Theba, Maricopa Co., Arizona. Fine specimens have been obtained from mines in the Central district, Grant Co., New Mexico, and perhaps the most exceptional specimens

from Villa Ahumada, Sierra de Los Lamentos, Chihuahua, Mexico.

The name is in honor of Franz Xaver von Wulfen (1728–1805), Austrian mineralogist. Wulfenite is a minor ore of lead.

Silicates

The silicates constitute the largest and commonest class of minerals. They are translucent, at least in thin splinters, and on the average are lower in specific gravity and harder than most minerals. Water is present in a number of them, especially in the zeolites, where it is loosely bound. In other species, water is strongly held and cannot be removed without destroying the mineral. Regardless of their complex nature, silicates all contain the silicate atomic structure, whose fundamental building block is the tetrahedron, in which one silicon atom is surrounded by four equally spaced oxygen atoms. The structure of the tetrahedron corresponds to the four-sided tetrahedron in the isometric crystal system. The silicon atom is inside the tetrahedron at the center, and the oxygen atoms occupy the four corners of the tetrahedron. The number and manner of linking of the silicon-oxygen tetrahedrons are the basis upon which the different silicate structures are formed.

Tectosilicates (Framework Silicates)
In the tectosilicates every silica
tetrahedron shares the oxygen ion at
each of its corners with another
tetrahedron. These tend to be stable,
strongly bonded minerals of low specific
gravity; quartz and the feldspars are
typical.

153–156, 160,
370, 372, 385,
396, 431,
526, 545, 661,
673, 674, 690,
699

Quartz
Silicon dioxide
SiO_2

Color and luster: White, colorless, and in various shades
as follows: *rock crystal,* transparent,
colorless; *amethyst,* purple; *rose quartz,*
pink, rose-red; *citrine,* clear yellow;
smoky quartz, pale brown to black; *milky
quartz,* milk-white; *aventurine,*
glistening with enclosed scales of mica
or hematite; *cat's eye,* opalescent from
inclusions of asbestos; and *tigereye,* with
lustrous yellow to brown parallel fibers;
vitreous, greasy luster; streak white.

Hardness: 7

Cleavage: Generally none; rarely indistinct
rhombohedral parting.

Other data: *Specific gravity* 2.65; *fracture* conchoidal;
transparent to subtranslucent.

Crystals: Hexagonal; usually prismatic crystals
striated crosswise and frequently
terminated by double rhombohedrons
(like hexagonal pyramids); also
granular, disseminated, massive.

Best field marks: Luster, striated hexagonal crystals,
good conchoidal fracture, and hardness.

Similar species: White and colorless beryl has one poor
cleavage, is harder than quartz, and
lacks the crosswise striations. Feldspar
is softer and has perfect cleavage.

Environment: Quartz is an important rock-forming
mineral and developed in many
different environments. It is a
constituent of granite and grandodiorite
of plutonic rocks, and is usually

associated with albite and orthoclase in granite pegmatites. It is present in rhyolite and dacite of volcanic rocks, and a very common constituent of sandstone, a clastic sedimentary rock. Quartz is the principal constituent of metaquartzite of contact metamorphic rocks and is usually present in hornfels of contact metamorphic rocks and amphibolite, gneiss, schist, and metaquartzite of regional metamorphic rocks; is the principal constituent of hypothermal, mesothermal, and epithermal veins; and is present in most lode and disseminated hydrothermal replacement deposits.

Occurrence: There is an abundance of excellent collecting localities in North America. Fine clear to milky quartz in prisms occurs in a quartz mine at Black Rapids, Leeds Co., Ontario. Fine deep-colored amethyst occurs in the quarries in Paterson, Passaic Co., New Jersey. Outstanding clusters of transparent crystals up to 20 cm (8″) in length have come from quartz veins in the Ouachita Mts. of Arkansas, and fine smoky-quartz crystals have been obtained from pegmatites in the region surrounding Pikes Peak, Colorado. Large clear rock crystal, with crystals up to .8 metric tonnes (2,000 pounds), has been found in stream gravels near Mokelumne Hill, Calaveras Co., California, and smoky quartz up to .6 m (2′) in length has been found in a pegmatite on Greenhorn Mt., Kern Co., California. Large masses of milky quartz are not rare, and one such mass in S Riverside Co., California, has yielded a considerable amount of beautiful deep-pink rose quartz. Drusy amethyst, generally pale in hue, occurs abundantly in the silver mines at Guanajuato, Mexico.

Gemstone data: Violet to red-purple quartz is called *amethyst;* yellow to red-orange or orange-brown quartz is called *citrine quartz;* smoky or grayish brown to black quartz is called *smoky quartz* (Cairngorm); pink, rose-red, or pale rose quartz is called *rose quartz;* grayish, yellowish, brownish, or green quartz with small platy mica inclusions (hematite or goethite also) is called *aventurine;* and the strongly chatoyant quartz is called *tigereye.* Most highly valued are amethyst and citrine quartz. Citrine quartz, smoky quartz, and amethyst are faceted. Aventurine, rose quartz and tigereye are fashioned into cabochons, and tigereye often used for cameos. Amethyst comes from Brazil and Uruguay; citrine quartz from Brazil and Madagascar; smoky quartz from Brazil, Switzerland, and Colorado; rose quartz from California, Maine, Montana, South Dakota, Brazil, India, and Madagascar; aventurine from Brazil, India, and Russia, and tigereye from Austria and South-West Africa.

The name is from the German *Quarz,* of uncertain origin. Quartz is used as a gemstone, in the manufacture of glass, and as oscillators and filters in radio and telephone services. Amethyst is the birthstone for February. All minerals with the composition SiO_2 are included in the *silica group,* which includes quartz, chalcedony, and opal.

82, 132, 218,   **Chalcedony**
220, 270, 281,   A variety of quartz (silicon dioxide),
452, 491, 501,   often with some iron and aluminum
554–556, SiO_2
558, 656, 662,
663, 701

Color and luster: White to gray, brown, blue, black, and in several varieties as follows: *carnelian* and *sard,* clear red to brownish red; *sardonyx* and *onyx,* sard and carnelian in layers; *heliotrope* and *bloodstone,* bright green with spots of red; *agate,* variegated, banded; *moss agate,* with mosslike or treelike inclusions; *chrysoprase,* apple-green; *jasper,* variegated and mottled red, yellow, brown; *flint,* whitish, dull gray, smoky brown to black; luster waxy, vitreous, dull; streak white.

Hardness: 7

Cleavage: None.

Other data: *Specific gravity* 2.6 to 2.64; *fracture* conchoidal; transparent to translucent; sometimes weakly fluorescent; brittle to tough.

Crystals: None; chalcedony is a microcrystalline variety of quartz. Usually occurs as crusts showing botryoidal and mammillary forms, also compact, banded.

Best field marks: Hardness, botryoidal form, gravity, and range in color.

Similar species: Very few minerals are readily confused with chalcedony.

Environment: Chalcedony is formed in several environments, generally near the surface of the earth where temperatures and pressures are relatively low. It commonly forms in the zone of alteration of lode and massive hydrothermal replacement deposits and as bodies of chert in chemical sedimentary rocks.

Occurrence: Banded agates and colorful chalcedony occur as amygdules in basalt on the north shores of the Great Lakes in Ontario. Pseudomorphs of chalcedony after coral and shells may be found in the floor of Tampa Bay in Florida, and especially beautiful are the magnificent trees that have been replaced by chalcedony at the Petrified Forest National Monument, Arizona. Agates of many colors are obtainable in a wide area in Chihuahua, Mexico.

Gemstone data: Apple-green chalcedony is called *chrysoprase;* dark red or orange-red to reddish brown chalcedony is called *carnelian;* dark green spotted with red inclusions is called *heliotrope* (bloodstone); distinctly banded specimens, in which adjacent bands differ in color and in degree of translucency, are called *agate;* and mottled yellow, red, brown, or green chalcedony is called *jasper.* Very fine chrysoprase is sometimes mounted with diamonds in platinum jewelry and commands a good price. All of these materials are fashioned as cabochons or carved into cameos. Fine chrysoprase comes from Australia, Arizona, California, and Oregon; carnelian from India and South America; agate from Brazil, United States, and Uruguay; heliotrope from India and Germany; and jasper from California, Arkansas, and Texas.

The name derives from Chalcedon, an ancient Greek city of Asia Minor. Chalcedony and varieties are used as gem and ornamental stones. Bloodstone is a birthstone for March; agate for May; carnelian or sardonyx for August.

219, 280, 470, 547, 551, 553, 557, 665, 700 **Opal**

Hydrous silica, often with some iron and aluminum

$SiO_2 \cdot nH_2O$; amount of water varies up to 10 percent

Color and luster: White, yellow, red, pink, brown, green, gray, blue, colorless; frequently shows rich internal play of colors (opalescence) in precious opal or fire opal; vitreous, pearly; streak white.

Hardness: $5\frac{1}{2}$–$6\frac{1}{2}$

Cleavage: None.

Other data: *Specific gravity* 2.0 to 2.2; *fracture* conchoidal, conspicuous when compact; transparent to translucent; fluorescent.

Crystals: None; usually massive, botryoidal, reniform, stalactitic, earthy.

Best field marks: Vitreous or pearly luster, opalescence, conchoidal fracture, and brittleness.

Similar species: Dense opal resembles quartz, but it is softer and has a lustrous conchoidal fracture.

Environment: Opal is a low-temperature mineral and usually develops in a wide variety of rocks as cavity and fracture fillings. It frequently develops as amygdules in basalt and rhyolite of volcanic rock and replaces the cells in wood and the shells of clams.

Occurrence: Common opal is widespread and can be readily obtained at many places, but localities for precious opal are rare and seem to be localized in W United States and Mexico. Magnificent examples of opalized wood can be found in Idaho, Nevada, Oregon, Utah, and Washington, and lively green fluorescing opal (hyalite) occurs in seams in pegmatites in New England and North Carolina and in cavities in basalt near Klamath Falls, Oregon. Beautiful precious opal, as a replacement in wood, has been obtained in Virgin Valley, Humboldt Co., Nevada. Excellent fire and precious opal occur in lava flows in N Mexico, and excellent material has been mined in Queretaro and Jalisco states, Mexico.

Gemstone data: Black, dark blue, dark green opal with dark gray body color and fine play of colors is called *black opal;* opal with white or light body color and fine play of color is called *white opal;* and transparent to translucent opal with body color ranging from orange-yellow to red and a play of colors is called *fire opal.* Play of colors depends upon interference of light and is not dependent upon body color. Black opal is the most highly prized, and fire opal is the most valued of the orange and red varieties. Most opal is fashioned into cabochons, but some fire opals are faceted. Nevada, Australia, and Honduras are sources for black opal; Australia and Czechoslovakia for white opal; Mexico and SW United States for fire opal. Birthstone for October.

The word is from the Sanskrit *upala,* meaning "precious stone."

13, 25, 88, 89,   **Orthoclase**
150, 254, 302,   Potassium aluminum silicate,
338, 399,   sometimes with considerable sodium
414, 466, 657 $KAlSi_3O_8$

Color and luster: White, pink, brown, gray, green, colorless, yellowish; vitreous; streak white.

Hardness: 6–6½

Cleavage: Good, two directions at 90°.

Other data: *Specific gravity* 2.5 to 2.6; *fracture* uneven; transparent to translucent. Orthoclase, adularia, sanidine, and microcline are called the potash feldspars. *Adularia* is transparent or opalescent (moonstone); *sanidine* is glassy; and *microcline* is white to pale yellow, rarely red; when bright-green, microcline is called amazonstone.

Crystals: Monoclinic (orthoclase, sanidine) or triclinic (microcline); predominately as single crystals of rectangular or square cross section and as tabular crystals; twin crystals very common; also cleavage masses, granular, disseminated grains.

Best field marks: Perfect cleavage in two directions at 90°; color; twinned crystals common.

Similar species: Plagioclase feldspars show twinning striations on fresh cleavage surfaces; spodumene breaks with splintery fracture; other similar silicate minerals lack the right-angle cleavage.

Environment: The potash feldspars are important rock-forming minerals in plutonic, volcanic, and metamorphic rocks. Orthoclase commonly occurs in granite, and microcline in granite pegmatites, carbonatites, and hornfels of contact metamorphic rocks. Adularia and sanidine are found usually in volcanic rocks. Microcline is the potash feldspar that usually forms intergrowths with quartz (called "graphic granite") and with albite (called "perthite") in granite pegmatite.

Occurrence: Because these minerals are so widespread in their distribution in North America, only a few of the more important localities will be listed. Sharp crystals of orthoclase up to 7.5 cm (3″) in length occur in volcanic rocks on the W side of Sandia Mt., Bernalillo Co., New Mexico; and sharp twinned orthoclase crystals up to about the same length occur in small bodies of volcanic rock near Cinco, Kern Co., California. White adularia crystals up to 2.5 cm (1″) across have been found in gold-bearing quartz veins at Bodie, Mono Co., California, and in the silver mines of the Silver City district, Owhyee Co., Idaho. Large sanidine crystals have come from rhyolite on Ragged Mt., Gunnison Co., Colorado, and from the W slope of the Black Range, Grant Co., New Mexico. The finest crystals of microcline— amazonite—occur in the pegmatites in the Pikes Peak area, Teller Co., Colorado. Gem amazonite has been obtained from the Rutherford No. 1 Mine and Morefield Mine, Amelia, Amelia Co., Virginia.

Gemstone data: The light bluish-green variety of microcline is called *amazonite* or *amazonstone*. Laminations (striae), which are common, and white streaks are not desirable. Good material is rare, but it polishes into flats, beads, and cabochons. Fine amazonite has come from Colorado, Pennsylvania, and Virginia, but the finest is obtained from Russia.

Orthoclase takes its name from the Greek *orthos*, "upright," and *klasis*, "fracture," in allusion to its two prominent cleavages at right angles to each other. Adularia is named for a locality in the Adula Mts., Switzerland; sanidine from the Greek *sanis*, "tablet," and *inos*, "like," in allusion to the tabular habit of the mineral; and microcline from a combination of the Greek *mikros*, "small," and *klinein*, "to incline." The potash feldspars are used as gemstones

and in ceramics. Moonstone adularia is
a birthstone for June.

131, 319, 360,   **Plagioclase Feldspar Group**
401, 409, 444,   A series of mixtures of sodium and
458, 465,   calcium aluminum silicates, from albite
497, 549, 550,   (the sodium-rich end member) through
552, 660,   oligoclase, andesine, labradorite, and
664   bytownite to anorthite (the calcium-
rich end member)
$NaAlSi_3O_8$ (albite)
$CaAl_2Si_2O_8$ (anorthite)

Color and luster: White, colorless, gray, green, bluish,
reddish; sometimes play of colors (albite
and labradorite), blue, green, yellow,
red; vitreous; frequently pearly on
cleavage; streak white.
Hardness: 6
Cleavage: Good in two directions at nearly right
angles, poor in a third direction;
twinning striations often on cleavages;
cleavages frequently curved.
Other data: *Specific gravity* 2.62 to 2.76; *fracture*
uneven; transparent to translucent;
brittle.
Crystals: Triclinic; crystals rare except for albite
and oligoclase; usually flattened,
forming thin blades (cleavelandite, a
variety of albite) in matrix; also
lamellar, granular, disseminated,
rosettes. Forms twin crystals that
resemble thin platy crystals sandwiched
together and giving striated cleavage
surfaces.
Best field marks: Mineral association and striations (fine
parallel lines) on cleavage surfaces that
are too hard to be scratched with a
knife. The plagioclase feldspars are
important rock-forming minerals and
should always be suspected in any rock
specimen. Recognition of individual
members is difficult, but fairly accurate
results can be obtained by careful
specific-gravity determinations. In
general, however, the twinning
lamellae are narrower in the soda-lime

feldspars (albite, oligoclase, and andesine) than in the lime-soda feldspars (labradorite, bytownite, and anorthite).

Similar species: Cleavage surfaces of orthoclase will not show numerous twinning striations.

Environment: The plagioclase feldspars are important rock-forming minerals and are found in many kinds of igneous and metamorphic rocks. Labradorite and bytownite occur with hornblende and augite in gabbro of plutonic rocks; labradorite with hornblende in basalt of volcanic rocks; andesine with biotite and hornblende in diorite and monzonite of plutonic rocks; andesine with augite in andesite of volcanic rocks; oligoclase with biotite and hornblende in monzonite of plutonic rocks; albite with nepheline and acmite in nepheline syenite pegmatites and carbonatites; albite in greenstone of contact metamorphic rocks; albite in schist, metaquartzite, and blue schists of regional metamorphic rocks; albite as bladed masses in granite pegmatites; and anorthite in serpentinite of hydrothermal metamorphic rocks and with calcite and spinel in hornfels of contact metamorphic rocks.

Occurrence: Fine labradorite showing beautiful colors comes from E Labrador. Excellent albite (cleavelandite) has come from the Rutherford mines, near Amelia, Amelia Co., Virginia, and from the pegmatites of San Diego Co., California. Bytownite occurs at Ottawa, Ontario, and transparent oligoclase occurs in the Hawk mica mine, Mitchell Co., North Carolina. Rounded masses of anorthite have been collected from a body of serpentinite near Middletown, Lake Co., California.

Gemstone data: Only the finest labradorite, showing distinct change of color (labradorescence), is considered a gemstone. Greenish, bluish, yellowish, or reddish change of color may occur; blues and greens are most common, and the color change may be only in patches. Light-colored opalescent oligoclase (moonstone) also finds occasional use as a gemstone. Labradorite and moonstone are used for cabochons. Excellent gem-quality has been found in Labrador and Newfoundland, but the specimens of greatest beauty usually come from Finland and the USSR.

The plagioclase feldspars are also called the soda-lime feldspars and lime-soda feldspars. They range in composition from mostly albite (Ab) to mostly anorthite (An):

Feldspar	Composition
Albite	$Ab_{100}-An_0$
Oligoclase	$Ab_{90}-An_{10}$
Andesine	$Ab_{70}-An_{30}$
Labradorite	$Ab_{30}-An_{70}$
Bytownite	$Ab_{10}-An_{90}$
Anorthite	Ab_0-An_{100}

These proportions are approximate and may vary by as much as 20 percent.

The name "albite" is from the Latin *albus,* "white," in allusion to its color. "Oligoclase" is of Greek origin, from *oligos,* "little," and *klasis,* "fracture," since it was thought to have a less perfect cleavage than albite. "Andesine" is named after a locality in the Andes; "labradorite" after Labrador; "bytownite" from the locality at Bytown, now Ottawa, Ontario. "Anorthite" is compounded from the Greek negative prefix *an-* with *orthos,* "upright," in allusion to the oblique crystal form. The plagioclase feldspars are used as gemstones and in ceramics.

313, 383, 425 Danburite
Calcium borosilicate
$CaB_2Si_2O_8$

Color and luster:	White to colorless, also pale pink to straw yellow; vitreous; streak colorless.
Hardness:	7
Cleavage:	Poor, one direction.
Other data:	*Specific gravity* 3.0; *fracture* uneven to conchoidal; transparent to translucent; brittle.
Crystals:	Orthorhombic; usually prismatic, resembling topaz. Crystals striated lengthwise.
Best field marks:	Hardness and poor cleavage.
Similar species:	Topaz, barite, and celestite. Danburite has poor cleavage and is softer than topaz, but it is harder than barite and celestite.
Environment:	Danburite develops in hypothermal veins, where it is associated with quartz, cassiterite, fluorite, and orthoclase, and in contact metamorphic rocks, where it occurs with andradite, wollastonite, and sulfides.
Occurrence:	Excellent crystals of danburite have come from mines at Charcas, San Luis Potosí, Mexico, of which some were suitable for faceting into gemstones. Danburite occurs as pale reddish-brown crystals near Russell, St. Lawrence Co., New York. The original locality was at Danbury, Fairfield Co., Connecticut.
	Danburite is named for its first reported occurrence in Danbury, Connecticut; the original locality has since been buried by the growth of the city.

413, 482 Leucite
Potassium aluminum silicate
$KAlSi_2O_6$

Color and luster:	Colorless or white to gray, may have yellowish or reddish tinge; vitreous, greasy; streak white.
Hardness:	5½–6

Cleavage: None, or very poor.

Other data: *Specific gravity* 2.4 to 2.5; *fracture* conchoidal; translucent to transparent; brittle.

Crystals: Tetragonal; usually in pseudoisometric, trapezohedral crystals; also rounded, disseminated grains.

Best field marks: Dull luster, hardness, and crystal shape.

Similar species: Garnet is harder than leucite, and analcime has greater luster.

Environment: Leucite develops in basalt of volcanic rocks and is usually associated with olivine and labradorite.

Occurrence: Good crystals have been found at Magnet Cove, Garland Co., Arkansas, and leucite occurs as a principal constituent of some of the volcanic rocks in the Leucite Hills of Wyoming.

The name is from the Greek *leukois*, "white," in reference to the common hue of the mineral.

480, 502   Nepheline
Sodium, potassium aluminum silicate
$(Na,K)AlSiO_4$

Color and luster: Colorless, white or gray, with reddish, brownish, greenish tints; greasy, vitreous; streak white.

Hardness: 5½–6

Cleavage: Good in three directions, parallel to prism faces.

Other data: *Specific gravity* 2.6; *fracture* subconchoidal; transparent to translucent; brittle.

Crystals: Hexagonal; crystals rare; commonly small to large grains and granular masses (eleolite).

Best field marks: Greasy luster and good three-directional cleavage.

Similar species: The greasy luster will distinguish nepheline from cryolite and feldspars. Cleavage is not as good as in the feldspars, nor at 90° angles as in scapolite.

Environment: Nepheline is a rock-forming mineral and is commonly found in nepheline syenites and nepheline syenite pegmatites, both plutonic rocks. The finest material comes from the pegmatites, where it is associated with albite and apatite.

Occurrence: Localities in North America for collecting nepheline are uncommon. It occurs as large grains in pegmatites in Hastings Co., Ontario, and as crude crystals in nepheline syenites at Litchfield, Kennebec Co., Maine.

The name is from the Greek *nephele*, "cloud," because the mineral becomes clouded when placed in strong acid. It is used as a raw material in the glass and ceramics industries.

124, 125 Sodalite

Sodium aluminum silicate with chlorine

$Na_4Al_3(SiO_4)_3Cl$

Color and luster: Blue, gray, white, colorless, green; vitreous, greasy; streak white.

Hardness: $5\frac{1}{2}-6$

Cleavage: Poor, six directions.

Other data: *Specific gravity* 2.2 to 2.3; *fracture* uneven to conchoidal; transparent to translucent; fluorescent; brittle.

Crystals: Isometric; crystals rare; usually dodecahedrons; also compact, disseminated grains, nodular.

Best field mark: Blue color.

Similar species: Sodalite is more translucent than lazurite and lazulite, and lazurite is usually accompanied by pyrite.

Environment: Sodalite develops in nepheline syenite pegmatites.

Occurrence: Beautiful sodalite occurs in masses in the Princess Quarry, Dungannon Township, Hastings Co., Ontario, and massive sodalite has been obtained from Kicking Horse Pass and Ice River, British Columbia.

Sodalite is named in allusion to its sodium content. It is used as a gemstone.

127, 666 Lazurite

Silicate of sodium calcium and aluminum, with some sulfur; sodalite group

$(Na,Ca)_8(Al,Si)_{12}O_{24}(S,SO)_4$

Color and luster:	Azure-blue, violet-blue, greenish blue; dull to greasy; streak pale blue.
Hardness:	5–5½
Cleavage:	Poor, six directions.
Other data:	*Specific gravity* 2.4 to 2.5; *fracture* uneven; translucent; brittle.
Crystals:	Isometric; dodecahedral; crystals rare; usually granular, compact, massive.
Best field marks:	Deep-blue color and frequent association with pyrite.
Similar species:	Lazurite is deeper in color and usually finer-grained than sodalite, and is softer and lighter in weight than lazulite.
Environment:	Lazurite forms in association with pyrite, calcite, and diopside in hornfels of contact metamorphic rocks. Lapis lazuli is a mixture of lazurite, calcite, pyrite, and diopside.
Occurrence:	Lazurite is a rare mineral in North America, but it does occur on Italian Mt. in the Sawatch Mts. of Colorado; on Ontario Peak in the San Gabriel Mts., Los Angeles Co., and in Cascade Canyon in the San Bernardino Mts., San Bernardino Co., California.
Gemstone data:	The opaque, vivid blue, light blue, greenish-blue, or violet-blue stone, consisting largely of lazurite but with appreciable amounts of calcite, diopside, and pyrite, is a rock called *lapis lazuli.* The stone is usually veined or spotted. Its value depends largely upon excellence and uniformity of color and absence of pyrite, although some purchasers prefer lapis with pyrite. Lapis lazuli is fashioned into cabochons, beads, and flat slabs or carved into

ornamental objects. Finest lapis lazuli has come from Badakshan in Afghanistan, and less valuable material has come from Russia and Chile.

The name is from the Arabic *lazaward*, "heaven," which was also applied to sky-blue lapis lazuli. Lazurite (lapis lazuli) is used as a gemstone and is a birthstone for December.

14, 76, 264, 336, 420, 486, 694

Scapolite

A two-member series consisting of marialite, the sodium end member, and meionite, the calcium end member.

$Na_4(Al_3Si_9O_{24})Cl$ (marialite)
$Ca_4(Al_6Si_6O_{24})CO_3$ (meionite)

Color and luster: Colorless, white, gray, greenish; rarely bluish, pink, violet, brown, yellow; vitreous; streak white.

Hardness: 5–6

Cleavage: Distinct, two directions.

Other data: *Specific gravity* 2.5 to 2.8; *fracture* conchoidal to uneven; transparent to translucent; fluorescent.

Crystals: Tetragonal; usually crude short prisms with square cross section; also compact, fibrous, granular; sometimes striated on prism faces and on cleavage surface.

Best field marks: Short square prisms, color, and fluorescence.

Similar species: Its color, crystal form, and fluorescence distinguish scapolite from any of the similar feldspar minerals.

Environment: Scapolite is principally a product of metamorphism. It is found associated with almandine and andalusite in gneiss and hornfels of regional and contact metamorphic rocks and with andradite and actinolite in skarn of hydrothermal metamorphic rocks. It also occurs in granite pegmatites, where it is associated with microcline and muscovite.

Occurrence: Scapolite is abundant in metamorphosed limestone in Quebec and occurs as large crude yellowish-white prisms near Eganville, Renfrew Co., Ontario. Good crystals have been found at Grasse Lake, near Rossie, St. Lawrence Co., New York, and in the marble of Franklin, Sussex Co., New Jersey. Opaque white crystals occur with dark-green diopside and have been obtained from metamorphic rocks near Oaxaca, Mexico.

The name is from the Greek *skapos*, "shaft," in allusion to the prismatic crystal form. It is used as a gemstone.

Zeolites

The zeolites are a group of related hydrous tectosilicate minerals, popular among collectors, that commonly occur in cavities in basic igneous rocks, especially vesicular basalt. They contain water in microscopic channels within a framework of aluminum silicate units; the water can be driven off (by heat) or replaced without altering the structure of the zeolite minerals.

143, 403, 455   Heulandite

Hydrous sodium, calcium, potassium, aluminum silicate; potassium may substitute for sodium; zeolite group
$(Ca,Na)(Al_2Si_7O_{18}) \cdot 6H_2O$

Color and luster: White, grayish, colorless, greenish, red; vitreous, pearly on cleavage; streak colorless.

Hardness: $3\frac{1}{2}-4$

Cleavage: Perfect, one direction.

Other data: *Specific gravity* 2.2; *fracture* uneven; transparent to translucent; brittle.

Crystals: Monoclinic; usually in coffin-shaped or tabular single crystals; radiating aggregates of nearly parallel crystals; also foliated, globular, granular.

Best field marks: Crystal form, vitreous and pearly

lusters, and association with other zeolites.

Similar species: Stilbite has the wheat-sheaf form, and apophyllite has neither the wheat-sheaf form nor the coffin shape.

Environment: Heulandite is a low-pressure mineral, and commonly develops in cavities in basalts. It is usually associated with calcite and other zeolites.

Occurrence: Generally, where there is excellent stilbite one will also find equally beautiful heulandite. White crystals up to 7.5 cm (3″) in length have come from cavities in basalt at Teigarhorn, Berufjord, Iceland, and at Wasson's Bluff, Cumberland Co., Nova Scotia. The basalts in the Watchung Mts., Passaic Co., New Jersey, have yielded beautiful snow-white crystals up to 5 cm (2″) in length, and pink and white crystals occur in cavities in basalt near Edwards, Tillamook Co., Oregon.

The name is after a 19th-century English mineralogist, Henry Heuland.

268, 428 Stilbite

Hydrous calcium, sodium, aluminum silicate; zeolite group
$NaCa_2Al_5Si_{13}O_{36} \cdot 16H_2O$

Color and luster: White, grayish, yellowish, red to brown; vitreous, pearly on cleavage; streak colorless.

Hardness: 3½–4

Cleavage: Perfect, one direction.

Other data: *Specific gravity* 2.1 to 2.2; *fracture* uneven; transparent to translucent.

Crystals: Monoclinic; commonly in bladed aggregates of numerous twinned crystals, pinched in the middle to resemble wheat sheaves; also radial, globular, rarely as tabular crystals.

Best field marks: Wheat-sheaf aggregates and association with other zeolite minerals.

Similar species: The wheat-sheaf aggregate form will suffice to distinguish stilbite from heulandite and apophyllite. Also, apophyllite crystals have striated faces, which are lacking in stilbite.

Environment: Stilbite forms at low pressures and generally in cavities of some plutonic or volcanic rocks, commonly associated with calcite and other zeolites.

Occurrence: Outstanding snow-white bladed crystals have come from Teigarhorn, Berufjord, Iceland, and equally fine specimens from basalt at Cape d'Or, Horseshoe Cove, Partridge Island, Cumberland Co., Nova Scotia. Pale-brown crystals have come from basalts in the Watchung Mts., Passaic Co., New Jersey, and excellent white crystals up to 2.5 cm (1″) in length were found near Mitchell, Wheeler Co., Oregon.

The name is derived from the Greek *stilbein*, "to glitter," in allusion to the mineral's luster.

---

437 Laumontite
Hydrous calcium aluminum silicate; zeolite group
$CaAl_2Si_4O_{12} \cdot 4H_2O$

Color and luster: White, colorless, yellowish, brownish; vitreous; streak colorless.
Hardness: 4
Cleavage: Perfect, two directions.
Other data: *Specific gravity* 2.2 to 2.3; *fracture* uneven; transparent to translucent; brittle.
Crystals: Monoclinic; usually short prismatic crystals with oblique terminations; also massive and recently found in long prismatic crystals up to 7.5 cm (3″) in length.
Best field marks: White powdery surface on mineral due to loss of water.
Similar species: Apophyllite and heulandite do not have a white powdery surface.
Environment: Laumontite is formed at relatively low temperatures and develops in cavities in basalt of volcanic rocks along with

calcite and zeolites. It has recently been found in cavities in hornfels of contact metamorphic rocks, associated with grossular, epidote, scheelite, and molybdenite.

Occurrence: Exceptional crystal clusters of laumontite with single crystals up to 7.5 cm (3″) in length have recently come from a tungsten mine in Pine Creek, Inyo Co., California. Crystals up to 2.5 cm (1″) in length have come from Sunnyside, Cochise Co., Arizona, and small white crystals occur at the zeolite localities in Paterson, Passaic Co., New Jersey.

It is named in honor of Gillet de Laumont (1747–1834), French mineralogist, who first found the mineral in the lead mines at Brittany in 1785. Laumontite loses water readily upon exposure to the atmosphere and converts to a white powder unless first immersed in a plastic or other sealant.

142 Chabazite

Hydrous calcium, sodium, aluminum silicate, usually with some sodium and potassium; zeolite group
$CaAl_2Si_4O_{12} \cdot 6H_2O$

Color and luster: White, yellow, pink, red; vitreous; streak white.
Hardness: 4–5
Cleavage: Poor in three directions, parallel to rhomb faces.
Other data: *Specific gravity* 2.0 to 2.2; *fracture* uneven; transparent to translucent brittle.
Crystals: Hexagonal; usually rhombohedro resemble cubes because the angle between the faces are near 90°; al compact, usually showing penetr twins.
Best field marks: Rhombohedral crystals, pseudoc outline, and lack of pearly luster cleavages.

Similar species: The rhombohedral outline and lack of pearly luster on cleavages are sufficient to distinguish chabazite from heulandite and analcime; calcite can be distinguished by its effervescence in dilute acid.

Environment: Chabazite forms at low temperatures and is generally associated with zeolites and calcite in cavities in basalt of volcanic rocks.

Occurrence: Excellent glassy crystals occur in the basalt at Berufjord, Iceland, and large flesh-red rhombohedrons up to 3.75 cm (1½″) on the edge have come from Wasson's Bluff, Cumberland Co., Nova Scotia. The crystal cavities in the basalt in the Watchung Mts., Passaic Co., New Jersey, have produced many chabazite specimens, and fine translucent crystals have been obtained with other zeolites from basalt near Goble, Columbia Co., Oregon.

The name is from the Greek *chabazios*, an archaic term for "stones."

412 Analcime (Analcite)
Hydrous sodium aluminum silicate; zeolite group
$NaAlSi_2O_6 \cdot H_2O$

Color and luster: White, colorless, gray, with greenish, yellowish, or reddish tints; vitreous; streak colorless.

Hardness: 5–5½

Cleavage: None.

Other data: *Specific gravity* 2.2 to 2.3; *fracture* uneven to subconchoidal; transparent to translucent; brittle.

Crystals: Isometric; generally as simple trapezohedrons; also granular, compact.

Best field mark: Occurrence as shiny, glass-clear crystals lining cavities.

Similar species: Leucite crystals have dull luster, and pale-colored garnet is harder than analcime.

Environment: Analcime usually develops in cavities in

basalt of volcanic rocks and is associated
with zeolites, calcite, and prehnite.

Occurrence: Excellent specimens with crystals up to
10 cm (4″) in diameter have come from
zeolite localities at Cape Blomidon,
Nova Scotia, and smaller individual
crystals and druses of white analcime
have been obtained from basalts in the
Watchung Mts., Passaic Co., New
Jersey. Brilliant crystals occur at Table
Mt., Jefferson Co., Colorado, and
crystals as much as 2.5 cm (1″) across
have been collected near Point Sal, San
Luis Obispo Co., California.

The name is from the Greek prefix *an-*,
"not," and *alkimos*, "strong," in
reference to its weak pyroelectricity.

389, 440   **Natrolite**
Hydrous sodium aluminum silicate;
zeolite group
$Na_2Al_2Si_3O_{10} \cdot 2H_2O$

Color and luster: White, colorless, grayish, yellowish,
reddish; vitreous, silky; streak colorless.
Hardness: 5–5½
Cleavage: Perfect, one direction.
Other data: *Specific gravity* 2.2 to 2.3; *fracture*
uneven; transparent to translucent;
brittle.
Crystals: Orthorhombic; commonly slender to
acicular; also radial, granular, compact;
commonly in radiating groups, lining
cavities in volcanic rocks.
Best field marks: Crystal shape, hardness, and prismatic
cleavage.
Similar species: Crystals of natrolite are thicker than
those of mesolite, and natrolite is
harder than prismatic gypsum.
Environment: Natrolite usually occurs with the zeolite
minerals, calcite, and prehnite in
cavities in basalt.
Occurrence: Excellent specimens have come from
the Houdaille Quarry, Bound Brook,
Somerset Co., New Jersey, and crystals
up to 7.5 cm (3″) in length occur near

Livingston, Montana. Natrolite is the
matrix mineral in which occur beautiful
blue crystals of benitoite at the Gem
Mine, San Benito Co., California.

The name is from the Greek *nitron,*
"niter," and *lithos,* "stone," in allusion
to the composition of the mineral.

447 Mesolite
Hydrous sodium, calcium, aluminum
silicate; zeolite group
$Na_2Ca_2(Al_6Si_9)O_{30} \cdot 8H_2O$

Color and luster: White, colorless; vitreous, silky; streak
colorless.
Hardness: 5
Cleavage: Perfect, two directions.
Other data: *Specific gravity* 2.3; *fracture* uneven;
transparent to translucent.
Crystals: Monoclinic; usually acicular and
capillary; also fibrous, delicate,
divergent.
Best field mark: Usual occurrence in groups of fine,
silky-white needlelike crystals.
Similar species: Mesolite is slightly softer and lighter in
weight than natrolite, but because of its
fibrous and acicular habit, useful tests
for hardness and for specific gravity are
difficult to make.
Environment: Mesolite is a low-temperature mineral
and commonly occurs associated with
datolite, prehnite, and zeolites in
cavities in basalt of volcanic rocks.
Occurrence: North America has several outstanding
localities where excellent mesolite may
be obtained. Needles of mesolite up to
15 cm (6″) in length have come from
the basalt at Teigarhorn, Berufjord,
Iceland, and fine specimens containing
delicate white needles have come from
numerous places in New Jersey. Masses
of chatoyant mesolite occur at Mt.
Pisgah, Lane Co., Oregon.

The name is from the Greek *mesos,*
"middle," and *lithos,* "stone," in

allusion to the fact that it falls in composition midway between two other closely related minerals, natrolite and scolecite.

Phyllosilicates (Sheet Silicates)

In the phyllosilicates three oxygen atoms or ions of each silica tetrahedron are shared with the adjacent units, forming the sheet structure for which the class is named. Most phyllosilicates have a single prominent (basal) cleavage and a flaky or platy habit; muscovite and the other micas are typical.

7, 26, 346, 387, 411, 483

Apophyllite

Hydrous calcium potassium fluorsilicate, often with a small amount of iron and nickel
$KCa_4Si_8O_{20}(F,OH) \cdot 8H_2O$

Color and luster: Colorless, white, gray, greenish, yellowish, reddish; vitreous, pearly on cleavage; streak white.

Hardness: $4\frac{1}{2}$–5

Cleavage: Perfect, one direction.

Other data: *Specific gravity* 2.3 to 2.4; *fracture* uneven; transparent to translucent.

Crystals: Tetragonal; usually cubelike or tabular, square in cross section; also lamellar, granular, compact.

Best field marks: Cubelike crystals with pearly luster on the one perfect cleavage, striations on other faces, and association with zeolites.

Similar species: Stilbite develops as tabular monoclinic crystals that cluster together like wheat sheaves, and heulandite crystals usually have the shape of an old-fashioned coffin.

Environment: Apophyllite forms at low temperatures and is commonly found in cavities in basalt of volcanic rock, where it is associated with zeolites and prehnite.

Occurrence: There are many outstanding localities

in North America where apophyllite can be collected. Excellent glassy crystals occur with prehnite in the basalt in the Watchung Mts., Passaic Co., New Jersey, and the same association has recently been found in a diabase near Centreville, Fairfax Co., Virginia. Large glassy crystals have come from the copper mines on the Keweenaw Peninsula, Michigan, and fine pearly-white crystals, often forming large druses, have been found in the silver mines at Guanajuato, Mexico.

The name is from the Greek *apo*, "off," and *phyllon*, "leaf," in allusion to the fact that the mineral flakes apart when heated in a flame.

---

464 Kaolinite
Hydrous aluminum silicate
$Al_2Si_2O_5(OH)_4$

Color and luster:	White, gray, yellowish; dull, pearly on cleavage; streak white.
Hardness:	2–2½
Cleavage:	Perfect, one direction.
Other data:	*Specific gravity* 2.6; *fracture* earthy; plastic when wet; brittle.
Crystals:	Monoclinic; usually as submicroscopic grains or minute plates and in compact masses; friable; minute scaly crystals rare.
Best field mark:	Friable claylike masses or plates.
Similar species:	It is difficult to distinguish between kaolinite and similar clay minerals by gross physical properties. The professional uses heat-absorption, X-ray, or electron-microscope techniques.
Environment:	Kaolinite is a secondary mineral, formed by the alteration, usually at shallow depths, of aluminum silicates (generally feldspars) in soils and in rocks near the surface.
Occurrence:	Crystals of kaolinite are rare, but a few have been found in quartz veins near

Silverton, San Juan Co., Colorado.
Massive kaolinite is mined at various
places in North America: in a belt that
extends from Twiggs Co., Georgia, to
Lexington Co., North Carolina; in
Marion Co., Alabama; in Amador and
Inyo Cos., California; in Putnam Co.,
Florida; in Latah Co., Idaho; and near
Kosse, Texas.

The name, sometimes shortened to
"kaolin," derives from Kaoling, a
mountain in China that was an early
source of the mineral. Kaolinite is
widely used (as clay) in pottery and
ceramics, and as a filler in paper
products.

73, 74, 287, 474   **Serpentine Group**
Consisting of antigorite and chrysotile,
both basic magnesium silicates with
similar formula; chrysotile contains
some iron
$(Mg,Fe)_3Si_2O_5(OH)_4$

Color and luster: Olive-green, blackish to yellowish
green, brown, yellow, rarely white;
greasy, waxy, silky (chrysotile); streak
white.

Hardness: 3−5

Cleavage: None (chrysotile); perfect micaceous
(antigorite).

Other data: *Specific gravity* 2.5 to 2.6; *fracture*
conchoidal (antigorite), uneven,
splintery (chrysotile); brittle.

Crystals: Monoclinic; antigorite is unknown in
crystals, usually massive, and appears
cryptocrystalline. Chrysotile is fibrous;
also lamellar and columnar; fibers
flexible and tough.

Best field marks: Low hardness. Any rock mass of dark-
green color, hardness of 3 to 4, and a
greasy feel may be suspected to contain
the serpentine minerals. Chrysotile is
soft and flexible.

Similar species: The serpentine minerals are harder than
talc, but softer than nephrite.

Chrysotile is softer and more flexible than tremolite asbestos.

Environment: The serpentine minerals are the major constituents of the rock serpentinite, which is usually formed from peridotite by hydrothermal metamorphic processes.

Occurrence: Large masses of serpentinite occur at numerous places in North America, but the following localities are the best known for chrysotile and translucent serpentinite (principally antigorite). The finest specimens of long-fiber chrysotile asbestos have come from asbestos mines at Thetford, Megantic Co., Quebec. Bright-yellow chrysotile occurs in yellow translucent serpentinite near Lake Valhalla, Montville, Morris Co., New Jersey. Seams of beautiful pale-yellowish chrysotile occur in the Salt River Valley asbestos deposits in Gila Co., Arizona. Sheets of white chrysotile are common in fractures in shattered serpentinite near Coalinga, Fresno Co., and chrysotile asbestos is mined near Copperopolis, Calaveras Co., California. Fine green translucent serpentinite (called williamsite) occurs near Rock Springs, Pennsylvania.

The name "serpentine" alludes to the surface pattern of serpentinite rock, which recalls the skin of a serpent. "Chrysotile" is from the Greek *chrysos,* "gold," and *tilos,* "fiber," and antigorite is named after the locality of Antigorio in Italy. Some massive serpentinite rock is used for ornamental stone, and chrysotile asbestos has many industrial applications, including fireproof fabrics and brake linings.

286, 446, 488   **Pyrophyllite**
Basic aluminum silicate
$Al_2Si_4O_{10}(OH)_2$

Color and luster:	White, apple-green, gray, yellow; pearly to dull; streak white.
Hardness:	1–2
Cleavage:	Perfect, one direction.
Other data:	*Specific gravity* 2.8 to 2.9; *fracture* uneven, splintery; thin flakes flexible, not elastic; greasy feel; translucent to opaque.
Crystals:	Monoclinic; crystals rare; commonly foliated, fibrous, compact fine-grained masses.
Best field marks:	Greasy feel, micaceous habit and cleavage; difficult to distinguish from talc.
Similar species:	Pyrophyllite is softer than talc or any of the other fine-grained micas.
Environment:	Pyrophyllite forms principally in metamorphic rocks. It occurs with quartz, albite, andalusite, and muscovite in schists of regional metamorphic rocks; and with barite and gypsum in massive hydrothermal replacement deposits.
Occurrence:	Good examples of pyrophyllite may be found at many places in North America. Specimens showing silver or greenish bladed crystals in star-shaped groups up to 2.5 cm (1″) in diameter occur at Staley, Randolph Co., North Carolina; at Graves Mt., Lincoln Co., Georgia; and at Indian Gulch, Mariposa Co., California.

The name is from the Greek *pyr*, "fire," and *phyllon*, "leaf," in allusion to its exfoliating when heated. Pyrophyllite is used principally in ceramics and as a filler in paints and rubber products.

83, 467   Talc
Basic magnesium silicate
$Mg_3Si_4O_{10}(OH)_2$

Color and luster: Apple-green, white; pearly, greasy; streak white.

Hardness: 1

Cleavage: Perfect, one direction.

Other data: *Specific gravity* 2.7 to 2.8; *fracture* uneven; sectile; thin flakes flexible, not elastic; greasy feel; translucent to opaque.

Crystals: Monoclinic; crystals rare; usually foliated, granular; fibrous, compact, waxy.

Best field marks: Softness, greasy feel.

Similar species: Difficult to distinguish between talc and pyrophyllite by physical tests.

Environment: Talc is characteristic of metamorphic rocks derived from dolomite rock and peridotite. It occurs with tremolite and magnesite in talc schists of regional metamorphic rocks, and with tremolite in contact metamorphic rocks.

Occurrence: Massive talc or "soapstone," as it is commonly called, is quarried in Connecticut, New York, and Vermont. Light-green talc in micaceous blades has been found at Staten Island, New York, and in Chester Co., Pennsylvania. Cream-colored, coarsely foliated talc occurs near Dillon, Montana, and in Hastings Co., Ontario.

The name comes from the Arabic *talq*, "mica." Talc has many uses and perhaps is most familiar as talcum powder and in cosmetics. It is widely used as a lubricant and as an insulation in electrical equipment.

Mica Group

The mica minerals are sheet silicates with a three-layer sheet structure and with either K^+ or Ca^{++} and Na^{++} between the layers. The micas are varied in color, with low hardness and perfect basal cleavage; they are important essential minerals of metamorphic and igneous rocks.

75, 173, 272, 459, 498, 548

Muscovite
Basic potassium aluminum silicate; mica group
$KAl_3Si_3O_{10}(OH)_2$

Color and luster: White or colorless to yellowish, greenish, pink, brownish, multicolored; vitreous, pearly; streak colorless.

Hardness: $2-2\frac{1}{2}$

Cleavage: Perfect, one direction.

Other data: *Specific gravity* 2.7 to 3.0; thin flakes tough, very elastic; translucent to transparent.

Crystals: Monoclinic; commonly tabular parallel to the cleavage, often hexagonal in outline; also foliated, flaky; fine scaly to fibrous.

Best field marks: Highly perfect cleavage into thin, flexible, elastic flakes and tapering of the prism faces.

Similar species: Muscovite flakes are elastic, whereas those of chlorite and gypsum are not. Phlogopite is darker than muscovite. It is difficult to distinguish between pink muscovite and pink lepidolite by physical tests. Microscope tests are required to recognize the fine-grained compact forms of these micaceous minerals.

Environment: Muscovite is a common rock-forming mineral and is characteristic of many environments. It occurs with albite, quartz, and tourmaline in granite pegmatites; with quartz and almandine in metaquartzite of contact metamorphic rocks; with quartz, almandine, and albite in blue schist, schists, and gneisses of regional metamorphic rocks; and with quartz and calcite in mesothermal veins.

Occurrence: Almost without exception, good muscovite specimens are restricted to granitic pegmatites, which are widespread throughout North America. Well-formed and zoned green crystals of muscovite have been found near Salt Lake City, Utah; pink muscovite has been found at Goshen, Massachusetts; and pale-green crystals partly imbedded in albite have been found at the Rutherford No. 2 Pegmatite, Amelia, Amelia Co., Virginia.

The name is from the popular name "Muscovy glass" because of its use as a glass substitute in Russia. Thin transparent sheets of muscovite (often referred to as isinglass) are still used as windows in iron stoves. Muscovite is used as a filler in various industrial products and as an insulator in electrical equipment.

252, 509 **Phlogopite**
Basic potassium, magnesium, aluminum silicate, often with fluorine and iron; mica group
$KMg_3(AlSi_3O_{10})(OH)_2$

Color and luster: Yellowish or reddish brown, gray to green, rarely colorless; pearly, adamantine; streak colorless.
Hardness: 2–3
Cleavage: Perfect, one direction.
Other data: *Specific gravity* 2.8 to 2.9; thin flakes tough, very elastic; translucent, transparent in thin sheets; commonly asteriated (shows 6- or 12-ray star around small light source when viewed through a thin cleavage sheet), due to oriented inclusions of rutile.
Crystals: Monoclinic; often in well-formed prismatic crystals with hexagonal

outline; also plates, scales.

Best field marks: Asterism, mineral associations in marble, and dark color.

Similar species: Muscovite and biotite seldom occur in marble and do not possess the asterism of phlogopite.

Environment: Phlogopite is usually found in marbles (metamorphosed limestones and dolomites). It is a common constituent of hornfels of contact and regional metamorphic rocks, where it is associated with calcite, spinel, and pargasite.

Occurrence: Some of the finest phlogopite in North America has come from Canada. The largest recorded single crystal ever mined, weighing 75 tonnes (90 tons) and measuring 11 m (33′) in length and 4.5 m (14′) in diameter, was removed from the Lacy Mine in Ontario. Excellent well-formed phlogopite crystals have come from the zinc mines at Franklin, Sussex Co., New Jersey, and beautiful brown crystals as much as 2.5 cm (1″) across are known to occur in E Fresno Co., California.

The name is from the Greek *phlogopos,* "fiery-looking," in allusion to its red-brown color. Phlogopite is used as insulation in electrical equipment.

539 Biotite

Basic potassium, magnesium, iron, aluminum silicate; mica group
$K(Mg,Fe)_3(Al,Fe)Si_3O_{10}(OH,F)_2$

Color and luster: Black, brownish black, greenish black, dark green; pearly, submetallic; streak colorless.

Hardness: 2½–3

Cleavage: Perfect, one direction.

Other data: *Specific gravity* 2.8 to 3.4; thin plates tough, very elastic, becoming more brittle with alteration; opaque to translucent.

Crystals:	Monoclinic; good crystals common, usually tabular, sometimes barrel-shaped; also plates, scales.
Best field marks:	Dark color and generally small crystals.
Similar species:	Biotite has a darker color than muscovite and does not occur in metamorphosed limestone as does phlogopite.
Environment:	Biotite is a common accessory mineral in plutonic, volcanic, and certain metamorphic rocks (schist and gneiss). It occurs with quartz and orthoclase in granite pegmatites; in granite, granodiorite, diorite, and monzonite of plutonic rocks; in rhyolite, andesite, and dacite of volcanic rocks; with albite and hornblende in greenstone and hornfels of contact metamorphic rocks; and with albite, feldspar, andalusite, and almandine in schist and gneiss of regional metamorphic rocks.
Occurrence:	No specific localities for biotite can be cited, but frequently one can find good biotite specimens in pegmatites in which the feldspar is deep pink to brick-red in color.

Biotite is named after J. B. Biot (1774–1862), French physicist astronomer, and mathematician.

172 Lepidolite
Basic potassium, lithium, aluminum fluorsilicate mica group
$K(Li,Al)_3(Si,Al)_4O_{10}(F,OH)_2$

Color and luster:	Pink, lilac, yellowish, grayish white; pearly; streak colorless.
Hardness:	2½–3
Cleavage:	Perfect, one direction.
Other data:	*Specific gravity* 2.8 to 2.9; laminae tough, elastic; translucent to transparent.
Crystals:	Monoclinic; usually in scaly aggregates, rarely as well-developed crystals of sharp hexagonal outline; also foliated, compact.

Best field marks: Occurrence in granite pegmatites, lilac and pink colors, and rough surface on crystals.

Similar species: It is difficult to distinguish by physical tests between pink lepidolite and pink muscovite. Pink- and purple-colored chlorites are not found in pegmatites, as is lepidolite, and dumortierite is harder and heavier than lepidolite.

Environment: Lepidolite is confined to granite pegmatites, where it occurs either as fine-granular masses near the core of the pegmatite or as stubby or tabular crystals in cavities. It is commonly associated with microcline, quartz, and tourmaline.

Occurrence: There are several outstanding collecting localities in North America for lepidolite. It has been mined in substantial amounts in several New England states, in the Black Hills of South Dakota, and in S California. Large fine masses of lepidolite have been mined at the Stewart Pegmatite at Pala, and superb sharp crystals have been obtained from the Little Three Pegmatite near Ramona, both in San Diego Co., California.

The name is from the Greek *lepidos*, "scale," in allusion to the scaly aggregates in which the mineral commonly occurs. Lepidolite has been used as a source of lithium.

71, 540 **Chlorite**

Chlorite is a group name, and the description to follow will be that of a green mica whose general composition is that of a basic iron, magnesium aluminum silicate $(Mg,Fe)_6(AlSi_3)O_{10}(OH)_8$

Color and luster: Light to dark green, black; pearly, vitreous, dull; streak colorless.

Hardness: 2–2½

Cleavage: Perfect, one direction.

Other data: *Specific gravity* 2.6 to 3.3; *fracture* scaly, earthy; thin flakes flexible, tough, not elastic; slightly soapy feel; transparent to translucent.

Crystals: Monoclinic; usually forms tabular six-sided pseudohexagonal crystals; also foliated, scaly, granular, compact, earthy.

Best field marks: Green color, lack of elasticity, and hardness.

Similar species: Chlorite is not elastic, as are green muscovite and green phlogopite, and it is harder than talc.

Environment: Chlorite has several environments. It occurs as a secondary mineral along with calcite and zeolites in cavities in basalt of volcanic rocks; with albite and epidote in greenstone of contact metamorphic rocks; with actinolite, almandine, and glaucophane in amphibolite, schist, metaquartzite, blue schist and gneisses of regional metamorphic rocks; and with quartz and siderite in lode hydrothermal replacement deposits.

Occurrence: Beautiful crystals of chlorite have been found at the Tilly Foster iron mine, near Brewster, Putnam Co., New York. Small green crystals of tabular habit occur with magnetite near the benitoite locality, San Benito Co., and deep-green crystals up to 1.25 cm (½") across occur with magnetite in E Fresno Co., both in California.

The name is from the Greek *chloros,* "green," in reference to the mineral's characteristic color.

Inosilicates (Chain Silicates)
In the inosilicates the silica
tetrahedrons are joined together in the
form of linked single or double chains,
giving some of them an unusual
toughness. The inosilicates include two
important groups of rock-forming
minerals: the amphiboles (including
tremolite, actinolite, hornblende,
glaucophane, and riebeckite) and the
pyroxenes (including hypersthene,
diopside, hedenbergite, augite, jadeite,
and spodumene).

448, 477, 478, **Tremolite**
489 A basic calcium, magnesium, iron
silicate; when iron content becomes
appreciable, the mineral is called
actinolite; amphibole group
$Ca_2(Mg,Fe)_5Si_8O_{22}(OH)_2$

Color and luster: White to dark gray, yellowish, pink to
lilac, colorless; vitreous, silky; streak
colorless.

Hardness: 5–6

Cleavage: Perfect, two directions in the shape of a
diamond.

Other data: *Specific gravity* 2.9 to 3.1; *fracture*
uneven; small fibers flexible (amphibole
asbestos).

Crystals: Monoclinic; usually in fibrous,
radiating aggregates; also bladed,
compact.

Best field marks: Prismatic habit and cleavage angles.

Similar species: Wollastonite is commonly fluorescent
and lacks the prismatic cleavage of
tremolite; tourmaline has no cleavage.

Environment: Tremolite is a product of
metamorphism and occurs with calcite
and grossular in hornfels of contact
metamorphic rocks and with talc in
serpentinites of hydrothermal
metamorphic rocks.

Occurrence: There are many localities where fine
tremolite specimens may be obtained,
and only a few are noted here. Crystals
up to 7.5 cm (3″) in length occur in

marble at Haliburton and Wilberforce, Haliburton Co., Ontario, and granular masses of pink tremolite (hexagonite) at De Kalb, St. Lawrence Co., New York. White and greenish crystals occur in calcite at Canaan, Litchfield Co., Connecticut.

Gemstone data: The amphibole mineral nephrite, which consists of combined tremolite and actinolite, is dense, compact, tough. Semitransparent to translucent varieties of nephrite are called *jade*. Nephrite jade colors are white, all shades of green, gray, grayish (with tinge of blue, red, or green), brown, and lavender. Value increases with transparency, intensity and evenness of color, and freedom from flaws. Jade is fashioned into beads, earrings, and cabochons for rings and brooches, or carved into ornamental or religious objects. Nephrite jade comes from Alaska, British Columbia, Wyoming, China, and Siberia.

The name is from the occurrence in Val Tremolo in the Swiss Alps. Translucent nephrite jade is used as a gemstone and the finely fibrous form is used as asbestos in many industrial applications.

18, 518, 535   Actinolite
A basic calcium, magnesium, iron silicate; amphibole group
$Ca_2(Mg,Fe)_5Si_8O_{22}(OH)_2$

Color and luster: Bright to dark green, grayish green, black; vitreous, pearly, silky; streak colorless.

Hardness: 5–6

Cleavage: Perfect, two directions lengthwise in the shape of a diamond.

Other data: *Specific gravity* 3.0 to 3.5; *fracture* splintery, uneven; transparent to translucent.

Crystals: Monoclinic; usually long prismatic with

diamond-shaped cross section; also bladed, acicular, columnar, divergent.

Best field marks: Prismatic habit and cleavage angle.

Similar species: Wollastonite is usually fluorescent; tourmaline has no cleavage; and epidote lacks the cleavage angle of actinolite.

Environment: Actinolite results principally from metamorphic processes. It is associated with albite, chlorite, and epidote in greenstone of regional metamorphic rocks; with albite and muscovite in hornfels of contact metamorphic rocks; and with barite and anhydrite in massive hydrothermal replacement deposits.

Occurrence: Beautiful green blades of actinolite up to 12.5 cm (5″) in length occur in talc near Chester, Windsor Co., Vermont. Deep-green actinolite is common among the bodies of serpentinite in California, and masses composed of long bladelike crystals as much as 20 cm (8″) long were found near Hopland, Mendocino Co., California. Slender well-formed crystals of deep-green actinolite occur in cream-colored talc near Pleasanton, Alameda Co., California. Nephrite, which is usually a chemical mixture of actinolite and tremolite, has been found in substantial amounts in British Columbia, Alaska, California, and Wyoming.

The name is from the Greek *aktinos*, "ray," in reference to the common radiate habit of prismatic crystals.

16, 513, 536 Hornblende

A complex basic silicate of sodium, potassium, calcium, magnesium, iron, and aluminum, often with some titanium; amphibole group $(Ca,Na,K)_{2-3}(Mg,Fe^{2+},Fe^{3+},Al)_5(SiAl)_8 O_{22}(OH)_2$

Color and luster: Green, brown, black; submetallic, vitreous, pearly, silky; streak colorless.

Hardness: 5–6

Cleavage: Perfect, two directions in the shape of a diamond.

Other data: *Specific gravity* 3.0 to 3.4; *fracture* uneven, splintery; transparent to translucent on splinter edges; brittle.

Crystals: Monoclinic; usually in short to long prismatic crystals that have a diamond-shaped cross section; also granular, columnar, fibrous, radiated.

Best field marks: Cleavage angles of 56° and 124°, and greenish-black color.

Similar species: Tourmaline lacks the good cleavage of hornblende, and tremolite and actinolite are lighter in color than hornblende.

Environment: Hornblende is a rock-forming mineral of some plutonic and metamorphic rocks. It is an essential mineral in granite, granodiorite, diorite, and monzonite, and a plutonic rock that is composed largely of hornblende is called hornblendite. Hornblende is also present in dacite, andesite, and basalt of volcanic rocks, and occurs with acmite and nepheline in nepheline syenite pegmatites; with albite and epidote in greenstone; and with almandine, biotite, and corundum in schists and gneisses of regional metamorphic rocks.

Occurrence: Hornblende is a common mineral, but there are few localities where one might obtain fine crystals. Dark-green to black crystals occur in marble at High Falls and Ragged Chute on the Madawaska River, Lanark Co., Ontario, and in the marble associated with the zinc-ore bodies at Franklin, Sussex Co., New Jersey.

The name is from the German miners' term *Horn,* possibly with reference to the color of horn, and *blenden,* "to deceive," because the mineral resembled the metallic ores but did not produce a useful metal.

80 Pargasite

Basic sodium, calcium, magnesium, and aluminum silicate; amphibole group

$NaCaMg_4Al(Si,Al)_8O_{22}(OH)_2$

Color and luster:	Green or bluish green, brown; vitreous; streak white to pale tan.
Hardness:	5–6
Cleavage:	Perfect, two directions in the shape of a diamond.
Other data:	*Specific gravity* 3.0 to 3.4; *fracture* uneven, subconchoidal; transparent to translucent.
Crystals:	Monoclinic; usually short to long prismatic crystals showing diamond-shaped cross section; also massive, compact.
Best field marks:	Cleavage angles of 56° and 124°, occurrence in metamorphosed impure limestones, and tan streak.
Similar species:	The diamond-shaped cross section and good cleavage of pargasite will suffice to distinguish it from vesuvianite.
Environment:	Pargasite, a variety of hornblende, is a product of metamorphism and occurs commonly with phlogopite and vesuvianite in hornfels of contact metamorphic rocks.
Occurrence:	Pargasite from the original locality at Pargas, Finland, is green in color, but there is an occurrence in Fresno Co., California, where the pargasite is a deep chocolate-brown and occurs in sharp prismatic crystals up to 2.5 cm (1″) in length associated with phlogopite, spinel, and vesuvianite.

The name is from the locality at Pargas, Finland, where the mineral was first found.

537 Glaucophane

Basic silicate of sodium, magnesium, iron, and aluminum; amphibole group $Na_2(Mg,Fe^{2+})_3Al_2Si_8O_{22}(OH)_2$

Color and luster: Azure-blue, lavender-blue, bluish black; pearly, vitreous; streak grayish blue.

Hardness: 6

Cleavage: Perfect, two directions in the shape of a diamond.

Other data: *Specific gravity* 3.0 to 3.1; *fracture* uneven, splintery; translucent on thin edges; brittle.

Crystals: Monoclinic; usually prismatic crystals with a diamond-shaped cross section; also columnar, bladed, fibrous.

Best field marks: Blue color, cleavage, and diamond-shaped cross section.

Similar species: Tourmaline does not have cleavage lengthwise on the crystal; riebeckite is bluish black, whereas glaucophane is lighter blue.

Environment: Glaucophane is of metamorphic origin and commonly occurs with lawsonite, albite, and almandine in blue schist of regional metamorphic rocks.

Occurrence: Localities for collecting glaucophane in North America are principally in California, Oregon, and Washington. Bodies of blue schist generally occur near masses of serpentinite, and there are many such occurrences scattered throughout the Coast Ranges in California and into SW Oregon. Glaucophane has also been found in the Cascade Range in Washington.

The name is from the Greek *glaukos*, "bluish gray," and *phainelein*, "to appear," in allusion to its color.

527   **Riebeckite**
Basic silicate of sodium and iron;
amphibole group
$Na_2Fe_3^{2+}Fe_2^{3+}Si_8O_{22}(OH)_2$

Color and luster: Dark blue to black; vitreous, silky in
fibrous variety (crocidolite); streak
white to blue-gray.

Hardness: 5–6

Cleavage: Perfect, two directions in the shape of a
diamond.

Other data: *Specific gravity* 3.0 to 3.4; *fracture*
uneven, splintery; translucent to nearly
opaque.

Crystals: Monoclinic; usually as long prismatic
crystals showing a diamond-shaped
cross section; also fibrous, bladed,
acicular, columnar, radiating.

Best field marks: Color, diamond-shaped crystals in cross
section, and cleavage.

Similar species: Tourmaline lacks the good cleavage of
riebeckite, and glaucophane can be
distinguished, but not easily, from
riebeckite by its generally lighter color.

Environment: Riebeckite develops in igneous and
metamorphic rocks. The dark-blue to
black riebeckite that occurs as prismatic
crystals develops in rhyolite of volcanic
rocks and in granite pegmatites. The
fibrous variety—crocidolite—is
metamorphic in origin and develops
along with almandine, quartz, and
albite in blue schist of regional
metamorphic rocks.

Occurrence: Black prismatic crystals have come from
a pegmatite in Quincy, Norfolk Co.,
Massachusetts, and from rhyolite in the
San Francisco Mts., Coconino Co.,
Arizona. Riebeckite occurs as black
acicular crystals with acmite in cavities
in rhyolite in the mountains east of
Petaluma, Sonoma Co., California.
Crocidolite occurs at many places in the
Coast Ranges of N California and SW
Oregon. Of particular note are several
localities in Mendocino and Sonoma
Cos., California, where riebeckite
occurs with acmite in metamorphosed
cherts.

Riebeckite is named in honor of Emil Riebeck (d. 1885), German explorer and mineralogist.

---

260 Hypersthene
Magnesium iron silicate; pyroxene group
$(Mg,Fe)SiO_3$

Color and luster:	Grayish, greenish, and brownish to bronze; bronzy, pearly; streak brownish gray, grayish white.
Hardness:	5–6
Cleavage:	Perfect, one direction, less distinct in two other directions.
Other data:	*Specific gravity* 3.4 to 3.9; *fracture* uneven; transparent to translucent in thin splinters.
Crystals:	Orthorhombic; good crystals rare; usually in coarsely crystalline aggregates; also foliated cleavage masses.
Best field marks:	Bronze luster; cleavages at nearly right angles.
Similar species:	Hornblende has cleavage angles of 56° and 124°; those of hypersthene are close to 90°. Hypersthene is difficult to distinguish from augite by physical properties alone.
Environment:	Hypersthene is a rock-forming mineral. It occurs with olivine in gabbro and peridotite of plutonic rocks, and with almandine, biotite, and quartz in hornfels of contact metamorphic rocks.
Occurrence:	Good localities for hypersthene are scarce. It is found in dark plutonic rocks in the North Creek garnet occurrences in the Adirondack Mts. of New York, and hypersthene that shows a strong bronzy luster is associated with labradorite in Labrador.

The name is from the Greek *hyper,* "over," and *sthenos,* "strength," in reference to its greater hardness compared with hornblende, with which hypersthene was originally confused.

2, 34, 42, 528 **Diopside**
Calcium magnesium silicate; pyroxene group
$CaMgSi_2O_6$

Color and luster:	White, colorless, grayish, greenish; vitreous, dull; streak white, grayish, greenish.
Hardness:	5–6
Cleavage:	Good, two directions lengthwise at nearly right angles.
Other data:	*Specific gravity* 3.3 to 3.6; *fracture* uneven; transparent to translucent.
Crystals:	Monoclinic, commonly short prismatic with good terminations; also lamellar, granular, compact.
Best field marks:	Light green color and cleavage angles of 87° and 93°.
Similar species:	Olivine does not have the cleavage of diopside and is not found in marble. Epidote also lacks the cleavage of diopside and is usually a darker green.
Environment:	Diopside has two environments. It occurs with dolomite, fluorite, and andradite in carbonatites, and with phlogopite, chondrodite, and actinolite in hornfels of contact and regional metamorphic rocks.
Occurrence:	Transparent gem-quality diopside has been found in the Ala Valley, Piedmont, Italy, and other famous European localities have supplied choice crystals to many collections. Collecting localities in North America have also provided collectors and mineralogists with beautiful specimens. Fine crystals of pale green diopside occur at Cardiff, Haliburton Co., Ontario, and crystals up to 15 cm (6″) in length have been found in druses at Oxford, Sherbrooke Co., Quebec. Pale green diopside of gem quality has been obtained from marble near Richville, St. Lawrence Co., New York, and small masses of brilliant white diopside occur in marble in E Fresno Co., California.

The name is from the Greek prefix *di,* "two," and *opsis,* "appearance," in

allusion to the fact that crystals of
diopside commonly occur with two sets
of prism faces that appear to be similar.

17, 54, 520 **Hedenbergite**
Calcium iron silicate, often with some
magnesium; pyroxene group
$CaFeSi_2O_6$

Color and luster: Bright to dark green, black; vitreous,
dull; streak colorless to pale green.

Hardness: 5–6

Cleavage: Perfect, two directions lengthwise at
nearly right angles; parting sometimes
distinct.

Other data: *Specific gravity* 3.3 to 3.6; *fracture*
uneven; translucent to transparent;
brittle.

Crystals: Monoclinic; crystals (rare) are usually
short, prismatic; also granular,
columnar, rarely fibrous.

Best field marks: Dark-green color, cleavage angles of
87° and 93°, and associated minerals.

Similar species: Hedenbergite is darker green than
epidote and diopside and has the perfect
prismatic cleavage in two directions,
which epidote and tourmaline lack.

Environment: Hedenbergite is formed in
metamorphic rocks and occurs with
grossular, wollastonite, and magnetite
in hornfels of contact metamorphic
rocks, and with andradite, magnetite,
and actinolite in skarn of hydrothermal
metamorphic rocks.

Occurrence: Localities where hedenbergite is the
principal mineral species are rare.
Deep-green hedenbergite is a principal
constituent in both skarn and hornfels
in a body of metamorphosed impure
limestone in E Fresno Co., California.

Hedenbergite is named after Ludwig
Hedenberg, early 19th-century Swedish
chemist.

15, 510, 521 Augite
Silicate of calcium, magnesium, iron, and aluminum; pyroxene group
$Ca,Na(Mg,Fe,Al)(Al,Si)_2O_6$

Color and luster: Bright to dark green, grayish green, brown, black; vitreous, submetallic, dull; streak greenish.

Hardness: 5–6

Cleavage: Two directions lengthwise at nearly right angles; parting often prominent crosswise; diallage has fine lamellar parting in one direction lengthwise.

Other data: *Specific gravity* 3.2 to 3.6; *fracture* uneven; translucent; brittle.

Crystals: Monoclinic; commonly short prismatic; also granular, columnar, rarely fibrous; lamellar (diallage).

Best field marks: Nearly right-angle cleavages and generally short prismatic crystals.

Similar species: Diopside and hedenbergite are lighter in color than augite, and acmite crystals are more elongated.

Environment: Augite develops principally in igneous rocks, and in some of them it is an essential mineral. It occurs in diorite and gabbro of plutonic rocks; in basalt and andesite of volcanic rocks; with nepheline and albite in nepheline syenite pegmatites; with apatite and albite in carbonatites; and with antigorite and chrysotile (as diallage) in serpentinite of hydrothermal metamorphic rocks.

Occurrence: Sharp black augite crystals up to 1.25 cm (½″) across are abundant in basalt in the Trail Creek-Gold Run Creek area, Grand Co., Colorado, and greenish-black augite crystals up to 2 cm (¾″) across may be found in basalt at Cedar Butte, near Tillamook, Tillamook Co., Oregon. Large crystals of augite occur in St. Lawrence Co., New York, and in Renfrew Co., Ontario.

The name is from the Greek *augites,* "brightness," in reference to the luster of the crystals.

523 Acmite (Aegirine)

Sodium iron silicate; pyroxene group
$NaFe^{3+}Si_2O_6$

Color and luster:	Black, greenish black, brownish black; vitreous; streak gray.
Hardness:	6–6½
Cleavage:	Perfect, two directions at nearly right angles.
Other data:	*Specific gravity* 3.5 to 3.6; *fracture* tough, hackly, uneven; translucent on thin edges.
Crystals:	Monoclinic; usually in long and short prismatic crystals with steep pointed pyramids; also compact, fibrous, granular.
Best field marks:	Color and crystal habit.
Similar species:	The black color and especially the prismatic crystals with steep pyramids help to distinguish acmite from augite.
Environment:	Acmite occurs with albite, nepheline, and sodalite in nepheline syenite pegmatites; with andradite, barite, and albite in carbonates; and with quartz, spessartine, and riebeckite (crocidolite) in hornfels of contact metamorphic rocks.
Occurrence:	Splendid black crystals of acmite have been found at Narsarssuk Fjord, Greenland, and at Magnet Cove, Garland Co., Arkansas. Deep-green acmite occurs at widely scattered localities in the Coast Ranges of N California and SW Oregon.

The name derives from the Greek *akme,* "point," a reference to the steeply pointed pyramidal crystals. The old name, aegirine, was given to the mineral in Norway (where it was first discovered) after Aegir, the Teutonic god of the sea.

79, 421, 655   **Jadeite**
Sodium aluminum silicate, often with
some calcium and iron; pyroxene group
$NaAlSi_2O_6$

Color and luster: Apple-green or emerald-green to white;
vitreous, dull, waxy; streak white.

Hardness: $6\frac{1}{2}-7$

Cleavage: Distinct, two directions at nearly right
angles.

Other data: *Specific gravity* 3.3 to 3.5; *fracture*
splintery, uneven, difficult; translucent
to opaque; brittle.

Crystals: Monoclinic; crystals rare; usually in
tough, compact felted masses of
elongated blades.

Best field marks: Toughness, distinct cleavages at 87°
and 93°.

Similar species: Jadeite has higher gravity than nephrite
(variety of tremolite) or serpentinite,
and it is much harder and tougher than
serpentinite.

Environment: Jadeite is a metamorphic mineral and
occurs with glaucophane in blue schist
of regional metamorphic rocks, and
with prehnite and vesuvianite in lode
hydrothermal replacement deposits.

Occurrence: Finest gem-quality jadeite (jade) comes
from Burma, but masses of jadeite up
to about 11 m (35′) across occur
enclosed in serpentinite in San Benito
Co., California. Small pale-green
crystals up to .6 cm (¼″) in length
occur with calcite in veins in
glaucophane schist near Cloverdale,
Sonoma Co., California.

Gemstone data: Semitransparent to translucent
varieties of jadeite are called *jade*.
Jadeite jade colors are: white to green,
and white with greenish spots, the
most common; pale lavender is less
common; bluish lavender; emerald
green ("Imperial Jade"); silvery white;
reddish-brown; and brownish-red.
Value increases with transparency,
color, evenness of color, and freedom
from flaws. Jadeite jade is fashioned
into beads, earrings, bracelets, and
cabochons for rings and brooches, or

carved into ornamental or religious
objects.

The name is from the Spanish *piedra de
ijada,* "stone of the side," in allusion to
the belief that jade could cure kidney
disorders if applied to the side of the
body.

6, 20, 159, | **Spodumene**
678, 689 | Lithium aluminum silicate; pyroxene
group
$LiAlSi_2O_6$

Color and luster:	White, gray, yellowish, emerald-green (hiddenite), pink to purple (kunzite); vitreous, pearly; streak white.
Hardness:	6½–7
Cleavage:	Good, two directions lengthwise at nearly right angles; parting frequently prominent in one direction bisecting larger cleavage angle.
Other data:	*Specific gravity* 3.1 to 3.2; *fracture* uneven, splintery; transparent to translucent; brittle.
Crystals:	Monoclinic; mostly lathlike flattened crystals with deep grooves parallel to the elongation; also cleavage masses, columnar.
Best field marks:	Flattened and striated lathlike crystals and tough splintery fracture.
Similar species:	The tough splintery fracture is sufficient to distinguish spodumene from amblygonite and any of the feldspars.
Environment:	Spodumene is found only in granite pegmatites, where it generally occurs with tourmaline, albite, and lepidolite.
Occurrence:	The largest spodumene crystal in the world was mined in a pegmatite at the Etta Mine in the Black Hills of South Dakota. It measured 12.8 m (42′) in length and over 1.5 m (5′) in width, and is said to have weighed at least 75 metric tons (90 tons). The Pala district in San Diego Co., California, produces gem-quality kunzite, and excellent

hiddenite has come from Alexander Co., North Carolina.

Gemstone data: Pale greenish-yellow to almost emerald-green spodumene is called *hiddenite,* and pink, lilac, and amethystine spodumene is called *kunzite.* Although softer than quartz, their exquisite color and transparency make hiddenite and kunzite of considerable value. However, the mineral's good cleavage makes these stones likely to develop cleavage cracks and flaws. Kunzite fades slowly, especially upon exposure to sunlight. Both hiddenite and kunzite are popularly cut into faceted gems. Alexander County in North Carolina is the only known source for hiddenite, but fine kunzite has come from California and Maine, and from Brazil and Madagascar.

The name is from the Greek *spodoumenos,* "burnt to ash," in allusion to its ashy color. The pink to violet (kunzite) and emerald-green (hiddenite) varieties are used as gemstones, and the uncolored common variety as a source of lithium.

422, 450, 460 **Wollastonite**
Calcium silicate
$CaSiO_3$

Color and luster: Colorless, white, grayish, may have yellowish, reddish, brownish tint; vitreous, silky; streak white.
Hardness: 4½–5
Cleavage: Perfect, two directions at nearly right angles.
Other data: *Specific gravity* 2.8 to 2.9; *fracture* uneven, hackly, splintery; transparent to translucent; fluorescent; brittle.
Crystals: Triclinic; usually in fibrous masses of elongated crystals; also cleavage masses, compact.
Best field marks: Cleavage angles and mineral association.

Similar species: Cleavage angles will aid to distinguish wollastonite from tremolite, whose cleavage angles are 56° and 124°. Pectolite is usually associated with zeolites in basalt cavities, and with sillimanite in schists and gneisses.

Environment: Wollastonite is a product of both contact and regional metamorphism of impure limestones. It generally occurs with calcite and grossular in hornfels.

Occurrence: Large white crystals of wollastonite have been found at Diana, Lewis Co., New York, and at the Crestmore Quarry near Riverside, California. Beautiful fluorescent wollastonite has come from Franklin, Sussex Co., New Jersey.

The name is after W. H. Wollaston (1766–1828), British chemist and mineralogist. Wollastonite is used in ceramics and as a filler in paints.

368, 442, 443, **Pectolite**
445, 453   Hydrous calcium sodium silicate, often with some manganese
$NaCa_2Si_3O_8(OH)$

Color and luster: Colorless, white, grayish; vitreous, silky; streak white.

Hardness: $4\frac{1}{2}$–5

Cleavage: Perfect, two directions at 85° and 95°

Other data: *Specific gravity* 2.7 to 2.9; *fracture* splintery, uneven; translucent; fluorescent; brittle.

Crystals: Triclinic; distinct crystals rare; usually compact and botryoidal masses with radial fibrous structure.

Best field marks: Radial fibrous structure and association with zeolites.

Similar species: Tremolite and wollastonite rarely occur with zeolites or develop the radial fibrous structure seen in pectolite.

Environment: Pectolite most commonly develops in cavities in basalt of volcanic rocks, where the associated minerals usually are zeolites, datolite, calcite, and prehnite. Veins of pectolite occur in serpentinite, and its development here is related to the hydrothermal metamorphic processes that lead to the formation of the serpentinite.

Occurrence: Excellent specimens of pectolite have been found in the basalt at Prospect Park, Passaic Co., New Jersey, and at Bergen Hill, Hudson Co., New Jersey. Coarse gray to white crystals have been found at Magnet Cove, Garland Co., Arkansas, and massive white pectolite in veins up to a meter (several feet) thick occur in serpentinite near Middletown, Lake Co., California.

The name is from the Greek *pektos*, "compacted," in allusion to the mineral's compact fibrous nature.

148, 152, 199, 204, 217 **Rhodonite**
Manganese silicate, often with some calcium
$MnSiO_3$

Color and luster: Brownish red, flesh-red, pink; rarely yellowish or greenish; may tarnish brown or black upon exposure; vitreous; streak colorless.

Hardness: $5\frac{1}{2}$–6

Cleavage: Good, two directions at nearly right angles.

Other data: *Specific gravity* 3.5 to 3.7; *fracture* conchoidal, uneven; transparent to translucent.

Crystals: Triclinic; rare; blocky, tabular, or square prismatic in form; crystals usually in fine-grained masses, granular, compact, cleavable.

Best field marks: Distinctive pink or flesh-red color and (usually) associated black veining.

Similar species: Rhodonite is harder than rhodochrosite, and the massive form is usually cut by narrow veins of dense black manganese oxide, which are not present in pink feldspar.

Environment: Rhodonite forms in metamorphic rocks

and in hydrothermal replacement deposits. It occurs with spessartine and tephroite in hornfels of contact metamorphic rocks, and with willemite, franklinite, and calcite in massive and lode hydrothermal replacement deposits.

Occurrence: There are numerous localities where massive pink rhodonite occurs, but exceptionally fine crystals have been found only at the zinc deposits in the Franklin-Ogdensburg area, Sussex Co., New Jersey.

The name is from the Greek *rhodon*. "rose," in reference to the mineral's usual color. Rhodonite is used as an ornamental stone and gemstone.

---

517 Babingtonite
Basic calcium, iron silicate, often with some manganese
$Ca_2Fe^{2+}Fe^{3+}Si_5O_{14}OH$

Color and luster: Dark green to black; vitreous to splendent; streak light gray to colorless.
Hardness: 5½–6
Cleavage: Good, two directions at nearly right angles.
Other data: *Specific gravity* 3.36; *fracture* subconchoidal to uneven; translucent in thin splinters.
Crystals: Triclinic; usually small platy or rarely prismatic crystals.
Best field marks: Platy or prismatic crystals and weak magnetism.
Similar species: Acmite, augite, and hornblende have crystals that are more prismatic; none of these is magnetic.
Environment: Babingtonite is a secondary mineral occurring in association with zeolites in cavities in altered basalt.
Occurrence: Fine small crystals, seldom over 3 mm (⅛″), have been found at many localities in the basalts of New Jersey, and excellent crystals have come from quarries in Massachusetts, especially at

Blueberry Mt. in Middlesex Co., and near Westfield, in Hampden Co.

Babingtonite is named after William Babington (1757–1833), English mineralogist.

198, 525 **Neptunite**
A complex titanosilicate of sodium, potassium, iron, and manganese
$(Na,K)_2(Fe^{2+},Mn)TiSi_4O_{12}$

Color and luster: Black, with red-brown internal reflections; vitreous; streak cinnamon-brown.
Hardness: 5–6
Cleavage: Perfect, one direction lengthwise.
Other data: *Specific gravity* 3.23; *fracture* conchoidal; translucent red-brown on thin edges.
Crystals: Monoclinic; usually as well-formed prismatic crystals with square cross section.
Best field marks: Crystal form, perfect cleavage (with angles of 80° and 100°), and association with natrolite and benitoite.
Similar species: Black tourmaline, black acmite, and black hornblende. Tourmaline lacks the cleavage, and the cleavage angles of acmite and hornblende differ from those of neptunite.
Environment: Neptunite forms along with benitoite and natrolite in lode hydrothermal replacement deposits. It is also formed in nepheline syenite pegmatites of plutonic rocks.
Occurrence: Neptunite was first found in bodies of nepheline syenite near Julianehaab, SW Greenland, and early in the 1900s it was discovered in California, where it occurs with benitoite and natrolite near the headwaters of the San Benito River, San Benito Co.

It is named after Neptunus, the Roman god of the sea.

56, 114, 115,   **Chrysocolla**
119, 120, 658   Basic copper silicate
$Cu_2H_2Si_2O_5(OH)_4$

Color and luster: Green, bluish green, blue; brown to
                    black from impurities; vitreous, greasy,
                    dull; streak white to pale blue or green.
Hardness: 2–4
Cleavage: None.
Other data: *Specific gravity* 2.0 to 2.2; *fracture*
              uneven to conchoidal; translucent; very
              brittle.
Crystals: Monoclinic; microcrystalline; usually
            compact reniform, botryoidal masses,
            often opal-like in appearance.
Best field marks: Bright blue or green color, softness,
                    brittleness, and lack of crystals.
Similar species: Chrysocolla is harder than turquoise
                   and softer than chalcedony.
Environment: Chrysocolla is a secondary mineral and
               usually forms in the zone of alteration
               in all types of hydrothermal
               replacement deposits, where it is
               frequently associated with azurite,
               malachite, and limonite.
Occurrence: Although most of the chrysocolla
              localities are in SW United States, it
              was also found at Cornwall, Lebanon
              Co., Pennsylvania. Fine specimens of
              glassy green chrysocolla were obtained
              from copper mines at Bisbee, Cochise
              Co., in the Globe district, Gila Co.,
              and in the Clifton-Morenci district,
              Greenlee Co., all in Arizona.

              The name is derived from the Greek
              chrysos, "gold," and *kolla,* "glue," in
              reference to a similar-looking material
              that was used in soldering gold.
              Chrysocolla is a minor ore of copper and
              is used as an ornamental stone. The
              name chrysocolla is also sometimes
              applied to chrysocolla-impregnated
              chalcedony, a much harder mineral.

110, 129 Shattuckite
Basic copper silicate
$Cu_5(SiO_3)_4(OH)_2$

Color and luster: Blue; vitreous, dull; streak blue.
Hardness: $3\frac{1}{2}$
Cleavage: Perfect, two directions.
Other data: *Specific gravity* 4.1; *fracture* uneven; translucent; brittle.
Crystals: Orthorhombic; slender prismatic, in radiating aggregates; also compact, granular, fibrous.
Best field marks: Blue color and occurrence with other copper minerals.
Similar species: Lazurite and lazulite are harder and less dense than shattuckite, and are not associated with malachite and chrysocolla.
Environment: Shattuckite is a secondary copper mineral and develops in the zone of alteration in massive and disseminated hydrothermal replacement deposits. It is associated with malachite, chrysocolla, and azurite.
Occurrence: Shattuckite is a rare mineral and occurs at the Shattuck Mine at Bisbee, Cochise Co., Arizona.

The name is after the Shattuck Mine in Arizona, where the mineral was first found. Shattuckite is used as an ornamental stone.

Cyclosilicates (Ring Silicates)

In this silicate group the basic building block is a ring structure, in which two oxygen ions of each silica tetrahedron are shared with the neighboring tetrahedrons. The cyclosilicates are typically very strong with elongated, striated crystals, as in beryl and tourmaline.

87, 91, 680   **Benitoite**
Barium titanium silicate
$BaTiSi_3O_9$

Color and luster:	Sapphire-blue, light blue, colorless; vitreous; streak colorless.
Hardness:	$6-6\frac{1}{2}$
Cleavage:	None.
Other data:	*Specific gravity* 3.6; *fracture* uneven to conchoidal; transparent to translucent; fluorescent.
Crystals:	Hexagonal; tabular, usually well-shaped crystals that are triangular in shape; triangular base duller in luster than pyramids and prisms.
Best field marks:	Locality (see below) and association with white natrolite and black neptunite.
Similar species:	None.
Environment:	Benitoite is a rare mineral and occurs associated with natrolite and neptunite in lode hydrothermal replacement deposits.
Occurrence:	Benitoite specimens come only from one principal locality, the Gem Mine in San Benito Co., California. Outstanding crystals up to 5 cm (2″) in diameter have been obtained, but most crystals are less than 2.5 cm (1″) across.

The name is after the occurrence in San Benito Co., California. Benitoite is used as a gemstone.

44 **Dioptase**
Basic copper silicate
$CuSiO_2(OH)_2$

Color and luster:	Emerald-green; vitreous, slightly greasy on fracture; streak pale greenish-blue.
Hardness:	5
Cleavage:	Perfect, three directions.
Other data:	*Specific gravity* 3.3 to 3.4; *fracture* uneven to conchoidal; brittle; transparent to translucent.
Crystals:	Hexagonal; commonly in short prismatic crystals capped by rhombohedrons; also granular, massive.
Best field marks:	Emerald-green color and hardness.
Similar species:	Dioptase is harder than brochantite or malachite.
Environment:	Dioptase is a secondary copper mineral and forms in the zone of alteration in all types of hydrothermal replacement deposits, usually associated with limonite and chrysocolla.
Occurrence:	Tsumeb in South-West Africa and mines in Katanga, Zaire, have both been sources for magnificent dioptase crystals up to 2.5 cm (1″) in length. In North America, fine microcrystals of dioptase have come from the Mammoth-St. Anthony Mine at Tiger, Pinal Co., and from the Ox Bow and Summit mines in the Payson district, all in Arizona.

The name derives from the Greek *dia,* "through," and *optasia,* "view," in reference to the fact that cleavage planes could be seen in the crystals. Dioptase is used as a gemstone.

274, 276, 348, 352, 534 **Axinite Group**
Basic calcium, manganese, iron, aluminum borosilicate
$(Ca,Mn,Fe,Mg)_3Al_2BSi_4O_{15}(OH)$

Color and luster:	Clove-brown, yellow, greenish, gray, black; vitreous; streak colorless.
Hardness:	6½–7

Cleavage: Good, one direction.
Other data: *Specific gravity* 3.3 to 3.4; *fracture* uneven to conchoidal; transparent to translucent; brittle.
Crystals: Triclinic; commonly in flattened tabular striated crystals bounded by knifelike edges; also lamellar, granular, bladed aggregates.
Best field marks: Clove-brown color, knife-edged tabular crystals, and striations.
Similar species: The distinctive color and the flattened striated crystals are sufficient to distinguish axinite from titanite.
Environment: Axinite has several environments, in which it is formed. It occurs with diopside and andradite in hornfels of contact metamorphic rocks, and with quartz and calcite in hypothermal veins.
Occurrence: Outstanding transparent crystals have come from Madera Co., California. Small bright-yellow crystals form druses in the zinc ores at Franklin, Sussex Co., New Jersey, and large bladed masses have been found near Luning, Mineral Co., Nevada.

The name is from the Greek *axine*, "ax," in allusion to the sharp-edged tabular crystals resembling a cutting tool.

19, 29, 139, **Beryl**
196, 327, 374, Beryllium aluminum silicate,
400, 676, 682, frequently with some sodium, lithium,
683, 688 and cesium
$Be_3Al_2Si_6O_{18}$

Color and luster: Bright green (emerald), blue, greenish blue (aquamarine), yellow (golden beryl), red, pink (morganite), white, colorless; vitreous; streak colorless.
Hardness: 7½–8
Cleavage: Indistinct, one direction.
Other data: *Specific gravity* 2.66 to 2.92; *fracture* uneven to conchoidal; transparent to translucent.

Crystals: Hexagonal; crystals common, usually six-sided prisms that are striated lengthwise.

Best field marks: Six-sided outline and occurrence in pegmatites.

Similar species: Beryl is harder than apatite, quartz, and the feldspars; does not have the cleavage of feldspars; and is striated the length of the crystal, whereas quartz is striated crosswise.

Environment: Beryl develops in pegmatites and certain metamorphic rocks. It occurs with quartz, microcline, and muscovite in pegmatites, and with quartz, muscovite, and almandine in schist of regional metamorphic rocks.

Occurrence: Beryl has been mined commercially from pegmatites in the New England states, where gem-quality aquamarine, golden beryl, and morganite were also frequently found. Many of the pegmatites in North Carolina have yielded both ore-grade and gem-quality beryl. Pegmatites on Mt. Antero in Chaffee Co., Colorado, have yielded some fine aquamarine crystals, and pale aquamarine and excellent morganite crystals have been obtained from the pegmatites at Mesa Grande and Pala, San Diego Co., California. Pale-green beryl occurs with scheelite in a pegmatite near Oreana, Pershing Co., Nevada.

Gemstone data: Transparent green to slightly bluish-green beryl of medium to dark tones is called *emerald,* one of the most highly prized gemstones. All of the other beryl gems may occur in light colors: light blue and light bluish-green beryl is called *aquamarine;* golden yellow beryl is called *golden beryl;* yellow and brown beryl is called *heliodor;* pink to light purplish-red beryl is called *morganite,* and colorless beryl is called *goshenite.* Fine emeralds have velvety body appearance; their value lies in their even distribution of color. Inclusions are common in emerald, but other stones of this group are usually most valuable when free of flaws. All stones are faceted. Best emerald comes from Colombia and fine morganite, aquamarine, heliodor, goshenite, and golden beryl have come from California, Maine, Connecticut, and North Carolina. Emerald is the birthstone for May; aquamarine, for October.

The name is from the Greek *beryllos,* indicating any green gemstone. Beryl is also valuable industrially as a source of beryllium for use in the manufacture of alloys.

126, 519   **Cordierite**
Magnesium aluminum silicate, often with some iron, calcium, and hydroxyl
$(Mg,Fe^{3+})_2Al_4Si_5O_{18}$

Color and luster:	Pale to dark blue or violet, also gray, brown, black; vitreous; streak colorless.
Hardness:	7–7½
Cleavage:	Poor, one direction.
Other data:	*Specific gravity* 2.6 to 2.7; *fracture* conchoidal, uneven; transparent to translucent; brittle.
Crystals:	Orthorhombic; crystals rare; usually massive or granular.
Best field marks:	Color and dichroism (see below).
Similar species:	None.
Environment:	Cordierite is generally considered a mineral found in metamorphic rocks, but it does occur in granite as well. It is associated with almandine and corundum in hornfels and metaquartzite of contact metamorphic rocks; with almandine, andalusite, and biotite in hornfels and gneiss of regional metamorphic rocks; and with biotite in granite of plutonic rocks.
Occurrence:	Localities where one may collect cordierite are not abundant. Massive cordierite occurs near Haddam, Middlesex Co., Connecticut, on the W side of the Connecticut River, and in

the Yellowknife district of Northwest Territories.

The name is after P. L. A. Cordier (1777–1861), French geologist. Cordierite is used as a gemstone, and is known in the gem trade as iolite, from its violet color (Greek *ion,* "violet").

Cordierite is dichroic: that is, its hue appears to change when it is viewed from different angles. A fragment of violet-blue cordierite will seem to change to grayish color as it is rotated from one crystal direction to another.

Tourmaline Group

32, 33, 40, 103, 157, 158, 201, 242, 506, 541, 542, 543, 672, 687

A complex silicate of boron and aluminum, whose composition varies widely because of substitutions

$Na(Mg,Fe)_3Al_6(BO_3)_3(Si_6O_{18})(OH,F)_4$

Color and luster:	Black (schorl), blue (indicolite), pink and red (rubellite), brown (dravite), green, multicolored, rarely white; vitreous; streak white.
Hardness:	$7–7\frac{1}{2}$
Cleavage:	None.
Other data:	*Specific gravity* 3.0 to 3.3; *fracture* uneven, conchoidal; transparent to opaque; brittle.
Crystals:	Hexagonal, usually short to long prismatic crystals that commonly have a rounded triangular cross section, striated lengthwise; also radiating, columnar, compact.
Best field marks:	Rounded triangular cross section of crystals; poor cleavage.
Similar species:	Tourmaline is harder than apatite and further distinguished from apatite and beryl by striations. It is distinguished from hornblende by its triangular cross section.
Environment:	Tourmaline forms in igneous and metamorphic rocks and veins. It occurs with lepidolite, microcline, and spodumene in granite pegmatites; with

andalusite and biotite in schist of
regional metamorphic rocks; with
siderite and quartz in hypothermal
veins, and with molybdenite and
cassiterite in massive hydrothermal
replacement deposits.

Occurrence: Magnificent prismatic crystals of color-
zoned tourmaline up to 20 cm (8″) in
length have come from the Malagasy
Republic, and gem-quality tourmaline
from Minas Gerais, Brazil. North
America also has some famous
localities. Beautiful green tourmaline
has come from Mt. Mica, Oxford Co.,
Maine, and exceptionally fine red, blue,
and green tourmaline crystals have
come from pegmatites in Riverside and
San Diego Cos., California. Large color-
zoned tourmaline crystals occur in
pegmatites near Alamos, Baja
California Norte, Mexico.

Gemstone data: Most gem tourmalines are color
varieties of elbaite, which may be
green, pink, or any of an enormous
range of tints and shades, including the
green-and-pink zoned crystals called
watermelon tourmaline and the blue
variety called *indicolite.* Red to
purplish-red varieties are often referred
to as *rubellite* and dark orange-brown
varieties as *dravite.* Many tubular
inclusions produce a catseye variety in
the greens, pinks, and blues. Rubellites
are the most highly prized.
Tourmalines are mounted or cut into
faceted gems. Fine gem-quality
tourmaline comes from California,
Maine, Brazil, Burma, the USSR, and
the Malagasy Republic.

The name is from the Singhalese
touramalli, "mixed colored stones," in
reference to varicolored water-rolled
gem pebbles from placer gravels in
Ceylon. The name actually refers to a
group of related minerals—buergerite,
dravite, elbaite, indicolite, rubellite,
schorl, and verdelite—that are treated
in some works as distinct species. The

colorless variety is very rare and is called *achroite*. Tourmaline is widely used as a semiprecious gemstone.

Sorosilicates (Double Tetrahedral Silicates)

Silicate minerals in which two silicon-oxygen tetrahedrons are linked by sharing one oxygen ion between them. Most are moderately hard and stable; epidote and vesuvianite are typical.

116, 378, 432   **Hemimorphite**
Hydrous zinc silicate
$Zn_4Si_2O_7(OH)_2 \cdot H_2O$

Color and luster:	White, colorless, yellowish, bluish, brownish; vitreous, adamantine, dull; streak colorless.
Hardness:	4½–5
Cleavage:	Perfect, one direction.
Other data:	*Specific gravity* 3.4 to 3.5; *fracture* uneven to subconchoidal; transparent to translucent; brittle.
Crystals:	Orthorhombic; usually thin tabular and in fan-shaped aggregates of platy crystals; also in divergent coxcomb groups, mammillary, stalactitic, granular; large crystals rare.
Best field marks:	Bladed crystals and radiating aggregates.
Similar species:	Hemimorphite is lighter than smithsonite and heavier than prehnite.
Environment:	Hemimorphite develops under low-temperature conditions in the near-surface oxidized portion of disseminated hydrothermal replacement deposits, where it is usually associated with gypsum, hematite, and calcite.
Occurrence:	Large mammillary masses of hemimorphite have been found at Sterling Hill, Sussex Co., New Jersey, but the finest North American specimens have come from the Ojuela Mine, Mapimi, Durango, Mexico, in

the form of sharp single blades up to 2.5 cm (1″) in length.

The name is from the Greek prefix *hemi-*, "half," and *morphe*, "form," in allusion to the fact that opposite ends of a hemimorphite crystal display different crystal forms. Hemimorphite is a minor ore of zinc.

144, 419, 454 Lawsonite
Hydrous basic calcium aluminum silicate
$CaAl_2Si_2O_7(OH)_2 \cdot H_2O$

Color and luster:	White or colorless to pale blue, pale gray; vitreous, greasy; streak white.
Hardness:	6
Cleavage:	Perfect in two directions and good in a third direction.
Other data:	*Specific gravity* 3.1; *fracture* uneven; transparent to translucent.
Crystals:	Orthorhombic; commonly prismatic and tabular; also massive, lathlike, granular; simple twinning common.
Best field marks:	Two perfect cleavages and hardness.
Similar species:	Lawsonite is distinguished from zoisite by its twinning and two perfect cleavages. Lawsonite is slightly softer than prehnite but has higher specific gravity and is softer than andalusite.
Environment:	Lawsonite is a product of metamorphism and is associated with chlorite, almandine, and glaucophane in blue schist of regional metamorphic rocks.
Occurrence:	In North America lawsonite localities appear to be restricted to the Coast Ranges of California and Oregon. Lawsonite was discovered on the Tiburon Peninsula, Marin Co., California, where pale-blue prismatic crystals up to 5 cm (2″) in length occur with chlorite, albite, almandine, and glaucophane. Near Valley Ford in Sonoma Co., California, veins of pinkish, coarsely crystalline lawsonite

occur in a blue schist composed almost wholly of glaucophane, and olive-green lawsonite in prismatic crystals occurs nearby in greenstone, a weakly metamorphosed basalt.

Lawsonite is named in honor of Professor Andrew C. Lawson (1861–1952) of the University of California.

52, 532 Pumpellyite

Hydrous calcium, magnesium, aluminum silicate, often with some iron, titanium, and manganese

$Ca_2MgAl_2(SiO_4)(Si_2O_7)(OH)_2 \cdot H_2O$

Color and luster:	Olive green to bluish green, black; vitreous, dull; streak white.
Hardness:	6
Cleavage:	Good, two directions.
Other data:	*Specific gravity* 3.2; *fracture* uneven; translucent; brittle.
Crystals:	Monoclinic; usually as narrow tabular or platy crystals; also fibrous, bladed.
Best field marks:	Platy or tabular crystal shapes, cleavage angle, and softness.
Similar species:	Pumpellyite is softer than epidote, clinozoisite, and zoisite, but harder than chlorite. The cleavage angle of pumpellyite is greater than that of epidote.
Environment:	Pumpellyite is a secondary mineral, and is also formed by metamorphic processes. It occurs as a secondary mineral with chlorite and calcite in basalt of volcanic rocks, and with glaucophane, albite, and lawsonite in schist of regional metamorphic rocks.
Occurrence:	Pumpellyite was found in the copper deposits on the Keweenaw Peninsula, Michigan, in the early 1920s, and since the publication of its description in 1925 it has been recognized at scattered places throughout North America and especially in California. Druses of olive-green crystals have been collected on Porter Creek, near Healdsburg, Sonoma

Co., and fine crystals, some, up to 6
mm (¼″) in length, on the Tiburon
Peninsula in Marin Co., California.

The name is after Raphael Pumpelly
(1837–1923), pioneer American
geologist.

35, 255, 326,	**Vesuvianite (Idocrase)**
692	Basic calcium, magnesium, aluminum silicate, often with some beryllium and fluorine
	$Ca_{10}Mg_2Al_4(SiO_4)_5(Si_2O_7)_2(OH)_4$

Color and luster: Brown, green, rarely yellow or blue;
vitreous; greasy, resinous; streak white.
Hardness: 6½
Cleavage: Poor, one direction.
Other data: *Specific gravity* 3.3 to 3.5; *fracture*
uneven to conchoidal; transparent to
translucent; brittle.
Crystals: Tetragonal; usually in short prismatic
crystals with square cross section; also
columnar, granular, compact like jade.
Best field marks: Square cross section of crystals and
color.
Similar species: Compact massive vesuvianite, which is
commonly referred to as californite, is
harder and heavier than jadeite and
nephrite. Zircon is usually fluorescent
and rarely occurs in crystals of the size
characteristic of vesuvianite.
Environment: Vesuvianite forms by igneous and
metamorphic processes. It commonly is
metamorphic and occurs with grossular,
wollastonite, and calcite in hornfels of
contact metamorphic rocks; with
chromite and magnetite in serpentinite
of hydrothermal metamorphic rocks;
and with wollastonite, andradite, and
diopside in carbonatites.
Occurrence: Gem-quality vesuvianite has been
obtained from a pegmatite in marble
near Sixteen Island Lake, Laurel,
Argenteuil Co., Quebec, and beautiful
micromount crystals of purplish-pink
color occur in massive vesuvianite at the

Montral chrome pit at Black Lake, Megantic Co., Quebec. The blue variety called *cyprine* has been obtained at Franklin, Sussex Co., New Jersey. Fine crystals up to 3.75 cm (1½") across occur in pale-blue calcite at Scratch Gravel, near Helena, Lewis and Clark Co., Montana, and spectacular material of similar nature occurs at the quarries near Riverside, California. Beautiful pale-green massive vesuvianite (californite) occurs in California at Pulga, Butte Co., and near Happy Camp, Siskiyou Co., and crude yellow prismatic crystals occur with grossular at Xalostoc, Morelos, and Lake Jaco, Chihuahua, Mexico.

Gemstone data: Translucent gray to green or nearly colorless vesuvianite with green streaks is called *californite,* and is often sold as "California jade." Californite is fashioned into cabochons. Principal sources are the USSR, Italy, Canada, and California.

The name "vesuvianite" is from the original locality at Mt. Vesuvius, Italy. The alternate name, "idocrase," comes from the Greek *eidos,* "form," and *krasis,* "mixture," because vesuvianite may appear to combine the crystal forms of several other minerals. It is used as a gemstone.

84, 108, 169, **Zoisite**
500, 681 Basic calcium aluminum silicate, often with some iron and manganese; epidote group
$Ca_2Al_3Si_3O_{12}(OH)$

Color and luster: Gray, yellowish brown, greenish, pink (thulite), blue (tanzanite); vitreous, pearly on cleavage; streak white.
Hardness: 6–6½
Cleavage: Good, one direction lengthwise.
Other data: *Specific gravity* 3.2 to 3.4; *fracture* uneven to conchoidal; transparent to

translucent; pink zoisite (thulite) fluoresces.

Crystals: Orthorhombic; usually in long prismatic crystals deeply striated along length; also columnar, bladed, fibrous, compact.

Best field marks: Single plane of cleavage, pearly luster on cleavage, and fluorescence of pink zoisite.

Similar species: Tourmaline has no cleavage. Pink tourmaline may be mistaken for thulite, but does not fluoresce.

Environment: Zoisite is not a common mineral and is restricted to metamorphic rocks. It occurs with chondrodite, tremolite, and wollastonite in hornfels of contact metamorphic rocks, and with hornblende, almandine, and glaucophane in blue schist of regional metamorphic rocks.

Occurrence: Attractive specimens of thulite have been found at Telemark, Norway, perhaps the type locality of the pink variety of zoisite. A blue gem-quality variety, tanzanite, has been found only at localities in Tanzania, East Africa. In North America thulite occurs in Mitchell Co., North Carolina, and in Tulare Co., California. Brown crystals of zoisite occur in zinc ore at Ducktown, Polk Co., Tennessee, and light-gray bladed crystals up to 15 cm (6″) in length occur in glaucophane schist in Mendocino Co., California.

Zoisite was named after Baron S. Zois van Edelstein (1747–1819), and thulite after Thule, an ancient name for Norway.

39, 503 **Clinozoisite**
Basic calcium aluminum silicate; epidote group
$Ca_2Al_3Si_3O_{12}(OH)$

Color and luster: Brown, or pale green to greenish gray; vitreous; streak white, grayish white.

Hardness: 7

Cleavage: Perfect, one direction.

Other data: *Specific gravity* 3.2 to 3.4; *fracture* uneven; translucent to transparent; brittle.

Crystals: Monoclinic; usually short to long prismatic, also tabular or equant, sometimes columnar; acicular, divergent, granular, massive.

Best field marks: Brownish color and good cleavage lengthwise.

Similar species: Epidote is usually green, with slightly higher gravity; tourmaline has no perfect cleavage.

Environment: Clinozoisite forms in metamorphic rocks and develops along with albite, almandine, and glaucophane in blue schist of regional metamorphic rocks, and with calcite and axinite in hornfels of contact metamorphic rocks.

Occurrence: There are not many collecting localities for clinozoisite. Beautiful crystals of clinozoisite up to 12.5 cm (5″) in length have come from scheelite deposits in the Los Gavilanes-Castillo del Real district, Baja California Norte, Mexico, and pinkish-brown masses with columnar structure have come from tungsten prospects near Gerlach, Washoe Co., Nevada.

The name is combined from the Greek *klinein,* "to incline" (a reference to the inclined axis of the monoclinic crystals), and *zoisite.*

41, 330, 522, 524 **Epidote**
Basic calcium, aluminum, iron silicate
$Ca_2Al_2FeOSiO_4Si_2O_7(OH)$

Color and luster: Yellowish green to brownish black; vitreous; streak colorless to gray.

Hardness: 6–7

Cleavage: Perfect, one direction lengthwise.

Other data: *Specific gravity* 3.3 to 3.6; *fracture* uneven; transparent to translucent; brittle.

Crystals:	Monoclinic; usually in long, slender, grooved prismatic crystals that are frequently terminated by two sloping faces; also thick tabular crystals; massive, columnar, divergent, acicular, granular.
Best field marks:	Pistachio or dark greenish-black color and slender grooved crystals.
Similar species:	Clinozoisite is usually brown in color; tourmaline has no cleavage; and actinolite has perfect cleavage in two directions.
Environment:	Epidote forms in several environments. It occurs with albite and andalusite in granite pegmatites; with calcite and zeolites in cavities in basalt of volcanic rocks; with chlorite and actinolite in hornfels and greenstone of contact metamorphic rocks; and with hornblende, almandine, and actinolite in amphibolite and blue schist of regional metamorphic rocks.
Occurrence:	Superb groups and single crystals have come from prospects and small mines near Sulzer, Prince of Wales Island, Alaska. Lustrous short crystals up to 3.75 cm (1½″) across were found in the Calumet iron mine, Chaffee Co., Colorado, and large crystals, as much as 30 cm (12″) in length, were found in several mines in the Seven Devils district, Adams Co., Idaho. Long pale-green crystals up to 15 cm (6″) in length have been obtained from several small tungsten mines in the Greenhorn Mts., Kern Co., California, and dark-green epidote occurs associated with black tourmaline, chlorite, and titanite in pegmatites in the Pino Solo-Alamos district of Baja California Norte, Mexico.

The name "epidote" is from the Greek *epi,* "over," and *didonai,* "to give," and was intended to describe the enlargement of one side of the crystal in some specimens. The name epidote is also used with reference to a group of related minerals (zoisite, clinozoisite, epidote, piemontite, and allanite) of extremely complex structure. Epidote is occasionally used as a gemstone.

Nesosilicates (Independent Tetrahedral Silicates)

The nesosilicates consist of isolated silicon-oxygen tetrahedrons with no direct linkages between adjacent tetrahedrons. Typical nesosilicates are moderately hard and form short, blocky, somewhat square crystals; olivine is typical.

9, 81, 685   ## Olivine Group

A series consisting of two end members, forsterite and fayalite, which occur as separate species; when chemically combined they form the magnesium iron silicate that is commonly called olivine

Mg_2SiO_4 (forsterite)
$(Mg,Fe)_2SiO_4$ (olivine)
Fe_2SiO_4 (fayalite)

Color and luster:	Yellowish green (peridot), yellowish brown, reddish; vitreous; streak colorless.
Hardness:	6½–7
Cleavage:	Indistinct, two directions at 90°.
Other data:	*Specific gravity* 3.2 to 4.3; *fracture* conchoidal, uneven; transparent to translucent; brittle.
Crystals:	Orthorhombic; crystals rare; usually in rounded grains, granular masses.
Best field marks:	Yellowish-green color and occurrence.
Similar species:	Apatite is softer and is fluorescent; green tourmaline is not found in volcanic rocks or gabbros, and green garnet lacks cleavage.
Environment:	Olivine is a rock-forming mineral and occurs as an essential mineral in gabbro, peridotite, and basalt.
Occurrence:	The finest olivine (peridot) comes from St. Johns Island in the Red Sea. Olivine

is widespread in various rocks in North America, but there are not many localities where one can collect the mineral in any size other than grains. Small grains up to 6 mm (¼″) across occur on Timothy Mt., near Lac La Hache, British Columbia, and subangular nodules composed of olivine in grains occur in basalt on the San Carlos Indian Reservation, Gila and Apache Cos., Arizona, and at Dish Hill, a breached volcanic cone near Ludlow, San Bernardino Co., California.

Gemstone data: Transparent gem-quality olivine is called *peridot,* and ranges in color from yellowish-green to olive green. Dark yellowish-green stones are most valuable, and flawless stones are common. Peridot is incorrectly known as "evening emerald" because it appears to lose its yellowish hue at night and then closely resembles emerald. Peridot gems are faceted. Fine quality peridot has come in small stones from New Mexico and Arizona, but large stones of exceptional beauty come from the Island of Zebirget in the Red Sea. Peridot is a birthstone for August.

Olivine is named for its olive-green color; fayalite after Fayal, an island in the Azores; and forsterite after Johann R. Forster (1729–1798), a German naturalist who sailed with the great explorer Captain James Cook.

279 Tephroite
Manganese silicate, often with some iron, magnesium, and zinc; olivine group
Mn_2SiO_4

Color and luster: Ash-gray, pink, brown; vitreous, greasy; streak pale gray.
Hardness: 6
Cleavage: Good, two directions at 90°.

Other data: *Specific gravity* 4.0 to 4.1; *fracture* uneven to conchoidal; translucent.

Crystals: Orthorhombic; usually blocky crystals; also cleavage masses, granular, compact.

Best field mark: Two cleavages at 90°.

Similar species: Tephroite can be easily distinguished from willemite by its good cleavage at 90° angle.

Environment: Tephroite is a mineral of metamorphic and hydrothermal replacement origin. It occurs with quartz, spessartine, and rhodonite in hornfels of contact metamorphic rocks, and with calcite and rhodonite in massive hydrothermal replacement deposits.

Occurrence: Massive tephroite and crystals up to 1.25 cm (½″) across were found in abundance in the zinc mines at Franklin and Ogdensburg, Sussex Co., New Jersey. Tephroite has recently been identified at a number of small manganese mines in the foothill belt of the Sierra Nevada, California.

The name is from the Greek *tephros,* "ash-colored."

---

359 **Phenakite**
Beryllium silicate
Be_2SiO_4

Color and luster: Colorless, white, yellow, pink, brown; vitreous; streak colorless.

Hardness: 7½–8

Cleavage: Poor, one direction.

Other data: *Specific gravity* 2.97 to 3.00; *fracture* conchoidal, uneven; transparent to translucent.

Crystals: Hexagonal; usually in well-developed flat rhombohedral to long prismatic crystals, striated lengthwise. Crystals are generally small, less than 2.5 cm (1″) across, and form penetration twins.

Best field marks: Rhombohedral crystals, high hardness, and lengthwise striations on crystals.

Similar species: Quartz and topaz. Phenakite is harder

than quartz and is striated lengthwise; quartz is striated across the prism face. Topaz has a perfect basal cleavage, and phenakite has a poor cleavage.

Environment: Phenakite forms in hypothermal veins along with topaz and cassiterite; in pegmatities, where it occurs with quartz, microcline, and albite; and in mica schist of regional metamorphic rocks, where it occurs with emerald and chrysoberyl.

Occurrence: Fine crystals of phenakite, up to 5 cm (2″) across, have come from pegmatites at the Morefield Mine, Winterham, Amelia Co., Virginia. Twinned crystals, as much as 3.75 cm (1½″) in length, have been found on Mt. Antero, Chaffee Co., Colorado.

The name is from the Greek *phenakos,* "deceiver," because it was formerly mistaken for quartz. Phenakite is used as a minor gemstone.

23, 31, 246, 284, **Willemite**
335, 371, 418   Zinc silicate, often with considerable manganese and iron
Zn_2SiO_4

Color and luster: Yellow, green, red, brown, white, colorless; resinous, vitreous; streak white.

Hardness: 5½

Cleavage: Good, three directions.

Other data: *Specific gravity* 3.9 to 4.2; *fracture* uneven to conchoidal; transparent to translucent; strongly fluorescent.

Crystals: Hexagonal; usually small short prismatic or rhombohedral; also compact, granular, disseminated.

Best field marks: Hardness, resinous luster, associated minerals, and strong fluorescence.

Similar species: Willemite has greater hardness than smithsonite and is generally associated with calcite, zincite, and franklinite.

Environment: Willemite occurs associated with calcite, franklinite, zincite, and rhodonite in massive hydrothermal replacement deposits.

Occurrence: The finest willemite comes from the zinc mines at Franklin and Ogdensburg, Sussex Co., New Jersey. Tiny crystals, considered ideal as micromounts, occur with wulfenite, vanadinite, and quartz in the Mammoth-St. Anthony Mine at Tiger, Pinal Co., Arizona.

Its name is after Willem I (1772–1843), king of the Netherlands. It is used as an ore of zinc and as a gemstone.

250, 485   Andalusite
Aluminum silicate
Al_2SiO_5

Color and luster: White, gray, pink, reddish brown, olive green; vitreous, dull; streak colorless.
Hardness: 7½
Cleavage: Good, two directions at 89° and 91°.
Other data: *Specific gravity* 3.1 to 3.2; *fracture* uneven to subconchoidal; transparent to translucent.
Crystals: Orthorhombic; usually in stubby crystals that lack sharp edges; nearly square shape in cross section; also columnar, granular, disseminated. Rough prisms that show cross or checkered pattern in cross section are called *chiastolite*.
Best field marks: The internal pattern (in chiastolite), squarish shape in cross section, and good cleavage.
Similar species: Tourmaline lacks the cleavage and squarish cross section of andalusite.
Environment: Andalusite is found principally in metamorphic rocks, but does occur in igneous rocks as well. It occurs with quartz, microcline, and muscovite in granite pegmatites; with biotite and corundum in hornfels of contact metamorphic rocks; with almandine,

cordierite, and muscovite in gneiss and schist of regional metamorphic rocks; and with quartz, pyrophyllite, and topaz in massive hydrothermal replacement deposits.

Occurrence: Masses of pinkish-gray and white andalusite, often with clusters of prismatic crystals, were mined in the White Mts. near Laws, Inyo Co.; crude pinkish-brown crystals of andalusite have come from granite pegmatites from Fresno Co.; and the variety chiastolite occurs in abundance in mica schist near Chowchilla, Madera Co., all in California. The best chiastolite comes from Lancaster, Worcester, and Middlesex Cos., Massachusetts.

Named for the Spanish province of Andalusia. Andalusite is used as a gemstone and in ceramics, particularly in the manufacture of spark plugs.

288 Sillimanite
Aluminum silicate
Al_2SiO_5

Color and luster: Grayish white, brown, greenish brown; vitreous, silky; streak colorless.

Hardness: 6–7

Cleavage: Perfect, one direction lengthwise.

Other data: *Specific gravity* 3.2 to 3.3; *fracture* uneven, splintery; transparent to translucent.

Crystals: Orthorhombic; usually fibrous masses, columnar, radiating; distinct prismatic crystals rare.

Best field marks: Hardness and brittleness.

Similar species: Sillimanite is harder and more brittle than tremolite, chrysotile, and similar fibrous minerals.

Environment: Sillimanite is a metamorphic mineral and is usually found in schist and gneiss of regional metamorphic rocks, where it occurs with almandine, biotite, and quartz.

Occurrence: Sillimanite is not a common mineral, but excellent material may be found at several places in North America. Fibrous masses occur at Worcester, Worcester Co., Massachusetts, and at Norwich, New London Co., and Willimantic, Windham Co., Connecticut. Dark-brown crystals up to 5 cm (2″) in length have been found in Oconee Co., South Carolina.

The name is in honor of Benjamin Silliman (1779–1864), first professor of mineralogy at Yale University. An earlier name was "fibrolite."

101, 386 **Kyanite**
Aluminum silicate
Al_2SiO_5

Color and luster: Blue, white, colorless, gray, green, nearly black; vitreous; streak colorless.
Hardness: Varies: lengthwise 4–5; crosswise 6–7.
Cleavage: Perfect, one direction lengthwise; good in a second direction.
Other data: *Specific gravity* 3.5 to 3.7; *fracture* splintery; transparent to translucent.
Crystals: Triclinic; usually in bladed crystal aggregates, less often in terminated crystals.
Best field marks: Different hardness in two directions and bladed habit.
Similar species: Kyanite is seldom white or gray, as are tremolite and wollastonite, and these minerals do not have two distinct hardnesses.
Environment: Kyanite is a product of regional metamorphism and occurs associated with quartz, biotite, and almandine in gneiss and schist.
Occurrence: Striking specimens composed of deep-blue kyanite and chocolate-brown staurolite in a matrix of white mica have come from Pizzo Forno, Switzerland. In North America, blue blades of kyanite clear enough to yield gemstones have been found in Yancy,

Co., North Carolina. Spectacular kyanite occurs with rutile on Graves Mt., Lincoln Co., Georgia, and large minable masses of kyanite occur in the Cargo Muchacho Mts., Imperial Co., California.

The name kyanite ("cyanite" in its original spelling) is derived from the Greek *kyanos*, "dark blue." It is used in ceramics.

37, 94, 256,	**Topaz**
285, 307, 357,	Aluminum fluorsilicate
358, 367, 698	$Al_2SiO_4(F,OH)_2$

Color and luster: White, colorless, yellow, pink, bluish, greenish; vitreous; streak colorless.

Hardness: 8

Cleavage: Perfect, one basal direction.

Other data: *Specific gravity* 3.4 to 3.6; *fracture* subconchoidal, uneven; transparent to translucent.

Crystals: Orthorhombic; usually in stubby to medium-long prismatic crystals striated lengthwise; also granular, massive.

Best field marks: Great hardness and excellent cleavage across the crystal.

Similar species: Topaz is harder than quartz and has excellent cleavage, which is lacking in beryl and quartz.

Environment: Topaz is a high-temperature mineral and is generally found in igneous rocks and high-temperature veins. It occurs with albite, beryl, and quartz in granite pegmatites; with orthoclase and quartz in cavities of rhyolite of volcanic rocks; and with rutile, pyrophyllite, and quartz in massive hydrothermal replacement deposits.

Occurrence: The finest topaz is said to come from the Ural Mts. in the USSR, but excellent specimens are also found in North America. Pale-blue and sherry-colored crystals have been found in cavities in the granitic rocks near Conway, Carroll Co., New Hampshire.

Pegmatites in the Pikes Peak area of Colorado have been the source of both blue and sherry-colored crystals. Beautiful colorless and sherry-colored topaz occurs with fluorite, quartz, garnet, and hematite in cavities in rhyolite on Thomas Mt., Juab Co., Utah, and beautiful well-formed crystals have come from the Little Three Pegmatite, near Ramona, San Diego Co., California.

Gemstone data: Gem-quality transparent topaz occurs in several colors, including colorless, pale greenish-yellow to yellowish-green, yellow to orange-yellow and blue. Dark orange to dark orange-red topaz is called *hyacinth*. The light red to light purplish-red topaz is produced by heat-treating sherry-colored or brownish-yellow stones. Flaws and inclusions are common in topaz, and clean fine stones are not common. Topaz gems are faceted. Fine yellow, blue, and sherry-colored stones have come from North America, but Brazil, Sri Lanka, and the USSR are the principal sources. Topaz is the birthstone for November.

The name is from the Greek *topazos,* a name said to be applied to a gemstone whose identity has been lost.

249, 538 **Staurolite**
Basic silicate of iron and aluminum, often with some magnesium and zinc
$Fe_2Al_9Si_4O_{22}(OH)_2$

Color and luster: Yellowish brown, reddish to brownish black, weathering to gray; vitreous, dull; streak white.

Hardness: 7–7½

Cleavage: Poor, one direction lengthwise.

Other data: *Specific gravity* 3.7 to 3.8; *fracture* uneven to subconchoidal; translucent to opaque; brittle.

Crystals: Monoclinic (pseudo-orthorhombic); in single or twinned crystals. Single crystals are prismatic and show pseudohexagonal cross section; twinned crystals show two individual crystals intergrown at nearly 60° or nearly 90°.

Best field marks: Twin crystals, with two prisms often forming a right-angle "cross."

Similar species: The twin crystal form is sufficient to distinguish staurolite from tourmaline or andalusite.

Environment: Staurolite occurs with albite, biotite, and sillimanite in gneiss and schist of regional metamorphic rocks.

Occurrence: The famous locality at Pizzo Forno, Switzerland, has yielded choice specimens containing deep-brown staurolite and blue kyanite in white mica. In North America, beautifully twinned and single crystals of staurolite occur at Windham, Cumberland Co., Maine; at Sugar Hill, Franconia, and Lisbon, Grafton Co., New Hampshire; and in Fannin Co., Georgia. Staurolite occurs as fine twinned crystals near Pilar, Rio Arriba Co., New Mexico, and as single crystals up to 13 cm (5″) in length in the Funeral Mts., Inyo Co., California.

The name is from the Greek *stauros,* "cross," in reference to the commonly crosslike twinned form. The right-angled staurolite penetration twins are popular as good luck charms. Transparent single crystals are occasionally cut into gems.

3, 4, 10, 11, **Garnet Group**

146, 171, 175, A group of very closely related

176, 177, 194, aluminum silicates (pyrope, almandine,

223, 238, 239, and spessartine) and calcium silicates

240, 243, 309, (grossular, andradite, and uvarovite)

311, 314, 363, $Mg_3Al_2Si_3O_{12}$ (pyrope)

507, 511, 512, $Fe_3^{2+}Al_2Si_3O_{12}$ (almandine)

669, 670, 671, $Mn_3Al_2Si_3O_{12}$ (spessartine)

693, 697, 702 $Ca_3Al_2Si_3O_{12}$ (grossular)

$Ca_3Fe_2^{3+}Si_3O_{12}$ (andradite)

$Ca_3Cr_2Si_3O_{12}$ (uvarovite)

Color: *Pyrope:* deep red to reddish black, rarely purple or rose to pale purplish red (var. *rhodolite*).

Almandine: deep red to brown, brownish black.

Spessartine: brownish red to hyacinth-red.

Grossular: colorless, white, yellow, pink, green, brown.

Andradite; wine red, greenish (var. *demantoid*), yellow (var. *topazolite*), brown, black (var. *melanite*).

Uvarovite: emerald-green.

Luster: Vitreous.

Streak: Colorless.

Hardness: 6½–7½

Cleavage: None; parting sometimes distinct in six directions.

Other data: *Specific gravity* 3.56 to 4.32, varies with composition; *fracture* conchoidal, uneven; brittle; transparent to opaque.

Crystals: Isometric; crystals very common as dodecahedrons and trapezohedrons; also granular, lamellar, compact, disseminated.

Best field marks: Crystal form (usually dodecahedron or trapezohedron) and hardness.

Similar species: Apatite is softer than any of the garnets; zircon has higher gravity and often fluoresces; tourmaline has lower gravity.

Environment: Some garnets are of igneous origin, but most of them are products of metamorphism. *Pyrope* occurs with olivine and hypersthene in peridotite of plutonic rocks. *Almandine* occurs in diorite of plutonic rocks, and with andalusite, hornblende, and biotite in hornfels and schist of contact and regional metamorphic rocks. *Spessartine* occurs with albite and muscovite in granite pegmatites and with quartz and riebeckite in blue schist of regional metamorphic rocks. *Grossular* occurs with wollastonite, calcite, and vesuvianite in hornfels of contact metamorphic rocks. *Andradite* occurs with albite and biotite in granite pegmatites; with orthoclase, calcite,

and wollastonite in carbonatites; with
calcite and hedenbergite in hornfels of
contact metamorphic rocks; and with
magnetite and hedenbergite in skarn of
hydrothermal metamorphic rocks.
Uvarovite occurs with olivine and
chromite in peridotite of plutonic rocks
and in serpentinite of hydrothermal
metamorphic rocks.

Occurrence: Garnet localities are abundant
throughout North America, and only a
few of the more important ones will be
listed here. *Pyrope* occurs in peridotite
in Kentucky, Arkansas, Arizona, New
Mexico, and Utah. Well-formed
crystals of *almandine* have come from
Wrangell, SE Alaska; from Emerald
Creek, Benewah Co., Idaho; and from
Michigamme, Michigan. Large
corroded crystals of *spessartine* have come
from the Rutherford No. 2 Mine,
Amelia, Amelia Co., Virginia; crystals
up to 2.5 cm (1″) in diameter have been
found in several pegmatites in the
Ramona district, San Diego Co.,
California; sharp, dark-red, well-formed
crystals occur in cavities in rhyolite near
Ely, White Pine Co., Nevada; and
brilliant crystals of spessartine have
been found with topaz at Ruby Mt.,
near Nathrop, Chaffee Co., Colorado.
Grossular is perhaps the commonest of
all garnets. Fine colorless crystals up to
6 mm (¼″) across occur in Gatineau
and Magantic Cos., Quebec, fine
lustrous pale brown crystals up to 7.5
cm (3″) across were found near Minot,
Androscoggin Co., Maine, and
beautiful white and pink crystals up to
10 cm (4″) across have been found near
Xalostoc, Morelos, Mexico. Brilliant
black crystals of *andradite* (var.
melanite) have been found at Franklin,
Sussex Co., New Jersey and at the
benitoite locality, San Benito Co.,
California. Dark olive-green andradite
crystals up to 5 cm (2″) across have
come from the French Creek mines,
Chester Co., Pennsylvania, and brown

to bronzy-green dodecahedrons have been found near Stanley Butte, Graham Co., Arizona. Pale green andradite (var. *demantoid*) occurs with magnetite on Erskine Creek, Kern Co., California. *Uvarovite* is rare, but fine specimens showing bright-green micro crystals of uvarovite on grayish diopside occur at Magog, Stanstead Co., Quebec, and in brilliant crystals up to 3 mm (⅛″) across on serpentinite at Thetford, Megantic Co., Quebec. Fine druses of uvarovite have been found in massive chromite and beautiful crystals up to 6 mm (¼″) across were found in a small chromite mine near the former site of Jacksonville, Tuolumne Co., California.

Gemstone data: The garnet species with red or purple varieties, including pyrope, almandine, and a variety intermediate between these two, called rhodolite, are considered gemstones. Pyrope is intense red, orange-red, brownish-red, and red-brown in color; almandine is dark red and purplish-red to reddish-purple; and rhodolite is purplish-red to rose red. Pyropes and rhodolites are usually free from flaws, whereas almandines are likely to contain flaws. Fine pyropes have been used as gems by royalty and the combined brilliance and fine purplish color of rhodolite have produced some exquisite transparent gemstones. Garnets can be faceted, and those of deep color are fashioned as cabochons and are called carbuncles. Gem-quality pyrope comes from Arizona and Utah; almandine from Alaska and Idaho; and rhodolite from North Carolina. Foreign sources include Australia, Ceylon, Czechoslovakia, South Africa, and South America. Garnet is the birthstone for January.

Pyrope is from the Greek *pyropos,* "fire-eyed." *Almandine* is named after Alabanda, a town of ancient Caria (Asia Minor). *Spessartine* is named after an

occurrence in the Spessart district,
Bavaria, Germany. *Grossular* is from the
New Latin *grossularia,* "gooseberry,"
because some grossular crystals are pale
green like the fruit. *Andradite* is named
after J. B. de Andrada e Silva (1763–
1838), Brazilian geologist. *Uvarovite* is
named after Count S. S. Uvarov (1785–
1855), Russian statesman and mineral
collector. The different garnets are used
industrially as abrasive materials.

231, 241, 244, **Zircon**
686   Zirconium silicate, often with some
         hafnium
         $ZrSiO_4$

Color and luster: Gray, brown, yellow, green, red
transparent (hyacinth), colorless, or
smoky (jargoon); adamantine, vitreous;
streak colorless.

Hardness: 7½

Cleavage: Indistinct, two directions parallel to
prism faces.

Other data: *Specific gravity* 4.6 to 4.7; *fracture*
uneven; transparent to translucent;
fluorescent; brittle.

Crystals: Tetragonal; generally in simple short
prismatic crystals showing square cross
section terminated by the pyramid; also
irregular lumps, disseminated grains.

Best field marks: Tetragonal crystals, high hardness, and
high gravity.

Similar species: Vesuvianite. Zircon has higher specific
gravity than vesuvianite.

Environment: Zircon develops in igneous and
metamorphic rocks, and is a common
accessory mineral in the common types
of plutonic rocks. It occurs with
orthoclase and biotite in nepheline
syenites of the plutonic rocks; with
albite and acmite in carbonatites; and
although it does not form in placer
deposits, they are the commercial
source for gem and industrial zircon.

Occurrence: Large brown crystals were found in
Dungannon Township, Hastings Co.,

and fine crystals have come from veins of apatite in Buckingham Township, Ottawa Co., Ontario. The Hill Mine at Franklin, Sussex Co., New Jersey, and the pegmatites on St. Peter's Dome, El Paso Co., Colorado, have yielded sharp lustrous black crystals of zircon. Well-formed, doubly terminated crystals up to 1.6 cm (⅝") long have been collected in the Wichita Mts. of Oklahoma.

Gemstone data: Transparent gem-quality zircon is produced by heat-treating natural zircon. Colorless or pale gray zircon is called *jargoon,* and yellow, orange, and red zircons are called *hyacinth.* Other gem varieties are blue, green, violet, and brown zircon. Colors produced by heat-treating stones are likely to fade upon prolonged exposure to sunlight. The blue zircon is said to be the most popular and valuable. All stones are faceted. Good specimens occur in North America, but gem-quality material comes from foreign sources, particularly Ceylon, Burma, and France. Zircon is a December birthstone.

The name is from the Persian *zargun,* "gold-colored." Zircon is a source of zirconium and hafnium.

---

236 Chondrodite

Magnesium fluorsilicate; may contain some iron; humite group
$Mg_5Si_2O_8(F,OH)_2$

Color and luster: Honey-yellow to reddish brown or red; vitreous, resinous; streak white.
Hardness: 6–6½
Cleavage: Poor, one direction.
Other data: *Specific gravity* 3.1 to 3.2; *fracture* subconchoidal to uneven; transparent to translucent; sometimes fluorescent.
Crystals: Monoclinic; usually prismatic or tabular; more commonly shapeless grains, disseminated.

Best field marks: Hardness, good one-directional cleavage, and low specific gravity.

Similar species: Chondrodite is softer than garnet; has a cleavage that is lacking in brown tourmaline; and is lighter in weight than staurolite (which is unlikely to be found in the same environment).

Environment: Chondrodite is a metamorphic mineral and occurs with diopside, spinel, and phlogopite in hornfels of contact and regional metamorphic rocks, and with magnetite in serpentinite of hydrothermal metamorphic rocks.

Occurrence: Collecting localities for chondrodite are uncommon. Perhaps the best North American material comes from the Tilly Foster Mine, near Brewster, Putnam Co., New York, where deep red-brown crystals up to 5 cm (2″) across occur with magnetite.

The name is from the Greek *chondros*, "grain," in reference to the generally granular appearance of the mineral.

230, 349, 516, **Titanite (Sphene)**
695 Calcium titanium silicate, often with some thorium
$CaTiSiO_5$

Color and luster: Brown to black, yellow, gray, green; vitreous; resinous, adamantine; streak white.

Hardness: 5–5½

Cleavage: Distinct in two directions parallel to prism faces; parting frequently distinct.

Other data: *Specific gravity* 3.4 to 3.6; *fracture* conchoidal; transparent to translucent; brittle.

Crystals: Monoclinic; usually as sharp-edged tabular crystals that may or may not be twinned; also lamellar, compact.

Best field marks: Wedge-shaped crystals, high luster, and color.

Similar species: Titanite has better cleavage than staurolite; is harder than sphalerite; and is denser but softer than axinite.

Environment: Titanite is a minor accessory mineral in many plutonic rocks and also occurs in some metamorphic rocks. It occurs as small crystals in granite, granodiorite, diorite, and monzonite of plutonic rocks, and in crystals up to 12.5 cm (5″) across in granite pegmatites and nepheline syenite pegmatites; albite and zircon in carbonatites; with almandine, glaucophane, and lawsonite in blue schist of regional metamorphic rocks; and with calcite in disseminated hydrothermal replacement deposits.

Occurrence: Large crystals of titanite, some weighing as much as 35 kg (80 lb), have been found near Eganville, Renfrew Co., Ontario, and tabular crystals up to 20 cm (8″) across have been found at Rossie and Oxbow, St. Lawrence Co., New York. The Tilly Foster iron mine, near Brewster, Putnam Co., New York, has yielded some sharp bright-yellow, gem-quality twinned crystals up to 5 cm (2″) across, and fine brown translucent crystals up to 2.5 cm (1″) across occur with adularia and black tourmaline near Whitehall, Jefferson Co., Montana. The small pegmatites near El Alamo in Baja California Norte, Mexico, yield good crystals of brown to vivid green color.

Titanite is named for its titanium content. The alternate name, "sphene," comes from the Greek *sphen,* "wedge," an allusion to the characteristic shape of the crystals. Titanite is used as a gemstone.

128, 165 **Dumortierite**
Aluminum borosilicate
$Al_7O_3(BO_3)(SiO_4)_3$

Color and luster: Blue, violet, rarely pink, brown; vitreous, dull; streak white.
Hardness: 7

Cleavage: Good, one direction, and poor in a second direction.

Other data: *Specific gravity* 3.3 to 3.4; *fracture* uneven, hackly; translucent; sometimes fluorescent.

Crystals: Orthorhombic; crystals rare; usually in compact fibrous and columnar masses.

Best field marks: Bright color and fibrous appearance.

Similar species: Lazulite and lazurite are not fibrous, and pink lepidolite is much softer than pink dumortierite.

Environment: Dumortierite occurs with quartz and andalusite in granite pegmatites, and with andalusite and muscovite in hydrothermal replacement deposits.

Occurrence: Dumortierite occurs with quartz and kyanite at Clip, N of Yuma, Arizona. Deep-blue and violet dumortierite was mined from extensive deposits near Oreana, Pershing Co., Nevada, and dumortierite was encountered in building excavations in New York City. The dumortierite from Dehesa in San Diego Co., California, has a purple fluorescence, and the blue dumortierite in gray quartz in Los Angeles Co., California, resembles lapis lazuli.

The name is after Eugene Dumortier, 19th-century French paleontologist. Dumortierite is used as a gemstone.

Silicates of Complex Structure

The last three minerals to be described have very complex atomic structures, combining structural features of two or more of the other silicate groups.

58, 60, 381 **Prehnite**
Basic calcium aluminum silicate, often with some iron
$Ca_2Al_2Si_3O_{10}(OH)_2$

Color and luster: Light green, oil-green, gray, white, colorless; frequently fading upon exposure; vitreous, waxy; streak colorless.

Hardness: 6–6½

Cleavage: Distinct, one direction.

Other data: *Specific gravity* 2.9 to 3.0; *fracture* uneven; translucent to almost transparent.

Crystals: Orthorhombic; crystals rare, usually in botryoidal masses, with ridged surfaces marked by edges of curving crystals; also stalactitic, radial fibrous.

Best field marks: Green botryoidal crusts.

Similar species: Prehnite has lower specific gravity and is harder than hemimorphite and smithsonite.

Environment: Prehnite develops in cavities in basalt of volcanic rocks and occurs with zeolites, calcite, and pectolite.

Occurrence: Some of the finest North American prehnite has come from quarries in basalt at Paterson and W Paterson, Passaic Co., New Jersey, and from quarries in Fairfax and Loudon Cos., Virginia. It also occurs on the Keweenaw Peninsula, Michigan, and at Farmington, Hartford Co., Connecticut.

Prehnite is named for an 18th-century Dutchman, Colonel van Prehn, who brought the first specimens to Europe from South Africa in 1774. It is a minor gemstone, usually being fashioned into cabochons.

317, 365, 392, 405 **Datolite**
Basic calcium borosilicate
$CaBSiO_4(OH)$

Color and luster: Greenish to colorless or white, with yellowish, reddish, grayish tinge; vitreous, dull, greasy; streak colorless.

Hardness: 5–5½

Cleavage: None.

Other data: *Specific gravity* 2.8 to 3.0; *fracture* uneven, conchoidal; transparent to translucent.

Crystals:	Monoclinic; usually short prismatic to blunt wedge-shaped complex crystals; also fine-grained porcelainlike masses, botryoidal.
Best field marks:	Glassy, pale-greenish, wedge-shaped crystals.
Similar species:	Analcime has no cleavage but occurs as isometric-trapezohedral crystals. Stilbite has good cleavage and is softer than datolite.
Environment:	Datolite develops in cavities in basalt of volcanic rocks and is usually associated with calcite, prehnite, and zeolites.
Occurrence:	Some of the finest crystals have come from basalt at the Lane Quarry, near Westfield, Hampden Co., Massachusetts. Beautiful glassy crystals up to 6.25 cm (2½″) across were found in cavities in copper mines on the Keweenaw Peninsula, Michigan, and pinkish fine-grained datolite nodules also occur at the Michigan localities.

The name is from the Greek *dateisthai*, "to divide," because the granular aggregates crumble easily. Datolite is used as a minor gemstone.

138, 162 Inesite
Hydrous calcium manganese silicate
$Ca_2Mn_7Si_{10}O_{28}(OH)_2 \cdot 5H_2O$

Color and luster:	Rose- to flesh-red, pink; vitreous; streak pale pinkish.
Hardness:	6
Cleavage:	Perfect, one direction, and good in second direction.
Other data:	*Specific gravity* 3.0; *fracture* uneven; translucent; brittle.
Crystals:	Triclinic; usually prismatic and fibrous; also spherulitic and radiating.
Best field marks:	Pink color and prismatic or fibrous habit.
Similar species:	None.
Environment:	Inesite occurs with rhodonite and axinite in serpentinite of hydrothermal metamorphic rocks.

Occurrence: Inesite has been found at several localities, but not too many occurrences have been noted in North America. It occurs with rhodonite and axinite in Trinity Co., California, and at Villa Carona, Durango, Mexico.

The origin of the name is not definitely known, but may derive from the Greek *ines,* "fibers."

PART II: ROCKS

A GUIDE TO ROCK IDENTIFICATION

All rocks fall into three great classes, which are named according to their origin: igneous rocks, sedimentary rocks, and metamorphic rocks. The first step in identifying a rock, therefore, is to decide, by examining its texture and structure, which class it belongs in. The second step is to make an exact identification, by identifying the minerals that make up the rock.

Igneous Rocks Igneous rocks form the first of the three great rock classes. The term igneous (from the Latin *ignis,* meaning "fire") indicates that these rocks solidified directly from molten rock or from the "volatile constituents" (hot aqueous or gaseous solutions) emanating from it. This rock melt, or magma, generally originates at great depths beneath the earth's surface and then makes a long, slow upward journey through the earth's crust.

The igneous rocks are identified, by origin, as either volcanic or plutonic. If the cooling magma solidifies before it reaches the earth's surface it forms plutonic (or intrusive) igneous rocks, such as granite or gabbro. If the magma travels all the way to the earth's surface before cooling it is called lava; when the lava solidifies it forms volcanic (or extrusive) igneous rocks, such as obsidian or basalt. Characteristic features of igneous rocks include considerable hardness (mostly greater than 5½), crystalline texture with a fabric of interlocking mineral grains (in plutonic rocks), dense, glassy, or sometimes spongelike appearance (in volcanic rocks), and a general lack of distinctive structures such as banding or layering.

Igneous Rock Textures   The following terms are commonly used to describe the textures of igneous rocks:

Glassy   Amorphous, lacking any crystalline mineral grains; may have the appearance of glass (obsidian) or have a cellular or vesicular structure like "glass foam" (pumice).

Aphanitic   Dense, composed of crystalline mineral grains too small to be seen with the naked eye.

Porphyritic   Having a relatively small number of clearly distinguishable crystals (phenocrysts) in a finer-grained groundmass.

Aphanitic-porphyritic   Visible but generally small phenocrysts distributed through an aphanitic groundmass.

Phaneritic   Even-granular, with all crystals visible to the naked eye and approximately of equal size.

Phaneritic-porphyritic   Uneven-granular, with relatively large phenocrysts in a phaneritic groundmass.

Pegmatitic   Very coarse uneven-granular, with crystals of all sizes distributed unevenly throughout the rock.

Fragmental   Consisting of pyroclastic fragments (produced by volcanic explosions) as in tuff and volcanic breccia. Fragmental rocks are classified as volcanic igneous rocks even though they actually form through a sedimentary process.

Igneous Rock Structures   The following terms are used to describe structural features in igneous rocks:

Spherulitic   Characterized by rounded or spherical bodies of needlelike crystals (mostly quartz or feldspars) radiating from a central point. These may vary in size from microscopic to several centimeters across. Spherulitic structure occurs mostly in glassy rocks (obsidian) or partly glassy rocks (rhyolite).

Vesicular   Having numerous vesicles (cavities) of varied shape. Vesicles are formed by the rapid solidification of gas bubbles in surface or near-surface lava flows (example: scoria). In extreme cases vesicular rocks may be cellular or spongy, representing a solidified "rock foam" with glassy texture and generally rhyolitic composition (pumice).

Amygdaloidal   Having vesicles that are filled with secondary minerals, usually quartz, chalcedony, opal, chlorite, calcite, or zeolites. The filled vesicles are called amygdules.

Flow banding   Alternating layers, with somewhat different minerals and texture, produced by continued flowing of magma or lava during solidification. Most common in lava flows (e.g. rhyolite).

Flow structure   An alignment of platy or prismatic minerals along linear directions (flow lines) or along planes of lamellar flowage, sometimes producing a wavy or swirling pattern or a streaky, gneissoid (gneisslike) appearance.

Orbicular   Containing numerous, more or less spherical bodies (orbicules), of any size up to many centimeters across. Orbicules consist of crystalline rock-forming minerals arranged in concentric layers and are most likely to occur in phaneritic rocks of granite composition.

Miarolitic   In plutonic igneous rocks (especially granite); having small irregular cavities into which small crystals of the rock-forming minerals project from the walls. An equivalent term is "drusy."

Xenolith   Literally a "stranger" rock, which was broken loose from the older surrounding rock during the movement of the magma to form an unrelated inclusion within the surrounding igneous rock.

Color Index
The identification of igneous rocks usually takes into account the chemical composition of the minerals present in the rock as well as their relative abundance.

Nature has provided us with a crude but convenient indication of mineral composition in the form of the color index. Color index is simply a measure of the proportion of dark to light minerals in the rock.

In general, light-colored igneous rocks are rich in the light-colored minerals: quartz, the alkali feldspars (or feldspathoids), and muscovite mica. Chemically, these rocks have an excess of silica (shown by the presence of quartz) and appreciable amounts of potassium, sodium, and aluminum in orthoclase, albite, oligoclase, andesine, or nepheline.

By contrast, dark-colored igneous rocks lack silica (quartz) but are rich in the ferromagnesian (iron- and magnesium-bearing) minerals, such as hornblende, augite, biotite, magnetite, and olivine, and in the calcium and sodium feldspars (mostly labradorite, but also bytownite and anorthite).

Using the color index, we may distinguish three groups of igneous rocks:

Leucocratic
Predominantly light-colored rocks, with one-third or less dark minerals by volume (e.g. rhyolite, trachyte, dacite, granite, syenite, monzonite, granodiorite).

Mesocratic
Rocks of intermediate color, with roughly one-half dark minerals by volume (e.g. dacite, andesite, diorite).

Melanocratic
Predominantly dark-colored rocks, with two-thirds or more dark minerals by volume (e.g. basalt, gabbro, peridotite).

Identification of Essential Minerals

The next step in identifying an igneous rock is to identify the essential minerals; essential minerals are those that must be present to qualify the rock as being of a certain type. For a rock to be called a granite, for instance, it must include quartz and specific feldspar minerals in certain stated proportions; these are essential minerals for granite. Each rock type has its own group of essential minerals. All non-essential minerals in a rock are called accessory minerals. They do not affect how a rock is classified and named, and ordinarily they are present in rather slight amounts. Because the mineral components of a rock are generally in small grains or fragments, the hand lens is indispensable in rock identification. The first minerals to look for are quartz and the feldspars, the most common of the rock-forming minerals.

It is suggested that you practice these identification procedures for specific minerals using a specimen of granite or similar igneous rock.

Quartz

Quartz, which is usually colorless and transparent when viewed as a separate crystal, generally appears as equant, gray, crystalline grains in the rock matrix. These produce more or less continuous twinkling reflections from the numerous conchoidal fracture surfaces when the specimen is slowly rotated in the sun or in a bright beam of light.

Feldspars

The feldspars, which are abundant in the rock, appear much lighter in color than quartz and they give momentary, sharp, mirrorlike reflections from their lustrous cleavage planes when rotated in the light. To distinguish between the potash feldspars (orthoclase, microcline) and the soda-lime (plagioclase) feldspars, the most useful feature is the multiple twinning of plagioclase. The multiple twinning is visible as fine parallel lines or striations on some cleavage surfaces, with adjacent lamellae (the areas between the lines) becoming alternately light and dark in the rotation test. Orthoclase feldspar sometimes occurs as a simple twin (Carlsbad twin), which on a reasonably well-formed crystal takes the form of just two relatively broad lamellae. Although microcline has a distinctive type of multiple cross-twinning, it is of microscopic size and therefore of no use in hand specimen examination. Finally, trying to distinguish between the several plagioclase feldspars is a difficult task. Labradorite has a distinctive play of colors, but it is usually not visible in hand specimens.

It is often possible to use color index as a guide to the particular plagioclase feldspars in a plutonic rock:

Color index	Associated feldspars
Leucocratic	*Albite, oligoclase*
Mesocratic	*Andesine*
Melanocratic	*Labradorite, bytownite, anorthite*

Muscovite Muscovite occurs as colorless or gray flakes or shreds, owing to its single perfect cleavage; it has a vitreous to pearly or silky luster, hardness $2-2\frac{1}{2}$, and is elastic; it is rather easy to recognize.

Ferromagnesian The essential dark minerals, most of
Minerals which contain iron and/or magnesium, are somewhat easier to distinguish from one another than are the feldspars. The most important are biotite, hornblende, and augite.

Biotite Biotite has virtually the same properties as muscovite in hand specimen, except that it is black (rarely dark brown or green) and has a splendent vitreous luster.

Hornblende Hornblende, the most common of the amphiboles, occurs as prismatic dark-green to black crystals of hardness 5–6 with two perfect prismatic cleavages with angles of 56° and 124° between them. The cleavages form diamond-shaped cross sections (basal sections) perpendicular to the prism. Cleavage surfaces frequently have a "woody" texture caused by numerous fine fractures cutting across their surfaces.

Augite Augite is a pyroxene and is not common in granites. It is rather similar in appearance to hornblende but has prismatic cleavages at nearly 90°, producing prisms with a square or rectangular cross section. The cleavage surfaces also seem to be smoother and are unmarked by hairline fractures.

Sedimentary Rocks Sedimentary rocks (from the Latin *sedimentum,* meaning "a settling") are formed at or near the earth's surface by the accumulation of particles ranging in size from submicroscopic to boulder size. As sediments accumulate, often to the astounding thickness of several miles, they exert increasing pressure (accompanied by rising temperature) upon the lower beds, causing them to become compacted and cemented into rock layers. In this manner mud becomes mudstone and then shale, sand is consolidated into sandstone, and so on.

The sedimentary rocks are placed in three groups, depending on the provenance or source area of the sediments:

Detrital (clastic) rock Rock formed by the accumulation of fragments derived from preexisting rocks and minerals by mechanical weathering (disintegration) and transported to their places of deposition by purely mechanical agents (water, wind, ice, and gravity).

Biogenic (organic) rock — Organic sedimentary rock formed directly or indirectly through the action of organisms, either plant or animal (e.g. coal, coral limestone, chalk); with or without fossil remains.

Chemical rock — Nonclastic sedimentary rock composed primarily of minerals produced by precipitation from a saline or freshwater solution (such as fine limestones); if the solution becomes concentrated by evaporation the result is a so-called "evaporite" (e.g. rock salt, gypsum rock).

Sedimentary rocks, on the whole, are relatively easy to recognize because they usually have a layered or "bedded" structure and may reveal their sedimentary environment by hardened ripple marks, mudcracks, and, above all, fossil evidence of former life on earth.

A number of specialized terms are used to indicate the origins of different types of sedimentary rock:

Hydrogenic — Precipitated from water by inorganic processes.
Aqueous — Deposited by water.
Eolian — Transported and deposited by wind.
Terrigenous — Derived from the land.
Lacustrine — Lake deposits.
Marine — Deposited in sea water.
Continental — Deposited on land.

The following terms are used specifically to describe the composition of specific types of sedimentary rock:

Argillaceous — Containing an appreciable amount of clay.
Arkosic — Containing appreciable amounts of feldspar (e.g. an arkosic sandstone, conglomerate, or limestone).
Calcareous — Containing appreciable quantities of calcium carbonate (calcite).
Carbonaceous — Rich in carbon or organic matter, sufficient to produce dark-gray or black coloring of the rock.

Cherty Containing chert in the form of nodules or as replacement lenses.

Dolomitic Containing an appreciable amount of calcium magnesium carbonate (dolomite) in addition to calcite.

Feldspathic Containing conspicuous feldspar fragments or grains.

Ferruginous Containing sufficient iron oxides (hematite or limonite) to be colored by them, usually reddish or yellowish brown.

Quartzose Containing quartz as a major constituent.

Siliceous Containing abundant free silica (SiO_2) rather than silicates as a principal constituent.

The textures of sedimentary rocks are described by four basic terms:

Coarse-grained Fragments coarser than sand (i.e. pebbles, cobbles, or boulders).

Medium-grained Sand-sized particles.

Fine-grained Particles finer than silt, i.e. clay particles; cannot be distinguished with the naked eye; also referred to as "dense."

Crystalline Consisting wholly of crystals or fragments of crystals.

In the field, the sedimentary rocks are most easily recognized by their structural features. The following structures are very commonly seen in sedimentary rocks:

Strata Also called layers or beds. Rock-forming sediments are often deposited in layers, which can be distinguished by differences in texture, hardness, cementation, color, internal structure, or composition in the successive layers. The layering is called stratification.

Lamination Also called thin-bedding; thin strata, as in shale.

Cross-bedding Arrangement of minor beds or laminae, within a stratified rock, more or less inclined to the depositional surface, with straight sloping or concave surfaces at various angles; cross-bedding may result from the deposition of sediments by flood waters, buildup and movement of sand dunes by wind, or accumulation of sediments in a delta.

Ripple marks   Small parallel ridges and hollows (called ripples) originally formed in loose sediments by the action of wind, water flow in streams, and waves and currents at the bottom of lake or ocean basins, and later preserved in the consolidated sedimentary rock.

Mudcrack casts   Irregular fractures in a crudely polygonal pattern, originally formed by the drying and shrinking of clay, silt, or mud in the open air; the cracks are later filled by hardened rock material and preserved in the consolidated sedimentary rock.

Concretions   Roughly spherical or rounded, more or less symmetrical structures in clastic sedimentary rocks; concretions are formed by the accumulations and concentration of mineral matter (usually present in the rock as cement) around a nucleus (often a fossil) in the approximate center of the structure.

Oolites   Small, round, concretionary bodies in a sedimentary rock, resembling fish roe, usually between 0.5 and 1 mm in diameter; oolites are composed of calcite, dolomite, quartz, hematite, limonite, pyrite, or other minerals arranged in concentric layers, commonly about a nucleus (a shell fragment, sand grain, etc.); some oolites have internal radial structures, and others are virtually structureless.

Pisolites   Pisolites are essentially the same as oolites, but have larger diameters (2–10 mm; pea size) and are somewhat more irregular in shape; the interiors are more commonly structureless or filled with radial mineral fibers.

Fossils   Fossils are any remains, trace, or imprint of a plant or animal preserved by natural processes in the earth's crust (particularly in sedimentary rocks); fossiliferous (fossil-bearing) rocks thus

give evidence of life during past
geologic periods.

Metamorphic Rocks Metamorphic rocks (from the Greek *meta*, meaning "change," and *morphe*, meaning "form") comprise the most complex group of rocks. They result from changes produced in preexisting igneous, sedimentary, or earlier metamorphic rocks by high pressures and temperatures as well as chemical activity deep within the earth's crust. Metamorphic rocks show several rather distinctive features. Minerals in such rocks generally appear in their crystalline forms. A dense, massive limestone, for instance, may change to a marble with a coarse, crystalline texture. Many minerals formed by recrystallization involving the chemical constituents of the parent rock (e.g. micas, chlorite, hornblende, etc.) tend to be elongated in certain directions or to be aligned in parallel layers, so that the rock has a foliated structure. This foliation may appear as bands of alternating colors and textures, as in gneiss, or as closely spaced flaky layers, as in schist. Some minerals, such as kyanite, sillimanite, and tremolite, are always metamorphic in origin.

The effects of this metamorphism depend upon the properties of the parent rock and upon the type of metamorphic environment and the duration of the process until the "changed" rock is finally exposed at the earth's surface. Lateral as well as vertical movements in the earth's crust provide tremendous compressive stresses and high temperatures for metamorphic change and also serve to bring the products of metamorphism ever closer to the earth's surface. The highest temperatures occur many kilometers beneath the earth's surface, near the borders of deep-seated magma bodies. These bodies commonly are made up of remelted metamorphic

608   A Guide to Rock Identification

rocks. Here the rock cycle begins again
with molten rock.

Types of Three basic metamorphic processes are
Metamorphism recognized: contact (thermal)
metamorphism, hydrothermal
metamorphism, and dynamothermal
(regional) metamorphism.

Contact Metamorphism due principally to heat;
Metamorphism also called thermal metamorphism.
When magma, with an average
temperature of 700°–1100°C, is
intruded into the earth's crust (forming
igneous-plutonic rock), the surrounding
rock may be altered, both by the
intense heat and by substances
emanating from the molten material.
The contact-metamorphic zone around
an igneous intrusion is called an
aureole. It characteristically shows a
steady decrease in metamorphic effects
with increasing distance from the
intrusive contact. Hornfels, marble,
calc-silicate rock, and metaquartzite are
common contact metamorphic rocks.

Hydrothermal Metamorphism, related to contact
Metamorphism metamorphism, due to the percolation
of hot solutions or gases through
fractures, causing changes in the
chemistry and mineralogy of the
surrounding rock. Skarn and
serpentinite are the principal rocks of
this type.

Dynamothermal Metamorphism due to the combined
Metamorphism heat and pressure that accompany large-
scale mountain-building processes;
also called regional metamorphism.
Dynamothermal (regional)
metamorphism affects extensive areas
(up to thousands of square kilometers)
to considerable depths within the
earth's crust, and operates over
enormous spans of time. It is possible
to distinguish several grades of
dynamothermal metamorphism,
depending on whether the temperatures
involved are low, moderate, or high
(see "Schist," p. 733). Important rocks

of this type include slate, schist, gneiss, amphibolite, greenstone, marble, calc-silicate rock, and metaquartzite.

Effects of Metamorphism
The changes that take place during metamorphism fall into three categories: the formation of new minerals; changes in the shape and size of mineral grains; and development of new structures in the rock.

Formation of New Minerals in Metamorphism
During metamorphism, new assemblages of minerals are created by the partial to complete reorganization of the minerals that constituted the parent rock. The result is that the metamorphic rock fabric is predominantly crystalline, whereas the parent rock may have been of a very different texture.
A number of minerals are formed exclusively or mostly by metamorphic action. These include:

Actinolite
Almandine
Andalusite
Andradite
Chlorite
Cordierite
Epidote
Glaucophane
Graphite
Grossular
Kyanite
Scapolite
Sillimanite
Staurolite
Talc
Tremolite
Vesuvianite
Wollastonite

A number of other minerals that originate in igneous and sedimentary rocks are also common in metamorphic rocks. Such minerals, e.g. quartz, are stable enough to undergo the metamorphic processes and remain unchanged; since they have persisted in their original form despite the destructive action of metamorphism, they are described as "relict" (i.e. remnant) minerals.

The following table indicates some of the minerals and rocks that may be derived from particular parent rocks by metamorphic action:

Source rocks	Resulting minerals and rocks
Ferromagnesian igneous rocks	*Hornblende (in amphibolites, schists, and gneisses)*
Calcareous and dolomitic sedimentary rocks	*Calcite and dolomite (in marbles); wollastonite and diopside (in skarn and calc-silicate rock)*
Argillaceous and feldspathic sedimentary rocks	*Muscovite and biotite (in slates, schists, and gneisses)*
Argillaceous or dolomitic sedimentary rocks	*Phlogopite (in marbles); tremolite and actinolite (in schists and marbles)*
Ferruginous sedimentary rocks	*Specularite and hornblende (in schists)*
Carbonaceous sedimentary rocks	*Graphite (in slates, marbles, and schists)*

Changes in Mineral Grains Metamorphism usually causes a change in grain shape toward well-formed crystals and change in grain size toward production of larger crystals and coarser rock textures. Metamorphic minerals, whether newly formed or recrystallized from earlier minerals, tend to show good crystal outlines and to be somewhat larger than the crystals or grains of the parent rock. The crystals seem to fit together like the tiles of a mosaic rather than in the interlocking fashion seen in igneous rock fabrics. In many respects, crystalline metamorphic textures resemble those seen in plutonic igneous rocks. In the metamorphic rocks, however, there is a strong tendency for flaky and prismatic minerals to assume a parallel alignment.

Of the many terms that have been coined to describe the textures of metamorphic rocks, we will be using only three:

Porphyroblastic   Distinct crystals (of garnet, staurolite, etc.) in a finer-grained matrix; analogous to the porphyritic texture of igneous rocks.

Granoblastic   Having equidimensional crystals, of metamorphic origin and of roughly uniform size, formed by recrystallization in a nonfoliated metamorphic rock; analogous to the phaneritic texture of some igneous rocks.

Crystalloblastic   Having a texture of mineral crystals entirely produced by metamorphic processes; the crystals may be of any size, from very fine to extremely large.

Development of New Structures   Metamorphism often includes the development of new structures within the rock. Alignment of minerals is an especially common structural change, caused by the pressures that are common in metamorphic processes. A number of minerals tend to grow perpendicular to the direction in which pressure is applied, and the growth of minerals can therefore have a strong influence on the development of rock structures. A number of metamorphic minerals have characteristic shapes or habits, as shown in the following table, which may be useful in rock identification:

Common shape	Metamorphic minerals
Flakes	*Micas, chlorite, talc, specularite, graphite*
Prisms (stout, columnar, flat, bladed)	*Staurolite, hornblende, andalusite, tremolite, actinolite, kyanite, sillimanite*
Equant	*Garnet, calcite, dolomite, quartz, pyrite, some feldspars*

Structural Terms   In describing metamorphic rocks, it is necessary to distinguish several kinds of structural features. The most important of these are the following:

Linear structure   A parallel or subparallel alignment of prismatic minerals in a linear direction, but without any planar orientation (also called "lineation").

Platy structure (foliation)   A parallel or subparallel planar arrangement of flaky as well as prismatic minerals; also called "foliation," because rocks with this structure have a texture resembling overlapping leaves.

Four types of foliation are usually distinguished:

Slaty foliation   An incipient (beginning) foliation produced by the planar arrangement of microscopic mica flakes and producing smooth, somewhat lustrous fracture surfaces, along which the rock splits readily. Also called "slaty cleavage," although strictly speaking the term "cleavage" should be restricted to minerals.

Phyllitic foliation   A better-developed foliation; mica flakes are large enough to be seen without a hand lens, and the foliation surfaces are somewhat "scaly" and irregular.

Schistose foliation   A well-developed, rather coarse-grained foliation, commonly produced by the parallel or subparallel orientation of flaky or prismatic minerals, such as micas or hornblende, which account for more than 50% of the minerals in the rock (also called "schistosity").

Gneissic structure   Layers of granular minerals sometimes showing discontinuous or streaky foliation at best, alternating with bands of well-foliated micaceous and prismatic minerals representing less than 50% of the minerals in the rock (also called "gneissic banding").

VISUAL KEY TO ROCKS

This Key is in two parts: a Key to Rock Classes, and the Visual Key itself, a series of color plates that will help you to recognize most of the rocks you are likely to find in North America.

Key to Rock Classes Use the Key to Rock Classes, beginning on p. 618, to find the most likely class—igneous-volcanic, igneous-plutonic, sedimentary, or metamorphic—for each specimen. These are given in the right-hand column. Whenever possible the names of some specific rocks in each class are also included as a further clue to identification. The rocks listed in *italic* type are also illustrated with black-and-white drawings. The preceding chapter, "A Guide to Identifying Rocks," explains the terms used in the Key and in the rock descriptions beginning on p. 681.

This Key makes use of four basic physical properties: rock fabric, hardness, texture, and structure:

Rock Fabric Rock fabric refers to the shapes, sizes, and distribution of the mineral grains or crystals in a rock.

Hardness In rocks, hardness (indicated as "H" in the key) is usually approximate, and refers to the average hardness of the constituent minerals, whether generally higher than 5½ (5½+) or lower (5½−). The softer rocks (with hardness lower than 5½) can be scratched with the blade of an ordinary pocket knife; the harder ones cannot.

Texture and Other Distinguishing Properties   These include several physical properties that can be seen readily in a hand specimen, such as density, smoothness or roughness, color, and color index (i.e., the proportion of dark-colored minerals in the rock).

Rock Structures and Field Occurrence   Properties under this heading include larger-scale features, which may be observed in an outcrop or larger formation, but usually not in a hand specimen. These include several types of layering and folding, fractures, rock domes, and relationships to other rocks. There is not always a clear dividing line between textural and structural features. Where a choice had to be made, the descriptions of texture and structure were arranged so as to make the Key as practical as possible, even though this meant placing some textural features in the "Rock Structures" column.

Visual Key   The rocks in the Visual Key are arranged in four groups, depending upon their mode of origin:

Igneous-Volcanic Rocks
Igneous-Plutonic Rocks
Sedimentary Rocks
Metamorphic Rocks

To identify a rock, compare it with the color plates in the appropriate group until you find the one that most resembles your specimen. Cross-references in the captions will direct you to the detailed description of each rock, so you can confirm your first identification, or try again.

Example   Suppose you want to identify an outcrop of grayish, layered rock. It is

brittle, soft enough to scratch with an
ordinary pocket knife, and dense—that
is, all the mineral grains are too small
to see without a hand lens.

First look in the Key to Rock Classes,
under the heading "Dense," for the
rocks with a hardness lower than 5½.
Compare the descriptions. Your rock is
light-colored, lacks the gritty texture of
Tuff and the waxy luster of
Serpentinite, and does not split into
thin slabs, like Slate. It therefore seems
to belong with the Sedimentary Rocks
(e.g. Limestone, Dolomite, Mudstone,
Shale).

Next, turn to the "Sedimentary Rocks"
section of the Visual Key. Find the
rocks that most resemble your
specimen. The page numbers in the
captions will lead you to the description
of each rock shown, where details about
texture, structure, field features, and
mineralogy will help you to make an
exact identification. (At this point you
may have to check for the specific
minerals in the rock, using the keys in
Part I.) In this instance, an abundance
of calcium carbonate, for example,
would identify your rock as Limestone;
an abundance of the mineral dolomite,
on the other hand, would identify it as
Dolomite Rock.

Be cautioned, though, that in many
cases you should expect to make only an
approximate identification. Under field
conditions, even an expert cannot
definitely distinguish between some
rocks, especially Igneous-Plutonic rocks
such as Granite and Granodiorite, that
are very similar in composition.
However, with a little practice you can
make a good identification in most
cases; and mineral clubs, museums, and
college geology departments will
usually be glad to help with difficult
specimens.

Rock Fabric	H	Texture
Glassy: no grains visible, even under microscope	5½+	Smooth surface with bright vitreous luster; conchoidal fracture; mostly black; may contain scattered crystals
		Porous, sponge-like; light in weight and color; H difficult to determine due to brittle structure; floats in water
Dense: mineral grains present but visible only under microscope	5½+	Dark-colored to black; may contain scattered crystals
		Predominantly light-colored; may contain scattered crystals
		Usually dark-colored; very dense; no luster; often conchoidal fracture
		Dark green color with pale green patches; dull luster; massive

Rock Structures	Rock Class
Generally massive, in irregular thick layers (lava flows)	**Igneous-Volcanic** *Obsidian*
Vesicular "glass foam"; usually in irregular layers at tops of lava flows	**Igneous-Volcanic** *Pumice (Rhyolite)*
Thick, often extensive layers (lava flows)	**Igneous-Volcanic**  *Andesite, Basalt*
Often strongly vesicular, showing flow-banding	**Igneous-Volcanic**  *Rhyolite, Trachyte, Dacite*
May show some remnant bedding; closely associated with plutonic igneous rocks	**Metamorphic** *Hornfels*
Thick, often extensive layers	**Metamorphic** *Greenstone*

Italics indicate rock shown in drawing.

Rock Fabric	H	Texture
Dense (continued)	5½+	Mostly light-colored; moderate luster; conchoidal fracture; may contain fossils
	5½−	Mostly light-colored; earthy to porous with rough, gritty feel; may show visible angular rock or mineral fragments
		Generally dense; white, shades of gray to black, less commonly yellow, brown, and red; even fracture, sometimes conchoidal
		Black, compact; relatively light weight; dull to strong vitreous luster
		Compact, dull to waxy luster; smooth to greasy feel; generally shades of yellow, brown, reddish-green; also black
		Soft, brittle, crumbly; dull luster; usually gray, but may appear in many other colors

Rock Structures	Rock Class
Occurs as lenses, nodules, or thin beds	**Sedimentary** *Chert*
Generally in layers of varying thickness	**Igneous-Volcanic** *Tuff*
Commonly thick-bedded; often cut by sets of rectangular rock fractures (joints); often contains fossils	**Sedimentary** 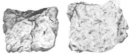 *Limestone, Dolomite*
In layers of varying thickness interbedded with other stratified rocks	**Sedimentary** *Coal*
Layered structure; also occurs in lens-shaped masses	**Metamorphic** *Serpentinite*
Well stratified in thin beds; splits unevenly more or less parallel to bedding plane; may contain fossils	**Sedimentary** 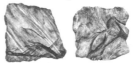 *Shale, Mudstone*

Italics indicate rock shown in drawing.

Rock Fabric	H	Texture
Dense (continued)	5½−	Moderately hard; color chiefly gray to black, but also green, brown, red, purple
Even-Granular: all mineral grains or crystals are visible to the naked eye (2–5 mm; up to ⅛″) and of approximately equal size	5½+	Interlocking crystal grains of light- and/or dark-colored minerals; see color index, below
		Leucocratic: at least ⅔ light-colored minerals by volume
		Mesocratic: light & dark minerals in approximately equal proportions
		Melanocratic: at least ⅔ dark minerals by volume
		Crystalline texture; consists essentially of rounded quartz grains cemented by crystalline quartz; fine- to medium-grained; generally white, light gray, or yellow to brown

Rock Structures	Rock Class
Thin-layered structure, causing it to split readily into thin, smooth, slightly lustrous slabs	**Metamorphic** *Slate*
Large, dome-like masses of rock, often forming prominent mountain peaks; also tabular sheet-like bodies within other rocks	**Igneous-Plutonic** Granite to Peridotite, see below
	Igneous-Plutonic 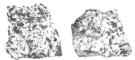 *Granite,* Syenite, *Monzonite,* Granodiorite
	Igneous-Plutonic *Diorite*
	Igneous-Plutonic 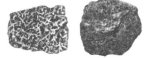 *Gabbro, Peridotite*
Thick-bedded; uneven to conchoidal fracture; breaks across (not around) quartz grains	**Sedimentary** or **Metamorphic** *Quartzite, Metaquartzite*

Italics indicate rock shown in drawing.

Rock Fabric	H	Texture
Even-Granular (continued)	5½+	Amphibole (usually hornblende) principal mineral; dark green to black; sparkling luster; medium- to coarse-grained
	Variable	More or less rounded rock or mineral grains cemented together; may contain fossils
	5½−	Crystalline texture; consists mostly of a single mineral (calcite or dolomite)
	2–2½	Mostly halite or gypsum; fine- to coarse-grained; generally white, but also in shades of gray, yellow, and red

Rock Structures	Rock Class
Slender prisms of hornblende in parallel alignment, resulting in schistose foliation	**Metamorphic** *Amphibolite*
Generally thick-bedded, varicolored; rough feel due to uneven surface produced by breaking around grains	**Sedimentary** *Sandstone*
Mostly fine-grained	**Sedimentary** *Limestone, Dolomite*
Generally medium- to coarse-grained; may be yellow, red, or black; lustrous due to reflections from cleavage planes	**Metamorphic**  *Marble,* Calc-Silicate Rock
Occurs in beds from less than 1 m to several hundred m thick; both rocks often interbedded	**Sedimentary**  *Rock Salt, Gypsum Rock*

Italics indicate rock shown in drawing.

Rock Fabric	H	Texture
Uneven-Granular: many grains of different sizes visible to the naked eye and scattered in a dense groundmass	5½+	Small well-formed crystals in a dense groundmass
		Predominantly light-colored
		Dark-colored to black
Uneven-Granular: all grains visible to the naked eye and of different sizes	5½+	Relatively large crystals scattered in an even-granular groundmass of smaller crystals
		Interlocking, often well-formed crystals of different minerals in all sizes up to 10 cm (3″) & larger, irregularly distributed
		Interlocking crystals, mostly calc-silicate minerals

Rock Structures	Rock Class
Generally in thick layers; may show flow banding	**Igneous-Volcanic** Porphyritic Rhyolite to porphyritic Basalt; see below
	Igneous-Volcanic  *Rhyolite, Trachyte, Dacite*
	Igneous-Volcanic  *Andesite, Basalt*
Large, dome-like masses of rock, often forming prominent mountain peaks; also tabular sheet-like bodies within other rocks	**Igneous-Plutonic** 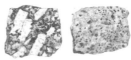 Porphyritic *Granite, Syenite,* Monzonite, Granodiorite, Diorite, Gabbro, *Peridotite*
Irregular rock bodies within plutonic rocks, or tabular bodies cross-cutting plutonic and other rocks	**Igneous-Plutonic** *Granite Pegmatite,* Nepheline Syenite Pegmatite, Carbonatite
Commonly close to or between bodies of marble and plutonic rock (e.g. granite)	**Metamorphic** *Skarn*

Italics indicate rock shown in drawing.

Rock Fabric	H	Texture
Uneven-Granular (continued)	5½+	Hardness variable; all crystalline texture; mineral crystals show distinct alignment along certain directions and in parallel or near-parallel layers
	5½−	Hardness extremely variable; consists of rounded or angular rock or mineral fragments cemented by silica, lime, iron oxide, etc.

Rock Structures	Rock Class
Mineral alignment; foliation, gneissic banding, or scaly structure common	**Metamorphic**

Gneiss, Schist |
| Mostly in thick, crudely stratified layers | **Sedimentary**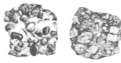

Conglomerate, Breccia |

Rocks

The color plates on the following pages
show all the rocks that are described in
this field guide. All rocks are shown
in hand specimens, measuring
approximately 7.5 x 10 cm (3" x 4").
For some, additional photographs are
included to show typical field features
or large-scale landforms.
The color plates are in four groups,
corresponding to the basic rock groups
or classes:

Igneous-Volcanic Rocks
Igneous-Plutonic Rocks
Sedimentary Rocks
Metamorphic Rocks

The Key to Rock Classes, on pages
618–629, will help you identify an
unknown rock by telling you which
class it belongs in. You can then turn
to the appropriate section of color plates
to make a precise identification; page
numbers in the captions indicate where
to find the rock descriptions, so you can
confirm your identification.

Thumb Index

To make it easy to locate the color plates for each rock class, a schematic symbol for each has been inset as a thumb spot at the left edge of each double-page group of plates.

The rock classes are indicated by the symbols on the opposite page.

Igneous-
Volcanic Rocks

Igneous-
Plutonic Rocks

Sedimentary
Rocks

Metamorphic
Rocks

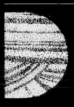

703   Scoria and Tuff; Mt. Lassen, *pp. 688, 691*

704   Basalt; Devil's Postpile, Calif., *p. 688*

705   Rhyolite cliffs; Yellowstone Park, *p. 684*

706   Basalt (Pahoehoe lava), *p. 688*

707   Tuff, *p. 691*

708   Rhyolite with flow banding, *p. 684*

709 Rhyolite with vesicles, *p. 684*

710 Trachyte, *p. 685*

711   Trachyte Porphyry, *p. 685*

712   Rhyolite Tuff, *p. 691*

713 Andesite Porphyry, *p. 687*

714 Mica Dacite Porphyry, *p. 686*

715 Olivine Basalt Porphyry, *p. 688*

716 Scoria (Pahoehoe lava flow), *p. 688*

717 Basalt, *p. 688*

718 Cindery Basalt (Aa), *p. 688*

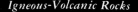

719   Basalt with amygdule of Chalcedony, *p. 688*

720   Olivine Basalt, *p. 688*

721 Obsidian, *p. 690*

722 Obsidian with lithophysae, *p. 690*

723   Granite boulders, *p. 694*

724   Granite blocks, *p. 694*

725 Gabbro (Anorthosite); Adirondack Mts., *p.* 707

726 Granodiorite batholith; Sierra Nevada, *p.* 704

727 Granite Pegmatite, *p. 696*

728 Granite Pegmatite (graphic Granite), *p. 696*

729 Nepheline Syenite, *p. 700*

730 Hornblende Granite, *p. 694*

731   Syenite, *p. 699*

732   Granite Pegmatite (graphic Granite), *p. 696*

733 Nepheline Syenite Pegmatite, *p. 701*

34 Carbonatite, *p. 710*

735   Hornblende Granite Pegmatite, *p. 696*

736   Zoned Granite Pegmatite, *p. 696*

737   Biotite Granite, *p. 694*

738   Hornblende Biotite Granite, *p. 694*

739 Granodiorite, *p. 704*

740 Monzonite, *p. 702*

741 Diorite, *p. 705*

742 Biotite Granite, *p. 694*

743   Peridotite, *p. 708*

744   Hornblende Pyroxene Diorite, *p. 705*

745   Gabbro, *p. 707*

746   Gabbro (Diabase), *p. 707*

747 Shale and Sandstone, *pp. 714, 715*

748 Sandstone (with cross-bedding), *p. 715*

749 Eroded Sandstones; Bryce Canyon, *p. 715*

750 Limestone, *p. 719*

751 Rock Salt, *p. 726*

752 Anthracite Coal, *p. 728*

753   Gypsum Rock, *p.* 724

754   Chert, *p.* 723

755   Shale (Siltstone), *p. 714*

756   Limestone, *p. 719*

757 Argillaceous Shale, *p. 714*

758 Dolomite Rock, *p. 722*

759   Sandstone (Graywacke), *p. 715*

760   Sandstone, *p. 715*

761 Quartzite, *p. 715*

762 Mudstone, *p. 714*

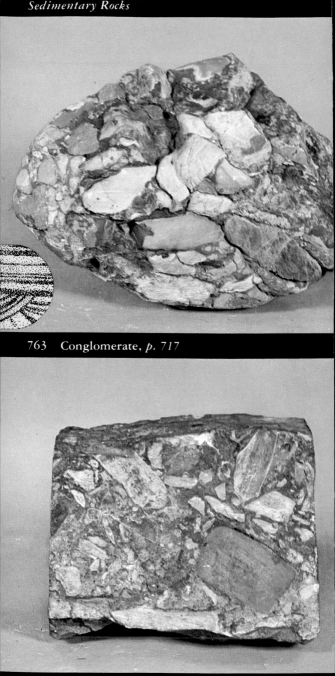

763 Conglomerate, *p. 717*

764 Breccia, *p. 717*

765   Fossiliferous Sandstone, *p. 715*

766   Green Mudstone, *p. 714*

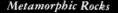

767   Schist, *p. 733*

768   Greenstone, *p. 741*

769 Slate, p. 732

770 Slate with Quartz veins, *p.* 732

771　Marble, *p. 742*

772　Dolomitic Marble, *p. 742*

773   Diopside Marble, *p. 742*

774   Calc-Silicate Rock, *p. 742*

775   Calc-Silicate Rock, *p. 742*

776   Skarn in Marble, *pp. 745, 742*

777 Skarn, *p. 745*

778 Marble with Hematite on fracture, *p. 742*

779   Serpentinite, *p. 748*

780   Greenstone, *p. 741*

781 Hornfels with Metaquartzite, *pp.* 739, 747

782 Met...........ite with relict bedding, *p.* 747

783   Slate, *p. 732*

784   Slate, *p. 732*

785 Slate with Pyrite crystals, *p. 732*

786 Slate, *p. 732*

787   Phyllite, *p. 732*

788   Granite Gneiss, *p. 735*

789 Augen Gneiss, *p.* 735

790 Biotite Gneiss, *p.* 735

791   Garnet Phyllite, *p. 732*

792   Quartz-Mica Schist, *p. 733*

793 Amphibolite (Hornblende Schist), *p. 738*

794 Garnet-Mica Schist, *p. 733*

THE COMMON ROCKS
OF NORTH AMERICA

The rocks described on the following
pages are grouped, according to their
mode of origin, in four sections:

For details and explanations of
terminology, refer to the "Guide to
Rock Identification," beginning on
page 597.
The number of numbers preceding each
rock description correspond to the
illustration number(s) in the Visual Key
to Rocks, pages 633–680.

Igneous-Volcanic Rocks

Rocks formed directly from molten rock that cooled quickly on or near the earth's surface. Textures are glassy to dense, usually without visible mineral crystals (aphanitic texture) or with relatively few crystals scattered in a dense groundmass (porphyritic texture). Prominent structures may include flow banding, vesicles, and amygdules, although there may be a distinct, rough lava texture, especially in some types of basalt.

705, 708, 709 Rhyolite

Texture: Aphanitic to partly glassy; commonly aphanitic-porphyritic with small phenocrysts.

Structure: Frequently shows pronounced flow banding with attendant alignment of phenocrysts in the flow direction; some of the flow bands have a glassy texture with small spherulites and vesicles; swirling flow structures are not uncommon. *Pumice* is an extremely porous, brittle variety of rhyolite, spongelike in appearance and light enough to float in water.

Color index: Leucocratic with mostly light-colored minerals (e.g. quartz and feldspar) as phenocrysts.

Color: Shades of gray, yellow, pale to deep red.

Hardness: Approximately 6–6½.

Composition: Rhyolite is the volcanic equivalent of plutonic granite, having excess silica.

Mineralogy: *Essential minerals* Quartz (var. tridymite common), alkali feldspar (sanidine), biotite (brown to deep green in hand specimen), amphibole (usually hornblende); *Accessory minerals* Magnetite.

Field features: Occurs as lava flows and small intrusive

bodies such as dikes and sills and in contact zones of large intrusions; the upper portions of rhyolitic flows commonly have a vesicular structure;

some compact, very fine-grained sedimentary rocks (e.g. fine-grained sandstones) may be confused with rhyolite but the latter's flow banding, with spherulitic and vesicular structures, is distinctive.

Origin: Rhyolite is formed when magma of granitic composition erupts at the earth's surface or intrudes the crust at shallow depths. Owing to the rapid cooling of the lava flow, only small crystals (mostly of microscopic size) are able to develop.

Environment: Associated minerals are biotite, hornblende, opal, orthoclase, magnetite, quartz, sanidine, and topaz. Prominent mineral occurrences in rhyolite have been found in Mexico (San Luis Potosí) and Utah (Juab Co.).

710, 711   Trachyte

Texture: Aphanitic to aphanitic-porphyritic; phenocrysts are usually lath-shaped crystals of feldspar, but ferromagnesian minerals may also appear as phenocrysts.

Structure: Flow banding is uncommon despite the subparallel flow alignment of feldspar crystals under the microscope (called trachytic structure); visible phenocrysts may show a similar subparallel orientation.

Color index: Leucocratic with mostly light-colored minerals as phenocrysts.

Color: Light to medium gray, pink, green, or tan; occasionally dark gray.

Hardness: 5½–6

Composition: Trachyte is the volcanic equivalent of plutonic syenite, having little, if any, excess silica.

Mineralogy: *Essential minerals* Potash feldspar (usually sanidine), biotite or hornblende; *Accessory minerals* Quartz (less than 5%), microcline, albite.

Field features: Occurs as surface lava flows and small intrusive dikes, also in contact zones of larger intrusive bodies. The trachytic structure, which is so prominent under the microscope, is quite inconspicuous in the field but does permit the rock to split fairly easily along it.

Origin: Trachyte is formed when magma of syenitic composition is erupted as a lava flow or intruded at shallow depths. Rapid cooling as well as movement of the increasingly viscous lava account for the development of small crystals and of the trachytic structure.

Environment: Trachyte as such is not considered an environment for the development of interesting or colorful minerals. The only notable exception is turquoise, which may occur as thin seam fillings.

714 Dacite

Texture: Aphanitic to aphanitic-porphyritic with often abundant phenocrysts of both light- and dark-colored minerals.

Structure: Flow banding is common and phenocrysts, when abundant, show flow alignment; vesicles are rare.

Color index: Owing to the rather variable amount of ferromagnesian minerals (never more than 50% of rock), color index may be leucocratic or mesocratic.

Color: From white through shades of gray, also buff, pale to deep red, brown, and (rarely) black.

Composition: Dacite is the volcanic equivalent of plutonic quartz diorite, a rock similar in composition to granodiorite. Quartz content is at least 5% of the rock by volume.

Mineralogy: *Essential minerals* Plagioclase feldspar (andesine), quartz, biotite, hornblende, and augite; *Accessory minerals* Potash feldspar (sanidine), magnetite, ilmenite, apatite, titanite, garnet.

Field features: Occurs as surface lava flows and in narrow dikes or sills, and in the chilled contact zones of larger intrusions. Also in small, steep-sided, circular bodies called volcanic domes.

Origin: Dacite is formed when magma of approximately granodiorite composition erupts on the surface as lava flows or is intruded in the vent of a volcano to form a dome. The minerals that occur as abundant phenocrysts evidently started crystallizing in the magma some time before its eruption.

Environment: Dacite itself is seldom considered an environment in which to look for mineral specimens; however, dacite bodies do act as the host rock for several types of hydrothermal veins, which are

the source of valuable and interesting
minerals.

713 Andesite

Texture: Aphanitic-porphyritic; less commonly
aphanitic; also glassy groundmass at
times; phenocrysts are plagioclase and
ferromagnesian minerals.

Structure: Flow banding is uncommon but under
certain conditions of cooling closely
spaced parallel joint planes are
developed, producing a platy structure.

Color index: Mesocratic.

Color: Brown, greenish, and dark gray.

Hardness: 5–6

Composition: Andesite is the volcanic equivalent of
plutonic diorite, having little, if any,
excess silica.

Mineralogy: *Essential minerals* Plagioclase feldspar
(andesine), amphibole (hornblende),
pyroxene (diopside or augite), biotite;
Accessory minerals Quartz or
feldspathoids (less than 5% of rock),
pyroxene (hypersthene).

Field features: Occurs principally as lava flows and
secondarily as shallow-depth dike
intrusions. Commonly porphyritic,
often with phenocrysts of
ferromagnesian minerals in a mesocratic
matrix. Some dark-colored varieties
with few phenocrysts have been
mistakenly identified as basalts, a
problem that can be solved only by
microscopic study.

Origin: Andesite forms when magma of dioritic
composition is erupted as lava flows or
injected into fractures of volcanic vents
and cones in the form of dikes and
domes.

Environment: Associated minerals include andesine,
augite, biotite, cordierite, diopside,
hornblende, hypersthene. Mineral
occurrences have been found in andesite
in California (Lake Co.).

| 703, 704, 706, | **Basalt** |
| 715–720 | **Scoria** |

Texture: Aphanitic, less commonly aphanitic-porphyritic; phenocrysts, often having the same dark color as the matrix (e.g. pyroxene), are not readily seen but may be recognized upon close examination by their crystalline nature and the light reflections from cleavage planes.

Structure: Vesicular structure is prominent and particularly well developed near the top of the lava flow, where the rock may be called scoriaceous or just *scoria*. The vesicles are formed by the expansion of gases trapped in the cooling and increasingly viscous lava. After solidification of the vesicle walls, the cavities are eventually filled by secondary minerals (e.g. quartz and zeolites) precipitated from volcanic gases and fluids. Such filled vesicles are then called amygdules and the resulting structure amygdaloidal.

Color index: Melanocratic.

Color: Dark gray to black; fresh basalt flows often have a dark-brown to reddish rust color.

Hardness: 5–6

Composition: Basalt is the volcanic equivalent of plutonic gabbro and is rich in ferromagnesian minerals.

Mineralogy: *Essential minerals* Plagioclase feldspar (labradorite in matrix, bytownite and anorthite in phenocrysts), pyroxene (augite or, less commonly, hypersthene), olivine (particularly as phenocrysts); *Accessory minerals* Biotite, amphibole (hornblende), magnetite, ilmenite, hematite, apatite, quartz (or its polymorphs tridymite or cristobalite); *Secondary minerals* Quartz, zeolites (in amygdules).

Field features: Basalt is one of the most widespread volcanic igneous rocks. It occurs particularly as massive lava flows, accumulating to astounding thicknesses of many thousands of feet and covering vast areas measured in thousands of square kilometers. Such outpourings of basaltic lava are known as "basalt floods" or "plateau basalts." Also many of the presently active volcanoes erupt lava of basaltic composition. Recent lava flows (e.g. in Hawaii) also illustrate the contrasting shapes in which basalt may solidify. They are either "molded" into twisted coils of rope or form cindery, jagged blocks, which are referred to by their Hawaiian names, "pahoehoe" and "aa" respectively. Polygonal or cylindrical jointing, called columnar structure, is particularly well developed in basaltic lava flows and sill intrusions. Chemical weathering in well-jointed basalts often causes the development of a "spheroidal" structure of near-spherical, onionlike, and somewhat crumbly, exfoliating shells.

Origin: Basalt forms when magma of gabbroic composition erupts on the earth's surface as lava flows or intrudes at shallow depths to form dikes and sills.

Environment: Associated minerals (both primary and secondary) include adularia, analcime, anorthite, apatite, apophyllite, arsenic, augite, biotite, bytownite, calcite, chabazite, chalcocite, chlorite, cinnabar, copper, epidote, hematite, heulandite, hornblende, hypersthene, ilmenite, labradorite, laumontite, leucite, magnetite, natrolite, olivine, pectolite, prehnite, pumpellyite, quartz, silver, stibnite, stilbite, and sulfur. Prominent mineral occurrences in basalt have been noted in British Columbia (Ice Valley region), California (Kern, Lake, Sonoma, and Tehama Cos.), Colorado (Jefferson Co.), Greenland (Disco Bay), Iceland (Berufjord and Bogarfjord), Michigan (Alger, Houghton, and Keweenaw Cos.), New Jersey (Passaic, Essex, Union, Somerset, and Mercer Cos.), Nova Scotia (Annapolis Co.), Ontario (Abitib River, Cobalt district, Sextant Portage, and Sudbury), Oregon

(Columbia and Grant Cos.), Quebec
(Megantic Co.), Utah (Juab Co.), and
Mexico (San Luis Potosí).

721, 722   Obsidian

Texture: Glassy with occasional spherulites and
lithophysae (see below); luster is
brilliantly vitreous.

Structure: Prominent conchoidal fractures owing
to the homogeneity of this amorphous
rock. Spherulites of feldspar fibers with
interstitial crystalline silica are
common; they represent very rapid
crystallization prior to the chilling of
the surrounding glass. Flow banding is
shown by layered bands of color or by
streaks of closely spaced spherulites.
Lithophysae (meaning "stone bubbles")
frequently accompany the spherulites.
They are somewhat larger cavities,
more or less filled by concentric shells
of crystalline material, often consisting
of fragile crystals of different minerals,
such as quartz, feldspar, topaz, and
tourmaline. Lithophysal cavities were
formed by gases escaping from the
obsidian lava flow, with the gases also
supplying the chemical constituents for
the minerals lining them.

Color: Generally black but more or less smoky
along translucent to transparent edges;
other colors are gray, reddish brown,
mahogany, dark green. Black is
sometimes mixed with any of these
colors to form thin bands or produce a
marbled effect.

Hardness: 6–7; obsidian scratches window glass.

Composition: Obsidian is so silica-rich that upon slow
crystallization a very light-colored
granite with about 35% quartz, 63%
feldspars, and only 2% ferromagnesian
minerals would have formed.

Field features: Obsidian occurs as volcanic lava flows
that are thick and of limited area. Its
black, glassy, lustrous, and often flow-
banded appearance makes it rather easy

to distinguish from the other volcanic rocks with which it is commonly associated.

Origin: Obsidian forms when a silica-rich magma of granitic composition flows onto the earth's surface, where it solidifies before minerals can develop and crystallize. It is, therefore, an amorphous solid or glass rather than an aggregate of minerals.

Environment: Obsidian is an environment for very few minerals. Lithophysae and spherulites may contain small but beautiful crystals of feldspar, tridymite, and cristobalite (both higher-temperature forms of quartz, not described in this book), ordinary quartz, and less commonly, iron olivine (fayalite), topaz, tourmaline, and garnet. These minerals have been found in obsidian bodies in California (Inyo, Imperial, and Modoc Cos.), Oregon (Crater Lake), Wyoming (Yellowstone Park), and Mexico (near Pachuca).

Economic use: Primitive peoples once valued obsidian highly, chipping and flaking it into knives, spearheads, and many other implements with razor-sharp edges resulting from the intersecting conchoidal fractures.

703, 707, 712 Tuff

Texture: Dense to fine-grained fragmental texture; tuff is composed of small volcanic rock fragments and ash, moderately compacted into a coherent rock material of earthy consistency. Has a rough, gritty "feel."

Structure: None of importance.

Color index: Predominantly light-colored.

Color: White, pink, pale brown, yellow, or gray.

Hardness: Even at its hardest, it can be scratched with a knife blade.

Field features: Occurs in well-defined layers, each representing a separate volcanic outburst; thickness of each layer depends on the intensity and duration of the explosive volcanic action. Although loosely compacted tuff is easily eroded, mountain ranges have been carved out of well-compacted and indurated (or "welded") tuff and volcanic breccia. The latter is composed of larger fragments including those derived from older, nonvolcanic rocks through which the eruptive lava had to pass. Tuff also commonly provides the bonding material for volcanic breccia.

Origin: Tuff is formed by the accumulation of pyroclastic material ejected violently by explosive volcanic eruptions. It is composed only of the finer fragments from about 2 mm ($\frac{1}{16}$″) in diameter down to volcanic ash and dust particles. It is quite porous in the early stages of formation, thus permitting mineralizing solutions to percolate through it and precipitate cementing material (usually silica). The result is a progressive hardening (induration) of the rock with time.

Environment: Tuff is seldom a mineral environment, but it will often become the host rock for mineral veins, which are environments for many metallic and nonmetallic minerals.

Igneous-Plutonic Rocks

Rocks formed directly from molten
rock that cooled slowly at considerable
depth beneath the earth's surface,
allowing the mineral crystals to grow to
visible (and in some cases to giant) size.
Textures are phaneritic to extremely
coarse (pegmatitic), with the mineral
crystals that make up the rock usually
closely interlocked; most are rather hard
(H = 5½ to 6 or more).

723, 724, 730,   Granite
737, 738, 742

Texture: Commonly phaneritic, medium- to
coarse-grained, occasionally porphyritic
with phenocrysts of well-formed
crystals of potash feldspars (orthoclase
or microcline with Carlsbad twinning).

Structure: Sometimes early-crystallized minerals
(e.g. dark-colored hornblende) show
linear as well as platy flow alignment,
giving the rock a streaky gneissoid
(gneisslike) appearance which is often
difficult to distinguish from the
gneissic structure of some metamorphic
rocks. When orbicules of concentrically
arranged biotite and hornblende are
present in sufficient quantities the rock
is called orbicular granite. Miarolitic
cavities are also abundant in some
granites.

Color index: Leucocratic.

Color: Depends largely on that of the
abundant feldspars and on their
proportion to the dark minerals.
Generally speaking, white to gray or
dark gray colors result from the
predominance of plagioclase feldspars
and the darkening influence of
ferromagnesian minerals; on the other
hand, pink, flesh-colored, red to deep
red colors are more likely to be from
orthoclase containing varying quantities
of hematite flakes.

Hardness: Average is greater than $5\frac{1}{2}$.

Composition: Granite is high in silica, potassium,
and sodium (feldspars $\pm$ 45% and
quartz up to 35%), but low in calcium,
iron, and magnesium (ferromagnesian
minerals 30% or less).

Mineralogy: *Essential minerals* Quartz, potash
feldspar (orthoclase and/or microcline),
plagioclase feldspar (albite-oligoclase)
with smaller quantities of muscovite,
biotite, and/or hornblende, and less
commonly pyroxene (augite);
intergrowths of potash and plagioclase
feldspars, called *perthite,* though mostly
observable only under the microscope,

may sometimes be recognized on cleavage surfaces of larger feldspar crystals. *Accessory minerals* Common are apatite, garnet, hematite, magnetite, ilmenite, pyrite, rutile, titanite, and zircon.

Field features:

Granite bodies are characteristically block-jointed on a large scale; three distinct sets of joints are at nearly right angles to each other, with one set being approximately horizontal. This feature is of importance in mining, tunneling, and quarrying because it facilitates excavation and removal of rock material. Jointing also largely determines the topographic forms produced by erosion. In high mountain areas where severity and intensity of erosion is great, granite frequently occurs as sharp crags, spires, and castlelike forms. In deeply eroded ranges where continental glaciation has been effective, granite masses appear as rounded, dome-shaped forms that tend to maintain their shapes by a weathering process called "exfoliation." Rock surfaces appear rather smooth when exfoliated but rough and pitted after having been exposed to weather for some time.

Origin: Granite is formed by the slow cooling and crystallization of magma at some depth in the earth's crust, as indicated by its characteristic phaneritic and phaneritic-porphyritic texture.

Environment: Associated minerals include almandine and topaz. Prominent mineral occurrences in granite have been found in California (Tuolumne Co.) and Texas (Mason Co.). Compare the environment of granite pegmatite, which usually occurs within or in close association with large intrusive granite bodies.

Economic use: Owing to its great crushing strength, resistance to weathering, and ability to take a high polish, granite is widely used for architectural construction, as ornamental stone (interior and exterior), and for monuments. Powdered potash-

Comments: rich granite has been used as fertilizer. The term "granite" has not only been applied to the common rock described above, but has also been used as a collective term for a number of related, leucocratic, plutonic rocks that have similar chemical and mineralogical compositions. Among these are syenite, monzonite, and granodiorite, all described in this chapter.

727, 728, 732, 735, 736 **Granite Pegmatite**

Texture: Uneven-granular, pegmatitic, very coarse-grained and highly variable both as to grain size and mineral distribution.

Structure: Complex pegmatite dikes commonly exhibit zones, which, proceeding from the walls inward, are border zone, wall zone, intermediate zone and the core (see chapter on mineral environments, under the heading "Pegmatite"). Drusy cavities with large crystals projecting into them may be found in the more coarse-grained interior portion of the pegmatite body.

Color index: Leucocratic.

Color: Quite variable due to uneven distribution of the dominant minerals. Refer to description of rock color under "Granite."

Hardness: Average approximately 6.

Composition: The bulk composition is essentially the same as that of granite, but much more variable over short distances owing to the highly irregular distribution of the component minerals.

Mineralogy: *Essential minerals* Quartz, potash feldspar (orthoclase, microcline, perthite), plagioclase feldspar (albite-oligoclase), muscovite, with biotite and/or hornblende as dark minerals; *Accessory minerals* Apatite, lepidolite, monazite, spodumene, topaz, and tourmaline, to mention just a few (see

"Environment" below). An intergrowth of quartz and feldspar, which looks roughly like cuneiform writing and is called "graphic granite," is common.

Field features: Granite pegmatite commonly occurs as tabular or discoidal elongate bodies, called dikes, cutting across the granitic parent rock body (stock or batholith) or intruding the surrounding rocks. Such dikes may vary in thickness from a few inches to tens of feet and extend a mile or more in length. They generally have definite walls that emphasize the extreme coarse grain of the pegmatite against the finer and more even-grained surrounding rock. Granite pegmatite may also form irregular masses having indistinct, gradational borders within the parent granite. The previously mentioned "zoning" as well as the great variability of crystal size and mineral distribution make granite pegmatites rather easy to recognize in the field.

Origin: Granite pegmatite represents the very rapid crystallization of minerals from residual fluids and gases escaping from the cooling and thickening granitic magma under high pressure and elevated temperature. Such "volatiles" are rich in water, silica, and gaseous chemical elements. Under these conditions large, well-formed mineral crystals can form in a low-density, igneous environment whose high degree of mobility accounts for the irregular mineral distribution.

Environment: Associated minerals include albite, amblygonite, andalusite, andradite, apatite, autunite, beryl, biotite, bismuth, bismuthinite, cassiterite, chrysoberyl, columbite-tantalite, corundum, cryolite, epidote, goethite, grossular, hematite, heulandite, kunzite, laumontite, lazulite, lepidolite, manganite, microcline, monazite, muscovite, oligoclase, opal, orthoclase, psilomelane, pyrite, quartz, siderite, spessartine, spodumene, topaz, tourmaline, and zircon. Prominent mineral occurrences in pegmatites have been found in Alabama (Cleburne, Larmar, and Randolph Cos.); Arizona (Maricopa, Mohave, and Yavapai Cos.); California (San Diego Co.); Canada (Manitoba and Ontario); Colorado (Chaffee, Fremont, Gunnison, and Larimer Cos.); Connecticut (Hampton, Middleton, and Portland Cos.); Greenland; Georgia (Cherokee, Monroe, Pickens, and Upson Cos.); Maine (Oxford and Sagadahoc Cos.); Massachusetts (Norfolk and Worcester Cos.); Montana (Cascade, Gallitin, and Madison Cos.); New Hampshire (Cheshire, Grafton, Merrimack, and Sullivan Cos.); New Mexico (Rio Arriba, San Miguel, and Taos Cos.); North Carolina (Catawba, Cleveland, Gaston, Lincoln, Macon, Mitchell, Rockingham, Rutherford, Stokes, and Yancy Cos.); South Carolina (Anderson, Greenville, Oconee, Pickens, and Spartanburg Cos.); South Dakota (Custer, Lawrence, and Pennington Cos.); Virginia (Amelia, Bedford, Caroline, Charlotte, Goochland, Halifax, Hanover, Henry, Louisa, Pittsylvania, Powhatan, Rockingham, and Spotsylvania Cos.), and Wyoming (Albany Co.).

Economic use: Granite pegmatite is the source of several important industrial minerals: feldspar (used in ceramic and glass manufacture), mica (used as insulating material in electronics), spodumene and lepidolite (a source of lithium for special alloys and in nuclear energy), beryl (for hardening of copper alloys and manufacture of refractory materials), and gem minerals (topaz, beryl, tourmaline, kunzite, etc.). For the collector it is one of the most productive mineral environments.

731   Syenite

Texture: Phaneritic, medium- to coarse-grained, occasionally phaneritic-porphyritic with lath-shaped, tabular feldspar phenocrysts in subparallel flow alignment.

Structure: Like granite, syenite has a tendency toward forming miarolitic cavities and gneissoid flow structure of tabular and prismatic minerals. Orbicular structures are rare.

Color index: Leucocratic.

Color: May be pink, white, light gray, pale green, or pale brown.

Hardness: Average 5½–6

Composition: Similar to granite but without excess silica; syenite has little or no quartz and may contain some feldspathoids.

Mineralogy: *Essential minerals* Potash feldspar (orthoclase, microcline, microperthite), plagioclase feldspar (albite—mostly as late magmatic replacement of K-feldspars); dark minerals are biotite and hornblende, or acmite, and riebeckite; *Accessory minerals* Muscovite, apatite, titanite, and corundum.

Field features: Syenite (unlike granite) is not a common rock. It occurs as small intrusive bodies or dikes, and as quartz-poor border facies of large granitic bodies. Its jointing and erosional forms are similar to those of granite, except that craggy and jagged outcrop shapes are rare.

Origin: The controversy that surrounds the origin of nepheline syenite applies also to the origin of syenite. Some syenite bodies are clearly intrusive and of magmatic origin, whereas the origin of others, especially those adjacent to limestone masses, has never been determined with certainty.

Environment: Associated minerals include albite, acmite, apatite, biotite, corundum, hornblende, microcline, microperthite, muscovite, riebeckite, orthoclase, titanite, and zircon. Prominent mineral localities in syenite have been found in

Arkansas (Garland Co.), California
(Inyo and San Bernardino Cos.),
Colorado (Fremont Co.), Maine
(Kennebec Co.), and Ontario (Hastings
Co.).

Economic use: Syenite has the same value as granite for
constructional and industrial purposes
but is not often used owing to its
relative rarity.

729   Nepheline Syenite

Texture: Phaneritic, medium- to coarse-grained,
rarely porphyritic.

Structure: Pronounced flow structure in the form
of streaks and aligned clots of dark
minerals, both in hand specimens and
in field exposures. Angular xenoliths
may be numerous.

Color index: Leucocratic.

Color: Usually light to medium gray, also
occasionally shades of pink, brown, and
green.

Luster: Distinctive greasy luster from abundant
nepheline.

Hardness: 5½–6

Composition: Similar to syenite but with still lower
percentage of silica, permitting the
appearance of feldspathoids in quantity.
Dark minerals are sodium- and iron-
bearing amphiboles and pyroxenes.

Mineralogy: *Essential minerals* Potash feldspar
(orthoclase, microcline, sanidine in
some porphyritic varieties), plagioclase
feldspar (albite, microperthite),
nepheline, biotite (lepidomelane),
amphibole, and pyroxene (acmite);
Accessory minerals Sodalite, analcime,
apatite, titanite, magnetite, and
andradite (var. melanite).

Field features: Occurs in rather small bodies that
appear to be intrusive. Like syenite, it
is rather well jointed and appears in the
same subdued erosional forms.

Origin: There is still considerable controversy as
to the origin of nepheline syenite. In
some localities the rock seems to pass

gradually into another soda-rich granitic rock rather than appear as a product of a separate and distinct magma. It also frequently occurs in contact with or in the vicinity of limestone deposits. At least a partial replacement origin has been suggested for nepheline syenite, but most evidence points to its formation from intrusive magma.

Environment: Associated minerals include acmite, albite, analcime, andradite, apatite, lepidomelane, magnetite, nepheline, orthoclase, sodalite, and titanite. Prominent mineral localities in nepheline syenite have been found in Arkansas, Maine (Kennebec Co.), and Ontario (Hastings and Haliburton Cos.). Compare the environment notes for nepheline syenite pegmatite.

Economic use: The commercial use of nepheline syenite is rather limited owing to its uncommon occurrence. In some localities (e.g. Magnet Cove, Arkansas) it has been used as an excellent building stone. More recently, it has been utilized as ceramic raw material. It is of interest that nepheline syenites are the parent rocks of the Arkansas bauxite deposits.

733   Nepheline Syenite Pegmatite

Texture: Uneven-granular, pegmatitic, usually very coarse-grained and highly variable in both grain size and mineral distribution.

Structure: Dikes, often zoned, with drusy crystal-lined cavities; same as given for granite pegmatite.

Color index: Leucocratic.

Color: Gray to pink, brown, green (as for nepheline syenite); variable owing to the highly variable mineral distribution and sizes.

Hardness: Average 5½–6

Composition: Same as nepheline syenite but with a

greater range of volatile and rare elements contained in a great variety of minerals.

Mineralogy: Same as nepheline syenite.

Field features: Generally occurs in close association with bodies of nepheline syenite, from which it is derived, and showing a gradational rather than a sharp contact between the two rocks. The great range of crystal sizes, up to 1.5 m (5′) or more in length, makes identification of the many different minerals rather easy.

Origin: As for granite pegmatite, but forms from magma containing much less silica and more sodium, iron, and rare elements.

Environment: Associated minerals include acmite, albite, andradite, apatite, augite, biotite, brucite, calcite, corundum, fluorite, hornblende, ilmenite, magnetite, microcline, nepheline, orthoclase, pyrite, pyrrhotite, sanidine, sodalite, titanite, wollastonite, and zircon. Outstanding mineral occurrences in nepheline syenite pegmatites have been found in Arkansas (Garland Co.), Maine (Kennebec Co.), Ontario (Hastings and Haliburton Cos.), and Quebec (Rouville Co.).

Economic use: Generally of little economic importance except as an unusually fine source of interesting and rare mineral specimens. Some of these have been collected from time to time for the extraction of rare elements in research laboratories.

740   Monzonite

Texture: Phaneritic to phaneritic-porphyritic; medium- to coarse-grained; feldspar phenocrysts often large and well-formed.

Structure: Monzonite (like syenite and granodiorite) is one of the many leucocratic plutonic rocks that have been classified under the general heading of "Granites." Thus it has essentially the same structural features as granite, such as linear and platy flow structures, giving the rock a gneissoid appearance. Miarolitic cavities are common.

Color index: Leucocratic; generally somewhat darker than granite.

Color: Light to medium gray, less commonly pink, dark gray or greenish gray.

Hardness: 5½–6

Composition: Like granite, but quartz content is 10% by volume or less; potash feldspar and plagioclase occur in approximately equal amounts. When quartz content exceeds 10% the rock is called quartz monzonite.

Mineralogy: *Essential minerals* Potash feldspar (orthoclase or microcline), plagioclase feldspar (oligoclase or more commonly andesine); dark minerals are hornblende, augite, and biotite; *Accessory minerals* Apatite, magnetite, ilmenite, titanite, zircon, and quartz (10% or less); hypersthene and olivine in the more ferromagnesian varieties.

Field features: Monzonite is not an abundant rock and is generally found along the borders of larger plutonic masses of granodiorite and diorite. It has essentially the same properties as other granitic rocks, from which it can be distinguished with certainty only by microscopic study.

Origin: Same as granite, by slow cooling and crystallization of magma at depth in the earth's crust.

Environment: Associated minerals, principally in miarolitic cavities, include topaz, beryl, and microcline. Prominent occurrences of these cavities are in the Conway region of New Hampshire, Pikes Peak region of Colorado, and the Llano Uplift, Mason Co., Texas.

Economic use: Potentially the same as granite but infrequently used because of limited quantities available and lack of easy accessibility.

726, 739 Granodiorite

Texture: Phaneritic, sometimes phaneritic-porphyritic; medium- to coarse-grained; phenocrysts usually plagioclase feldspars with multiple twinning striations and compositional zoning.

Structure: Virtually the same as granite; commonly has well-developed flow lineation and flow layering as well as xenoliths in the marginal portions of its large intrusive mass; orbicular structure and miarolitic cavities occasionally present.

Color index: Leucocratic.

Color: Similar to granite but somewhat darker gray; less commonly pink.

Hardness: 5½–6

Composition: Similar to quartz monzonite, having the same light-colored minerals but in somewhat different proportions: quartz content is that of granite (10–30%), with the plagioclase feldspars (oligoclase-andesine) more abundant than the alkali feldspars (orthoclase, microcline, and perthite).

Mineralogy: *Essential minerals* Quartz (more than 10%), orthoclase, microcline, oligoclase-andesine, hornblende, biotite; *Accessory minerals* Augite, apatite, titanite, and magnetite.

Field features: As for granite.

Origin: Formed, like granite, by slow cooling and crystallization of magma at depth in the earth's crust.

Environment: Granodiorite, as the principal rock in batholithic intrusions, has supplied the heat and chemicals necessary for the formation of contact-metamorphic and hydrothermal rocks and minerals. It is, therefore, the host for many ore-bearing veins.

Economic use: As for granite.

Comment: Granodiorite (and quartz monzonite) are, next to granite, the most abundant plutonic igneous rocks in large-scale intrusions such as batholiths, large stocks, thick sills, and dikes. The "granitic" Sierra Nevada batholith is actually composed of a complex combination of granodiorite, granite, monzonite, and diorite bodies.

741, 744   Diorite

Texture: Phaneritic, medium- to coarse-grained, less commonly phaneritic-porphyritic; phenocrysts are zoned plagioclase feldspars with multiple twinning striations, hornblende, and biotite.

Structure: In the marginal portions of a diorite intrusion the rock will show distinct flow banding both by parallel orientation of lath-shaped feldspar crystals and in the form of streaks and oriented clots of hornblende and biotite, which are formed by early crystallization of ferromagnesian minerals in the more-or-less fluid magma. Xenoliths of the wall rocks are also quite common in the marginal zones of the diorite body.

Color index: Mesocratic.

Color: Gray to dark gray, occasionally greenish to brownish gray.

Hardness: 5½–6

Composition: A comparison of the chemical composition (in weight %) of mesocratic diorite with that of leucocratic syenite (as a representative of the granite family) shows silica (SiO_2) percentage somewhat lower but percentages of iron ($FeO + Fe_2O_3$), magnesia (MgO), and lime (CaO) appreciably higher for diorite. This explains the increase of ferromagnesian minerals in the rock (to approximately 50% of the total volume). Quartz content is normally 5% or less by volume. The term "quartz diorite" is applied when the quartz content rises to 10% or more.

Mineralogy: *Essential minerals* Plagioclase feldspars (mostly andesine, some oligoclase), potash feldspar (orthoclase, less commonly microcline), hornblende, biotite, and pyroxene (augite); *Accessory minerals* Quartz (less than 5%), apatite, zircon, titanite, magnetite, ilmenite, hypersthene.

Field features: Occurs as stocks, sills, and dikes; often forms in marginal portions of large granite-granodiorite masses (e.g. Sierra Nevada batholith). Erosional shapes of diorite are similar to those of granite, but topographically less prominent. Differential weathering sometimes emphasizes the flow banding by leaving dark streaky mineral segregations, which stand out in relief against the more rapidly weathered light-colored minerals (mostly feldspars).

Origin: Slow, deep-seated cooling and crystallization of a magma richer in ferromagnesian constituents than those that produced the plutonic rocks of the granite family.

Environment: Some of the minerals associated with diorite are found as a result of contact metamorphism where diorite intrudes other rocks. The same intrusion also supplies the materials as well as the heat energy for the formation of mineral veins and hydrothermal replacement deposits. A xenolith of impure limestone, for instance, is engulfed by the intruding magma and encased in the crystallizing diorite. This intense contact metamorphism results not only in the formation of such minerals as diopside and grossular in the xenolith, but also of diopside, plagioclase feldspar, and hornblende in the diorite host. Associated minerals in diorite then include almandine, andesine, apatite, biotite, magnetite, spinel, and titanite. Noteworthy mineral occurrences in diorite have been found in California (Kern and Tuolumne Cos.) and Ontario (Dungannon Co.).

Economic use: Diorite has good strength and durability, and can take a high polish. It is little used as an architectural or ornamental stone, however, because of its dark and unimpressive color.

725, 745, 746   Gabbro

Texture: Phaneritic, mostly rather coarse-grained; phaneritic-porphyritic texture is rare but very coarse-grained where found, with phenocrysts exceeding the groundmass in volume.

Structure: Generally massive, but may exhibit a layered structure produced by successive layers of different mineral composition, analogous to the stratification in sedimentary rocks. When tabular feldspars are present, their subparallel orientation may also reveal a distinct flow structure. Orbicular structure is very distinctly developed in some types of gabbro.

Color index: Melanocratic.

Color: Essentially dark gray, greenish black, and rarely reddish. Depending on the ferromagnesian minerals and their grain sizes, some gabbros are somewhat lighter colored (i.e. medium or greenish gray); these rocks may appear mottled in hand specimen.

Hardness: Variable, but average above $5\frac{1}{2}$

Composition: Gabbros contain less silica (SiO_2) and alkali ($K_2O + Na_2O$) than diorite, but more iron ($FeO + Fe_2O_3$), magnesia (MgO), and lime (CaO). Hence two-thirds of the rock by volume consists of dark ferromagnesian minerals, and the feldspar is calcic plagioclase.

Mineralogy: *Essential minerals* Plagioclase feldspar (labradorite, rarely bytownite or anorthite), pyroxene (diallage, augite, or orthopyroxene), amphibole (hornblende), and olivine; *Accessory minerals* Biotite, quartz, magnetite, ilmenite, chromite, pyrope, spinel, apatite, hematite, rutile, titanite, and corundum.

Field features: Occurs as sheetlike, saucer-shaped intrusions called lopoliths; also as dikes and stocks. The layered structure is usually visible on large vertical exposures. Gabbro weathers and erodes more rapidly than granitic rocks, so that its outcrops are relatively small and partly covered by crumbly, decomposed rock particles.

Origin: Gabbro forms by slow cooling and crystallization at depth in the earth's crust from a magma that is more fluid than granite magma. Because of this fluidity, olivine crystals, which form early, tend to sink to the bottom of the intrusion. The accumulating crystals eventually form a layer rich in olivine, followed by successive layers of other minerals that crystallize later.

Environment: Associated minerals are anorthite, apatite, augite, bytownite, chromite, corundum, diallage, diopside, hematite, hornblende, hypersthene, ilmenite, labradorite, magnetite, olivine, pyrope, quartz, rutile, titanite, and spinel. Prominent mineral occurrences in gabbro have been found in California (Nevada Co.), Greenland, Labrador, New York (Adirondack Mtns. and Rockland Co.), New Jersey (Bergen and Hudson Cos.), and Wyoming (Albany Co.).

Economic use: Diabase (or dolerite), a variety of gabbro, is composed principally of labradorite, augite, and some olivine and magnetite with a tightly interlaced microscopic crystal structure that is responsible for the rock's toughness and high crushing strength. Known by the commercial name "trap rock," it is widely used as crushed stone for concrete aggregate, road metal, railroad ballast, roofing granules, and riprap. Smaller quantities of diabase are cut and polished for dimension stone (called "black granite").

---

743 Peridotite
Dunite

Texture: Phaneritic; medium- to coarse-grained.
Structure: In the coarser-grained varieties, (i.e. those rich in pyroxenes and amphiboles) the numerous cleavage surfaces have a

spotted appearance owing to enclosed grains of olivine; this is known as "luster mottling."

Color index: Melanocratic.

Color: Dull green to black; dunite, a variety of peridotite composed almost entirely of olivine, has a light-green to yellowish-green color (the natural color of olivine).

Luster: Luster mottling is common, due to enclosures of randomly oriented crystals of olivine in pyroxenes (particularly bronzite, a variety of enstatite) and amphiboles.

Hardness: Highly variable depending on the type and abundance of ferromagnesian minerals present and on the degree of alteration they have undergone; fresh peridotite specimens have a hardness of approximately 5½–6.

Composition: Entirely ferromagnesian, but chemical composition varies with the particular minerals of which the rock is composed. Typically has less silica (SiO_2) than most igneous rocks, high magnesia (MgO) and iron (FeO + Fe_2O_3) content, with little alumina (Al_2O_3) and virtually no alkali (K_2O + Na_2O). Monomineralic peridotites are named after their particular minerals, e.g. pyroxenite or hornblendite. (Dunite, an exception to this rule, is named for Dun Mountain, New Zealand).

Mineralogy: *Essential minerals* Olivine, pyroxene (diopside, augite, hypersthene, enstatite), amphibole (hornblende); *Accessory minerals* Chromite, biotite, magnetite, pyrrhotite, pyrope, spinel, and uvarovite; *Secondary minerals* Serpentine and talc may be present as secondary minerals, formed by the alteration of primary ferromagnesian minerals.

Field features: Peridotites occur as dikes, sills, laccoliths, and stocks, some of which may be of large dimensions; they also appear as stratiform layers in gabbro lopoliths. Fresh peridotite is generally

dull green in color. Weathering
changes the color to medium or dark
brown, and also tends to reduce
exposures of the rock to rounded
hillocks with pitted to crumbly
surfaces.

Origin: Peridotites form at depth, by the slow
cooling and crystallization of a magma
of ferromagnesian silicate composition
with little, if any, alumina and alkalis.
Extrusive (volcanic) rocks of peridotite
composition are rare.

Environment: Associated minerals include augite,
biotite, chromite, diamond, enstatite,
hornblende, hypersthene, magnetite,
olivine, pyrope, pyrrhotite, spinel,
and uvarovite. Prominent mineral
occurrences in peridotite have been
found in Arkansas (Pike Co.),
California (Del Norte, Siskiyou, and
Trinity Cos.), Arizona (Apache Co.),
Kentucky, New Mexico (McKinley and
San Juan Cos.), North Carolina (Macon
Co.), and Northern Cascades,
Washington.

Economic use: Peridotites have been a source of
valuable minerals such as chromite, the
principal chromium ore, nickel ore
(concentrated from weathered olivine
peridotite), and native platinum (in
placer deposits derived from completely
decomposed peridotite). Diamond is
mined from a mica peridotite called
kimberlite. The metamorphic minerals
talc and chrysotile, commonly formed
by alteration of olivine and pyroxene,
are also of commercial value (see
"Serpentinite").

734 Carbonatite

Texture: Uneven-granular, pegmatitic, medium-
to coarse-grained, occasionally
phaneritic-porphyritic.

Structure: None of importance.

Color: Medium to dark, but highly variable
and often mottled in appearance.

Hardness: Hardness and tenacity extremely variable owing to the widely divergent physical properties of the constituent minerals.

Composition: Fundamentally a carbonate rock of calcite and dolomite with a variety of ferromagnesian silicate minerals.

Mineralogy: *Essential minerals* Calcite and dolomite with varying quantities of alkali feldspars (albite, orthoclase), nepheline, pyroxene (diopside, acmite), biotite, and olivine; *Accessory minerals* Considerable variety, including andradite, apatite, barite, chalcopyrite, fluorite, monazite, and pyrite.

Field features: Bodies of carbonatite occur in close association with soda-rich rocks such as nepheline syenite. They have irregular shapes and are generally of small size, probably less than 5 km² (2 sq. mi.) in North America. Outcrops are dark-colored, weathered, and rather inconspicuous.

Origin: Considered by many to be of deep-seated magmatic origin, like peridotite (var. kimberlite), with which it is often associated. Another close association is with soda-rich nepheline syenite, whose plutonic origin has also been questioned. In any event, the precise mode of carbonatite origin and emplacement is still a matter of much discussion and disagreement among geologists.

Environment: Associated minerals are acmite, albite, andradite, anhydrite, apatite, augite, azurite, barite, biotite, bornite, calcite, cerussite, chalcopyrite, chlorite, chrysotile, columbite, diopside, dolomite, fluorite, galena, goethite, gold, hematite, ilmenite, magnetite, malachite, molybdenite, monazite, orthoclase, pyrite, pyrrhotite, quartz, riebeckite, rutile, scapolite, siderite, sphalerite, strontianite, tetrahedrite, titanite, uraninite, vesuvianite, wollastonite, wulfenite, and zircon. Prominent mineral occurrences in carbonatites are known in Arkansas

(Garland Co.), California (San Bernardino Co.), Colorado (Gunnison Co.), Montana (Blain and Hill Cos.), and Ontario (Haliburton and Ontario Cos.).

Sedimentary Rocks

Rocks formed under moderate pressure from layers of accumulated sediment. Clastic sedimentary rocks consist of fragments of older, weathered rock, ranging in size from submicroscopic particles to boulders. Other sedimentary rocks are of organic or chemical origin. Texture is extremely varied, depending on the character of the original sediments, but is typically rough and relatively loosely consolidated or cemented, with distinct signs of layering. Hardness varies but is often rather low (roughly 3–4 for many types). The layered or bedded structure is distinctive in hand specimens and outcrops, and fossils are fairly common.

747, 755, 757,   **Shale**
762, 766   **Mudstone**

Texture: Dense, clastic, with particles of silt size
(microscopic) and clay size (sub-
microscopic); mudstone is compacted
and somewhat indurated (hardened) but
may break apart when wet; shale is
better compacted, harder, and thin-
bedded.

Structure: Mudstone is generally massive with
layers up to several feet in thickness;
shale is well laminated and tends to
split into flat, shell-like fragments
parallel to bedding. Some shales
contain many fossils; ripple marks and
fossil mudcracks are not uncommon.

Color: Normally light to dark gray depending
on the amount of carbonaceous
(organic) debris present; admixture of
iron oxides (limonite and hematite) may
color some shales buff, brown, reddish
brown, or deep red.

Hardness: Easily scratched by a knife, mudstone
more readily than shale.

Composition: Clay minerals (e.g. kaolinite), which
are derived from the decomposition
(chemical weathering) of original
feldspars, with silt-size grains of quartz
and flakes of mica as relict minerals by
disintegration (mechanical weathering)
of the source rocks.

Field features: The structural characteristics (massive
vs. laminated) are quite apparent on a
clifflike exposure, with shale beds
standing out in some relief against the
mudstone layers, which have eroded
more deeply owing to their rapid
disintegration in wet weather. In moist
regions both rock types erode quite
readily compared to other sedimentary
rocks such as sandstones, and rarely
form any prominent topographic
features by themselves. But in arid and
semiarid localities they may stand out
in bold relief, supporting mesas,
buttes, and similar cliffed topographic
features.

Origin: Detrital, from sediments deposited in

the quiet environment of lake and ocean bottoms.

Environment: Shale and mudstone are seldom environments for minerals.

Varieties: Determined chiefly by the presence of accessory materials. Most important are carbonaceous shale (which with increasing content of organic carbon grades into coal shale and coal), oil shale (shale containing bituminous material that can be distilled to yield oil), and calcareous shale (which passes into limestone upon continued addition of calcite).

Economic use: Used in the manufacture of bricks, pottery, and other ceramic products. Oil shales represent a great potential supply of fossil fuel.

747–749, 759, 760, 761, 765 **Sandstone Quartzite**

Texture: Even-granular, medium-grained, clastic; particles generally rounded, of sand size, .05–2 mm (up to .08″) in diameter, held together by compaction in the presence of clay or through cementation by silica, carbonates, clay, or iron oxides.

Structure: Mostly well stratified, thin- to thick-bedded, sometimes massive; several types of cross-bedding and ripple marks are quite common. Some sandstones also have an appreciable fossil content.

Color: Extremely varied, depending first on quantity and color of the cement, and then on overall color of mineral grains. Light colors seem to prevail where sandstone is either devoid of cement or is cemented by calcite or quartz. The presence of limonite and hematite is responsible for buff, brown, and red colors. Glauconite grains in sufficient quantity cause the color of the green variety called "greensand."

Hardness: Variable, owing to the wide range of hardness of the cementing materials.

Composition: Quartz is the dominant mineral, occurring as mostly rounded, sometimes angular, detrital grains; when feldspar is added in sufficient quantities, the rock is called arkose sandstone or simply "arkose"; garnet, magnetite, tourmaline, hornblende, mica, and zircon may also be present in small amounts. Silica (quartz or chalcedony), carbonates (calcite, dolomite, or siderite), clay, and iron oxides (limonite and hematite) are the common cementing agents.

Other data: *"Feel"* Sandstones usually have a gritty feel because they tend to fracture through the cement and around the detrital grains.

Field features: Layers of thin-bedded or massive sandstone, whether flat-lying or steeply inclined, usually stand out in relief against over- or underlying sedimentary rocks that have less resistance to erosion; sandstones are therefore often called "ridge formers."

Origin: Detrital, from sediments accumulated in a wide variety of environments such as beaches, deltas, floodplains, and deserts.

Environment: Sandstone or quartzite as such is rarely considered to be a mineral environment for the collector. Deep beneath the earth's surface, sandstone provides the principal reservoirs for petroleum resources. Closer to the surface, the more porous and permeable sandstone horizons become important aquifers (reservoirs and conductors of groundwater).

Varieties: Sandstone varieties are commonly distinguished according to the kind of cement or by the admixed minerals, such as calcareous, argillaceous, ferruginous, siliceous, micaceous, or arkose sandstones. When the cement as well as the detrital grains is quartz, a hard, crystalline rock results, which will fracture through the grains rather than around them. Such a rock, which has no porosity at all, is called quartzite or orthoquartzite to distinguish it from the metaquartzite formed by metamorphism. These two quartzites are difficult to tell apart without either microscopic examination or knowledge of the field terrain in which they occur. Another variety is graywacke, an impure, "dirty" sandstone composed of rounded to angular fragments of shale, slate, chert, granite, basalt, etc., in addition to quartz and feldspar grains. Its color is gray, sometimes greenish and black.

Economic use: Sandstone is used principally for construction. It is rather easy to work, and thick-bedded or massive structures permit quarrying of uniform, large-size blocks (often called freestones). The red-brown sandstone of Triassic age, better known as "brownstone," has been used extensively for building construction in the cities of E United States. It proved suitable for architectural design because it was easy to carve and retained sculptured details longer owing to the chemical stability and insolubility of the iron oxide cement. Greensands (glauconitic sandstones) have been used as a source of potash (potassium carbonate) for use in fertilizer.

763, 764 Conglomerate
Breccia

Texture: Uneven-granular, coarse-grained, clastic, with well-rounded rock fragments of pebble, cobble, or boulder size, 2 mm (.08") to 25 cm (10") or more in diameter, held together by various kinds of cementing materials; if fragments are angular the rock is called *breccia*.

Structure: Characteristically thick-bedded to massive; may contain fossils, particularly in the cement.

Color: Varies greatly owing to the large size

and varied colors of the minerals and rock fragments and cement.

Hardness:
Highly variable because both fragments and cementing materials may have wide range of hardness.

Composition:

Conglomerate pebbles may consist of any mineral or rock; the most common constituents are resistant materials such as quartz, quartzite, chert. Depending on the provenance, however, fragments of feldspar, limestone, dolomite, granite, gneiss, and schist may predominate locally in either conglomerate or breccia. Cementing materials are the same as in sandstone, i.e. silica, carbonates, clay, and iron oxides.

Other data:
"Feel" Freshly broken surface generally very rough, because rock fractures around the sizable fragments.

Field features:
Conglomerates are not as common as sandstones and shales, but they do occur interbedded with them. A well-indurated conglomerate or breccia will form prominent outcrops or cliffs, whereas a poorly compacted conglomerate tends to disintegrate into a layer of loose pebbles, cobbles, and boulders.

Origin:

Detrital, from coarse sediments; the rounding of the conglomerate fragments is the result of impact, grinding, and abrasion during transport. Transporting agents capable of moving the larger fragments (cobbles and boulders) are swift-flowing streams, storm waves, glacial flow, or gravity; hence suitable environments for conglomerate deposition include river channels, alluvial fans, and ocean beaches. In breccia the angularity of the fragments indicates they were not subjected to the rigors of turbulent and long-distance transport. Depositional environments for breccia include talus slopes (at base of cliffs), landslides, some glacial moraines, and movements along fault planes.

Environment:
Generally, conglomerates and breccias

are not productive mineral environments. But a special, loosely consolidated conglomerate, which is commonly referred to as "placer gravel," was a source of much of the gold mined in California and Alaska. Associated minerals are chromite, corundum, diamond, gold, platinum, sapphire, and zircon. Prominent mineral occurrences in conglomerates (placer gravels) have been found in Alaska (Nome), California (Amador, Butte, Calaveras, Del Norte, El Dorado, Nevada, Placer, Sierra, Siskiyou, Trinity, and Tuolumne Cos.), Florida (coast), Montana (Lewis & Clark Co.), and Oregon (Coos, Curry, and Josephine Cos.).

Economic use: Conglomerates are of limited use as source material for concrete aggregates, which are more commonly derived from unconsolidated gravel deposits. Some tightly cemented breccias are capable of taking a good polish and have been used as ornamental stone.

750, 756   Limestone

Texture: Dense to even-granular, fine-grained, essentially nonclastic. Usually so dense that it can be studied only under a microscope; grains of some crystalline limestones are large enough to be seen with the naked eye, and in these the even-granular fine-grained texture is apparent. In fossiliferous limestones, distinctive textural patterns are often produced by a multitude of visible fossils of many kinds.

Structure: Occurs in beds ranging in thickness from a few centimeters or inches to more than 30 m (11′) or as unstratified moundlike masses representing fossil reef structures; also may appear in many shapes as a result of its easy solubility and subsequent reprecipitation in suitable places such as fractures, caves, etc. Stalactites and stalagmites, fracture fillings, crystalline "sculptures" at hot springs and geysers are some examples. The most striking structural features, however, are found in biogenic limestones, with their vast variety of fossil remains. Oolitic structures occur in many chemically deposited limestones.

Color: Usually white or light to dark gray to black, with organic material being the darkening agent; yellow and brown colors result from iron oxides; red is uncommon.

Hardness: 3–4; easily scratched or cut by a knife.

Composition: In order to be called a limestone, the rock must consist of 50% or more of calcite (or aragonite). The remainder is made up of impurities, which may be grains of dolomite, quartz, clay, iron oxides, or rock particles of many kinds.

Other data: *Tenacity* Very dense varieties break with a conchoidal fracture; *Solubility* The most distinctive property is the solubility of limestone in cold, dilute hydrochloric acid accompanied by brisk effervescence, thus providing an easy test for the presence of calcite in a rock.

Field features: Limestone, frequently interbedded with shale and sandstone, is easily weathered due to its solubility, resulting in crumbly, pitted, pockmarked outcrops.

Origin: Detrital, chemical, or biogenic sediments.

Environment: Limestone is usually not a mineral environment, but owing to its solubility in slightly acid groundwater, calcite is frequently redeposited in favorable places (e.g. fractures) as well-formed crystals, sometimes with minute crystals of other minerals carried in the solution. Limestone is also susceptible to alteration by various mineralizing solutions, so that valuable mineral deposits are frequently associated with limestones. Some of the minerals formed in this manner are barite, calcite, celestite, fluorite, galena, gypsum, marcasite, and sphalerite. Prominent mineral occurrences in limestone have been found in Mexico (Chihuahua), Ohio (Ottawa and Putnam Cos.), Oklahoma (Ottawa Co.), and Ontario.

Varieties: *Clastic limestones* are the least common; they are composed of broken shell fragments, parts of calcite crystals, and fragments of other limestones; they are often beach deposits.

Chemical limestones are precipitates in warm seas, hot springs, saline lakes, and limestone caves.

Oolitic limestone is a typical warm, shallow sea-water deposit.

Travertine is a color-banded, crystalline deposit formed in caves and hot springs.

Organic or *biogenic limestones* include the greatest number of varieties, which are named after the most abundant type of fossil contained, such as coral, algal, or foraminiferal limestones.

Coquina is a pale-brown, porous, poorly cemented organic limestone composed of marine or freshwater mollusk shells and shell fragments.

Chalk is a white, soft, porous, dense-textured organic limestone composed of shells of microscopic organisms and deposited in shallow marine water but beyond the reach of detrital grains from the shore. Many limestones that contain no recognizable fossil remains, and once thought to have been precipitated from sea water, are now interpreted as having been secreted by marine algae, which, lacking hard parts, were not preserved in the rock.

Economic use: Limestone is widely used for structural purposes, both interior and exterior. It is an important ingredient in the manufacture of mortar and Portland cement, and is used as flux in iron- and steel-smelting operations. Certain argillaceous limestones are the essential ingredient of hydraulic cement. Dense limestones are crushed for concrete aggregates and road metal.

758   Dolomite Rock

Texture:	Dense, rarely even-granular, nonclastic; essentially the same texture as limestone.
Structure:	As for limestone, but with less variety and abundance of fossil structures.
Color:	As for limestone, but more commonly light gray to tan.
Hardness:	3–4, essentially as for limestone; slightly harder than calcite.
Composition:	Composed almost entirely of dolomite. In most cases varying amounts of calcite are present in addition to other impurities, such as quartz and feldspar, with gradations from pure limestone to magnesian limestone to dolomitic limestone to calcitic dolomite and dolomite. To be called dolomite, the rock should consist of at least 50% of the mineral dolomite.
Other data:	*Solubility* Effervesces in dilute hydrochloric acid, but only if the acid is hot or the specimen is finely powdered.
Field features:	As for limestone, although the effects of weathering upon dolomite rock are produced over a somewhat longer period of time owing to its lower solubility.
Origin:	Chemical sediments; most dolomite rock was formed by replacement of calcite in limestone by magnesium-rich water before complete lithification of the limestone and before its subsequent burial by other sediments. There is also evidence for this replacement action having taken place long after formation of the limestone. Some dolomite rock may have formed by direct precipitation from sea water on the ocean bottom, but this is still being debated by geologists.
Environment:	Dolomite rock is rarely a mineral environment in itself. It is readily subject to the effects of metamorphism and is often the host rock for mineral veins and hydrothermal replacement deposits.

Economic use: Dolomite rock, like limestone, has many industrial uses, including as asphalt filler, concrete aggregate, riprap, and roofing granules. It is also used as flux in iron smelting and is a source for metallic magnesium.

754   Chert

Texture: Dense, smooth; rough on weathered surface.

Structure: Chert commonly occurs in masses ranging in size from nodules to formations reaching thicknesses of 275 m (900') or more (as in the Coast Ranges of California and Oregon) and having wide areal extent. Bedded cherts, often in the form of wedgelike, discontinuous beds, are found intercalated with other sedimentary and sometimes volcanic deposits.

Color: Not a useful criterion for recognition; ranges from white to gray to black (flint), with varieties appearing in yellow, brown, green, and red (jasper).

Hardness: 7; hardness is distinctive.

Other data: *Tenacity* Extremely hard, tough, dense; *Fracture* Conchoidal.

Field features: Strongly resistant to erosion; therefore stands out in relief on weathered surfaces as nodules, beds, or massive outcrops.

Origin: Study of some cherts under the microscope reveals the presence of microscopic siliceous skeletons (whole or broken) of certain algae and protozoans, which, having accumulated on the ocean bottom, were compacted and partly recrystallized to form chert of opaline composition. Some cherts appear to have been formed by precipitation of silica from sea water. A different mode of origin involves the formation of chert nodules and lenticles by partial replacement of limestone with silica (chalcedony); this is a purely chemical process, although the silica involved may have come from dissolved skeletons of marine organisms. A similar process is the formation of petrified wood, which involves silica replacement of wood by groundwater action.

Environment: Associated minerals include pyrolusite and rhodochrosite. Prominent mineral occurrences in chert are largely limited to California (Humboldt, Mendocino, San Joaquin, Stanislaus, and Trinity Cos.).

Economic use: Flint and other forms of chert were used by early man for weapons and implements and for striking fire. Also used to ignite the charge in early (flintlock) firearms.

753 Gypsum Rock

Texture: Even-granular, fine- to medium-grained, nonclastic, crystalline. The fine crystalline texture is generally only visible under the microscope, but partial recrystallization often produces well-formed crystals of selenite (pure mineral gypsum) that can easily be observed with the unaided eye, giving the rock a pseudo-porphyritic texture.

Structure: Occurs in rather massive beds that range in thickness from a few centimeters or inches to tens of meters, normally interbedded with shale, limestone, and rock salt. Some deposits are delicately laminated due to seasonal deposition of fine clay layers.

Color: Mostly white to light gray; yellow or red colors may result from iron oxide pigments and dark gray from clay or organic impurities.

Luster: A freshly broken fragment of hand specimen will sparkle in the sun with a pearly to vitreous luster because of the many exposed cleavage planes of tiny selenite crystals. *Satin spar,* a fibrous variety of gypsum, has a silky luster.

Hardness: 2; scratches easily with fingernail; low

hardness is the most distinctive property.

Composition: Consists mainly of interlocking crystalline grains of selenite, often mixed with other evaporite minerals such as anhydrite and halite; clay and bituminous material are common impurities.

Field features: In arid and semiarid regions gypsum rock is relatively resistant to erosion and sometimes forms the cap rock on the tops of mesas and buttes. In moister climates it is rather easily eroded, like some of the softer limestones and shales with which it is associated.

Origin: Chemical (evaporite) sediment; gypsum rock originates by evaporation of saline lakes or sea water in restricted or cut-off bays, and requires an arid or semiarid climate for its formation as an evaporite. There is good field evidence, however, that gypsum ($CaSO_4 \cdot 2 H_2O$) may be a secondary mineral formed by hydration of anhydrite ($CaSO_4$) in the zone of weathering. This would then suggest that the original composition of the gypsum evaporite was anhydrite.

Environment: Minerals associated with selenite are anhydrite and halite. Noteworthy mineral occurrences in gypsum rock have been found in California (Imperial, Inyo, Kern, Los Angeles, Riverside, San Bernardino, San Luis Obispo, and Ventura Cos.), Colorado, Dominican Republic, Idaho (Bear, Lake, Lemhi, and Washington Cos.), Iowa (Webster Co.), Kansas (Barber and Marshall Cos.), Mexico (State of Chihuahua and San Marcos Island), Michigan (Ottawa Co.), Montana (Cascade and Meagher Cos.), Nevada (Clark, Lincoln, Ormsby, and Pershing Cos.), New Brunswick, New Mexico (Chaves, De Baca, Eddy, Lincoln, Otero, Socorro, and Terrance Cos.), New York (Genesee, Madison, Monroe, Niagara, Onondaga, and Seneca Cos.), Nova Scotia, Ohio (Mahoning Co.), Utah (Duchesne, Emery, Grand, Iron, Juab,

Kane, San Juan, Sanpete, Uintah, Washington, and Wayne Cos.), and Wyoming (Albany Co.).

Economic use: The chief use of gypsum is for the manufacture (by heating) of calcined gypsum or plaster of Paris, a material which has been utilized by man since the ancient Egyptian civilization. The modern construction industry depends heavily on the use of gypsum plaster in laths, wallboards, and other building materials. Relatively small quantities are also used in Portland cement manufacture, iron smelting, and (in pulverized form) as soil conditioner and fertilizer. Large deposits of anhydrite are presently of little economic value, but experiments are being carried out to greatly accelerate nature's process of changing anhydrite to gypsum by hydration. If these are successful, anhydrite deposits may be of considerable value in the future.

751 Rock Salt

Texture: Even-granular, fine- to coarse-grained, nonclastic, crystalline; halite grains generally coarse enough to be visible to the unaided eye.

Structure: Rock salt occurs in well-defined beds

ranging in thickness from a few meters or feet to as much as 400 m (1,300') in some localities and extending in sheets over areas up to 260,000 km (100,000 sq mi). One of the important characteristics of rock salt is its ability to flow at relatively low pressures and temperatures. Deeply buried thick salt beds may rise and "intrude" overlying rocks, forming salt plugs and domes, which may measure from 4,500 m to 11,000 m (appr. 15,000' to 35,000') or more, top to bottom. Such structures are of great importance because oil and gas accumulations and sulfur deposits are closely associated with them.

Color: Colorless to white when pure; impurities may produce a gray color or tints of pale blue, pink, and yellow.

Luster: A freshly broken specimen will have the vitreous luster of halite from its many excellent cleavage surfaces.

Hardness: 2; scratches easily with a fingernail.

Other data: *Taste* The salty taste of halite is distinctive.

Composition: Halite constitutes 95% to 99% of rock salt. Chief impurity is anhydrite, but small amounts of gypsum, dolomite, and shale may be present, and (less commonly) quartz and pyrite. In some localities valuable potassium and magnesium chlorides and sodium and magnesium sulfates (thenardite) may occur as impurities.

Field features: Because of the solubility of halite in surface waters, outcrops of rock salt can only be found in desert climates, as in Death Valley, California.

Origin: Chemical (evaporite) deposits. The origin of rock salt, like that of gypsum, is by evaporation of saline lakes and restricted or cut-off bodies of sea water. The great thickness of salt beds and their areal extent require that the evaporation basin had to subside and be refilled with ocean water from time to time under continued arid conditions to explain such great accumulations.

Environment: Minerals commonly associated with halite are anhydrite, gypsum, and dolomite; in some deposits thenardite (sodium sulfate) may also be found. Mineral occurrences in rock salt can be found in California (Imperial, Inyo, Kern, and San Bernardino Cos.), Dominican Republic (Port of Barahona), Kansas (Saline Co.), Louisiana (off coast), Manitoba, Mexico (Chiapas, Chihuahua, Durango, Hidalgo, Michoacán, Nuevo León, Oaxaca, Puebla, Querétaro, San Luis Potosí, Sinaloa, Sonora, Tabasco, Tamaulipas, Yucatan, and Zacatecas), Michigan (Manistee and Mason Cos.), Nevada, New Brunswick, New Mexico

(Eddy and Lea Cos.), New York (Livingston, Tompkins, and Schuyler Cos.), Nova Scotia, Ontario, and Saskatchewan.

Economic use: Rock salt is one of the four most essential mineral materials for the chemical industry, the others being coal, limestone, and sulfur. Extensive use is made of both the sodium and chlorine of the salt in the manufacture of chemicals for many industries, especially in the production of glass, paper, textiles, leather, soap, meat and fish packaging, dairy products, and table salt. Salt is also a minor ore of metallic sodium. Salt plugs are economically important for their associated deposits of sulfur and fossil fuels.

752 Coal

Texture: Dense, sometimes subvitreous nonclastic; visibly biogenic.

Structure: Varies according to grade of coal. *Peat* is a porous, spongy mass of partly decayed plant remains; *lignite* retains a fibrous, woody structure; *bituminous* coal is well jointed, breaking into rectangular pieces, often thinly laminated, tending to splintery or conchoidal fracture, with some fossil plant remains visible with a hand lens; *anthracite* is massive, homogenous, tends to break with a pronounced conchoidal fracture.

Color: *Peat* is brown to yellowish, *lignite* generally chocolate brown, sometimes yellowish or black to velvet-black; *bituminous coal* and *anthracite* are iron-black to velvet-black.

Luster: Dull (peat, lignite, and bituminous coal); anthracite is bright vitreous to submetallic.

Hardness: 1–1½ (peat and lignite), 2 (bituminous coal), 2–2½ (anthracite).

Composition: Principal constituents are the elements

carbon, hydrogen, and oxygen, with some sulfur and nitrogen.

Field features: Coal, regardless of grade, occurs in layers, which miners call *seams,* that range in thickness from about 2.5 cm (1″) to a usual maximum of about 3.6 m (12′), though a few are much thicker. Coal seams are interbedded with shales and sandstones and are easily recognized by their dark color in contrast to the lighter-colored enclosing rocks.

Origin: Coal is formed by destructive distillation of plant remains under anaerobic conditions and progressively rising pressures and temperatures until coal with a very high fixed carbon content is attained. During this long-term process several distinct ranks or grades of coal are formed as follows: (1) *peat,* an accumulation of partly decomposed plant remains in swampy lowlands; (2) *lignite* (brown coal), a more solid material covered by sediments causing compaction of peat; the fixed carbon content is a low 25%; (3) *bituminous coal* (soft coal), resulting from deeper burial with rising pressures and temperatures, driving off hydrogen and other volatiles and leaving a fixed carbon content of 50% to 65%; (4) *anthracite* (hard coal), formed from bituminous coal by pressures and temperatures existing in the metamorphic environment of deepest burial accompanied by folding deformation of the enclosing rocks. The fixed carbon content reaches a maximum of 85% to 95%. Under still more intensive folding deformation and metamorphism, graphite or pure carbon is formed from anthracite.

Environment: Coal is essentially a mineral fuel rather than a mineral environment. However, in the process of converting lignite into bituminous coal, some sulfur is released and combines with iron to form either pyrite or marcasite. These minerals occur as concretions in the form of spherical or lenticular aggregates of small crystals.

Economic use: Coal is the most abundant and important fossil fuel of the world. Bituminous coal occurs in the greatest quantities. It has the highest caloric heat value but burns with a yellow flame, developing smoke and giving off a bituminous odor. Anthracite requires strong heat to ignite and has a somewhat lower heat value than the highest-grade bituminous coal, but burns with a pale-blue flame and without smoke or odor. It is the most suitable coal for household use but is also the most expensive grade of coal.

Metamorphic Rocks

Rocks formed under conditions of intense heat, pressure, or both, at considerable depths within the earth, from older ("parent") rocks. The minerals of the parent rock are often altered, becoming more coarsely crystalline in the metamorphic rock, and tending to become aligned in layers. In rocks that have undergone extreme pressure the mineral layers may be conspicuously bent and folded.

769, 770,   **Slate**
783–787, 791   **Phyllite**

Texture: Dense; crystalline on microscopic scale (slate); or small crystals visible to the naked eye (phyllite); may contain porphyroblasts (e.g. garnet, andalusite).

Structure: Slaty foliation produced by alignment of mica flakes in parallel planes along which rock splits readily into thin sheets; larger, visible mica flakes and wavy to crinkly foliation are characteristic of phyllite. Relict bedding may be visible as color bands cutting across the foliation.

Color: Usually medium to dark gray to black (from enclosed carbonaceous matter and graphite), occasionally green (from chlorite), or red, purple, brown, or yellow (from iron oxides).

Luster: Distinct but weak on slaty foliation planes; pronounced silky sheen on phyllitic foliation.

Hardness: Easily scratched with knife blade.

Field features: Commonly occurs as steeply tilted outcrops with jagged or irregular outlines due to weathering, which also causes flaking and separation along foliation surfaces.

Metamorphism: Dynamothermal (regional) metamorphism under compressive stress—low-grade for slate, and medium-grade for phyllite.

Parent rock: Generally mudstone or shale.

Mineralogy: Muscovite and chlorite principal constituents; observable with the naked eye only in phyllite.

Environment: Not an environment for any specific minerals; may be transected by veins (often quartz); may contain porphyroblasts of such minerals as andalusite (var. chiastolite).

Economic use: Quarried for roofing slate, flagstone, blackboards, etc., and manufacture of roofing granules; phyllite has no particular economic value.

Comments: Phyllite, resulting from continued dynamothermal (regional) metamorphism of slate, represents an intermediate stage in the progressive metamorphic series:

shale→slate→phyllite→mica schist

767, 792, 794   Schist

Texture: Uneven-granular, medium- to coarse-grained, crystalline, with prominent parallel mineral orientation.

Structure: Prominent schistose foliation produced by plane-parallel alignment of crystalline minerals having the tendency to occur in thin plates or flakes (owing to crystal habit or single plane cleavage) and making up more than 50% of the rock; relict bedding may sometimes be recognized in the fine-grained varieties of schist as cross-cutting bands of somewhat different color or texture. The foliation is rather irregular and wavy owing to the scaly overlapping of the mineral flakes and is commonly bent, crumpled, and folded in response to the dominant compressive stress of regional metamorphism. Porphyroblasts frequently "make room for themselves" by causing the foliation minerals to bend around them, producing a feature called augen (eye) structure and a rock called augen schist.

Color: Silvery white, all shades of gray, with yellow to brown tones, depending on the color of the foliation-producing mineral or minerals and the concentration of accessories in the form of lenses or intercalated layers. Chemical weathering of biotite and other Fe-bearing minerals produces iron oxides (e.g. limonite), which cause the yellow and brown colors.

Luster: Fresh specimens have a sparkling luster produced by light reflections from the oriented cleavage flakes of the foliation minerals; luster dulls with time because of the rust-forming weathering processes.

Hardness: Hardness and firmness (ease of splitting) of schists depend on the proportions of micaceous minerals (micas, chlorite, talc with H = 1–3) in relation to hornblende (H = 5–6) and intercalated quartz (H = 7) as well as sometimes abundant accessories, e.g. garnet (H = 6.5–7.5).

Field features: Outcrops commonly show foliation structures in tilted or folded attitudes; when weathered, colors are dark with variable shades of brown (rust).

Metamorphism: Schists are characteristically formed by dynamothermal (regional) metamorphism under temperature and pressure conditions ranging from low to high grade. The grade of metamorphism is indicated by the so-called "index minerals," which are formed under the conditions prevailing in a particular grade zone, as follows:

Metamorphism	Index minerals
Low-grade (150°–250° C)	*Chlorite, albite*
Medium-grade (250°–450° C)	*Garnet (almandine), epidote*
High-grade (450°–700° C)	*Staurolite, kyanite, sillimanite*

Parent rock: Schists may be formed from sedimentary rocks (e.g. feldspathic shale, sandstone, conglomerate), from volcanic igneous rocks (e.g. rhyolite, basalt), or from other metamorphic rocks (e.g. slate, phyllite).

Mineralogy: "Schist" is a descriptive term. Specific schistose rocks (e.g. chlorite schist) are named after the principal foliation-producing minerals: muscovite, biotite, chlorite, talc, or hornblende; frequently well-formed crystals of epidote,

almandine, staurolite, or kyanite are
present in such quantities that they are
included in the rock name (e.g.
chlorite-epidote schist, almandine-
muscovite schist).

Environment: Associated minerals in schists of all
grades include, in addition to those
listed above, acmite, actinolite, albite,
andalusite, antigorite, aragonite, beryl,
calcite, chalcopyrite, chrysoberyl,
clinozoisite, glaucophane, graphite,
jadeite, lawsonite, lazulite, lepidolite,
magnetite, monazite, pumpellyite,
pyrite, pyrophyllite, riebeckite, rutile,
siderite, sillimanite, spessartine,
titanite, tremolite, and zoisite.
Prominent mineral occurrences in
schists have been found in Alaska
(Wrangell district), California (Inyo,
Madera, Marin, Mendocino, San
Benito, and Sonoma Cos.), Connecticut
(Litchfield, Middlesex, Norwich, and
Windham Cos.), Georgia (Fannin Co.),
Massachusetts, New Hampshire
(Grafton Co.), North Carolina
(Cherokee Co.), Ontario (Hastings
Co.), Oregon (Curry Co.), Virginia
(Patrick Co.), and Washington (N
Cascades).

Economic use: Some schists are minor source rocks for
minerals of economic value, such as
graphitic schist for graphite. Some
firm, erosion-resisting schists (e.g.
quartz-muscovite schist) are used locally
as building stones.

788–790 Gneiss

Texture: Uneven-granular, medium- to coarse-
grained, crystalline, with more or less
parallel mineral orientation.

Structure: Gneissic structure or gneissic banding,
composed of layers of granular minerals
(quartz, feldspar) sometimes showing
discontinuous or streaky foliation (of
biotite or hornblende) alternating with
relatively narrow bands of well-foliated

micaceous or prismatic minerals (e.g. micas, hornblende), but representing less than 50% of the minerals in the rock. The granular layers, often of granitic composition, frequently contain relict phenocrysts or porphyroblasts. The latter have a tendency to take on ovoid shapes with their long dimensions parallel to the foliation. This feature is called augen (eye) structure and the rock augen gneiss.

Color: Too variable to be of diagnostic value. The granular layers are generally light-colored (usually gray, tan, or pink, the colors of the predominant feldspar and quartz); the foliated bands are more likely to be dark-colored, as are the common foliation minerals, biotite and hornblende.

Luster: Both intensity and type of luster are highly variable, depending on the size and number of mineral grains providing reflecting surfaces such as good cleavages or conchoidal fractures.

Hardness: Variable. The granular, quartz-feldspar layers are relatively hard (H = 6–7); foliated bands with abundant micas are softer (H = 2½–3).

Field features: Gneisses, on the whole, have the same erosional resistance as granitic rocks so that they commonly underlie prominent hills and mountains. Their gneissic banding, however, distinguishes them readily from plutonic igneous rocks of similar composition. Also their origin is revealed by the usual intense folding deformation of gneisses, which must have taken place in the plastic state at depth in the earth's crust.

Metamorphism: Dynamothermal (regional) metamorphism under great compressive stress, high-grade, at temperatures from 450° to 700° C and correspondingly high pressures. Refer to discussion on metamorphism of "Schist." The index minerals for metamorphic grades are the same.

Parent rock: Just as the term "gneiss" encompasses an unusually diverse group of rocks, their parental rocks are likewise of many types. Generally speaking, the most common parent rocks are igneous plutonic rocks (granite, syenite, diorite, gabbro), sedimentary rocks (such as argillaceous and feldspathic shales, sandstones, and conglomerates), and many low-grade metamorphic rocks.

Mineralogy: Principal constituent minerals are feldspar (orthoclase), quartz, biotite, hornblende; well-formed crystals of almandine, corundum, and staurolite may occur in distinct bands.

Environment: Associated minerals include, in addition to those mentioned above, andalusite, apatite, cordierite, monazite, and titanite. Prominent mineral occurrences in gneiss have been found in Montana (Gallatin and Madison Cos.) and New York (Adirondack Mts., Hudson Highlands).

Economic use: Owing to the physical and chemical similarity between many gneisses (e.g. granite gneiss) and plutonic igneous rocks (e.g. granite), such gneissic rocks are used as building stones and for other structural purposes. Their usefulness decreases with an increase in mica content and foliation.

Comments: There is no sharp demarcation between schist and gneiss. They are both descriptive terms referring to the relative abundance of foliation minerals. Schistose foliation is presumed to involve more than 50% of the rock, while gneissic foliation is supposed to fall below the 50% figure. It is actually left to the judgment of the observer whether to call a foliated crystalline rock in the 40% to 60% abundance range a schist or a gneiss.

A specific gneiss may be named for the parent rock (e.g. granite gneiss) or for its characteristic minerals (e.g. biotite gneiss) or structures (e.g. augen gneiss).

793 Amphibolite

Texture: Even-granular, granoblastic, fine- to coarse-grained; with or without distinct parallel orientation of the amphibole crystals.

Structure: The term "amphibolite" refers to a group of metamorphic rocks that consist primarily of amphibole-group minerals, particularly hornblende. Their structure ranges from massive (lacking preferred mineral orientation) to weakly foliated to strongly schistose; the schistosity is produced by the alignment of slender, prismatic amphibole crystals parallel to each other as well as in more or less parallel planar surfaces, which determine the foliation. The schistose amphibolites are often classified under "schists," e.g. hornblende schist, glaucophane schist (blue schist).

Color: Depends largely on the color of the particular amphibole present; ranges from light to dark green to black, with the darker colors occurring more commonly. Sometimes a lighter green shade is produced by admixed chlorite.

Luster: Light reflections from the numerous oriented cleavage surfaces of the abundant amphibole crystals produce a sparkling silky luster.

Hardness: Amphibolites are rather hard rocks that are not easily scratched by a knife blade (H = 5–6¼).

Other data: *Tenacity* The schistose varieties are brittle but do not split readily along foliation surfaces. The more massive kinds are tough and difficult to break; *Specific gravity* Amphibolites are rather heavy, with a specific gravity of 3–3.4.

Field features: Usually in dark-colored, weathered outcrops, easily distinguishable from the lighter-colored schists and gneisses with which they are commonly associated. In a terrain of folded, high-grade metamorphic rocks, amphibolites exhibit a rather high degree of plastic flow deformation.

Metamorphism: Dynamothermal (regional) metamorphism at medium- to high-grade conditions of temperature and pressure; amphibolites are among the most common rocks in metamorphic regions.

Parent rock: Amphibolites have a dual origin; they are most frequently derived from ferromagnesian igneous rocks containing pyroxene (e.g. gabbro or peridotite) or they may originate from impure calcareous rocks, such as limestones or dolomites containing clay, sand, and iron oxides.

Mineralogy: Chief constituent mineral is hornblende, but plagioclase feldspars, micas, and quartz may be present in appreciable quantities.

Environment: Associated minerals include, in addition to those mentioned above, almandine, chlorite, diopside, epidote, labradorite, oligoclase, and zoisite. Prominent mineral occurrences in amphibolite have been found in California (Amador, Calaveras, Nevada, Placer, and Sierra Cos.) and New York (Adirondack Mts.).

781   Hornfels

Texture: Dense; granoblastic on a microscopic scale.

Structure: Very compact and massive, breaking with a splintery to conchoidal fracture; relict bedding may be observed particularly away from the immediate vicinity of the igneous contact. Spotting or knotting may appear along relict bedding, indicating incipient crystallization of minerals (e.g. cordierite, andalusite).

Color: Dark gray to black.

Luster: Dull.

Hardness: 6–7

Field features: A dark, compact hard rock that breaks into sharp, angular pieces; located in contact with or at close proximity to a plutonic igneous body of some magnitude. Hornfels is very similar in appearance to basalt but is generally harder. Microscopic study may be necessary to distinguish between these two rocks, unless the precise field relations with respect to the contact of an igneous intrusion is known.

Metamorphism: Hornfels is formed by contact metamorphism of argillaceous sediments involving recrystallization of the original sedimentary rock constituents (at high temperatures, but without shearing stress) and introduction of some additional chemical ingredients by volatiles escaping from the magma.

Parent rock: Argillaceous sediments: clay, silt, mudstone, shale, or slate.

Mineralogy: Because a great number of minerals may be present, virtually any one of the associated minerals listed below may be a principal constituent in a given hornfels. In any event, their microscopic size precludes their use in field identification.

Environment: Associated minerals of hornfels include actinolite, albite, almandine, andalusite, andradite, anorthite, apatite, axinite, biotite, brucite, cordierite, corundum, diopside, enstatite, fluorite, hedenbergite, hypersthene, magnetite, orthoclase, plagioclase, quartz, rhodonite, sillimanite, spessartine, spinel, and tephroite. Prominent mineral occurrences in hornfels have been found in Arizona (Clifton-Morenci district), California (Inyo and Kern Cos.), Idaho (Mackay region), Nevada (Pershing Co.), New Jersey (Bergen and Hudson Cos.), and New York (Rockland and Westchester Cos.).

Economic use: Minor use as crushed stone where quarrying of trap rock (diabase) has crossed the contact and proceeded into hornfels.

Comments: The term "hornfels" is used here in its original restricted sense as a contact-metamorphic rock derived from argillaceous sediments. Subsequent expansion of the term to include metamorphic products from calcareous sediments is not followed. Such rocks are discussed as calc-silicate rocks under the heading "Marble."

768, 780   Greenstone

Texture:	Dense, crystalline, and crystalloblastic (metamorphic crystals) only on microscopic scale.
Structure:	Massive, compact; relics of amygdules of calcite and quartz from original basalt are not uncommon.
Color:	Pale gray-green to yellowish green or dark green, depending on the proportions of chlorite, epidote, and actinolite (which are responsible for the rock color) to the other minerals present in the rock.
Luster:	Dull.
Hardness:	Variable, depending on which of the green minerals is the most abundant; H approximately 5–6.
Field features:	Usually found in folded mountain ranges. Outcrops are well-fractured, producing sharp, angular fragments. Narrow veins of quartz and calcite often traverse the rock.
Metamorphism:	Mild dynamothermal (regional) metamorphism under moderate compressive but low shearing stress; with increasing shearing force, foliation of chlorite begins to develop and the rock becomes a greenstone (chlorite) schist or just greenschist (see "Schist").
Parent rock:	Ferromagnesian igneous rocks (e.g. basalt and gabbro).
Mineralogy:	Principal constituents, chlorite, epidote, actinolite, and feldspar (albite).
Environment:	Associated minerals, in addition to the ones mentioned above, are biotite, calcite, hornblende, quartz, and zoisite. Mineral occurrences in greenstone have

been found in California (Marin,
Mendocino, and Sonoma Cos.).

Economic use: Used mainly as a crushed stone in
highway construction.

Comments: It should be pointed out that the term
"greenstone" is an old field term, now
rarely used, which applies only to the
compact, massive variety of this rock.
When a schistose foliation of the green
minerals begins to appear, the rock is
classified as a chlorite schist.

771–776, 778 Marble
Calc-Silicate Rock

Texture: Even-granular, granoblastic, fine- to
medium-grained; may be uneven-
granular and coarse-grained in calc-
silicate rock.

Structure: Marble composed of only calcite or
dolomite is generally massive and
devoid of foliation; if mineral
impurities are present they may cause
weak to distinct foliation (see
"Metamorphism" below); sometimes
bands or streaks of impurities result
from plastic flow during extreme
deformation.

Color: The normal color is white, even snowy
white, but accessory minerals acting as
coloring agents may produce a variety
of colors: black (from carbonaceous
matter), green (from diopside,
hornblende, serpentine, or talc), red
(from hematite) and yellow to brown
(from limonite); uneven distribution of
these coloring substances frequently
causes color spots, blotches, or veinlike
patterns, an effect described as
"marbled."

Luster: On fracture surfaces marble has a soft
vitreous luster that can be observed
even on fine-grained specimens where
the individual grains and their
cleavages are visible only with the aid
of a hand lens.

Hardness: With a hardness of 3, marble can easily

be scratched with a knife blade. In the transition to calc-silicate rock the hardness increases to 5½ or more, depending on the type and abundance of the silicate minerals.

Other data: *Solubility* Calcitic marble effervesces vigorously with cold, dilute (1:5) hydrochloric acid, but dolomitic marble will do so only if first reduced to powder or if the acid is hot; the presence of calcite or dolomite in calc-silicate rock may also be determined in this manner.

Field features: Marble characteristically occurs in regions of metamorphic rocks and is commonly interbedded with mica schists and gneisses or is adjacent to bodies of intrusive igneous rocks. On weathered outcrops it appears "recessed" and crumbly owing to its poor resistance to erosion, particularly in temperate and moist climates, where the weather activity is greatest. However, the erosional resistance increases perceptibly in calc-silicate rock, which may actually stand out in relief among regionally metamorphosed rocks.

Metamorphism: Marble is formed by contact metamorphism of pure limestone or dolomite or by dynamothermal (regional) metamorphism of mostly impure limestones or dolomites; the metamorphic grade may vary from low to high. Some structural features appear to be related to the type of metamorphism, i.e. massive structure is common in contact-metamorphosed marble, while dynamothermal metamorphism with its shearing stress under strong confining pressure is more likely to produce marble with moderate to well-developed foliation.

Parent rock: Pure calcitic or dolomitic marbles are evidently the contact-metamorphic equivalent of equally pure calcitic and dolomitic limestones. However, marbles with increasing amounts of calc-silicate minerals are derived from limestones with variable quantities of admixed clay, silt, sand, and ferruginous materials.

Mineralogy: In pure marbles, calcite and dolomite are the only principal constituents; impure marbles and calc-silicate rocks contain various other minerals, depending on the chemical composition of the original impurities: wollastonite, pyroxene (diopside) amphibole (tremolite), garnet (grossular), epidote, and feldspar (anorthite).

Environment: Pure marble is not a mineral environment owing to the fact that the few accessory minerals that may be present are small and rarely identifiable with the unaided eye or the hand lens. Impure marbles grading into calc-silicate rocks, however, are a fertile field for the mineral collector. Associated minerals, in addition to the ones listed above, are: apatite, axinite, brucite, chondrodite, fluorite, graphite, hedenbergite, hematite, hornblende, laumontite, magnetite, olivine, orthoclase, pargasite, phlogopite, scheelite, spinel, vesuvianite, and zoisite. Important mineral occurrences in marbles have been found in California (Fresno, Inyo, Kern, Madera, and Riverside Cos.), Colorado, Idaho, Montana, Nevada (Pershing Co.), New York (Willsboro, Essex Cos.), and Utah (Iron Co.).

Economic use: Marble is one of the more important "industrial rocks." Depending on its purity, texture, color, "marbled" pattern, etc., it is quarried for use as dimension stone for statuary, architectural, and ornamental (interior and exterior) purposes. As crushed stone (particularly the more impure varieties including calc-silicate rock) it is usable as concrete aggregate, road metal, railroad ballast, filter beds, etc. Dolomite-rich marble may be a source rock for magnesium and is used as an ingredient in the manufacture of refracting materials.

Comments: With reference to its industrial use, the term "marble" (by law) includes all crystalline calcium carbonate or calcium magnesium carbonate rocks that can take a high polish. Thus the widely used "Tennessee marble" is a fossiliferous sedimentary limestone with a crystalline texture. Another very attractive stone (used for the Lincoln Memorial in Washington, D.C.) is the "Yule marble" from Colorado, which is a totally recrystallized metamorphic rock.

776, 777 Skarn

Texture: Uneven-granular, medium- to coarse-grained; crystalloblastic (crystalline fabric entirely produced by metamorphic processes).

Structure: No unusual structural features except porphyroblasts, irregularly distributed and frequently of different minerals in different parts of the same exposure.

Color: Varied; depends on the color of the most abundant mineral present, which may sometimes change over short distances, even within a hand specimen. Some of the typical colors are green (from actinolite), reddish brown (from andradite), white (from calcite), gray (from diopside), black (from magnetite), and yellow (from pyrite).

Luster: Generally sparkling reflections from the many cleavage planes but variable in kind owing to the different minerals involved.

Hardness: Constrasting hardness of 3 (calcite) and greater than 5.5 for most of the other minerals.

Field features: Skarn and calc-silicate rock have rather similar mineral composition so that they are not easy to tell apart in hand specimen. Their field relations, however, are distinctive. Skarn occurs in sharply defined zones at contacts between marble and plutonic rock bodies. Calc-silicate rock, on the other hand, grades peripherally away from the intrusive contact into less metamorphosed rocks of similar chemical composition.

Metamorphism: Skarn is derived from nearly pure limestone and dolomite by the addition of large amounts of silicon, aluminum, iron, and magnesium, which combine with the calcium carbonate to form metamorphic silicate minerals. The transfer of elements is accomplished by a contact-metamorphic process, called metasomatism, involving emanations (gases and/or hot liquids) from the magmatic intrusion (commonly of granitic composition) across its contacts with the invaded limestone. In addition to the elements mentioned, such magmatic "volatiles" may also transport concentrations of metallic elements such as copper, lead, tin, and tungsten, causing the formation of ore deposits of pyrite, galena, bornite, scheelite, etc. in the contact zone.

Parent rock: Nearly pure limestone and dolomite.

Mineralogy: Probably the most common mineral constituents are diopside, epidote, garnet (grossular, andradite), hedenbergite, and wollastonite. But any of the associated minerals listed below (except calcite) may be a principal constituent of a skarn specimen.

Environment: Associated minerals, in addition to those mentioned above, include actinolite, bornite, calcite, chalcocite, chalcopyrite, chlorite, cassiterite, galena, hematite, laumontite, magnetite, scheelite, and titanite. Prominent mineral occurrences in skarn have been found in California (Fresno, Kern, and Tulare Cos.), New Mexico (Grant Co.), New York (Adirondack Mtns., Essex Co.), Pennsylvania (Lebanon Co.), and Utah (Beaver and Iron Cos.).

Economic use: Skarn zones composed of wollastonite and diopside have been mined for use in the ceramic, paint, and electrical industries for the manufacture of tile, porcelain, paint filler, and insulators. Garnetiferous zones have supplied garnet as a by-product for use as an abrasive.

781, 782 Metaquartzite

Texture: Even-granular, granoblastic, fine- to medium-grained, rarely dense.

Structure: Massive, thick-bedded; may have a weak, discontinuous foliated structure, sometimes indicating relict bedding, provided sufficient muscovite is present.

Color: White when pure, light to dark gray, or brownish to pinkish from included accessory minerals.

Luster: Vitreous luster of quartz.

Hardness: 7; tough but brittle, with an uneven, splintery to conchoidal fracture.

Field features: Outcrops are usually prominent, forming ledges, cliffs, and sharp crags in mountainous regions.

Metamorphism: Contact or dynamothermal (regional) metamorphism, and confined to any metamorphic grade; outlines of original sedimentary quartz grains have become generally imperceptible owing to the recrystallization of the original quartz cement.

Parent rock: Quartz-rich sandstones, sometimes with detrital grains of other minerals (e.g. feldspar) or other than silica cement (clay, calcite).

Mineralogy: Mostly quartz (original grains and crystalline cement); also almandine and muscovite.

Environment: Associated minerals are, in addition to those mentioned above, biotite, chlorite, cordierite, epidote, graphite, hornblende, kyanite, magnetite, orthoclase, sillimanite, tourmaline, and zircon. Prominent mineral occurrences in metaquartzite have been found in New York (Adirondack Mts.).

Comments: Metaquartzite is difficult to distinguish from sedimentary quartzite without microscopic study or knowledge of the larger field terrain. Care must be taken when collecting specimens in this rock; wear goggles and gloves, because sharp blows with a geologist's pick will produce sharp, flying chips of quartz.

---

779 Serpentinite

Texture: Dense, crystalloblastic (all crystals of metamorphic origin) on an extremely microscopic scale.

Structure: Though massive, serpentinite has many slick, polished-looking, and often striated surfaces, called "slickensides," which are the result of minor shearing movements during folding deformation of the region.

Color: Generally green, particularly yellow-green, but yellow, yellow to reddish brown, and dark green to black colors occur.

Luster: Dull to waxy.

Hardness: If composed principally of serpentine minerals, the rock is soft and can be cut by a knife; if secondary silica is introduced, rock is much harder but can still be scratched with a knife blade.

Other data: *"Feel"*   Somewhat greasy and very smooth to the touch.

Field features: Occurs as layers or discontinuous, lenticular bodies along "lines" of mountain-building activity; outcrops often show steeply tilted layers indicating attitude of originally steep-sided intrusions of ultrabasic (wholly ferromagnesian) rock from which serpentinite was derived. Serpentinite soil is infertile and will not support most vegetation because it lacks alkalies and lime.

Metamorphism: Hydrothermal metamorphism at low to moderate temperature and moderate pressure; sometimes involves two stages of metamorphism (e.g. dolomite rock metamorphoses first into amphibolite and then into serpentinite).

Parent rock: Peridotite or pyroxenite (both ultra-basic rocks) or amphibolite (originally metamorphosed from dolomite rock).

Mineralogy: Principally the serpentine minerals (antigorite and chrysotile).

Environment: Associated minerals are antigorite, brucite, chlorite (purple-red chromium var.), chromite, chrysotile, diamond, inesite, magnesite, magnetite, talc, and uvarovite as well as remnants of minerals from original igneous rock (e.g. olivine, pyroxene, and hornblende). Mineral occurrences in serpentinite have been found in Arizona (Gila and Pima Cos.), California (Amador, Butte, Calaveras, Del Norte, El Dorado, Fresno, Lake, Mendocino, Napa, Plumas, San Benito, San Luis Obispo, Santa Clara, Siskiyou, Sonoma, and Trinity Cos.), Georgia (Cherokee Co.), Maryland, New Jersey (Morris Co.), Oregon (Grant Co.), and Quebec (Megantic, Ottawa, and Richmond Cos.).

Economic use: Source of platinum in placer deposits (Ural Mts. of the USSR); vast iron ore deposits from weathering of serpentinites (Cuba); also host rock for nickel and chromium ores in many localities. Serpentinite is the principal source of asbestos, which occurs as chrysotile veins in serpentinite; also widely used as interior decorative stone, particularly when multicolored.

Comments: The term "serpentinite" (like greenstone) applies to the compact, massive variety. With development of schistose foliation it is classified as a schist and is then called serpentine schist.

PART III: MINERAL COLLECTING

TOOLS AND TECHNIQUES FOR COLLECTORS

Mineral collecting need not involve elaborate equipment. All that is required are a few tools for gathering, labelling, and identifying specimens; equipment for transporting and storing them; and a method of organizing and displaying the mineral collection.

Mineral Collecting
The essential items here are a hammer or a geologist's pick, a small cold chisel, a prybar or crowbar, a carrying bag, and a pocket knife, almost all of which can be obtained at a hardware store or hobby shop. A notebook is essential for recording such data as collection sites, distances traveled, the date, associated minerals, and the type of rock where the specimens were found.

The size of your specimens is of course a matter of choice. If the specimen is too bulky, it is generally possible to find undesirable portions and trim them off. Each specimen should be given a field number as it is collected. Adhesive tape makes good specimen labels. Specimens should be wrapped for protection. Newspaper will do for most pieces. Any that are fragile and contain delicate crystals should either be carried by hand or wrapped in tissue paper. It is not advisable to use cotton, especially around delicate crystals, since cotton fibers become entangled with the crystals and are difficult to remove. When packing wrapped specimens in a wooden box or cardboard carton, place the more massive specimens at the bottom.

Mineral Identification Equipment The basic equipment for identifying minerals can be very simple. A hand lens, with a magnifying power between 6x and 10x, is essential for examining small crystals. Also necessary is a small, white unglazed porcelain tile for use as a streak plate, and some sort of hardness testing kit. The latter may be ordered from a scientific supply house, but simpler equipment will do in most cases: your fingernail (H: 2½), a copper penny (H: 3), a pocket knife or a small piece of window glass (both H: 5½), a hardened steel file (H: 6½), and a small piece of quartz (H: 7). A magnet is useful for testing some iron-bearing minerals, and a small plastic bottle of dilute (1:5) hydrochloric acid is very helpful in identifying the carbonate minerals. The acid can be purchased from some drugstores or scientific supply houses, and should always be handled and stored carefully. Instructions for using these materials are given in the "Guide to Mineral Identification," pages 19 to 38.

Field Safety When exploring in a quarry or in mine dumps, use leather work gloves and a hardhat, stay on the uphill side of boulders that may be dislodged, and keep an eye open for loose material from overhead.
A geologist's pick should never be used as a chisel, or struck with another hammer. The steel may chip, sending dangerous fragments flying. To enlarge a hole or widen a seam in rock, use a cold chisel, which will not chip. Goggles should be worn when working in chert, metaquartzite, or any other quartz-rich rock. As it is struck with a

pick or chisel, the quartz fractures and sends off razor-sharp chips that can cause serious injury.

Finally, if you are going into a wild or inaccessible area, especially in mountainous regions, investigate the local conditions first. Bad weather, lack of drinking water, black flies, or snakebite can turn a pleasure trip into a trying and dangerous excursion.

Collecting on Private Land There are still many places in North America where you can collect minerals and rocks and not be trespassing on private property. But because of urban expansion and the large-scale development of mineral and range-lands, many famous collecting areas are now privately owned, and generally posted with "No Trespassing" signs. Before collecting in such places, permission should always be obtained from the owner. If you have questions about an area, get in touch with a local museum or mineral club.

Care of Specimens Many mineral specimens will require nothing more than gentle brushing before they are ready for storage, study, or exhibit. Other specimens may need some trimming. This should be done very carefully. Light, sharp tapping blows with a geologist's pick will usually remove undesirable materials. Most minerals can be cleaned in water, but some are soluble or crumble easily when wet. A stiff brush can be used on hard, massive specimens, but not those that include delicate crystals. After a specimen has been cleaned, dry it with a paper towel or cotton cloth and place it in a well-ventilated area to dry completely. An acid bath may be required to remove undesirable materials from some specimens, but a beginner should get the advice of an experienced collector before attempting an acid treatment.

Because minerals are formed under a

wide variety of conditions, they have different degrees of stability. Some minerals are readily affected by changes in temperature, pressure, and humidity, and need special handling if they are to be preserved and enjoyed. For example, autunite, borax, chalcanthite, epsomite, and laumontite, among others, will lose the water contained in their crystals at normal conditions of temperature and humidity, while halite and melanterite will absorb water from the atmosphere. For best effect, these minerals should be stored or displayed in moisture-proof cases.

Among the other minerals described in this guide, sulfur should be protected from rapid changes in temperature, and chlorargyrite, cinnabar, proustite, pyrargyrite, realgar, topaz, and some varieties of quartz should be kept from exposure to light in order to preserve their color. A number of other species tarnish quickly in the open air. For some of these a coating of clear plastic spray will give adequate protection without damage to the specimen and without causing any great change in its appearance.

Organizing a Mineral Collection
There are at least six types of mineral collection: (1) the study or systematic collection, (2) the display or exhibit collection, (3) the thumbnail collection, (4) the micromount collection, (5) the dealer's collection, and (6) the rock collection.

Systematic Collection
The study or systematic collection can be simple or elaborate, depending upon the interest of the individual and the availability of specimens and storage facilities. The pieces in such a collection are arranged by class, family, and series according to their chemical properties, with separate groupings for the native elements, sulfides, sulfosalts, oxides, and so on. The arrangement

used in this field guide or in any mineralogical reference book may serve as a guide to the arrangement of specimens.

Exhibit Collection An exhibit collection is usually assembled for the sake of the intrinsic beauty of the specimens rather than for their scientific interest. Usually many of the best specimens in such a collection are not found in the field, but are purchased from dealers. Building a collection through purchase is costly and should be done slowly and with discretion. The result can be a collection to be proud of.

Thumbnail and Micromount Collections The thumbnail and micromount collections deserve special attention. Thumbnail specimens are small, generally 2.5 cm (1″) or less across, and micromount specimens are smaller still, generally 1.5 mm (1/16″) or less across. Thumbnail or micromount specimens are mounted with glue in small transparent plastic boxes of various sizes. A hinged base allows the box to be opened in order that the specimen may be conveniently examined with a hand lens or binocular microscope. Data about the specimen can be written on the back of the base of the box. The specimens in the thumbnail collection are large enough to be viewed without a hand lens, but a binocular microscope is needed to study micromount specimens.

There are several advantages to these small-scale collections. Because of their size, many specimens can be stored in a cabinet. For example, a good-sized drawer can hold 160 thumbnail specimens in convenient cube-shaped boxes. Moreover, small crystals are usually more perfect in form than larger crystals and hence help the mineralogist make determinations of crystal shape. Micromounting has become very popular and is worth investigating after you have been exposed to the broader aspects of mineralogy.

Dealer's
Collection
Mineral dealers often collect some of the minerals they offer for sale, but much of their stock is obtained from professional mineral collectors or by the purchase of collections. It is rewarding and instructive to visit a mineral shop whose stock is well organized and displayed.

Rock
Collection
A rock collection, although it may not have all the possibilities of a mineral collection, may still be interesting and attractive. Because rocks are composed of several minerals, rock specimens should be about the size of a fist in order to reveal clearly the textural and mineralogical features of the rock. Each specimen should have a number, and a record should be kept of its name, where it was collected, and its relationships to other nearby rocks.

Ultimately it does not matter much which way your collection is organized—whether it is simple or elaborate. Any mineral collection can provide many hours of relaxation and pleasure, as well as an understanding of some of nature's most elegant and beautiful creations.

MINERAL ENVIRONMENTS AND ASSOCIATIONS

Once you have learned to identify a number of minerals and rocks in the field it is possible to go about collecting in a more systematic way.

For most collectors, any given rock is of interest mainly because it is a source of particular minerals. We know, for instance, that a granite pegmatite outcrop may contain excellent crystals of beryl, feldspar, mica, tourmaline, or quartz; the granite pegmatite is the "environment" for this group of associated minerals.

To begin with, a collector should be able to recognize six basic types of environment: igneous (plutonic and volcanic) environments; sedimentary environments; metamorphic environments; hydrothermal replacement deposits; veins; and secondary replacement deposits. In the following descriptions, more detailed distinctions are made within each type of environment on the basis of the minerals and geological processes involved.

Igneous Mineral Environments The formation of minerals in igneous rocks depends upon three conditions in the magma that forms the rock: chemical composition, temperature, and the surrounding physical pressure. Temperature and pressure vary considerably within the earth, but the widest variations in mineral composition are due largely to the nature of the raw materials of the magma.

The magmas that form the igneous rocks consist of a mutual solution of silicate compounds. Silicates contain silicon and oxygen, the two elements that are most abundant in the earth's crust. Other abundant elements in the magma are aluminum, iron, calcium, and magnesium. Usually sodium and potassium are also present, as well as variable amounts of water.

Most minerals found in igneous rocks form in one of three ways: from a melt, by precipitation out of hot aqueous solutions, or by precipitation out of a gas or vapor.

In the first case, minerals are formed directly out of the magma. As the magma cools, minerals crystallize in a specific sequence, depending upon the kinds and quantities of chemical elements present and on the melting points of the various minerals that are formed when the elements combine into compounds. As each mineral crystallizes, its various component elements are extracted from the magma, thus changing the composition of the remaining molten material. The new composition determines what mineral forms next. As each new mineral forms, this process is repeated, until all the material in the magma is used up.

The size of the mineral grains or crystals that form out of the magma depends largely on the rate of cooling. Slow cooling produces large grains or crystals; rapid cooling produces small ones. Thus a magma of a given composition may crystallize to yield several types of rock, each with its own texture and physical characteristics. In general it is the plutonic rocks that are of interest to the mineral collector.

However, cavities in volcanic rock may often yield excellent crystals of certain minerals.

The formation of minerals from aqueous solutions is possible because the rocks of the earth's crust contain numerous openings, ranging in size from microscopic spaces between rock and mineral grains to fissures many meters across.

At depth, this water is part of the volatile constituents escaping from the magma. It penetrates upward through the crust, in the form of superheated steam, under great pressure. This "magmatic" or "juvenile" groundwater dissolves soluble materials out of the rocks it traverses and becomes increasingly mineral-laden. Closer to the earth's surface the temperatures and pressures gradually diminish, openings become larger, and much additional water is added from above. This so-called "meteoric" groundwater comes from rain and sometimes from sea water, which can percolate downward through the rocks as deep as 1,600 m (1 mi). Less soluble minerals now begin to precipitate, coating the enclosing walls with mineral crystals. When such crystalline material fills a relatively narrow fissure it is called a vein. Well-formed crystals of quartz and other minerals often occur in cavities, called "vugs," where the crystals have grown inward from the walls.

This type of mineral environment is considered igneous as long as precipitation takes place from hot groundwater rising under considerable pressure. Details on mineral precipitation at different levels of this vertical depth zone are given under the heading "Vein Environments," on pages 776 to 779. Near the surface of the crust, where groundwater is mostly meteoric, at low temperature and pressure, mineral precipitation still takes place but becomes part of the

chemical sedimentary environment.
In areas of volcanic activity minerals
may develop from vapors or gases.
These minerals precipitate out when
hot, mineral-laden gases, part of the
volatile magmatic constituents, come
into contact with relatively cool rock
surfaces. Small, well-formed crystals of
sulfur, cinnabar, and stibnite are often
found along the margins of hot springs
and volcanic vents or fumaroles, where
they crystallize out of such gases.
The most common minerals of igneous
environments are, not surprisingly, the
important rock-forming minerals:
quartz, orthoclase and plagioclase
feldspars, nepheline, muscovite,
biotite, hornblende, pyroxenes (augite,
acmite, hypersthene), and olivine.
Well-formed crystals are fairly
common, especially in the plutonic
rocks of this group. In some igneous
rocks the important accessory minerals
include apatite, corundum, hematite,
magnetite, rutile, titanite, and zircon,
but these generally form very small
crystals and are not easy to see without
a lens.

Minerals of Igneous Environments The following minerals or mineral
groups are among those often collected
in igneous—especially plutonic—
rocks:
Acmite, amazonite, apatite, augite,
beryl, biotite mica, cassiterite,
cinnabar, copper, corundum,
danburite, diamond, gold (in quartz),
gummite, hematite, labradorite,
magnetite, muscovite mica, pectolite,
prehnite, pyrope garnet, quartz,
scheelite, silver, sodalite, stibnite,
sulfides (pyrite, etc.), titanite, topaz,
tourmaline, turquoise, uraninite,
zircon.
In addition, minerals commonly found
in volcanic igneous rocks include:
Analcime, apophyllite, chabazite,
chalcedony, datolite, heulandite,

leucite, opal, pectolite, prehnite, sulfur, stilbite.

Pegmatites Among the igneous rocks, none is as rich in spectacular minerals as pegmatite. Pegmatite actually has the same general composition as ordinary plutonic rock (e.g. granite or nepheline syenite), but pegmatite contains far more well-formed mineral crystals and these may be much larger than those in other plutonic rocks. Whereas rock-forming minerals usually crystallize in sizes between 1 mm (.04″) and about 3 cm (1″), pegmatites often contain crystals a meter or more in diameter. In pegmatites in the Black Hills of South Dakota crystals of spodumene have been found that measure up to 15 m (50′) and weigh more than 88 metric tons (80 tons).

The term "pegmatite" referred originally to the rock type described earlier, but this rock always occurs in distinctively shaped structures, or bodies. Thus the word "pegmatite" is also used to refer to these bodies as well. The shape of a pegmatite body is determined by the type of rocks that enclose it. Pegmatites are usually tablelike or lenslike, but they may also be pipelike, tear-shaped, arcuate, or irregularly branched. Although they may extend several kilometers in length, most pegmatites are between 30 and 300 m (about 100′ to 1,000′) in length, and from 1.5 to 30 m (5′ to 100′) thick. Pegmatites are scattered throughout North America and are meccas for mineralogists. They are significant sources of gemstones and of several important metallic and nonmetallic minerals used in industry. Pegmatites that contain only common minerals (quartz, alkali feldspars, and micas) are called simple pegmatites. Even simple pegmatites, however, contain far more minerals than ordinary plutonic rocks, and many have been mined commercially for mica, feldspar, and quartz. Complex pegmatites result from the crystallization of the last hydrous and gaseous portion of magma, with its higher concentrations of rare elements. Because of this they usually contain an even greater variety of minerals, including rare ones. Complex pegmatites are thus among the best sites for mineral collectors, and are a source of several industrially significant minerals: lepidolite, spodumene, and amblygonite for their lithium content; cassiterite for tin; and columbite-tantalite, fergusonite, pyrochlore, microlite, euxenite, and samarskite for their niobium, tantalum, and rare-earth elements.

Most pegmatites are characterized by four zones. The outermost, or border, zone (1) is fine-grained, usually consisting of aplite (even-granular mixture of quartz, feldspar, and muscovite); it is rarely more than 1 m (3.3') thick. The wall zone (2) is coarser-grained and thicker than the border zone and irregular in shape, generally conforming to the pegmatite body. It contains both common minerals (quartz, feldspars, muscovite, biotite, and tourmaline) and rarer minerals (apatite, columbite-tantalite, garnet, and beryl). The intermediate zone (3) is less well developed and may be absent in some pegmatite bodies. It is very coarse-grained and is usually the site of giant crystals of spodumene, amblygonite, and perthite. If present, the core (4) is irregular in shape and usually small compared to the entire pegmatite body. The core is simple, generally consisting of quartz, perthite, spodumene, and amblygonite.

Pegmatite   Excellent specimens of the following
Minerals   minerals, among others, have been
              found in granite pegmatite or nepheline
              syenite pegmatite environments:

Acmite, albite, amblygonite,
andalusite, andradite, apatite, augite,
beryl, biotite, bismuthinite, brucite,
calcite, columbite-tantalite, corundum,
epidote, fluorite, goethite, grossular,
hematite, heulandite, hornblende,
ilmenite, kunzite, laumontite,
lepidolite, manganite, microcline,
monazite, natrolite, nepheline,
oligoclase, opal, orthoclase, pyrite,
pyrrhotite, quartz, sanidine, sericite,
sodalite, spessartine, spodumene,
titanite, topaz, tourmaline,
wollastonite, zircon.

Carbonatites   Carbonatite is an unusual type of
plutonic rock, and like pegmatite it
deserves particular notice as a mineral
environment. The uniqueness of
carbonatite is that, although it is
believed to be an igneous rock, it
contains substantial amounts of calcium
carbonate (usually in the form of
calcite); all other igneous rocks have
had all their carbonate constituents
driven off by the intense heat of their
formation. Carbonatite, it is assumed,
precipitated out of hot migrating
solutions, which picked up minerals
from igneous rocks rich in sodium- and
potassium-bearing minerals.
Carbonatite bodies, or "carbonatites,"
are thus the environment for a wide
variety of interesting minerals.
Like other plutonic rocks, carbonatites
have a range of textures. Some resemble
granite in appearance, while others
show well-defined foliation. Still others
are porphyritic, with carbonate or
silicate minerals forming the large
crystals. The mineral grain size ranges
from fine to coarse, and crystals have
been found up to 5 cm (2″) in size.
Carbonatites occur as dikes, but more
commonly as irregular-shaped bodies in
stocks or plugs. There they are called
alkalic igneous complexes because they
frequently contain both plutonic and
volcanic rocks. It should be stated,

however, that the origin and formation of carbonatite is still very controversial; this rock could just as easily belong to the environment of hydrothermal replacement deposits.

Carbonatite The following are some of the minerals
Minerals that have been collected in carbonatite environments:
Acmite, albite, andradite, anhydrite, apatite, augite, azurite, barite, biotite, bornite, calcite, cerussite, chalcopyrite, chlorite, chrysotile, columbite, diopside, dolomite, fluorite, galena, goethite, gold, hematite, ilmenite, magnetite, malachite, molybdenite, monazite, orthoclase, pyrite, pyrrhotite, quartz, riebeckite, rutile, scapolite, siderite, sphalerite, strontianite, tetrahedrite, uraninite, titanite, vesuvianite, wollastonite, wulfenite, zircon.

Sedimentary Mineral collectors are generally
Mineral interested in three main types of
Environments sedimentary mineral environments: the clastic sedimentary rocks, placer deposits, and chemical sedimentary rocks.

Clastic Clastic sedimentary rocks are the
Sedimentary mechanical accumulations of weathered
Rocks rock debris. This debris—gravel, sand, and mud—is called detrital because the sediments are transported mechanically and deposited by water, ice, and wind. Upon compaction and cementation, gravel, sand, and mud form conglomerate, sandstone, and shale respectively, according to the grain size of the sediments.
Because clastic sedimentary rocks are composed of rock and mineral particles derived principally from the disintegration of preexisting rocks, their composition is similar to that of the parent rocks. A sandstone whose source material is olivine basalt is likely to contain olivine, augite, and

labradorite. On the other hand, a sandstone composed largely of quartz and orthoclase was probably derived from a coarse-grained leucocratic plutonic rock such as granite. Some minerals, however, cannot withstand the rigors of decomposition or disintegration and transport, and are completely broken down. The sedimentary rocks derived in this way rarely have the same composition as the original material.

During the transportation of sediments by water, ice, and wind, very few chemical changes occur, but because the particles are bounding around, rubbing together and fracturing as a result of impact, they undergo physical changes in shape and size. The harder minerals, naturally, are the most likely to survive transportation and retain anything like their original form.

Placers   A substantial number of minerals at the earth's surface are chemically stable and do not appreciably decompose as do the rocks in which they develop. When the rocks decompose and disintegrate and are carried away by rain, streams, waves, wind, or ice, the heavy stable minerals remain behind in the soil or are transported as part of the sands and gravels of streams or beaches. Movements of stream currents or ocean waves aid in producing sands and gravels with high concentrations of heavy stable minerals. The surficial mineral deposits formed by this process are referred to as placers or placer deposits.

The minerals most commonly associated with placers include gold, the platinum group, monazite, chromite, rutile, zircon, magnetite, ilmenite, sapphire, garnet, scheelite, andalusite, and kyanite. It was placer deposits that prospectors searched for frantically during the 1880s gold rush in Colorado.

Placer and The following minerals, among others,
Clastic have been collected in placer deposits
Sedimentary and clastic sedimentary environments:
Minerals Aragonite, barite, bauxite, cassiterite,
chalcedony (jasper, agate), chromite,
corundum, diamond, garnet, goethite,
gold, hematite, ilmenite, limonite,
magnetite, opal, platinum, quartz,
rutile, sapphire, zircon.

Chemical Chemical sediments originate, usually,
Sedimentary through solution and precipitation.
Environments Chemical sedimentary rocks, such as
travertine, rock salt, dolomite, chert,
phosphate rock, and borax deposits, are
fairly widespread and many of them are
of tremendous economic importance to
man.

Chemical sedimentary rocks that result
from the evaporation of water
containing dissolved solids are called
evaporites. Rock salt, gypsum, and the
borate deposits are all chemical
evaporites. Rock salt is composed of
halite and forms in a shallow arm of a
sea, when the rate of evaporation is
greater than the inflow of water. The
famous Bonneville Salt Flats in Utah
and Searles Lake in California are
excellent examples of salt deposits
formed by the evaporation of inland
bodies of water, which, however, must
have been connected with the ocean for
some time in their history.

The evaporite potash deposits in the
Permian Basin in Kansas, New Mexico,
Oklahoma, and Texas, and in strata of
Devonian age in Saskatchewan, Canada,
contain interbeds of clay, halite, and
potash minerals. The famous borate
deposits in California are considered to
be evaporites, as are the deposits of
strontianite and celestite at several
places in Arizona and California.

Since gypsum and salt commonly occur
in the same sedimentary deposits, their
origins are similar in many respects.
The less soluble gypsum forms by
precipitation from sea water, and

frequently occurs in layered deposits several hundred meters thick. Salt (halite) dissolves readily in water; it therefore stays in solution longer and is precipitated later than gypsum.

These complex processes give rise to a series of rocks and minerals that are a delight to the mineral collector and are of great importance to industries that derive their raw materials from deposits containing potash.

Chemical Sedimentary Minerals The following are some of the commonest minerals of chemical sedimentary environments. Analcime, anhydrite, aragonite, apatite, borax, calcite, celestite, colemanite, dolomite, glauberite, gypsum, halite, kernite, marcasite, pyrite, realgar, sulfur, thenardite, ulexite.

Metamorphic Mineral Environments The great pressures and high temperatures that develop deep within the earth can alter existing rocks and create new ones: the metamorphic rocks. Sometimes this involves only a deformation, breakage, or "smearing out" of mineral grains. At other times, the conditions of change are so severe that mineral stability is affected. A mineral formed under high temperature and pressure in the earth's interior and considered stable under those conditions may not be stable under the vastly different conditions at the earth's surface. When mineral stability is affected, existing rocks must undergo fundamental changes in their molecular framework and the chemical components must rearrange themselves into configurations that are stable under the new conditions, thus forming new minerals. Many such minerals are uniquely characteristic of the metamorphic rocks, forming only in metamorphic environments. Metamorphic rocks develop in the earth's crust at depths ranging from 3 to 20 km (2–12.5 mi). At such depths there are two types of pressure: lithostatic or load pressure, which operates on the rock equally from all directions; and directed pressure or shearing stress, which operates on the rock from a particular direction. These pressures cause different types of rock to form; for example, marble forms under lithostatic pressure, whereas slate is produced by directed pressure. Most metamorphic reactions take place at temperatures of several hundred degrees Celsius; under great pressure and over a long period of time this temperature is sufficient to effect drastic changes in a rock. These take place essentially in the solid state, i.e. without involving the melting of rocks. Three types of metamorphism are of interest to us here: contact metamorphism, dynamothermal (regional) metamorphism, and hydrothermal metamorphism.

Contact Metamorphism   Heat is the dominant agent in contact metamorphism, assisted by some pressure and chemically active aqueous fluids. This metamorphism occurs in zones adjacent to intrusive bodies of plutonic rocks; hence the name contact metamorphism. For example, a narrow dike of granite may intrude into shale. Because of the heat at the contact between the dike and the shale, a narrow hardened zone will develop in which the original clay minerals of the shale have been changed to new materials.

Marble—pure metamorphosed limestone—is a good example of a contact metamorphic rock. Calc-silicate rock forms from impure limestone and may be composed of many minerals, depending on the impurities in the original limestone. Some of the minerals in this rock may have formed as a result of intruding plutonic rocks. Hornfels forms generally from shale or mudstone; metaquartzite derives from quartz-rich sandstone.

Minerals of The following are among the minerals
Contact most commonly collected in contact
Metamorphic metamorphic rocks:
Environments Actinolite, albite, almandine, andalusite, anorthite, biotite, brucite, bytownite, chlorite, chondrodite, cordierite, corundum, diopside, dolomite, epidote, grossular, hedenbergite, hornblende, hypersthene, magnetite, muscovite, orthoclase, pargasite, phlogopite, quartz, scheelite, spessartine, spinel, tremolite, vesuvianite, wollastonite, zoisite.

Dynamothermal This process is also referred to as
Metamorphism "regional metamorphism" because it is a part of the large-scale process that results in the formation of large, usually folded mountain ranges. Such metamorphism can affect many thousands of square kilometers. Dynamothermal metamorphic rocks are often grouped according to the degree of metamorphism involved. Low-grade metamorphism involves relatively low temperatures and pressures and typically produces such rocks as slate and low-grade chlorite schist; high-grade metamorphism involves higher temperatures and pressures and typically produces such rocks as amphibolite, high-grade schist, and gneiss. The type of pressure involved is also important. If directed pressures are dominant, the metamorphic rock will be foliated (slate, schist, gneiss); if lithostatic pressures are dominant, the rock will be nonfoliated (high-grade marble, metaquartzite, hornfels). During metamorphism, entirely new minerals may be formed from the minerals of the original, "parental" rock. The presence of biotite, calcite, chlorite, epidote, spessartine, or tremolite, for instance, is usually a sign of low-grade metamorphism; medium-

and high-grade minerals include almandine garnet, diopside, grossular garnet, hornblende, kyanite, olivine, and sillimanite.

Minerals of Dynamothermal Metamorphic Environments   The following minerals are among those most commonly collected in dynamothermal metamorphic rocks: Actinolite, albite, almandine, andalusite, andesine, andradite, anorthite, apatite, axinite, biotite, calcite, cassiterite, chlorite, chondrodite, cordierite, corundum, diopside, epidote, fluorite, glaucophane, hedenbergite, hornblende, kyanite, labradorite, lawsonite, magnetite, microcline, muscovite, oligoclase, orthoclase, phlogopite, quartz, riebeckite, scapolite, scheelite, sillimanite, spinel, staurolite, titanite, tremolite, vesuvianite, wollastonite, zoisite.

Hydrothermal Metamorphism   Hydrothermal metamorphism is a relatively small-scale process. It occurs when hot gases or fluids are driven into fractures in rock, usually by the action of intruding magma. The migrating fluid carries mineral constituents of its own, and it picks up additional material from the surrounding rock as it moves. As they are carried upward, these substances react with the preexisting rocks to form new minerals and new rocks, principally skarn, serpentinite, or low-grade schist. This process is also referred to as hydrothermal metasomatism.

Hydrothermal Metamorphic Minerals   The following minerals typically occur in hydrothermal metamorphic rocks: Actinolite, andalusite, andradite, biotite, bornite, calcite, chalcocite, chalcopyrite, chlorite, covellite, diopside, galena, hedenbergite, hematite, laumontite, magnetite, marcasite, molybdenite, pyrite, pyrrhotite, quartz, scapolite, scheelite, sphalerite, tourmaline.

Hydrothermal Replacement Environments

Hydrothermal replacement is similar to hydrothermal metamorphism. It involves the replacement of a preexisting rock mass by hydrothermal solutions that come from a magma while it is cooling and solidifying. All kinds of rocks can be replaced, but the limestones, because of their composition, are most easily attacked by the hydrothermal solutions. Hydrothermal replacement is complex, and it is not restricted to mineral matter: for instance, wood, an organic substance, may be replaced by silica to form petrified wood. The process by which one mineral replaces another but still retains the shape and size of the earlier mineral is orderly; while the new substance is being deposited, the original one is being transported away. Replacement can take place either in the solid rock or in open spaces within the rock.

The agents of replacement are principally solutions and gaseous emanations in which water is the main component. Water solutions may be alkaline or acidic, and their composition will depend largely on the composition of the magmatic source from which the solution derives, as well as from the rocks through which it passes. Gaseous emanations, on the other hand, are generally acidic, usually containing chlorine, fluorine, sulfur, and boron. After the gases escape from the magma chamber, they usually condense to form liquids, which then react with the rocks. But hot, chemically active gases can also enter directly into the chemical reactions. Hydrothermal solutions containing sulfur tend to form sulfates, such as brochantite; those rich in the arsenic and phosphoric acids form arsenates and phosphates. Because carbon dioxide is common in hydrothermal solutions, many carbonate minerals are also formed. All generally form at relatively low pressures and temperatures, so they are usually found in mineral deposits near the surface of the earth.

Replacement takes place at any pressure and temperature, but is most effective at higher temperatures. Because the mineralizing solutions are more reactive at high temperature and pressure they can attack siliceous rocks, which are less easily attacked under normal conditions. Thus, every type of rock is vulnerable to replacement, but the carbonate rocks composed of calcite and/or dolomite are favored sites for these transformations. Just as rock composition plays an important role in the replacement process, the fractured condition and grain size of the rock being attacked are significant in determining replacement sites.

Three types of replacement deposits concern the mineral collector: massive deposits, disseminated deposits, and replacement lode deposits.

Massive deposits may be lens-shaped or very irregular in shape. They may measure as much as several thousand meters in their largest dimension. The famous pyrite deposits at Noranda, Quebec, and Flin Flon, Manitoba, are massive replacement deposits.

Disseminated replacement deposits may be of any size, but they are generally huge bodies of rock, many containing 500,000,000 tons or more of minable ore. The great "porphyry copper" deposits in Arizona and Utah are of this type, as are the gold deposits of Juneau, Alaska, and the lead deposits of SW Missouri. In such deposits, the introduced materials are scattered through the host rock as small mineral grains or as clusters of small grains, and rarely exceed 10 percent of the entire rock. To a great extent, the structural features of the host rock determine the form and size of the mineral deposit: deposits can be irregular, tabular, pipe-shaped, or even blanket-shaped.

Replacement lode deposits are not massive. They form along fissures, and range from a few centimeters to tens of meters in width. Replacement ore minerals occur in massive form or scattered irregularly throughout the rock in which they form. The lead veins at Coeur d'Alene, Idaho, and gold veins at Kirkland, Ontario, are examples of replacement lodes.

No account of hydrothermal replacement mineral deposits would be complete without some mention of the famous zinc deposits at Franklin and Sterling Hill, New Jersey. These have been the subject of scientific interest since 1810, and active metal-ore mining has continued there since 1840. A mineralogist's paradise, this area has produced well over 200 minerals, of which many were new, rare, or unique species. The host rock for the mineralization was marble, and the zinc ore minerals are oxides and silicates, rather than the sulfides that are common in hydrothermal replacement deposits.

Hydrothermal Replacement Minerals The following minerals have commonly been collected in massive hydrothermal replacement deposits:
Acanthite, actinolite, anglesite, anhydrite, barite, bismuth, bismuthinite, bornite, cassiterite, cerussite, chalcocite, chalcopyrite, chlorargyrite, covellite, dolomite, galena, gypsum, jarosite, marcasite, magnetite, molybdenite, pyromorphite, pyrrhotite, rhodochrosite, sphalerite, tetrahedrite, tourmaline, vanadinite, wulfenite.
The following minerals have frequently been collected in disseminated hydrothermal replacement deposits:
Aragonite, aurichalcite, azurite, bornite, calcite, cerussite, chalcocite, chalcopyrite, copper, cuprite, dolomite, enargite, epsomite, erythrite, galena, gypsum, hematite, hemimorphite,

malachite, marcasite, melanterite, millerite, molybdenite, psilomelane, pyrite, pyrolusite, pyromorphite, quartz, smithsonite, sphalerite, vivianite.

The following minerals have frequently been collected from hydrothermal replacement lodes:

Arsenopyrite, barite, bornite, chalcocite, chalcopyrite, chlorite, covellite, enargite, fluorite, galena, garnet, gold, hematite, magnetite, marcasite, pyrrhotite, pyrite, quartz, siderite, sphalerite.

Vein Environments
A vein is a sheetlike or tabular mass of mineral that occupies a fracture or set of fractures. Because veins form in the earth's crust at different depths and under varying conditions of temperature, pressure, and wallrock composition, they have been classified as hypothermal ("high temperature"), mesothermal ("medium temperature"), or epithermal ("low temperature"). Veins occupy fractures in rocks, and because these fractures may trend in any direction, veins may do likewise. Often the veins will form in closely spaced, parallel fractures. These veins are separated from one another by narrow slivers of altered wallrock and form what is called a vein zone. Such zones occur in all types of veins.

Quartz is common in all three types of veins because it is the earliest mineral to be deposited. The next minerals to be deposited are, in order, iron sulfides, sphalerite, enargite, chalcopyrite, gold, the silver minerals, stibnite, and cinnabar. This sequence of deposition follows a decreasing order of solubility of the minerals in solution under decreasing temperature and pressure. Thus each vein type listed above, because it formed under different temperature and pressure conditions, will consist of a different series of different minerals.

Hypothermal
Veins

Hypothermal veins form at great depth and at high temperatures, between 300° and 500°C (575° to 930°F). The vein minerals are coarse-grained. The veins range in width from a fraction of a centimeter to tens of meters; some have been mined for distances of several thousand meters, and to depths exceeding a kilometer. Such veins originally formed in metamorphic and igneous rocks of older geological periods, later appearing at the earth's surface through the uplift and erosion of overlying material. Hypothermal veins are important sources of valuable metals. Ore minerals, from which valuable metals are extracted, are the main minerals sought in mining. Other minerals, which are usually nonmetallic and of lesser value or of no importance in mining operations, are called gangue minerals. A typical gold vein might contain pyrite and arsenopyrite as the ore minerals and quartz (with minor amounts of calcite) and rhodochrosite as the gangue minerals.

Mesothermal
Veins

Mesothermal veins are formed at moderate temperatures (200° to 300°C; 390° to 575°F) and at moderate pressures. Minerals common in hypothermal veins are seldom found in mesothermal veins.
Mesothermal veins range in width from a fraction of a centimeter to as much as 3 m (10'); many have been traced along their strike, or compass direction, for 2,500 m (8,250') and mined to a depth of 2,700 m (8,900').

Epithermal
Veins

Epithermal veins are shallow, normally forming at low temperatures (100° to 200°C; 212° to 390°F) and within 1,000 m (3,300') of the surface. The veins are often irregular and branching and tend to form a network of veinlets in the wallrock. The fissures into which the vein materials are deposited connect directly to the surface of the earth, and some hot springs are probably the surface expression of an underlying epithermal plumbing system. The minerals in most epithermal veins came originally from the plutonic or volcanic rocks in which the veins occur.

Because of their shallow depths and subsequent erosion, many epithermal vein mineral deposits in North America have been completely mined out. However, others still produce ore and a few, including those at Zacatecas, Guanajuato, and Pachuca in Mexico, Cripple Creek in Colorado, and Keweenaw in Michigan, continue to yield valuable metals.

Epithermal veins also yield nonmetallic minerals, including quartz, fluorite, and barite, all exceedingly useful in industry. Most fluorite mined in the United States comes from fissure veins and replacement bodies. The veins range considerably in size; the famous Rosiclare vein in Illinois has been mined for 3,000 m (9,900') along its strike length, and was as much as 10 m (33') wide in places. Although fluorite was the principal mineral raw material sought, substantial amounts of barite, galena, and sphalerite were obtained, as well as beautiful specimens of calcite.

Quartz is a common and abundant vein mineral. The quartz deposits of W Arkansas have been important for economic and scientific purposes. The quartz occurs as massive milky veins in thick-bedded sandstones and shales. The quartz veins contain cavities from which beautifully formed clear crystals, up to a meter in length, have been obtained. Magnificent clusters of clear quartz crystals are not uncommon, and many such specimens are on exhibit at museums throughout the United States.

Many interesting minerals can be collected from veins of hypothermal, mesothermal, and epithermal environments. The waste rock dumps or heaps at metal mines are choice places to look for these minerals, and if permission is granted by the mine management it is sometimes possible to gain access to the underground workings and collect choice minerals from their original sites.

Vein Minerals The following minerals have frequently been collected in hypothermal vein environments:
Arsenopyrite, bismuthinite, calcite, cassiterite, chalcopyrite, dolomite, galena, gold, molybdenite, quartz, rhodochrosite, scheelite, sphalerite, tourmaline, uraninite.
The following minerals have frequently been collected from mesothermal vein environments:
Acanthite, adularia, barite, bornite, calcite, chalcocite, chalcopyrite, cobalt arsenides, nickel arsenides, dolomite, enargite, galena, gold, pyrargyrite, pyrite, quartz, rhodochrosite, sphalerite, tetrahedrite.
The following minerals have frequently been collected from epithermal veins:
Acanthite, adularia, barite, calcite, chalcedony, chlorargyrite, cinnabar, dolomite, fluorite, gold, orpiment, proustite, pyrargyrite, quartz, realgar, rhodochrosite, scheelite, stephanite, stibnite, sylvanite, tetrahedrite.

Secondary Replacement Deposits Many spectacular minerals have been collected from environments that were subjected to chemical alteration at or near the surface. These altered minerals are called secondary minerals, because they develop from the primary minerals in the original rock or deposit. The alteration takes place when surface water, containing dissolved oxygen and carbon dioxide, seeps downward into the rock. The water reacts with the minerals in the rocks to form sulfates, sulfuric acid, and other active solutions; these solutions continue moving downward, where they react with other primary minerals to form secondary minerals, at the same time carrying their dissolved minerals to greater depths.

The sulfide minerals are easily attacked by weathering, and their secondary products are especially colorful and interesting. Hydrothermal veins and replacement deposits, because they are often rich in a wide variety of sulfide minerals, are readily altered to produce a large number of brilliantly colored species. Chalcopyrite, for instance, alters readily to bornite, covellite, bronchantite, and other minerals; galena alters to anglesite and cerussite; sphalerite alters to hemimorphite, smithsonite, and willemite (troostite); and pyrite alters to melanterite and others.

Sulfates, however, are not the only secondary minerals. If the original deposits contain arsenic- and phosphorus-bearing minerals, secondary arsenates and phosphates will be formed, and so on, many such minerals making superb micromount specimens. In hydrothermal vein and replacement deposits, the upper, leached zone is referred to as the oxidized zone, because it is here that the oxygen in the downward-seeping water begins its activity. As the chemically active water continues downward it reacts with the primary sulfide minerals to develop new sulfide minerals, and the zone in which these develop is called the enriched zone or secondary enriched zone. The chemically active waters rarely descend below the enriched zone; at greater depths, only the unaltered primary minerals are usually found.

Fine and delicately crystalline secondary minerals are often found in the oxidized zone, because the chemically active waters have dissolved out the primary minerals, honeycombing the rock and creating open spaces into which delicate crystals of secondary minerals could grow.

Secondary Replacement Minerals The following are a few of the minerals that have been collected in the oxidized zones or the secondary enrichment zones of hydrothermal veins and replacement deposits:
Adamite, anglesite, aragonite, aurichalcite, autunite, azurite, bornite, brochantite, calcite, cerussite, chalcanthite, chalcocite, chlorargyrite, chrysocolla, covellite, crocoite, cuprite, cyanotrichite, dioptase, enargite, epsomite, fluorite, goethite, gypsum, hemimorphite, jarosite, linarite, malachite, melanterite, mimetite, pyromorphite, smithsonite, torbernite, vanadinite, vivianite, wulfenite.

PART IV: APPENDICES

GLOSSARY

Accessory mineral A mineral that occurs in a rock in minute quantities, and does not affect the way the rock is named or classified.

Acidic rock A type of igneous rock (e.g. granite) that consists predominantly of light-colored minerals and more than 66% free or combined silica (see Basic rock, Intermediate rock, and Ultrabasic rock).

Alkaline rock A rock containing more than average amounts of potassium- and sodium-bearing minerals.

Alteration Any physical or chemical change in a mineral or rock subsequent to original formation; usually results in the formation of new minerals or in textural changes in the rock.

Amorphous Literally, "without form"; applied to rocks and minerals that lack definite crystal structure.

Amphiboles A group of closely related, dark-colored rock-forming silicate minerals (e.g. actinolite, hornblende, glaucophane, and tremolite).

Amygdaloidal rock A volcanic rock containing numerous gas cavities (amygdules) filled with such secondary minerals as calcite, quartz, and zeolites.

Amygdule   A mineral-filled cavity formed in an igneous rock by escaping gas.

Anthracite coal   A hard, black, lustrous coal.

Aphanitic rock   A rock in which the crystalline constituents are too small to be distinguished with the unaided eye.

Argillaceous   Containing or composed largely of clay (e.g. argillaceous shale, etc.).

Arsenates   Minerals (e.g. adamite) in which the arsenate radical (AsO_4) is an important constituent.

Basic rock   An igneous rock (e.g. gabbro) with low silica content and a high percentage of pyroxene, hornblende, and labradorite (see Acidic rock, Intermediate rock, and Ultrabasic rock).

Batholith   A huge body of plutonic rock that has been intruded deep into the earth's crust and later exposed by erosion.

Bedding   The arrangement of sedimentary rocks in approximately parallel layers (strata, or "beds"), which correspond to the original sediments that formed the rock.

Bituminous rocks   Rocks that contain (and sometimes smell of) asphalt, tar, or petroleum.

Bituminous coal   A medium-hard, highly carbonaceous black coal; also called "soft coal."

Borates   A group of minerals (e.g. borax, colemanite) in which the borate radical (BO_3) is an important constituent.

Botryoidal   Resembling a bunch of grapes; describes hematite and a number of other minerals in which very small radiating crystals are arranged in massive clumps, giving a surface covered with spherical bulges (from Greek *botrys*, "bunch of grapes").

Calcareous Containing calcium carbonate or calcite.

Calcic Containing calcium.

Carbonaceous Composed largely of organic carbon (i.e., carbon derived from plant and animal tissue).

Carbonates Minerals (e.g. calcite) in which the carbonate radical (CO_3) is an important constituent.

Cataclastic rock A metamorphic rock produced by the crushing and grinding of preexisting rocks, which are still visible as crushed and flattened minerals and as angular fragments (from the Greek *klastos*, "broken").

Cataclastic metamorphism A metamorphism due principally to directed pressure and resulting in rocks with cataclastic texture.

Characterizing accessory mineral A mineral that gives a specific name to an igneous rock. In hornblende granite, for example, hornblende is the characterizing accessory mineral.

Chemical sedimentary rock A rock formed by chemical processes; gypsum is a chemical sedimentary rock, formed by chemical precipitation.

Clastic rock A sedimentary rock that is made up of fragments of preexisting rocks, transported mechanically into the place of deposition.

Clay Any soft sediment or deposit that is plastic when wet and consists of very fine-grained, micalike materials, mainly hydrous aluminum silicates.

Cleavage The tendency of some minerals to break along one or more regular, smooth surfaces.

Concordant Describes an intrusive igneous body whose surfaces are parallel to the bedding (or foliation) of the surrounding rocks.

Concretion An accumulation of mineral matter, formed when particles of silica, pyrite, gypsum, etc. become cemented together into an orderly, rounded, often artificial-looking form.

Contact metamorphism Metamorphism directly related to the intrusion of magmas and taking place at or near the contact with the molten rock.

Cross-bedding An arrangement of layers within a sedimentary rock, such that minor layers lie at an angle to the main layers of sediment; usually a sign of changing wind or water currents acting on the original sediments forming the rock.

Crystal A solid mass of mineral, having a regular geometric shape and bounded by smooth, flat surfaces (crystal faces).

Crystal habit The actual form of a crystal; determined by the shape and relative proportions of the crystal faces.

Crystal symmetry The repeat pattern of crystal faces, caused by the ordered internal arrangement of a mineral's atoms.

Detrital sediment A deposit of mineral and rock fragments that have been transported to their place of deposition.

Differentiation A process by which different types of igneous rocks are derived from the same parent magma.

Dike A wall-like body of igneous rock, usually intrusive, that cuts across the layers of the surrounding rocks.

Discordant Describes an intrusive igneous body whose margins cut across the bedding (or foliation) of the surrounding rocks.

Dynamothermal metamorphism Metamorphism resulting from the combined effects of heat and pressure; also called regional metamorphism.

Epithermal vein A vein formed at shallow depths from ascending hot solutions.

Equigranular rock A rock whose mineral particles are of the same general size.

Essential minerals The mineral constituents of a rock (usually an igneous rock) that are used to classify and name the rock.

Extrusive rock An igneous rock that solidifies on the surface of the earth.

Feldspar A group of abundant rock-forming silicate minerals, including orthoclase and microcline (potash feldspars) and albite, oligoclase, andesine, labradorite, bytownite, and anorthite (the plagioclase, or soda-lime, feldspars).

Feldspathic rock A rock that contains feldspar as a principal constituent.

Feldspathoids A group of minerals (e.g. leucite, nepheline, and sodalite) that are similar in composition to the feldspars, but contain less silica.

Ferruginous Containing iron.

Flow banding A structure (in some volcanic rocks) consisting of alternating layers of unlike mineralogical composition and formed as a result of flowing lava.

Foliation The laminated structure present in regionally metamorphosed rocks that results from segregation of different minerals into roughly parallel layers.

Fragmental rock Sedimentary rock consisting of rock and mineral fragments.

Friable Easily crumbled or pulverized.

Fusion	The process of being melted or dissolved by heat.
Gneissose rock	A rock that has the banded appearance of a gneiss but is not formed by metamorphism.
Granulose	A metamorphic texture characterized by granular minerals, such as quartz, feldspars, and garnet, in alternating streaks and bands.
Groundmass	See Matrix.
Halides	A group of minerals (e.g. halite and fluorite) that are primarily compounds of the halogen elements: bromine, chlorine, fluorine, and iodine.
Hardness	Resistance of a mineral to abrasion or scratching.
Hydrothermal alteration	An alteration of minerals or rocks by the action of superheated mineral-rich fluids, usually water that has been heated to very high temperatures within a crystallizing magma.
Hydrothermal metamorphism	Changes in the structure or composition of rock, caused by the action of hydrothermal fluids.
Hydrothermal replacement	A change in a rock or mineral deposit due to the addition or removal of minerals by hydrothermal fluids.
Hypothermal vein	A vein formed at relatively great depth and at relatively high temperatures ($300°–500°$ C).
Igneous rock	Rock formed by the solidification of magma.
Intermediate rock	Igneous rock (e.g. syenite or diorite) that is transitional between acidic and basic rock, having a silica content of between 54% and 65% (see Acidic rock, Basic rock, and Ultrabasic rock).

Intrusive rock An igneous rock that formed underground, from magma that was squeezed into cracks or crevices, or between layers of older rocks.

"Japanese" twins Simple contact twins (in quartz) in which two single crystals, usually broad flattened prisms, are joined in the same plane at an angle of about 84°.

Laccolith A lens-shaped body of igneous rock with a dome-shaped upper surface and a flat bottom surface, and with both surfaces parallel to the bedding or foliation of the enclosing rocks.

Lamellar Composed of thin layers, plates, or scales.

Laminated rocks Sedimentary rocks that are formed of numerous very thin layers.

Lava Molten rock material extruded onto the surface of the earth.

Lava flow A body of rock formed by a single outpouring of lava.

Lenticular Lens-shaped.

Lopolith A large, lenticular, centrally sunken mass of igneous rock whose surfaces are concordant with the enclosing rocks.

Luster The surface appearance of a substance, or the manner in which it reflects light.

Magma Molten rock material, beneath the solid crust of the earth, that solidifies to form igneous rocks at or below the earth's surface.

Magmatism Any process by which magma solidifies into volcanic or plutonic rock.

Massive mineral A mineral that occurs either without any definite external crystal form or in poorly defined masses of small crystals.

Matrix The fine-grained material (groundmass) that surrounds the larger crystals or particles in a porphyritic or sedimentary rock. Also, any material, such as clay or rock, in which a crystal, fossil, etc. is embedded.

Mesothermal vein A vein that forms at intermediate depth and temperature.

Metamorphic rock Any rock (e.g. schist, gneiss, etc.) that was formed in some fashion from a pre-existing rock, through heat, pressure, the effect of superheated fluids, or any combination of these forces.

Mica A group of soft silicate minerals (e.g. biotite, muscovite) that have perfect basal cleavage in one direction and can easily be split into characteristic thin, elastic, pearly sheets.

Microcrystalline rock A rock whose crystals are too small to be seen without a microscope (see Aphanitic rock).

Mineral environment The rock (or rock type) in which a mineral or a group of associated minerals forms and occurs. Mineral environments include igneous, sedimentary, and metamorphic rocks, as well as several types of veins and replacement deposits.

Mineral stability The ability of a mineral to remain unaltered over a stated range of pressure and temperature.

Molybdates A group of minerals (e.g. wulfenite) in which the molybdate radical (MoO_4) is an important constituent.

Nodular Having the shape of or composed of irregular lumps of rock or mineral (e.g. nodular chert).

Organic compounds Compounds produced in or by plants and animals and containing carbon as the essential ingredient.

Outcrop A mass of bedrock that is exposed at the surface of the earth.

Oxides A group of minerals (e.g. cuprite and magnetite) in which oxygen, combined with a metal, is a major constituent.

Oxidized zone The part of an ore body (usually the upper part) that has been altered by downward percolating groundwater, containing dissolved oxygen and carbon dioxide.

Parting The tendency of some minerals to separate along certain planes, which are not related to the crystal symmetry of the mineral; usually due to twinning or deformation.

Pegmatite An igneous rock of extremely coarse grain size. Usually found as dikes within a larger plutonic or metamorphic rock mass, pegmatites are often excellent sources of large, fine crystals, especially of quartz, tourmaline, feldspar, and mica.

Petrography The branch of geology that deals with the description and classification of rocks.

Petrology The study of rocks, specifically their composition, origin, and modes of occurrence.

Phaneritic rock An igneous rock in which all of the essential minerals can be distinguished with the unaided eye.

Phenocryst A prominent crystal (in a porphyritic rock) surrounded by smaller mineral grains.

Phosphates A group of minerals (e.g. apatite) in which the phosphate radical (PO_4) is an important constituent.

Pipe A vertical, cylindrical mass of igneous rock.

Pisolitic Consisting of rounded grains like peas or beans.

Placer A deposit of heavy mineral particles (e.g. gold) that have weathered out of the bedrock and been concentrated mechanically, usually by the action of streams.

Playa A desert plain; a shallow basin in which water collects following a rain and is evaporated.

Plug The solidified core of an extinct volcano.

Pluton Any deep, intrusive igneous body, of any size, whose exact form has not been determined.

Plutonic rock A granular igneous rock that has solidified at great depth and shows distinct grain texture (e.g. granite, granodiorite).

Porphyritic rock An igneous rock in which larger crystals (phenocrysts) are enclosed in a fine-grained groundmass, which may be crystalline or glassy.

Precipitation The process by which a suspended or dissolved solid is separated out of a liquid.

Pseudomorph A mineral that has taken the outward crystal form of a different mineral.

Pyroelectricity An electric charge produced in a crystal by heat.

Pyroxenes A group of closely related, dark-colored rock-forming minerals (e.g. augite, diopside, and acmite).

Radical A group of oxygen atoms clustered about a nonmetallic atom (e.g. silicon, phosphorus, sulfur) so as to form a "structural unit" that behaves like a single atom.

Replacement A process by which one mineral replaces another, while often retaining the physical form of the first mineral.

Secondary minerals Minerals that are formed by the alteration of preexisting (primary) minerals.

Sedimentary rock A layered rock, formed through the accumulation and solidification of sediments, which may originally be made up of minerals, rock debris, or animal or vegetable matter.

Silica Silicon dioxide (SiO_2), a tremendously abundant mineral that occurs widely and in many forms, including quartz, chalcedony, opal, and chert.

Silicates A group of minerals (e.g. quartz and orthoclase) composed essentially of SiO_4 tetrahedra in different arrangements.

Sill A tabular, sheetlike body of intrusive igneous rock, which has been injected between layers of sedimentary or metamorphic rock.

Slaty cleavage A variety of foliation typical of slates and characterized by parallel arrangement of clay minerals.

Stock A small, irregularly shaped body of intrusive igneous rock with a surface area of less than 65 square kilometers.

Streak The color of the powder of a mineral produced by rubbing the mineral over the surface of a piece of unglazed, white porcelain.

Striations Minute parallel grooves or narrow channels on crystal faces.

Structure Large features of rock masses, such as flow banding and bedding; in minerals, structure refers to the shapes and forms of crystal groups and masses.

Sulfates   A group of minerals (e.g. gypsum and barite) in which the sulfate radical (SO_4) is an important constituent.

Sulfides   A group of minerals (e.g. pyrite, galena, and sphalerite) in which sulfur is in combination with one or more metals (copper, iron, or zinc).

Sulfosalts   A group of minerals in which sulfur combines with the semi-metals (arsenic, antimony, and bismuth) to form what are called negative ions, which then combine with the metals (lead, silver, copper, and zinc) to form such minerals as enargite, tetrahedrite, and pyrargyrite.

Tenacity   The ability of a substance to resist separation.

Texture   The surface appearance of a homogenous rock or mineral aggregate. The degree of crystallization, the size of the crystals, and the shape and interrelations of the crystals or other components all contribute to the texture of a rock.

Tungstates   A group of minerals (e.g. scheelite) in which the tungstate radical (WO_4) is an important constituent.

Twin   A specimen that consists of two or more single crystals of the same mineral, intergrown in a definite systematic arrangement.

Ultrabasic rock   Any plutonic igneous rock (e.g. peridotite) with very low silica content (less than that of a basic rock) (see Acidic rock, Basic rock, and Intermediate rock).

Vanadates   A group of minerals (e.g. vanadinite) in which the vanadate radical (VO_4 is an important constituent).

Vein A tabular or sheetlike body of mineral matter (e.g. quartz) cutting across preexisting rock (e.g. granite or gneiss).

Vesicle A small cavity in a volcanic rock.

Vitreous Glasslike in appearance or texture.

Volcanism The movement of molten rock, by way of volcanos, fissures, vents, etc., to the earth's surface, where it cools into extrusive (volcanic) igneous rocks.

Volcano A vent or hole in the earth's crust through which magma (in the form of lava), gases, ashes, and other products escape onto the surface.

Zeolites A group of hydrated aluminosilicates of potassium, sodium, and calcium that can lose part or all of their water (reversibly) without changing crystal structure. This open structure allows the zeolites to absorb other compounds, making them commercially valuable as purifiers and water softeners.

BIBLIOGRAPHY

General Works
on Minerals

Gary, Margaret, Robert McAfee, Jr.,
and Carol L. Wolf (editors).
Glossary of Geology. Washington, D.C.:
American Geological Institute, 1973.

Hurlbut, Cornelius S. *Minerals and
Man*. New York: Random House,
1970.
A fully illustrated, highly
knowledgeable account of the role of
minerals in human affairs.

Hurlbut, Cornelius S., Jr., and
Cornelis Klein. *Manual of Mineralogy*
(after James D. Dana), 19th edition.
New York: John Wiley & Sons, 1977.
An abridged and slightly simplified
edition of the most authoritative and
widely used reference on minerals and
mineralogy; technical.

Mason, Brian, and Leonard G. Berry.
*Mineralogy: Concepts, Descriptions and
Determinations*, 2nd edition. San
Francisco: W.H. Freeman, 1967.
Introduction to mineralogy; a college-
level textbook.

Sinkankas, John. *Mineralogy for
Amateurs*. New York: Van Nostrand
Reinhold, 1964.
A standard reference for serious
amateurs, touching almost every aspect

of mineralogy and thoroughly
illustrated by the author.

Sinkankas, John. *Prospecting for
Gemstones and Minerals.* New York:
Van Nostrand Reinhold, 1970.
A convenient, comprehensive
introduction to mineral collecting, for
amateurs and beginners, with unusually
clear explanations of the processes that
create rocks and mineral deposits.

Periodicals   *Lapidary Journal.* 60 Chestnut
Ave., Suite 201, Devon, PA 19333.
The May issue is the *Annual Buyers'
Guide.*

Mineralogical Record. Published by the
Mineralogical Record, P.O. Box 35565,
Tucson, AZ 85740.

Rocks and Minerals. Heldref
Publications, 1319 18th St. NW,
Washington, D.C. 20036-1802.

Mineral Guides Fay, Gordon S. *The Rockhound's
for North *Manual.* New York: Harper & Row,
America 1972.

MacFall, Russel P. *Gem Hunter's Guide*
(5th ed.) New York: Thomas Y. Crowell
Co., 1975.

MacFall, Russel P. *Minerals and Gems.*
New York: Thomas Y. Crowell Co.,
1975.

Oles, Floyd and Helga Oles. *Eastern
Gem Trails.* Mentone, Cal.: Gembooks,
1967.

Pough, Frederick H. *A Field Guide to Rocks and Minerals* (4th ed.). Boston: Houghton Mifflin Co., 1976.

Ransom, Jay Ellis. *Gems and Minerals of America*. New York: Harper & Row, 1974.

Zeitner, June C. *Appalachian Mineral and Gem Trails*. San Diego, Cal.: Lapidary Journal, Inc., 1968.

Zeitner, June C. *Midwest Gem Trails Field Guide* (3rd ed.). Mentone, Cal.: Gembooks, 1964.

ROCK-FORMING MINERALS

The following are the major rock-forming minerals, organized by mineral group, approximately in order of decreasing abundance. The following symbols are used to indicate the rocks or deposits in which each is likely to occur as an essential or common mineral:

I   Igneous rocks
S   Sedimentary rocks
M   Metamorphic rocks
P   Pegmatites
H   Hydrothermal veins and replacement deposits
C   Carbonatites

Silica	Quartz (I, S, M, P, H)
Potash Feldspars	Microcline (I, M, P, H)
	Orthoclase (I, M, P, H)
Plagioclase Feldspars	Albite (I, S, M, H)
	Oligoclase (I, M)
	Andesine (I, M)
	Labradorite (I, M)
	Bytownite (I)
	Anorthite (I, M)
Feldspathoids	Nepheline (I, P)
	Leucite (I)
Chlorite Group	Chlorite (M, H)

Micas Biotite (I, M, P)
Muscovite (I, S, M, P)
Phlogopite (I, M)

Pyroxenes Augite (I, M)
Acmite (I, S, M, P, C)
Diopside (I, M, H)
Enstatite (I, M, P)
Hypersthene (I, M)

Amphiboles Hornblende (I, M)
Tremolite (M)
Actinolite (M)
Glaucophane (M)

Miscellaneous Olivine (I, M)
Silicates Serpentine group (M, H)
Talc (M, H)
Kyanite (I, M, P)
Andalusite (M; rarely I, P)
Sillimanite (I, M)
Staurolite (M)
Garnet (I, M)
Epidote (M, H)
Vesuvianite (M, H; rarely I)
Wollastonite (M; occasionally I)

Carbonates Calcite (S, M, H, C)
Dolomite (M, H; rarely S)

Oxides Hematite (S, M, H; occasionally I)
Magnetite (I, M, P, H; rarely S)

THE CHEMICAL ELEMENTS

The chemical formulas for minerals employ
the following standard abbreviations for the
chemical elements:

Al	Aluminum
Sb	Antimony
A	Argon
As	Arsenic
Ba	Barium
Be	Beryllium
Bi	Bismuth
B	Boron
Br	Bromine
Cd	Cadmium
Ca	Calcium
C	Carbon
Ce	Cerium
Cs	Cesium
Cl	Chlorine
Cr	Chromium
Co	Cobalt
Cu	Copper
Dy	Dysprosium
Er	Erbium
Eu	Europium
F	Fluorine
Gd	Gadolinium
Ga	Gallium
Ge	Germanium
Au	Gold
Hf	Hafnium
He	Helium
Ho	Holmium
H	Hydrogen
In	Indium
I	Iodine
Ir	Iridium

Fe	Iron
Kr	Krypton
La	Lanthanum
Pb	Lead
Li	Lithium
Lu	Lutecium
Mg	Magnesium
Mn	Manganese
Hg	Mercury
Mo	Molybdenum
Nd	Neodymium
Ne	Neon
Ni	Nickel
Nb	Niobium*
N	Nitrogen
Os	Osmium
O	Oxygen
Pd	Palladium
P	Phosphorus
Pt	Platinum
K	Potassium
Pr	Praseodymium
Ra	Radium
Rn	Radon
Re	Rhenium
Rh	Rhodium
Rb	Rubidium
Ru	Ruthenium
Sm	Samarium
Sc	Scandium
Se	Selenium
Si	Silicon
Ag	Silver
Na	Sodium
Sr	Strontium
S	Sulfur
Ta	Tantalum
Te	Tellurium
Tb	Terbium
Tl	Thallium
Th	Thorium
Tm	Thulium
Sn	Tin
Ti	Titanium
W	Tungsten
U	Uranium

Niobium (Nb) may appear as Columbium (Cb) in older references.

V	Vanadium
Xe	Xenon
Yb	Ytterbium
Y	Yttrium
Zn	Zinc
Zr	Zirconium

LOCALITIES

This list indicates the place of origin of each mineral or rock specimen illustrated. The numbers correspond to the color plate numbers in the Visual Keys. If the specimen is part of a notable private or public collection, that information may be included; specimens in the Smithsonian Institution, Washington, D.C., are indicated by the initials "SI."

1 Conn. (Gillette quarry, Haddam, Middlesex Co.); coll. N. Yedlan

2 N.Y. (DeKalb, St. Lawrence Co.)

3 N.J. (Franklin, Sussex Co.)

4 Quebec (Asbestos, Richmond Co.); coll. M. Ridding

5 Chihuahua (Naica)

6 N.C. (Hiddenite, nr Stony Point, Alexander Co.)

7 N.J. (Paterson, Passaic Co.); SI

8 Ariz. (Copper Queen Mine, Bisbee, Cochise Co.); SI

9 Ariz. (San Carlos, Gila Co.); SI

10 Calif. (Jackson, Amador Co.)

11 Quebec (Jeffrey Mine, Asbestos, Richmond Co.); coll. V. Anderson

12 Colo. (Silverton, Ouray Co.)

13 Colo. (Crystal Peak, Teller Co.); coll. Joe Urban

14 N.Y. (Pyrites, St. Lawrence Co.)

15 N.Y. (E. Pitcairn, St. Lawrence Co.); SI

16 N.Y. (Warwick, Orange Co.)

17 N.Y. (Warwick, Orange Co.)

18 Quebec (Montreal)

19 N.C. (nr Hiddenite, Alexander Co.); coll. D. Wilbur

20 N.C.; coll. D. Wilbur

21 Ariz. (Bisbee, Cochise Co.)

22 Idaho (Lemhi Co.)

23 N.J. (Franklin, Sussex Co.)

24 Maine (Topsham, Sagadahoc Co.); G.V. Brush Coll., Yale Univ.

25 Utah (Fairfield, Utah Co.)

26 India (Poona, Bombay Prov.)

27 Locality unknown

28 Colo. (Leadville, Lake Co.)

29 Maine (Topsham, Sagadahoc Co.)

30 Zacatecas (Concepcion de Oro)

31 N.J. (Franklin, Sussex Co.)

32 Maine (Newry, Oxford Co.)

33 Maine (Dunton Mine, Newry, Oxford Co.)

34 Quebec (Brompton Lake, Stanstead Co.)

35 Quebec (Asbestos, Richmond Co.)

36 Nev. (Majuba Hill, Pershing Co.)

37 Brazil (Virgem de Lapa, Minas Gerais); coll. J. Lowell

38 Durango (Cerro del Mercado, nr Ciudad Durango); coll. Joe Urban

39 Penn. (Cornog, Chester Co.)

40 Calif. (San Diego Co.)

41 N.C. (Snow Camp, Alamance Co.)

42 Italy (Mussa Alp, Piedmont)

43 Ariz. (No. 79 Mine, Hayden, Gila Co.)

44 Ariz. (Gila Co.)

45 Nev. (Douglas Hill Mine, Ludwig)

46 Utah (Gold Hill, Tooele Co.)

47 Va. (Lynch Station, Campbell Co.)

48 Ariz. (No. 79 Mine, Hayden, Gila Co.); coll. W. Thomson

49 Ariz. (Bisbee, Cochise Co.)

50 Nev. (Majuba Hill, Pershing Co.)

51 Ark. (Mt. Ida, Montgomery Co.)

52 N.J. (Fort Lee, Bergen Co.)

53 Va. (Richmond, Henrico Co.); SI

54 Calif. (Baird, Shasta Co.); SI

55 Durango (Mapimi)

56 Ariz. (Miami, Gila Co.); Arizona-Sonora Desert Muscum

57 Wash. (Mudhold Mine, Mt. Spokane, Spokane Co.); coll. Karl Fair

58 N.J. (Paterson, Passaic Co.)

59 Calif.; coll. J.D. Minette

60 Va. (Centreville, Fairfax Co.); coll. W. Smith

61 Durango (Mapimi)

62 Ark. (Avant, Garland Co.)

63 Ark. (Hot Springs, Garland Co.)

64 Ariz. (Bisbee, Cochise Co.)

65 Ariz. (Bisbee, Cochise Co.)

66 N.M. (Kelly Mine, nr Magdalena, Socorro Co.)

67 N.C. (Chalk Mt. Mine, Mitchell Co.)

68 Ariz. (Bisbee, Cochise Co.)

69 N.C. (Chalk Mt. Mine, Mitchell Co.)

70 England (Weardale, Durham); George Vaux coll., Bryn Mawr College

71 Calif. (Calaveras Co.)

72 N.H. (Smith Mine, Chandler's Mills, Sullivan Co.)

73 N.J. (Morris Co.)

74 Penn. (Chester Co.)

75 Ariz. (Mariposa Co.)

76 Quebec (Grenville, Argenteuil Co.)

77 Ariz. (Kingman, Mohave Co.); Arizona-Sonora Desert Museum

78 Utah (Fairfield, Utah Co.)

79 Burma (Uru River Valley)

80 N.Y. (Edenville, Orange Co.); SI

81 Ariz. (San Carlos Reservation, Gila Co.)

82 Calif. (Tulare Co.)

83 Vt. (Roxbury, Washington Co.)

84 Locality unknown

85 Ontario (Craig Mine, Renfrew Co.)

86 Ga. (Lincoln Co.); SI

87 Calif. (San Benito Co.)

88 Colo. (Crystal Peak, N of Lake George, Teller Co.)

89 Colo. (Pike's Peak, El Paso Co.)

90 Ga. (Graves Mt., Lincoln Co.)

91 Calif. (San Benito Co.)

92 Ariz. (Ajo, Pima Co.); coll. C. Van Scriver

93 Yukon (Big Fish River-Blow River, NE Yukon); coll. V. Anderson

94 Baja California (Rancho Viejo, Las Delicias); coll. J. Scripps

95 Chihuahua (Naica)

96 N.M. (Bingham, Socorro Co.)

97 Colo. (El Paso Co.)

98 Ontario (Dundas Co.)

99 N.H. (Palermo Mine, North Groton, Grafton Co.)

100 Chihuahua (Naica); SI

101 N.C. (nr Spruce Pine, Mitchell Co.)

102 N.H. (Smith Mine, Chandler's Mills, Sullivan Co.)

103 Calif. (San Diego Co.)

104 N.M. (Bingham, Socorro Co.)

105 Ariz. (Morenci, Greenlee Co.)

106 Zacatecas (Concepcion de Oro)

107 Ariz. (Bisbee, Cochise Co.)

108 Tanzania (Arusha); SI

109 N.M. (Bingham, Socorro Co.)

110 Ariz. (Ajo, Pima Co.)

111 Ariz. (Grandview Mine, Coconino Co.)

112 Chihuahua

113 Va. (Lynch Station, Campbell Co.)

114 Ariz. (Bagdad, Yavapai Co.); coll. Harvard Univ.

115 Zacatecas

116 Ariz. (No. 79 Mine, Hayden, Gila Co.)

117 Ariz. (Bisbee, Cochise Co.); coll. J. Sinkankas

118 N.M. (Magdalena, Socorro Co.)

119 Ariz. (Inspiration Mine, Miami, Gila Co.)

120 Ariz. (Miami, Gila Co.)

121 Ariz. (Grand Reef Mine, Graham Co.)

122 Ariz. (Bisbee, Cochise Co.)

123 Mont. (Butte, Silver Bow Co.)

124 Maine (Kennebec Co.)

125 Ontario (Princess Mine, Bancroft, Hastings Co.)

126 British Columbia (Prince Rupert, NW coast of Kaien Island, Coast District); SI

127 N.Y. (Edwards, St. Lawrence Co.); SI

128 Ariz. (Yuma Co.)

129 Ariz. (Ajo, Pima Co.)

130 N.M. (Cerrillos, Santa Fe Co.)

131 Ontario

132 Calif. (Death Valley, Inyo Co.); SI

133 N.M. (Catron Co.)

134 N.Y. (Amity, Orange Co.)

135 Calif. (Searles Lake, San Bernardino Co.)

136 Maine (Pulsifer quarry, Auburn, Androscoggin Co.)

137 Conn. (Strickland quarry, Portland, Middlesex Co.)

138 Calif. (Hale Creek Mine, Trinity Co.)

139 Calif. (White Queen Mine, Queen Mt., Pala, San Diego Co.); coll. D. Wilbur

140 Colo. (Silverton, San Juan Co.)

194 N.C. (Spruce Pine, Mitchell Co.); SI

195 Ariz. (Apache Mine, Globe District, Gila Co.)

196 Utah (Wah Wah Mt., Millard Co.); coll. B. Larson

197 Ontario (Renfrew Co.); SI

198 Calif. (nr Gem Mine, San Benito Co.)

199 Australia (Zinc Corp. Mine, Broken Hill, New South Wales); coll. A. Chapman

200 N.J. (Franklin, Sussex Co.); SI

201 Calif. (Pala, San Diego Co.)

202 Ariz. (Ajo, Pima Co.)

203 England (Palla Flat Mine, Cumberland Co.); British Museum (Natural History)

204 N.J. (Franklin, Sussex Co.); SI

205 Nev. (Getchell Mine, nr Golconda, Humboldt Co.)

206 Ariz. (Hamburg Mine, Yuma Co.)

207 Ontario (O'Brien Mine, nr Cobalt, Timiskaming District)

208 Zacatecas (Guadelupe Mine)

209 Colo. (Ouray Co.); SI

210 Peru; coll. D. Wilbur

211 Ariz. (Morenci, Greenlee Co.)

212 Australia (Dundas, Tasmania); coll. A. Chapman

213 Australia (Dundas, Tasmania)

214 Calif. (Aetna Mine, Napa Co.)

215 Nev. (Humboldt Co.); SI

216 N.M. (Georgetown, Grant Co.)

217 N.J. (Franklin, Sussex Co.); coll. B. Larson

218 Ariz. (Mesa, Maricopa Co.)

219 Mexico

220 Ontario (Ottawa)

221 Calif. (Sonora Co.)

222 N.J. (Franklin, Sussex Co.)

223 Quebec (Asbestos, Richmond Co.)

224 Mo. (nr Joplin, Jasper and Newton Cos.)

225 Chihuahua

226 Chihuahua (Santa Eulalia)

227 Nev. (Pershing Co.)

228 N.C.

229 N.C. (Foote Mine, at Kings Mt., Cleveland Co.)

230 N.J. (Fort Lee, Bergen Co.)

231 Colo. (El Paso Co.)

232 Sonora; SI

233 Ohio (Clay Center, Ottawa Co.); Kee coll., Canadian National Museum

234 England (Cumberland); British Museum (Natural History)

235 N.Y. (Washington Heights, New York City)

236 N.Y. (Tilly Foster Mine, Putnam Co.); Hancock coll., Harvard Univ.

237 N.M. (Lake Valley, Sierra Co.); coll. J. Rodekohr

287 Quebec (Asbestos, Richmond Co.)

288 Conn. (Yantic, New London Co.); SI

289 British Columbia (Anaconda British Columbia Mine)

290 Chihuahua (Los Lamentos)

291 Ariz. (Old Yuma Mine, Pima Co.)

292 Durango; SI

293 Nev. (Getchell Mine, Golconda, Humboldt Co.)

294 Ariz. (Rawley Mine, nr Thebe, Maricopa Co.); SI

295 Ariz. (Rawley Mine, nr Thebe, Maricopa Co.)

296 Sonora (San Francisco Mine, Cerro Prieta, nr Magdalena)

297 N.J. (Franklin, Sussex Co.)

298 Chihuahua (Los Lamentos)

299 Ariz. (No. 79 Mine, Gila Co.)

300 Ariz. (Red Cloud Mine, Trigo Mts., Yuma Co.); coll. W. Wilson

301 Brazil (Linopolis, Minas Gerais); coll. M. Sklar

302 Madagascar; SI

303 Ind. (nr Fort Wayne, Allen Co.); coll. J. Kurtzeman

304 Texas

305 N.C. (placer deposit)

306 Ind. (Fort Wayne, Allen Co.); coll. W. Wilson

307 Utah (Thomas Mt., Juab Co.)

308 Conn. (Norwich, New London Co.)

309 Quebec (Mt. St. Hilaire, Rouville Co.)

310 N.C. (placer deposit)

311 Quebec (Asbestos, Richmond Co.)

312 Ind. (North Vernon, Jennings Co.); coll. W. Wilson

313 Baja California (Mina La Verde, La Huerta, Ojos Negros); coll. J. Scripps

314 Utah (Milford, Beaver Co.); British Museum (Natural History)

315 Calif. (Searles Lake, San Bernardino Co.)

316 Maine (Newry, Oxford Co.)

317 N.J. (Prospect Park, Passaic Co.); coll. R. Drift

318 Germany (Dudweiler, Saarland); SI

319 Sonora (Pinacata Mts.)

320 Okla. (Cardin, Ottawa Co.)

321 Ariz. (Dragoon Mts., Cochise Co.); SI

322 Left: N.C. (Rutherford Co.); middle: Calif. (El Dorado Co.); right: Ky. (Russell Co.)

323 Ariz. (Santa Teresa Mts.); coll. Robert W. Jones

324 Maine (Newry, Oxford Co.); G.V. Brush coll., Yale Univ.

325 Mo. (89 Mine, St. Joe Lead District)

326 Quebec (Asbestos, Richmond Co.)

327 Maine (Mt. Mica, Paris, Oxford Co.)

328 Durango (Mapimi)

329 Durango (Cerro del Mercado, nr Ciudad Durango)

330 Mass. (Lane's quarry, Westfield, Hampden Co.)

331 Texas

332 Nev. (Getchell Mine, Golconda, Humboldt Co.)

333 Durango (Ojuela Mine, Mapimi); coll. W. Wilson

334 S.D. (Elk Creek, Meade Co.)

335 N.J. (Franklin, Sussex Co.); SI

336 N.J. (Franklin, Sussex Co.); SI

337 Durango (Mapimi)

338 Penn. (Cornog, Chester Co.)

339 N.M. (Lake Valley, Sierra Co.)

340 Durango (Mapimi)

341 Durango (Mapimi)

342 Chihuahua (San Pedro Corralitos)

343 Ariz. (Superior, Pinal Co.); coll. Rey Barnes

344 Chihuahua (San Pedro Corralitos); SI

345 Ariz. (Rawley Mine, nr Thebe, Maricopa Co.); Davis coll., SI

346 Va. (Centreville, Fairfax Co.); coll. Robert W. Jones

347 N.C. (Piney Flats Mine, Mitchell Co.)

348 N.J. (Franklin, Sussex Co.); SI

349 R.I. (Manton Hill, Providence, Providence Co.)

350 N.H. (Grafton Center, Grafton Co.)

351 Utah (La Sal Mts., nr Moab, Grand Co.)

352 N.J. (Franklin, Sussex Co.)

353 N.H. (Ruggles Mine, Grafton Center, Grafton Co.)

354 Utah (Mercur, Tooele Co.)

355 Spain (Eugui, Navarra); coll. R. Gaines

356 Ontario (Madoc, Hastings Co.)

357 Calif. (Chihuahua Valley, Riverside Co.)

358 N.H. (Baldface Mt., Chatham, Carroll Co.); coll. R. Bartsch

359 Colo. (Mt. Antero, Chaffee Co.); SI

360 Alaska (Aleutian Islands)

361 Utah (Eureka, Tintic District, Juab Co.)

362 South Africa; SI

363 Quebec (British Canadian Mine, Black Lake, Megantic Co.)

364 Guanajuato

365 Md. (Luck Goose Creek, Howard Co.)

366 Calif. (Death Valley, Inyo Co.)

367 Utah (Thomas Range)

368 Quebec (De Sourdy quarry, Mt. St. Hilaire, Rouville Co.)

369 Mich. (Scofield quarry, Maybee, Monroe Co.); coll. W. Wilson

370 France (La Gardette); British Museum (Natural History)

371 N.J. (Franklin, Sussex Co.)

372 Ark. (nr Mt. Ida, Montgomery Co.)

373 Colo. (Sterling, Logan Co.)

374 Colo. (Mt. Antero, Chaffee Co.)

375 Ga. (Cartersville, Bartow Co.)

376 Ariz. (No. 79 Mine, Hayden, Gila Co.)

377 Mich. (Ellsworth, Mahoning Co.)

378 Durango (Mapimi)

379 Utah (Gold Hill, Tooele Co.)

380 Calif. (Boron, Kern Co.)

381 Quebec (Asbestos, Richmond Co.); coll. F. Spertini

382 Chihuahua

383 San Luis Potosí (Charcas)

384 Calif. (Boron, Kern Co.); SI

385 Chihuahua (San Antonio Mine)

386 N.C. (Helderman's Mt., Lincoln Co.)

387 N.J. (Snake Hill, Secaucus, Hudson Co.)

388 Mich. (Iron Mt., Dickinson Co.)

389 Calif. (Tick Canyon, nr Lang, Los Angeles Co.)

390 Ill. (McHonning Mine, Cave-in-Rock, Hardin Co.)

391 Maine (Newry, Oxford Co.)

392 Mass. (Lane's quarry, Westfield, Hampden Co.)

393 Penn. (Wood Chrome Mine, Texas, Lancaster Co.); coll. Yale Univ.

394 Chihuahua (Naica)

395 Colo. (Creede, Mineral Co.)

396 Ark.; SI

397 N.H. (North Groton, Grafton Co.); SI

398 Ill. (Cave-in-Rock, Hardin Co.)

399 Nev. (Goodsprings, Clark Co.)

400 Calif. (White Queen Mine, Pala, San Diego Co.)

401 N.C.

402 Calif. (San Bernardino Co.)

403 N.J. (Paterson, Passaic Co.)

404 Calif. (Searles Lake, San Bernardino Co.)

405 Conn. (Roncari quarry, nr East Granby, Hartford Co.); coll. S. Ridell

406 Calif. (Searles Lake, San Bernardino Co.)

407 N.Y. (Rochester, Monroe Co.); SI

408 Calif. (Inyo Co.)

409 Italy (Mt. Vesuvius, nr Naples)

410 Ohio (Lime City, Wood Co.)

411 N.J. (Prospect Park, Passaic Co.); coll. D. Scholze

412 N.J. (Paterson, Passaic Co.)

413 Italy (Rocca Monfina, Vulcano Island); SI

414 Utah (Milford, Beaver Co.)

415 Ill. (Hardin Co.); coll. R. Sohn

416 Mass. (nr Shelburne, Franklin Co.)

417 Calif. (Boron, Kern Co.)

418 N.J. (Franklin, Sussex Co.)

419 Calif. (Sonoma Co.); SI

420 Oaxaca (La Panchita Mine)

421 Calif. (Cloverdale, Mendocino Co.); SI

422 N.Y. (Diana, nr Natural Bridge, Lewis Co.)

423 Calif. (Gower Gulch, Death Valley, Inyo Co.); coll. M. New

424 Ill. (Cave-in-Rock, Hardin Co.)

425 San Luis Potosí (Charcas)

426 Calif. (Boron, Kern Co.)

427 Ill. (Cave-in-Rock, Hardin Co.); Canadian National Museum

428 Wash. (Skookum Chuck Dam, Tenino, Thurston Co.); coll. R. Tschernich

429 San Luis Potosí (Charcas); coll. B. Van Scriver

430 Durango (Mapimi)

431 N.J. (Prospect Park, Passaic Co.)

432 Durango (Ojuela Mine, Mapimi); coll. M. Ridding

433 N.J. (Chimney Rock quarry, Bound Brook, Somerset Co.)

434 Calif. (Morro Bay, San Luis Obispo Co.)

435 Calif. (Boron, Kern Co.)

436 Ariz. (Flux Mine, Patagonia District, Santa Cruz Co.)

437 Ore. (Drain, Douglas Co.)

438 Calif. (Boron, Kern Co.)

439 Calif. (Boron, Kern Co.); coll. S. Alexander

440 N.J. (Erie RR cut at Bergen Hill, Bergen Co.)

441 Nev. (nr Beatty, Nye Co.)

442 N.J. (Erie RR cut at Bergen Hill, Bergen Co.)

443 N.J. (Paterson, Passaic Co.)

444 Ark. (Mount Ida, Montgomery Co.)

445 N.J. (Paterson, Passaic Co.)

446 Ga. (Graves Mt, Lincoln Co.); Denver Museum

447 Nova Scotia (Cape d'Or, nr Minas Basin)

448 Conn. (Canaan, Litchfield Co.)

449 Ill. (Rosiclare, Hardin Co.)

450 Ariz. (Patagonia Mts.)

451 Ariz. (Camp Verde, Yavapai Co.)

452 N.Y. (Genessee River Gorge, Monroe Co.)

453 N.J. (Paterson, Passaic Co.)

454 Calif. (Cazadero, Sonoma Co.)

455 Iceland (Berufjord)

456 Calif. (Jennifer Mine, Boron, Kern Co.)

457 Chile (Chuquicamata, Antofagasta); SI

458 Minn. (Crystal Bay, Hennepin Co.)

459 Quebec (Templeton, Ottawa); SI

460 N.Y. (Willsboro, Essex Co.)

461 Greenland (Ivigtut)

462 Calif. (Coast Range)

463 Mont. (Kelley Mine, Butte, Silver Bow Co.); SI

464 Guerrero (Coacoyula,

in Rio de las Balsas Valley, nr Iguala); SI

465 Md. (fr Baltimore City Water Tunnel); SI

466 N.Y. (Hudson Highlands)

467 Ontario (Madoc, Hastings Co.)

468 Calif. (Lang, Los Angeles Co.); SI

469 Colo. (El Paso Co.); SI

470 Nev. (Humboldt Co.)

471 Ariz.

472 Chihuahua (Naica)

473 Chihuahua

474 Quebec (Thetford, Megantic Co.)

475 Colo. (American Tunnel, Sunnyside Mine, Silverton, San Juan Co.); coll. J. Scripps

476 Greenland (Ivigtut); coll. K. Robertson

477 N.Y. (Gouverneur, St. Lawrence Co.); coll. Yale Univ.

478 (Gouverneur, St. Lawrence Co.); George Vaux coll., Bryn Mawr College

479 Calif. ("New Pit," Boron, Kern Co.)

480 Ontario (Dungannon)

481 Calif. (Soda Lake, San Luis Obispo Co.)

482 Ark. (Magnet Cove, Hot Springs Co.)

483 Penn. (French Creek Mines, Chester Co.); George Vaux coll., Bryn Mawr College

484 Mont. (Bozeman corundum deposit, Gallatin Co.)

485 S.D.

486 N.Y. (Newcomb, Essex Co.)

487 Ark. (Hot Springs, Garland Co.); Denver Museum

488 N.C.; coll. Llewellyn

489 Conn. (Canaan, Litchfield Co.)

490 Ark. (Magnet Cove, Hot Springs Co.)

491 Ill. (Hamilton, Hancock Co.)

492 Utah (Eureka, Tintic District, Juab Co.)

493 England (Cumberland); coll. D. Wilbur

494 Ga.; coll. W. Smith

495 Calif. (Saline Valley)

496 Ontario (Bancroft, Hastings Co.); SI

497 Sweden

498 Wash. (Pend Oreille Co.)

499 Penn. (Lancaster Co.); Denver Museum

500 Mass. (Conway, Franklin Co.); Denver Museum

501 Chihuahua

502 Ontario (Bancroft, Hastings Co.)

503 Mass. (Chester, Hampden Co.)

504 Ark. (Bauxite, Saline Co.); SI

505 N.J. (Sparta, Sussex Co.)

506 N.Y. (Pierrepont, St. Lawrence Co.)

507 N.C. (Senia, Avery Co.)

508 South-West Africa (Berg Aukas Mine, Grootfontein); coll. M. Ridding

509 Quebec

510 N.Y. (Diana, Lewis Co.); coll. N. Yedlan

511 Calif. (San Benito Co.)

512 Calif. (San Benito Co.)

513 Mass. (Chester, Hampden Co.)

514 N.C. (Bryson City, Swain Co.)

515 S.D. (Custer Co.)

516 Ontario (Wilberforce, Haliburton Co.)

517 Mass. (Westfield, Hampden Co.)

518 Calif. (Mendocino Co.)

519 N.H. (nr Richmond, Cheshire Co.)

520 Idaho (South Mt. Mine, Loxey); coll. A. McGuinness

521 Locality unknown

522 Alaska (Prince of Wales); SI

523 Quebec (St. Hilaire, Rouville Co.); coll. B. Baudin

524 Calif. (Calaveras Co.); SI

525 Calif. (San Benito Co.)

526 Colo. (Crystal Peak, nr Florissant, Teller Co.)

527 Colo. (St. Peter's Dome, Fleming Co.)

528 Quebec (Pontiac Co.); SI

529 N.J. (Red Bank, Monmouth Co.)

530 Iowa (Keokuk, Lee Co.)

531 Va. (Richmond, Henrico Co.); SI

532 Mich. (Isle Royale, Lake Superior); Denver Museum

533 Mich. (Ishpeming, Marquette Co.)

534 Calif. (Riverside Co.); coll. A. Montgomery

535 Vt. (Chester, Windsor Co.)

536 N.J. (Franklin, Sussex Co.); Denver Museum

537 Calif. (Fresno Co.); Denver Museum

538 Ga. (Morganton, Fannin Co.); Denver Museum

539 Ontario (nr Bancroft, Hastings Co.)

540 Conn. (West Torrington, Litchfield Co.)

541 Maine (Newry Hill, Oxford Co.)

542 Calif. (Himalaya Mine, San Diego Co.)

543 Calif. (Himalaya Mine, San Diego Co.)

544 Idaho (Blackbird Mine, Cobalt, Lemhi Co.)

545 N.J. (Burger's quarry, Paterson, Passaic Co.)

546 Ariz. (Olsen Mine, Superior, Pinal Co.)

547 Nev. (Virgin Valley, Clark Co.)

548 N.C. (Shelby, Cleveland Co.)

549 Labrador

550 N.Y. (Hudson Highlands)

551 Idaho (Spencer, Clark Co.)

552 Sweden

553 Nev. (Virgin Valley, Clark Co.)

554 Colo. (Rico, Dolores Co.)

555 Calif. (Morgan Hill, Santa Clara Co.)

556 Ariz.; Barrons coll., Univ. of Texas

557 Querétaro

558 Locality unknown

559 Chihuahua (Naica)

560 Mont. (Butte, Silver Bow Co.)

561 Ontario (Deloro, Hastings Co.)

562 Calif. (Placer Co.)

563 Chihuahua (La Bufa)

564 Zacatecas (El Cobre)

565 N.M. (Vanadium, Grant Co.); SI
566 Chihuahua
567 Penn. (French Creek Mine, Venango Co.)
568 Zacatecas
569 Chihuahua
570 Zacatecas
571 Mich. (Lucy Mine, Negaunee, Marquette Co.); SI
572 Morocco (Bou Azzer); SI
573 Chihuahua (Santa Eulalia); SI
574 Ariz. (nr Bouse, Yuma Co.); SI
575 Kansas (Treece, Cherokee Co.); SI
576 Mich. (Marquette Range, Marquette Co.)
577 Zacatecas (El Cobre); SI
578 Colo. (Clear Creek Co.); SI
579 Kansas (Treece, Cherokee Co.)
580 Mont. (Butte, Silver Bow Co.); SI
581 Bolivia (Colquechaca, Chayanta Prov., Potosí Dept.)
582 Chihuahua (Parral); coll. M. New
583 Utah (Thomas Mts.); SI
584 Ontario (Espanola, Merritt Township, Sudbury District); SI
585 Utah (Thomas Mts.); SI
586 N.J. (Franklin, Sussex Co.); SI
587 N.J. (Franklin, Sussex Co.); SI
588 Conn. (Litchfield Co.); SI
589 Penn. (Delaware Co.)
590 Calif. (San Benito Co.)
591 Guanajuato; SI
592 Conn. (Bristol, Hartford Co.)
593 Conn. (Strickland quarry, Portland, Middlesex Co.)
594 Mont. (Butte, Silver Bow Co.); SI
595 Colo. (Cripple Creek, Teller Co.)
596 Ontario (Espanola, Merritt Township, Sudbury District)
597 Calif. (Ambrose Mine, San Benito Co.)
598 Zacatecas
599 Guanajuato
600 Guanajuato
601 Mont. (Butte, Silver Bow Co.)
602 Conn. (Bristol, Hartford Co.); coll. A. Montgomery
603 Mich. (Neguanee, Marquette Co.); SI
604 Zacatecas (Noche Buena); SI
605 Switzerland (Binnenthal, Turpen Alps)
606 S.D. (Keystone, Pennington Co.); SI
607 Iowa (Keokuk, Lee Co.)
608 Zacatecas
609 Utah (Silver King Mine, Park City); SI
610 Zacatecas; SI
611 Colo. (Crystal Peak, nr Florissant, Teller Co.)
612 Colo. (Teller Co.); coll. R. Kosnar
613 Minn. (Cuyuna, Aitkin Co.)
614 Mich. (Negaunee, Marquette Co.)
615 Mich. (L'Anse, Baraga Co.)

616 Ill. (Sparta, Randolph Co.)
617 Ill. (Hardin Co.)
618 Ill. (Sparta, Randolph Co.)
619 Calif. (Socrates Mine, Sonoma Co.)
620 Ariz. (No. 79 Mine, Hayden, Gila Co.)
621 Mich. (Ishpeming, Marquette Co.)
622 Mich. (Ironwood, Gogebic Co.)
623 Conn. (Salisbury, Litchfield Co.)
624 Chihuahua (Santa Eulalia)
625 Colo. (Silverton, San Juan Co.); coll. J.D. Minette
626 Colo. (Silverton, San Juan Co.); SI
627 Ariz. (Quartzite, Yuma Co.); SI
628 Mont. (Butte, Silver Bow Co.)
629 Czechoslovakia (Joachimsthal, Bohemia); SI
630 Mont. (East Colusa Mine, Butte, Silver Bow Co.); SI
631 Nev. (Ludwig)
632 Zacatecas
633 Zacatecas
634 Ontario (Creighton Mine, Sudbury District); SI
635 Ore. (Grant Pass, Josephine Co.); SI
636 Conn. (West Torrington, Litchfield Co.)
637 Alaska (Yukon Territory); SI
638 Calif. (El Dorado Co.)
639 N.C. (Rutherford Co.)
640 USSR (Ural Mts.)
641 Wash. (Chelan); SI

642 Calif. (Kern Co.)
643 Ariz. (Santa Cruz Co.)
644 British Virgin Islands (Virgin Gorda)
645 Colo. (Climax, Lake Co.)
646 Chile (Chañarcillo, Atacama Prov.); SI
647 Australia (Broken Hill, New South Wales); SI
648 Colo. (Cripple Creek, Teller Co.)
649 Colo. (Aspen, Pitkin Co.)
650 Romania (Baia Sprie); SI
651 Guanajuato
652 Wash. (Kittitas Co.)
653 Calif. (Placer Co.)
654 Mich. (Mohawk Mine, Keweenaw Co.)

The specimens in plates 655–702 are all in the collections of the Smithsonian Institution.

655 Rough stones, Calif. (Monterey Co.); cabochons L to R, Wash.; Wyo.
656 Australia (Kalgoorlie)
657 Crystal, Colo. (Pike's Peak, El Paso Co.); cabochon, Penn.
658 Rough stone, Ariz. (nr Globe, Gila Co.); cabochon, Ariz.
659 Rough stones, Nev. (Lander Co.); cabochon, Nev.
660 Labrador
661 South Africa (Griqualand)
662 Chihuahua
663 Slab, Texas; cabochon, Colo.

664 Rough stone, N.C. (Mitchell Co.); cabochons, Penn.

665 Large rough stone, Mexico; small rough stone, Australia (Queensland); large cabochon, Australia; small cabochon, Mexico

666 Rough stone, Chile (Ovalle, Coquimbo); cabochon, N.H.

667 Crystals and smaller cut stone, Sri Lanka; larger cut stone, Burma

668 Rough stone, Burma (Balangoda); cut stones, N.C.

669 Crystal, Norway (Norland); cabochon, Sri Lanka; cut stone, Ariz.

670 Ariz.

671 N.C. (Rich Gap Mine, Avery Co.)

672 Calif. (Himalaya Mine, San Diego Co.)

673 Crystals, Brazil (Minas Gerais); cut stone, France

674 Crystal, Guanajuato; cut stone, Japan

675 Crystals, N.Y. (Penfield quarry, Monroe Co.); cut stone, Ill.

676 Brazil (Minas Gerais)

677 Crystal in matrix, South Africa (Kimberley); cut stones, India

678 Calif. (nr Pala, San Diego Co.)

679 Sri Lanka

680 Calif. (San Benito Co.)

681 Tanzania (Arusha)

682 Crystal, South-West Africa (Klein Spitzkopje); cut stones, L to R, N.C., USSR, Maine

683 Crystal, Colombia; cut stone, N.C.

684 Sri Lanka

685 Crystal, Egypt (St. John's Island); cut stones, L to R, N.M., Ariz., N.M.

686 Crystal, Ontario; cut stones, L to R, Sri Lanka, Sri Lanka, Indochina

687 Crystal, Maine (Newry, Oxford Co.); cut stones, Maine (Paris, Oxford Co.)

688 Crystal, Brazil (Minas Gerais); cut stones, L to R, USSR, Maine

689 N.C. (Hiddenite, Alexander Co.)

690 Crystal, N.H. (Intervale, Carroll Co.); cut stone, Brazil

691 Crystal, Brazil (Espíritu Santo); cut stones, Sri Lanka

692 Crystal, Italy; cut stone, locality unknown

693 Crystal, Italy; cut stones, USSR

694 Crystal, Brazil; cut stone, Tanzania

695 Crystal, Brazil (Minas Gerais); cut stones, L to R, Austria, N.Y.

696 Durango

697 Crystal, Quebec (Jeffrey Mine, Asbestos, Richmond Co.); cut stones, Sri Lanka

698 Brazil (Ouro Preto, Minas Gerais)

699 Crystal, Madagascar; cut stones, Brazil
700 Mexico
701 Rough stone, Honduras; cut stone, Scotland
702 Brazil (Rio Grande do Norte)
703 Calif. (Mt. Lassen, Lassen Volcanic National Park, Shasta Co.)
704 Calif. (Devil's Postpile, Madera Co.)
705 Wyo. (Yellowstone National Park)
706 N.M. (Valley of Fires State Park)
707 Colo. (Cripple Creek, Teller Co.)
708 Colo. (Chaffee Co.)
709 Colo. (Castle Rock, Douglas Co.)
710 Colo. (Cripple Creek, Teller Co.)
711 Hawaii (Mauna Loa)
712 Colo. (Douglas Co.)
713 Colo.
714 Colo. (Ward, Boulder Co.)
715 Hawaii (Mauna Loa)
716 Idaho (Craters of the Moon National Monument, Butte and Blaine Cos.)
717 Hawaii (Kilauea, E side of Mauna Loa)
718 Hawaii (Kilauea, E side of Mauna Loa)
719 N.J. (Great Notch, Passaic Co.)
720 Colo. (Jefferson Co.)
721 Calif. (Inyo Co.)
722 Locality unknown
723 Calif. (S of Pacheco Peak, San Gabriel Mts.)
724 N.Y. (Pine Meadow Lake, Hudson Co.)
725 N.Y. (summit, Wright Peak, Adirondack Mts.)
726 Calif. (High Sierra, Yosemite National Park)
727 N.C. (Shelby, Cleveland Co.)
728 N.Y. (Bedford, Westchester Co.)
729 Ontario (Bancroft, Hastings Co.)
730 N.Y. (Bear Mt., Rockland Co.)
731 N.Y. (Hudson Highlands)
732 Conn. (Hale quarry, Middletown, Middlesex Co.)
733 Ontario (Bancroft, Hastings Co.)
734 Calif.
735 N.Y. (Bear Mt., Rockland Co.)
736 N.Y. (Manhattan, New York City)
737 New Brunswick (St. George)
738 Minn. (Duluth, St. Louis Co.)
739 Minn. (St. Cloud, Benton, Sherburne, and Stearns Cos.)
740 Colo. (San Juan Co.)
741 N.J. (Bergen Co.)
742 N.Y. (Bear Mt., Rockland Co.)
743 Mass. (Belchertown, Hampshire Co.)
744 N.Y. (Lake Tiorati, Rockland Co.)
745 N.J. (Fort Lee, Bergen Co.)
746 N.J. (Edgewater, Bergen Co.)
747 Calif. (San Diego, San Diego Co.)
748 Utah (Checkerboard

Mesa, Zion National
Park)

749 Utah (Bryce Canyon
National Park)

750 N.J. (Franklin, Sussex
Co.)

751 Mich. (Detroit,
Wayne Co.)

752 Penn. (Wilkes-Barre,
Luzerne Co.)

753 Mich. (Grand Rapids,
Kent Co.)

754 Mo. (Joplin, Jasper
and Newton Cos.)

755 Calif. (nr Newhall, Los
Angeles Co.)

756 N.Y. (Tompkins
Cove, Rockland Co.)

757 N.Y. (Rochester,
Monroe Co.)

758 N.Y. (Clinton Point)

759 Ohio

760 N.Y. (Potsdam, St.
Lawrence Co.)

761 S.D. (Dell Rapids,
Minnehaha Co.)

762 Wyo.

763 N.Y. (Stony Point)

764 Penn.

765 N.Y. (Catskill Mts.)

766 Mont. (Red Lodge,
Carbon Co.)

767 Vt. (N of Townshend,
Windham Co.)

768 Va. (Skyline Drive, nr
Dark Hollow Falls,
Blue Ridge, Botetourt
Co.)

769 Calif. (Mono Co.)

770 N.Y. (New York
Thruway, Taconic
region)

771 Vt. (W Rutland Co.)

772 N.Y. (Thornwood,
Westchester Co.)

773 N.Y. (Hudson
Highlands)

774 N.Y. (Willsboro,
Essex Co.)

775 N.Y. (Willsboro,
Essex Co.)

776 N.Y. (Bear Mt.,
Rockland Co.)

777 Ontario (Burleigh
Falls, Harvey and
Burleigh Townships,
Peterborough Co.)

778 N.Y. (Bear Mt.,
Rockland Co.)

779 Md. (Cardiff, Harford
Co.)

780 N.Y. (Canaan,
Columbia Co.)

781 N.J. (Fort Lee, Bergen
Co.)

782 Wis.

783 N.Y. (Granville,
Washington Co.)

784 N.Y. (Granville,
Washington Co.)

785 Calif.

786 N.Y. (Dutchess Co.)

787 N.Y. (Dutchess Co.)

788 N.Y. (Bronx, New
York City)

789 N.H. (Bethlehem,
Grafton Co.)

790 Mass. (Uxbridge,
Worcester Co.)

791 N.Y. (Dutchess Co.)

792 N.Y. (Manhattan,
New York City)

793 N.Y. (Bronx, New
York City)

794 Vt. (Gassetts,
Windsor Co.)

PICTURE CREDITS

The numbers in parentheses are plate numbers. Some photographers have pictures listed under an agency name as well as under their own. Agency names appear in boldface.

Violet Anderson (11, 93)

Joel E. Arem (2, 42, 115, 151, 155, 186, 187, 240, 244, 247, 248, 263, 278, 282, 285, 315, 325, 350, 406, 414, 415, 436, 446, 456, 462, 487, 488, 499, 500, 505, 507, 519, 521, 532, 535–539, 544, 549, 605, 783)

Charles W. Chesterman (704, 769)

Rock H. Currier (1, 4, 24, 48, 57, 59, 60, 70, 92, 94, 108, 114, 117, 139, 141, 160, 162, 193, 196, 199, 203, 210, 212, 217, 219, 223, 234, 236, 245, 256, 261, 262, 264, 268, 271, 274, 276, 301, 302, 313, 314, 316, 317, 324, 355–357, 370, 381, 383, 393, 405, 411, 417, 423, 427–429, 431, 432, 434, 438, 439, 475–478, 481, 483, 493, 494, 508, 510, 520, 523, 524, 531, 534, 581, 582, 599–602, 611, 612, 624, 625, 627)

Ed Degginger (88, 124, 354, 616, 631, 726, 749)

Phil Degginger (25, 649)

Earth Scenes
Michael Gadomski (725)

Breck P. Kent (26, 63–65, 118, 142, 182, 197, 215, 258, 292, 342, 362, 394, 525, 575, 579, 586, 607, 608, 748) L. L. T. Rhodes (747) Jack Wilburn (703) Jerome Wyckoff (705, 706, 723, 724, 750, 767, 768, 770)

Floyd R. Getsinger (27, 84, 120, 161, 167, 168, 172, 220, 404, 451, 471, 551)

Maurice Giles (408, 484, 722, 727)

Studio Hartmann (66, 558)

Katherine H. Jensen (14, 79, 98, 130, 135, 146, 148, 169, 170, 173, 177, 251, 284, 298, 320, 329, 352, 372, 400, 412, 426, 452, 472, 486, 506, 618, 639)

Breck P. Kent (143, 194, 222, 403, 433)

Jeffrey J. Kurtzeman (5, 12, 13, 19–21, 37, 38, 56, 77, 81, 213, 270, 275, 296, 299, 303, 307, 323, 343, 346, 556, 620)

Reo N. Pickens, Jr. (22, 43, 61, 116, 138, 180, 228, 269, 388, 424, 490, 491, 509, 526, 533, 615, 621)

Mark W. Sexton (283, 349)

Benjamin M. Shaub (51, 78, 101, 149, 243, 252, 460, 461, 485, 541, 553, 555, 613, 614)

Julius Weber (3, 6, 10, 16–18, 23, 28, 30–33, 35, 36, 39–41, 44–47, 49, 50, 52, 55, 58, 62, 68, 69, 71–75, 83, 85, 87, 89, 90, 95, 96, 99, 103–107, 111, 119, 121–123, 125, 128, 129, 131, 137, 140, 145, 147, 150, 152–154, 156–158, 164–166, 171, 175, 176, 179, 183, 184, 188, 189, 191, 192, 195, 198, 201, 202, 205, 207, 208, 211, 214, 216, 218, 221,

INDEX

Numbers in bold-face type refer to plate numbers. Numbers in italic refer to page numbers. The major text entry for each subject is listed first, after the plate numbers. Circles preceding the rocks, minerals, and gems make it easy for you to keep a record of the specimens that you have seen or collected.

NOTES

NOTES

NOTES

STAFF

Prepared and produced by
Chanticleer Press, Inc.

Founding Publisher: Paul Steiner
Publisher: Andrew Stewart

Staff for this book:

Editor-in-Chief: Gudrun Buettner
Executive Editor: Susan Costello
Managing Editor: Jane Opper
Project Editor: Peter Salwen
Art Director: Carol Nehring
Drawings: Judy F. L. Clinton
Production Manager: Helga Lose
Visual Key: Carol Nehring

Original series design by
Massimo Vignelli

All editorial inquiries should be
addressed to:
Chanticleer Press
665 Broadway, Suite 1001
New York, NY 10012

To purchase this book, or other
National Audubon Society illustrated
nature books, please contact:
Alfred A. Knopf
201 East 50th Street
New York, NY 10022
(800) 733-3000

NATIONAL AUDUBON SOCIETY FIELD GUIDE SERIES

Also available in this unique all-color, all-photographic format:

African Wildlife

Birds *(Eastern Region)*

Birds *(Western Region)*

Butterflies

Fishes, Whales, and Dolphins

Fossils

Insects and Spiders

Mammals

Mushrooms

Night Sky

Reptiles and Amphibians

Seashells

Seashore Creatures

Trees *(Eastern Region)*

Trees *(Western Region)*

Tropical Marine Fishes

Weather

Wildflowers *(Eastern Region)*

Wildflowers *(Western Region)*